THE POLITICS OF SOCIAL CONFLICT

THE PEAK COUNTRY, 1520–1770

This book provides a new approach to the history of social conflict, popular politics and plebeian culture in the early modern period. Based upon a close study of the Peak Country of Derbyshire between *c.* 1520 and 1770, it has implications for understandings of class identity, popular culture, riot, custom and social relations.

A detailed reconstruction of economic and social change within the region is followed by an in-depth examination of the changing cultural meanings of custom, gender, locality, skill, literacy, orality and magic. The local history of social conflict sheds new light on the nature of political engagement and the origins of early capitalism. Important insights are provided into early modern social and gender identities, civil war allegiances, the appeal of radical ideas and the making of the English working class. Most of all, the book challenges the claim that early modern England was a hierarchical, 'pre-class' society.

ANDY WOOD is Lecturer in History, University of East Anglia

T0312095

Cambridge Studies in Early Modern British History

Series editors

ANTHONY FLETCHER
Professor of History, University of Essex

JOHN GUY
Professor of Modern History, University of St Andrews

JOHN MORRILL
*Professor of British and Irish History, University of Cambridge,
and Vice Master of Selwyn College*

This is a series of monographs and studies covering many aspects of the history of the British Isles between the late fifteenth century and early eighteenth century. It includes the work of established scholars and pioneering work by a new generation of scholars. It includes both reviews and revisions of major topics and books which open up new historical terrain or which reveal startling new perspectives on familiar subjects. All the volumes set detailed research into broader perspectives and the books are intended for the use of students as well as of their teachers.

For a list of titles in the series, see end of book.

THE POLITICS OF
SOCIAL CONFLICT

The Peak Country, 1520–1770

ANDY WOOD

CAMBRIDGE
UNIVERSITY PRESS

CAMBRIDGE UNIVERSITY PRESS
Cambridge, New York, Melbourne, Madrid, Cape Town, Singapore, São Paulo

Cambridge University Press
The Edinburgh Building, Cambridge CB2 8RU, UK

Published in the United States of America by Cambridge University Press, New York

www.cambridge.org
Information on this title: www.cambridge.org/9780521561143

First published 1999
This digitally printed version 2007

A catalogue record for this publication is available from the British Library

Library of Congress Cataloguing in Publication data
Wood, Andy.
The politics of social conflict: the Peak Country, 1520–1770 / Andy Wood.
p.   cm. – (Cambridge studies in early modern British history)
Includes bibliographical references and index.
ISBN 0 521 56114 0 (hb)
1. Derbyshire (England) – Social conditions.
2. Social conflict – England – Derbyshire – History.
I. Title.   II. Series.
HN398.D4W66   1999
306′.09425′1–dc21   98–48331   CIP

ISBN 978-0-521-56114-3 hardback
ISBN 978-0-521-03772-3 paperback

CONTENTS

List of figures	*page*	x
List of tables		x
List of maps		xi
Preface		xiii
List of abbreviations		xvi

Introduction   'Terms we did not understand': landscape, place
and perceptions   1

1 Social relations and popular culture in early modern England   10
  Class and social history   10
  Rethinking class in early modern England   18
  Local cultures and popular cultures   26

Part I   The structures of inequality

2 Economy and society in the Peak Country, *c.* 1520–1570   41
  Technology and industry   41
  Land, wealth and community   45
  Landscape and population   53

3 Industrialization and social change, *c.* 1570–1660   57
  Population change and technological innovation   57
  Enclosure and common right   66
  The mining industry and its workforce   72

4 The Peak Country as an industrial region, *c.* 1660–1770   89
  The economics of regional identity   89
  The priorities of capital   98
  Poverty and labour   102

5 Social conflict and early capitalism 113
    The Peak Country and the Industrial Revolution 113
    Custom and economic change 116

Part II The conditions of community

6 'The memory of the people': custom, law and popular culture 127
    Custom, law and popular culture in early modern England 127
    'Time out of memorie of man': mining custom in the early
        sixteenth century 137
    'A kind of levelling custom': the opponents of free mining 143
    The uses of literacy: speech, writing and custom 150

7 The politics of custom 163
    Law, order and the sense of the past 163
    Gender, place and the construction of social identity 169

8 Community, identity and culture 179
    Gender, work and identity 179
    Community and local culture 188
    The supernatural and the underworld 195

Part III The politics of social conflict

9 'Pyllage uppon the poore mynorz': sources of social conflict,
   1500–1600 203
    Late medieval quiescence 203
    The 'troublesome people' of the Tudor High Peak 209

10 'All is hurly burly here': local histories of social conflict,
   1600–1640 218
    The confrontation over free mining in the Wapentake of
        Wirksworth 219
    The politics of a parish and the King's Attorney-General 223
    The 'illegal combinations' of the High Peak 231
    Riot, litigation and free mining rights in the High Peak 238

11 The Peak in context: riot and popular politics in early
   Stuart England 249
    Redefining popular politics 249

Gender and the social basis of plebeian politics   254
Traditions of resistance   261

12 'Prerogative hath many proctors': the English Revolution and the plebeian politics of the Peak, 1640–1660   267
    War and allegiance   267
    The Levellers, the miners and the eighth Earl of Rutland   277
    The transformation and defeat of the miners' political project   286

13 The experience of defeat? The defence of custom, 1660–1770   295
    Changing interests, changing alliances   296
    Resistance, protest and survival   303

14 The making of the English working class in the Derbyshire Peak Country   316

Bibliography   326
Index   346

FIGURES

3.1 Total baptisms per decade, four parishes, 1560–1769   *page* 60
3.2 Surplus/deficit of baptisms over burials, four parishes,
    1560–1769   60
3.3 Price of lead ore per load, 1540–1770   75

TABLES

2.1 Comparison of the 1524–5 Lay Subsidy with lists of miners
    of the 1520s   *page* 47
2.2 Comparison of the 1543 Lay Subsidy with the 1541–2 list
    of miners   48
3.1 Occupational ascriptions in Youlgreave burial register,
    1558–1604   61
3.2 Landholding on Cavendish estates, 1610–17   70
3.3 1653 production totals for five townships, expressed in
    loads and dishes   87
4.1 Seasonality of marriage in three parishes, 1560–1770 (%)   95
4.2 Occupations of grooms in three parishes, 1754–70   96
6.1 Number and gender of deponents to Consistory, Exchequer
    and Duchy of Lancaster courts, 1517–1754   132
6.2 Literacy of Peak Country deponents at the Consistory Court
    of the Diocese of Coventry and Lichfield, 1593–1638   154
6.3 Literacy in eight mining townships, 1641–2   154
6.4 Literacy in three mining parishes, 1754–70   156
8.1 Structure of 1,463 Peak mining households in 1641   180

MAPS

1 The topography of the Peak Country   *page* 29
2 The parishes of the Peak lead field   31
3 The administrative divisions of Derbyshire   32
4 The township boundaries of the Peak Country lead field   34
5 The manorial structure of the Peak lead field, *c.* 1640   35
6 The growth of the Peak lead field, *c.* 1540–1600   42
7 The population of the Peak Country in 1563: the distribution of
  acres per household   54
8 The population of the Peak Country in 1638: the distribution of
  acres per able-bodied man   64
9 The population of the Peak Country in 1664: the distribution of
  acres per household   65
10 Free mining as an employer: free miners as a percentage of the
   adult male population, 1641   78
11 Wage dependency and marginality: percentage of the mining
   workforce described as 'cavers and hirelings' in 1641   79
12 Industry and society: total percentage of the population
   dependent upon mining, 1638–1641   80
13 Topographies of poverty: percentage of households exempted
   from the Hearth Tax, 1664   91
14 The assertion and defence of custom: the extent of free mining
   rights, *c.* 1580–1762   208

PREFACE

In the summer of 1988, I was present in Chesterfield, in the north-east of Derbyshire, to hear a speech given by the Member of Parliament for that town, Tony Benn. In that speech, Tony Benn referred to the presence of Levellers in Derbyshire. This intrigued me greatly. The Levellers were one of the most radical of the political movements of the late 1640s, and have been claimed by British socialists as their ideological ancestors. But historians of the Levellers have shown that the movement's base of civilian support was concentrated into the south-east of England, and into London in particular. What were Levellers doing in Derbyshire in the late 1640s?

At the time at which I first heard mention of the Levellers' connection with Derbyshire, I had it in mind to start a doctoral thesis on the organization of that movement outside London. I was, and remain, convinced that a closer understanding of grassroots Leveller politics and organization have important implications for the understanding of plebeian politics and culture in early modern England. My intention was to produce an argument about Leveller organization based upon a series of local case-studies. The Leveller presence in Derbyshire seemed as good a place to start as any, partly because it seemed so odd, and partly because of a long-standing personal affection for the Peak. In the autumn of 1989, I began my doctoral work. Checking the secondary literature on the Levellers, I found that the key source for their involvement in Derbyshire was a petition written in the name of the miners of that county, and published in September 1649 in the Levellers' newspaper *The Moderate*. Upon investigation, this petition raised more questions than it answered. It certainly demonstrated a degree of support for the Leveller movement amongst some of the miners of the Peak Country, in the north-west of Derbyshire. But for all that the petition was couched in the kind of language I had come to associate with the Leveller movement, it spoke to a local and peculiar politics of which I had no knowledge. It seemed that the miners were aggrieved by the denial of their customary rights, for which they blamed 'Great men' in general and the Earl of Rutland in particular. The denial of those rights had prompted the miners to declare their support for the Levellers. Yet much remained unclear. What were these customary rights? What did the Earl of Rutland have to do with the matter? And what did this apparently trivial, local dispute have to do with the radical politics of the Leveller movement?

This book attempts to answer these questions, and a host of others besides. I cannot remember the point at which, as a post-graduate student, I stopped telling people that I was researching the Leveller movement, and started saying that I was writing about the Derbyshire Peak Country in the seventeenth century. In 1993, I eventually wrote a doctoral dissertation on that subject. In 1995, I started working on the subject again, this time for publication, and with a rather more ambitious chronology. Over a decade after I first heard Tony Benn refer to Levellers in Derbyshire, the book is finally finished. In the course of its production, I have incurred a great many debts. First of all, enormous thanks are due to the supervisor of my doctoral work, Keith Wrightson, from whose imagination, enthusiasm and critical support I have long benefited. John Morrill and Rab Houston were careful but sympathetic examiners of my PhD dissertation; in another context, this time in the company of Anthony Fletcher, John Morrill enabled the production of this book. At the University of York, Jim Sharpe and David Parrott's inspired teaching turned me into an early modernist. In my time at the Universities of York, Cambridge, East London, Liverpool, East Anglia, and at University College London and the Institute of Historical Research, I have incurred many other debts. The British Academy have been generous: they funded my doctoral work between 1989 and 1992, awarded me a Postdoctoral Research Fellowship in 1995, and in 1997 even gave me a small grant to finish my work in Matlock. In 1992, the Institute of Historical Research awarded me a Scouloudi Research Fellowship, thereby keeping my head above water. I am grateful to John Arnold, Mick Brightman, Cathy Carmichael, Andy Davies, Michael Frearson, Dennis Glover, Paul Griffiths, Steve Hindle, Pat Hudson, Peter Martin, Simon Middleton, Kate Peters, Dave Rollison, Heather Shore, Tim Stretton, John Sutton, Eric Taplin and Garthine Walker for their ideas, criticisms and enthusiasms. Thanks to the staff of the repositories (listed in the Bibliography) where I consulted documents; but regrettably His Grace the Duke of Rutland refused access to his splendid holdings at Belvoir Castle. Pete Herdan and Ian Kirkpatrick have had to endure my conversation about the Peak Country for far too long. Deb Riozzie's friendship kept me going through my doctoral research, and much more. I reconceived and wrote this book between September 1995 and April 1998. I have shared those years with Lucy Simpson, and they have been the best of times.

The book is really about two things: it is about the history of working people, and it is about the Peak Country. I first learnt about both subjects from my parents, Jim and Joyce Wood, and I dedicate this book to them.

Andy Wood
Norwich

ABBREVIATIONS

AgHR	*Agricultural History Review*
APC	*Acts of the Privy Council*
BL	British Library
BPDMHS	*Bulletin of the Peak District Mines Historical Society*
CHT	Chatsworth House
CSPD	*Calendar of State Papers Domestic*
DAJ	*Derbyshire Archaeological Journal*
DCL	Derby Central Library
DRO	Derbyshire Record Office
DRS	Derbyshire Record Series
EcHR	*Economic History Review*
HLRO, MP	House of Lords Record Office, Main Papers series
JRL	John Rylands Library
LJRO	Lichfield Joint Record Office
LPL	Lambeth Palace Library
MCL	Manchester Central Library
NAO	Nottinghamshire Archives Office
P&P	*Past and Present*
PRO	Public Record Office
SA	Sheffield Archives
TT	Thomason Tracts
VCH	*Victoria County History of Derbyshire*

Introduction 'Terms we did not understand': landscape, place and perceptions

In 1724, Daniel Defoe published an account of his recent journey through the Peak Country of north-west Derbyshire.[1] In his mind's eye, he re-crossed the 'black mountains' which separated the Peak Country from its neighbours, and entered the hills and valleys of that region. Here Defoe saw again the dominant lead mining industry in its full bloom, moved through the small, compact, poverty-stricken mining villages, and encountered the 'Peakrills' ('the subterranean wretches . . . who work in the mines') who dwelt there. Yet for all its flair, Defoe's oft-cited responses to the Peak and its people followed a script established by earlier accounts of the place, and by the prejudices of his class.[2] Like so many other visitors to the region, Defoe was shown its geological and architectural 'wonders' – the baths at Buxton, the Duke of Devonshire's great mansion at Chatsworth, the immense cave known as the Devil's Arse at Castleton – and commented upon the folk-beliefs which attached to some of these sites. In leading his readers on a journey 'through this howling wilderness in your imagination', Defoe knew that he was speaking to prior assumptions held by his polite, educated readership about the Peak Country in particular, and about upland, industrial areas in general. In large measure, the Peak Country which Defoe invoked was not one which most of its inhabitants would have recognized. None the less, social historians of early modern England have all too easily turned to contemporary elite antiquaries and travellers for descriptions of local cultures. The result has been the unwitting reproduction of elite prejudices towards the plebeian inhabitants of regions perceived of as marginal, dangerous or backward.[3] This book will attempt to redress that balance.

---

[1] D. Defoe, *A tour through the whole island of Great Britain* (1724–6; abridged edn, London, 1971), 460–79.

[2] See for instance M. Berg, *The age of manufactures, 1700–1820* (London, 1985), 110–11.

[3] A. Fletcher and J. Stevenson, 'Introduction', in A. Fletcher and J. Stevenson (eds.), *Order and disorder in early modern England* (Cambridge, 1985), 39; C. Hill, *The world turned upside down: radical ideas during the English Revolution* (London, 1972), 13–56, 73–86;

Although few of Defoe's literate, urban readers were likely to have visited the place, the Peak Country was not unknown to them. Tutored by Thomas Hobbes' and Charles Cotton's published accounts of the region, the middling sort of Augustan England knew the Peak to be a backward, barbarous place inhabited by unruly miners and illiterate peasants. Famously, its hills contained the finest lead ore in Britain, from which was manufactured the pewter vessels which sat upon their table and the shot which their armies used to dominate Europe and the New World. But the hills also appeared to succour a peculiar, dangerous local culture. The thin resources of the wide, barren moors seemed to be given over to common use by poor households. Within those hills, and down below in the valleys, the men of the villages laboured in mineworkings. Here educated readers understood the miners to dig for lead under a custom of free mining which overrode private property in land. The polite culture of the early eighteenth century followed its forebears of the seventeenth century in seeing in material environment the germs of popular culture. Moors, fens and forests were thought to breed a rebellious and independent culture amongst the lower orders. Like the East Anglian fens or the forests of western England, the Peak Country was perceived by upper-class outsiders as a dark corner of the land occupied by troublesome people whose local cultures were nourished by the black water of custom.[4] In all of these regions, local customary law gave wide freedoms to poor people. But the customary laws of the Peak Country enshrined a special, almost unique, right: that of free mining. In many manors within the Peak Country, any man (whether newcomer or settled inhabitant) enjoyed the right to dig for lead on any land, regardless of its ownership. This right of free mining was guaranteed by a body of laws which dated back to 1288. Unsurprisingly, the right had been the subject of intense dispute between lord and miner for generations before Defoe's visit to the region. In the Peak Country more than perhaps anywhere else, therefore, early modern elite perceptions of environment helped to reproduce a larger social conflict.

That the Peak was also an industrial region spoke to other fears. The fiction of social hierarchy upon which early modern England's traditional elite founded their rule rested upon a perception of society and economy as simple, unchanging and non-industrial. Before the civil wars, patriarchal

---

D.E. Underdown, *Revel, riot and rebellion: popular politics and culture in England, 1603–1660* (Oxford, 1987), esp. chs. 2–4.

[4] W.C. Carroll, '"The nursery of beggary": enclosure, vagrancy and sedition in the Tudor–Stuart period', in R. Burt and J.M. Archer (eds.), *Enclosure acts: sexuality, property and culture in early modern England* (Ithaca, 1994), 34–47; C. Hill, 'Puritans and "the dark corners of the land"', in his *Change and continuity in seventeenth century England* (London, 1974), 3–47; K. Thomas, *Man and the natural world: changing attitudes in England 1500–1800* (Harmondsworth, 1983), 242–86.

theorists closed their eyes to the flux of social mobility and economic change which moved about them. Yet the increasingly numerous industrial communities of the period could not fit into the neat boxes prescribed by patriarchal theory. England's governors therefore tended to imagine industrial workers as disorderly, indolent and dangerous. This was as true of the miners of the Derbyshire Peak Country as it was of other industrial groups.[5] The poverty of upland, industrial areas tended to exacerbate such prejudices. Mining villages were seen by gentlemen and nobles as lawless places, and mining workforces presented as an undifferentiated, intimidating mass. Writing in 1700, Leigh commented that 'there is scarce a vicious act but [the Derbyshire miners] are guilty of it, their folly is as notorious as their vice'.[6] The absence of any significant elite presence in such areas was presented as a further cause for concern. Early seventeenth-century commentators observed 'the rudenes, incivility & disobedience of divers of the inhabitants of that country of the Peake' and connected this to 'the scarsetie of Noblemen and Gentlemen' there.[7] The absence of gentry meant that reports of crowd gatherings were greeted with concern. In the 1520s, the Duchy of Lancaster's officials were worrying over 'Love Ale', gatherings in the High Peak 'Whereby have growne amongst them many myschevous deds as riotts assaltes affrayes murdres and other many in convencees'. In the late sixteenth century, when John Tunstead was appointed as Bailiff of the High Peak by the Earl of Shrewsbury, the peer warned him that it was an office of much 'creditt thear by reason that few Justices doe inhabitt that wyld country'. In the 1690s, worries over 'how barren this Country is of gentlemen' were expressed in a letter telling of crowd gatherings against re-coinage. [8]

Defoe's descriptions of the Peak miners he encountered built on such perceptions. In his recollections, the 'Peakrills' were 'subterranean wretches . . . a rude, boorish kind of people'. Defoe pulled his audience's attention to one of the most remarkable features of local customary culture in the Peak:

[5] On stereotypes of early modern mining communities, see D. Levine and K. Wrightson, *The making of an industrial society: Whickham, 1560–1765* (Oxford, 1991), 274–8; A. Wood, 'Custom, identity and resistance: English free miners and their law, 1550–1800', in P. Griffiths, A. Fox and S. Hindle (eds.), *The experience of authority in early modern England* (Basingstoke, 1996), 254–6; M. Stoyle, *Loyalty and locality: popular allegiance in Devon during the English civil war* (Exeter, 1994), 208. On stereotypes of industrial workers more generally, see A. Randall, *Before the Luddites: custom, community and machinery in the English woollen industry, 1776–1809* (Cambridge, 1991), 30–1.

[6] C. Leigh, *The natural history of Lancashire, Cheshire and the Peak in Derbyshire* (London, 1700), 79. For earlier versions of these prejudices, see PRO, E134/13 Jas I/Mich 3; DRO, D258M/59/13L.

[7] R. Meredith, 'The Eyres of Hassop, 1470–1640: II', *DAJ*, 2nd ser., 85 (1965), 49, 67.

[8] PRO, DL37/62, fols. 23, 25; W. Braylesford Bunting, *Chapel-en-le-Frith: its history and its people* (Manchester, 1940), 187; BL, Add. MS 6668, fol. 211.

the administrative structure which attached to the customs of free mining.[9]
Recalling his visit to Wirksworth town, the ancient heart of the mining
industry, Defoe stated that 'The Barmoot Court kept here to judge
controversies among the miners . . . is very remarkable.' Ordered by an
officer called the barmaster, a jury of twenty-four miners constituted the
barmote. Defoe briefly explained the laws of the industry, which in his
recollection allowed 'any man' to dig 'in another man's ground, except
orchards and gardens', and which regulated the disposal of mineshares, the
conduct of the miners and a host of other matters: 'This court also
prescribes rules to the mines, and limits their proceedings in the works
under ground; also they are judges of all their little quarrels and disputes in
the mines, as well as out and, in a word, keep the peace among them.'
Through their control of the barmote court, the miners became 'judges of
all their little quarrels and disputes'. Defoe had been taken to the moothall
in Wirksworth, where the barmote for the manor of Wirksworth sat. It was
here that the mining customs of that manor had been explained to him, and
which he simplified and confused in his account.

Like other visitors, Defoe misunderstood the complex web of conflicting
jurisdictions and customs within which the Derbyshire lead industry
operated. For all that Defoe and others spoke easily of the operation of the
custom of free mining across the whole of the lead field of the Peak, by
1724 the spatial and social operation of that custom was much more
restricted than he thought. None the less, and for all the heavy condescen-
sion of his tone, Defoe's recognition of the large degree of control enjoyed
by the miners over matters of custom is important. We will return
frequently in the course of this book to the moothall in Wirksworth, and to
equivalent sites in other jurisdictions within the Peak, to hear the 'little
quarrels' fought out therein, and to witness the 'strange, turbulent, quarrel-
some temper' of the miners. The moothall, and the customs it supported,
will emerge as one of the key centres of plebeian politics in the Peak.

Social historians of the early modern period are currently redefining
politics as inherent to everyday life and communal practice. Thus, what
went on in places like the Wirksworth moothall could be just as political as
the affairs of state conducted in the great houses of the gentry and nobility.
Yet most contemporary political theorists would not have agreed with such
an assessment of politics. Instead, patriarchal theorists presupposed a rigid
social polarity, in which the gentry and nobility were born to command and
the common people to obey. For all that patriarchalism was challenged
after the mid-seventeenth century by more liberal models of political
participation, a rigid perception of the socio-political order remained

---

[9] Defoe, *Tour*, 460–2.

written into elite perceptions of landscape and local culture. Upon encountering the ordered, rational environment of Chatsworth House, seat of the Duke of Devonshire, both Defoe's and Charles Cotton's accounts of the Peak Country evidence a similar sense of relief.[10] Defoe contrasted this 'most regular piece of architect[ure]' to the 'waste and howling wilderness' which surrounded it, while Cotton saw the natural environment as a diseased, contorted body. For Cotton, the 'rudeness' of the hills mirrored a 'rudeness' and 'incivility' on the part of the 'Hob-nail Peakrills' and the 'Peak highlander'. The landscaped environment of Chatsworth helped to sequester its noble inhabitants from their lower-class neighbours. Defoe noted how a wood had been planted so as to exclude the surrounding hills and industry from the Duke's sight. Cotton observed 'A Tower of Antick model' at the entry to the House whose purpose was to 'securely shut' out the 'Peak rabble'.

The Duke of Devonshire tried to close out the plebeian world of the Peak by constructing physical barriers to social intercourse. By the early eighteenth century the Manners Dukes of Rutland, the other great noble family of the region, had removed themselves from their Peak estates to the more ordered environment of Belvoir Castle in Leicestershire. The political and social exclusions by which the gentry and nobility of early modern England defined their authority were therefore encoded upon the landscape of the Peak. Yet the authority of such exclusions could never be taken for granted. As we shall see, the conceptual and physical boundaries which separated plebeian from elite could be ruptured. The plebeian politics of the Peak spoke in a diversity of voices. These find an unequal expression in this book, and were articulated in diverse places: in the moothall, at the manor court, before the common law, before commissions of central law courts, before the Privy Council or the parliament, at the porch of the parish church, at the doorway, in the alehouse, the marketplace, the field and the street.

The politics of social conflict found their clearest expression in the historically retrievable encounter between the opposed interests of plebeian and elite. That opposition was at its clearest in disputes over free mining custom, as lords and entrepreneurs sought to undermine the miners' claims to custom, and as the miners responded with riot, petition, demonstration and litigation. The twists and turns of that long-running conflict over local custom and material resources are charted in Part III of this book. In that encounter, the miners in particular created a political culture which bore

[10] C. Cotton, *The wonders of the Peak* (London, 1681). For a fuller study of the relationship between elite values and the landscape park, see T. Williamson, *Polite landscapes: gardens and society in eighteenth century England* (Stroud, 1995).

distinct similarities to the artisanal politics of the early Industrial Revolution. In excluding women and unskilled men from participation in the institutions of their trade, the miners helped to define their own political identity. The structural and cultural processes by which that identity was created and reworked between 1520 and 1770 is explored in Part II. But the book begins with a consideration of the economics of the Peak Country. Part I describes the Peak's movement from early sixteenth-century isolation to become an industrial region by the mid-seventeenth century. Fundamental to that movement was the creation of an early form of industrial capitalism. Although the social structures of this poor, industrial region constrained human agency, so the distribution of wealth, resources and power were simultaneously produced and renewed out of conflict and political engagement. The book therefore explores the changing point of interconnection between politics, law, ideology, culture, economics and identity over some two and a half centuries as they developed within a region which has largely escaped the attentions of professional historians. Moreover, it approaches that story from the perspective of the Peak's plebeian inhabitants. That perspective has been chosen in deliberate reversal of the conventional historical privileging of the concerns of governing elites at the expense of people like the 'subterranean wretches' whom Daniel Defoe encountered.

Defoe's account of the 'Peakrills' was constructed through the establishment of social and cultural difference. On barren Brassington moor, he was surprised to discover a mining family living in a cave.[11] Defoe provides his readers with a sympathetic description of the woman of the house. He recalls discussing with the woman first her husband's earnings as a miner, and then her own as one who 'washed the ore' after it was brought to the surface. He noted that the family cultivated barley on a smallholding, and kept a cow and a few pigs. As such, the economic historian is provided with a pen-portrait of that now well-known species: the poor, near-landless rural household, dependent upon the exercise of common rights and industrial waged labour. We will occupy ourselves with the changing fortunes and structural typologies of such households in the Peak Country in Chapters 2 to 5. But for now we are concerned with the distance which Defoe placed between himself and the woman. For Defoe, the woman was a paid-up member of the deserving poor. In his memory, she was

tall, well shaped, clean and (for the place) a very well looking, comely woman; nor was there any thing [about her home that] looked like the dirt and nastiness of the miserable cottages of the poor; though many of them spend more money in strong drink than this poor woman had to maintain five children with.

[11] Defoe, *Tour*, 463–5.

Defoe recognized the Brassington woman as a fellow human being. There is nothing here of John Aubrey's nasty account of the people of north Wiltshire, or of Cotton's harsh contempt for the Peakrills.[12] None the less, his recollections were bred within a close recognition of social and cultural difference. This perceived difference becomes most evident as he recalls his subsequent encounter with a miner, who appeared suddenly out of a mine-shaft on Brassington moor.[13] Defoe remembered the man as a 'subterranean creature' and 'a most uncouth spectacle':

he was cloathed all in leather, had a cap of the same without brims, some tools in a little basket . . . not one of the names of which we could understand but by the help of an interpreter. . . he was as lean as a skeleton, pale as a dead corpse, his hair and beard deep black, his flesh lank . . . he looked like an inhabitant of the dark regions below.

Defoe and his companions tried to speak with the miner but found that though he 'was pretty free of his tongue . . . He answered us in terms we did not understand.'[14] Communication was only possible through an 'interpreter'. But it was not only the terms of the miner's speech which Defoe misunderstood; it was the terms of his culture. Just as Defoe and his readers imagined the material world of the Peak Country as constituted by threatening hills, strange geology and natural wonders, so they anticipated a social world of illiterate, stupid, isolated and potentially rebellious 'Peakrills'. Prebendary Gilpin spoke for his class when he looked first upon the Peak and then upon the Peakrills and concluded that 'the inhabitants of these scenes were as savage as the scenes themselves'.[15] To the gentry outsider, the Peak Country and its plebeian people were therefore defined within the interlocking of geological and social difference.

This study will reveal a considerable degree of heterogeneity within Peak society between 1520 and 1770. Yet contemporary elite travellers closed their eyes to the finer distinctions which the Peak's inhabitants drew between one another on the basis of gender, place, skill, status, age and class. Inspired by Cotton, Defoe and Hobbes, the eighteenth-century gentry visitor to the Peak came expecting to find 'subterranean people' inhabiting 'these territories of Satan'. And so they did, discovering that 'These People resemble the Troglodytes, or Cunicular Men who . . . lived under Ground

---

[12] D. Rollison, *The local origins of modern society: Gloucestershire, 1500–1800* (London, 1992), 254–8.

[13] Defoe, *Tour*, 465–7.

[14] For similar incomprehension of a 'Peakrill', see C.B. Andrews and F. Andrews (eds.), *The Torrington diaries: a selection from the tours of the Hon. John Byng (later Fifth Viscount Torrington) between the years 1781 and 1794* (London, 1954), 187.

[15] W. Gilpin, *Observations, relative chiefly to picturesque beauty made in the year 1772 on several parts of England*, 2 vols. (3rd edn, London, 1792), I, 212.

like Rabbits.'[16] But the subterranean people found their own voices. One such voice was that of William Hooson, a miner of Youlgreave, who in 1747 published a diverse book dealing with mining method, tradition, law and history. He made it clear that he was aware of the stereotypes offered of his region and his trade: 'I know that Miners are accounted at this Day by many who reap great benefit from their Endeavours to be a Set of dispiseable Men of no good Characters, but Tools to be imployed on Occasions in the Mines, and a great deal more they brand them with.' Yet Hooson did not regard himself as a 'Tool' of any mine-owner. He concluded his book with a series of remarks which speak volumes for the pride he took in his occupation:

WHETHER there be any Practical Miners that have written any thing of mining, is more than I yet know, but several Gentlemen have furnished us with bits and scrips taken on Information mixt and wrought up with [perhaps] some Guesswork of their own; but I do not see that a Man is either the wiser or better for them, for what I have delivered, is the very Practice as the Experienced Miner well knows . . . If any shall object against my Rough, yet Plain way of Writing &c., he may easily excuse me, when I tell him, I always was, am and hope by God's help so to continue the remainder of my days A MINER.[17]

Much of this book will be preoccupied with the origins and nature of the Peak miners' identity. We will see how the formation of that identity had larger implications for the region's social, cultural and political history. In the years *c.* 1590–1610, a closer sense of collective identity developed amongst the skilled free miners. The harder edge thereby given to the miners' identity resulted from the specification of skill and custom as the property of settled, plebeian adult men. This had important implications for gender relations and for understandings of work, law and local identity. The hardening of the miners' identity was bound up with a gathering political contest over material resources. After the 1570s, involvement in the lead industry became increasingly profitable. The vague customary laws by which free mining had hitherto been allowed to dominate the lead industry were challenged by wealthy gentlemen and nobles, anxious both to exert control over the industrial workforce and to gain possession of the lead mining industry. In developing a tradition of resistance to their rulers, the miners redefined themselves as a social group. From that confrontation emerged a plebeian political project which, although defined through the exclusion of women and of the unskilled men, set itself in overt and public opposition to the interests of the 'great men' of the Peak.

---

[16] BL, Add. MS 6670, fols. 333–53. See also BL, Add. MS 6668, fols. 477–9; Anon., *Account of the wonders of Derbyshire* (London, 1779); W. Bray, *Sketch of a tour into Derbyshire and Yorkshire* (London, 1777), for equivalent accounts.
[17] W. Hooson, *The miner's dictionary* (1747; repr. Ilkley, 1979), 198, 197.

The conflict of the *c.* 1590–1660 period raises important questions about the nature of social relations in early modern England. Still more important was the language in which plebeians came to describe that conflict, which identified society as harshly and simply divided into 'rich' and 'poor'. Local conflict was defined as the encounter of opposed social groups over the conceptual and legal battleground of custom. The stress placed by Peak plebeians upon custom and locality gives the disputes over mining rights a distinctly early modern feel. But other aspects of the politics of social conflict as practised in the Peak Country sit less easily upon the established foundations of early modern social history. For the polarized confrontation over free mining custom produced definitions of social conflict which anticipate nineteenth-century languages of class.

It is a central argument of this book that early modern plebeian cultures bequeathed important habits and traditions to the working-class culture of the early nineteenth century. Social historians have failed to communicate across the historiographical and conceptual divide of the Industrial Revolution. Early modern social historians have long been hesitant in using the term 'class' as an analytical category, convinced that it was a product of nineteenth-century modernity. Meanwhile, modern social historians are currently persuading themselves of the emptiness of the term. This book tries to speak to the agendas of both modern and early modern social history. In order to establish how its findings contribute to historical understandings of class identity and social conflict, we must turn first to how social historians have dealt with the issue of class.

1

Social relations and popular culture in early modern England

CLASS AND SOCIAL HISTORY

Class, we are told, is dead. It has been excised from contemporary political discourse, and is being torn from its place at the heart of the social history of modern Britain. For many observers, rapid deindustrialization and the decline of mass society have removed the structural context within which class identities thrived. Shorn of Marxist certainties, social historians of modern Britain have come under the influence of new postmodern sociologies. Whereas Marxian social history had perceived of class as an embedded, material fact produced out of exploitation, immiseration and resistance, for their postmodernist successors class exists nowhere but in discourse. Earlier histories which saw working-class identity as a social fact born within the cradle of the early factory system and given voice in political radicalism and organized labour are now disparaged. Instead, class is seen as 'an imagined form, not something given in a "real" world beyond this form'.[1] To the postmodern historian, the force possessed by class in the nineteenth century came from its wide acceptance as a material fact, yet its only reality lay in discourse.[2] Hence the language of class is seen as having provided momentary expression to the social opposition imagined by socialists and radicals. That language enabled socialists of the late nineteenth and early twentieth centuries to construct universal claims to political and economic equality. Postmodernist historians of the industrial period now reveal that universalism to have been a mere discursive tissue which covered over differences of gender, ethnicity, locality and religion.[3] Having done battle with the ghost of Marxist historiography, the

[1] P. Joyce, *Democratic subjects: the self and the social in nineteenth-century England* (Cambridge, 1994), 1.
[2] P. Joyce, 'The end of social history?', *Social History*, 20, 1 (1995), 82.
[3] P. Joyce, *Visions of the people: industrial England and the question of class, 1840–1914* (Cambridge, 1991); J. Vernon, *Politics and the people: a study in English political culture, c. 1815–1867* (Cambridge, 1993). On the unravelling of materialist definitions of class

postmodern historians of the industrial period now present us with the corpse of class analysis, revealing its 'spurious facticity' in the historical past at precisely the moment that its meaning is being denied in current political debate.[4]

There is some force to these claims. In its most developed and positive form, the postmodernist critique of class has allowed for a fuller appreciation of how difference operated within modern working-class culture, and has forced social historians to rethink key categories and assumptions. We shall see later how some postmodernist approaches might liberate social historians of early modern England from restrictive understandings of social relations and conflict. Yet we shall also see how the liberation of early modern social relations from the straitjacket of modernist historiography obliges its historians to reconfigure, rather than simply to eliminate, the role played by economics and exploitation in social conflict and popular politics. It is still too early to assess how enduring will be the impact of the new postmodernist sociologies within current political discourse. But it is certain that the collapse of Marxism has had far-reaching consequences for the theoretical foundations of modern social history.

The academic practice of social history was revolutionized in the West in the late 1960s. One of the few achievements of the middle-class student revolts of that era was the establishment of social history as a key contender in academic historical writing. Building upon the earlier work of the British Communist historians, a Marxian vision of social relations and structure came to predominate in studies of British industrial society after 1968. Heavily influenced by the culturalist Marxism of Edward Thompson, class formation became seen as a political process dragged out between the 1780s and 1832. None the less, even for Thompson, class was born within a structural context characterized by rapid industrialization, urbanization and immiseration. English working-class culture and politics were therefore simultaneously a product of the political agency of working men and women, *and* of the Industrial Revolution. Although Thompson could find class struggles in England before the Industrial Revolution, these were insufficiently choate for the plebeian labouring poor to be called a working

---

experience and politics, see especially J.W. Scott, 'The evidence of experience', *Critical Inquiry*, 17 (1991), 773–97; P. Joyce (ed.), *Class: a reader* (Oxford, 1995), 3–16; G. Stedman Jones, *Languages of class: studies in English working class history, 1832–1982* (Cambridge, 1983), esp. 1–24, 90–178. For hostile comment, see for instance B.D. Palmer, *Descent into discourse: the reification of language and the writing of social history* (Philadelphia, 1990), ch. 4 ; N. Kirk, 'History, language, ideas and post-modernism: a materialist view', *Social History*, 19, 2 (1994), 221–40.
[4] Quoting Joyce, 'End of social history?', 85.

class.[5] Hence, for all the agency and contingency written into Thompson's vision of class formation, he remained wedded to a Marxist conception of social change as arising ultimately out of economics.[6] For Thompson, class remained a product of nineteenth-century industrial modernity. Historiographically, the paradigmatic foundations of modern social history remained dominated into the early 1980s by Marxian formulations of social change. Subsequent studies challenged details of this formulation, but in order to do so critics had to endure an early immersion in the language and assumptions of dialectical materialism.[7] Both the paradigmatic foundations and the dominant language of modern social history were therefore so intimately bound up with Marxism after the 1960s that the contemporary crisis in one has in some quarters been perceived as inducing a crisis in the other. It should not therefore come as any surprise that the end of social history has recently been announced.[8]

Every historian, of course, loves a good crisis, whether to be identified in the past or manufactured in the present. None the less, the current 'decline of class' perceived by modern social historians has been greeted with a degree of bewilderment amongst their neighbours in the early modern period, amongst whom the postmodernist critique of Marxism has thus far had less impact. The reasons for this are partly historical and partly historiographical. Historically, students of class have tended to have been pulled towards the nineteenth and twentieth centuries, for it was in that period that class seemed to appear in its most commonsensical forms. The study of labour movements and class-based socialist parties, struggling in the shadows of the great ideologies of the post-Enlightenment age against a background of urbanization, industrialization and modernization, seemed to offer a more enticing prospect than anything on offer in earlier periods. Historiographically, Marxian formulations of social change had become critical to understanding the industrial period, even for those who wish to criticize Marxist assumptions.

[5] E.P. Thompson, 'Patrician society, plebeian culture', *Journal of Social History*, 7, 4 (1974), 382–405; *idem*, 'Eighteenth-century English society: class struggle without class?', *Social History*, 3, 2 (1978), 133–65; *idem, Customs in common* (London, 1991), ch. 2.
[6] E.P. Thompson, *The making of the English working class* (1963; 2nd edn, London, 1968). For a summary of Thompson's interpretation of class formation, see W.H. Sewell, 'How classes are made: critical reflections on E.P. Thompson's theory of working-class formation', in H.J. Kaye and K. McClelland (eds.), *E.P. Thompson: critical perspectives* (Cambridge, 1990), 50–77.
[7] This is most apparent in the twists and turns of Stedman Jones' work, from his *Outcast London: a study in the relationship between classes in Victorian society* (Oxford, 1971) to his *Languages of class*.
[8] Joyce, 'End of social history?'. In the same vein, see also J. Vernon, 'Who's afraid of the "linguistic turn"? The politics of social history and its discontents', *Social History*, 19, 1 (1994), 81–97.

In contrast, Marxism was almost absent from the 'new' social history of the early modern period which emerged after the late 1960s.[9] Whereas Marxism provided the questions (if not always the answers) that drove the engines of modern British social history in the 1970s, the 'new' social history of early modern England was developed at a conscious distance from the Marxist tradition. This was partly a by-product of an acrimonious debate then taking place on one of the contested borderlands of the 'new' social history. Within seventeenth-century political history, the 1970s and early 1980s saw a protracted exchange between Marxist historians of the English Revolution and their so-called 'revisionist' critics. Led by Christopher Hill, Marxist historians saw in the 1640s a revolutionary transformation which established the preconditions for the emergence of industrial capitalism in the following century.[10] In contrast, the 'revisionists' preferred to stress the short-term causes and consequences of the civil wars.[11] In an early reverse to the operation of the Marxist paradigm upon British historical writing, the 'revisionists' were seen by most observers by the mid-1980s to have had the best of the confrontation. Rather than enter into this debate, the 'new' social historians of early modern England chose to adopt a distanced neutrality.

The conscious removal of the 'new' social history from the debate over the English Revolution had three consequences for the subsequent development of the field. First, unlike modern social history the theoretical impulses of the 'new' social history thereafter came from sources other than Marxism. Structuralist anthropology allowed for an appreciation of culture and belief in the period, while an understated Weberianism provided a model of change in which England's 'early modernity' in the sixteenth and

---

[9] For the reflections of one of the best practitioners of that 'new' social history upon his subject, see K.E. Wrightson, 'The enclosure of English social history', in A. Wilson (ed.), *Rethinking social history: English society, 1570–1920 and its interpretation* (Manchester, 1993), 59–77.

[10] Emblematic titles included: C. Hill, *Reformation to Industrial Revolution* (Harmondsworth, 1967); idem, *World turned upside down*; L. Stone, *The causes of the English Revolution, 1529–1642* (London, 1972); B. Manning, *The English people and the English Revolution* (1976; 2nd edn, London, 1991). For an acerbic review of the Marxist interpretation of the English Revolution, see A. MacLachlan, *The rise and fall of revolutionary England: an essay on the fabrication of seventeenth-century history* (Basingstoke, 1996).

[11] Outstanding were: C. Russell, *Parliaments and English politics, 1621–1629* (Oxford, 1979); idem, (ed.), *Unrevolutionary England, 1603–1642* (London, 1990); idem, *The causes of the English civil war* (Oxford, 1990); J.S. Morrill, *The revolt of the provinces: conservatives and radicals in the English civil war, 1630–1650* (London, 1976); idem, *The nature of the English Revolution* (London, 1993), esp, chs. 3, 8–10; M.A. Kishlansky, *The rise of the New Model Army* (Cambridge, 1979); idem, *Parliamentary selection: social and political choice in early modern England* (Cambridge, 1986). For a review of the Marxist-revisionist debate, see R.C. Richardson, *The debate on the English Revolution revisited* (1977; 2nd edn, London, 1988), chs. 7–11.

seventeenth centuries was assured as the 'new' social historians' special area of scrutiny.[12] Secondly, the absence of Marxism meant that the category of class was removed from the 'new' social history's agenda as a potential subject for enquiry. Thirdly, the 'new' social history was defined in opposition to political history. Whereas modern social historians overtly connected the history of social identities and cultural practice to political movements and debate, early modern social historians tended to avoid such subjects, and settled for a more descriptive, less analytic approach. Politics and class were not to be discussed at the dinner table of the 'new' social history.

None the less, the social historians of early modern England found much to occupy their time: there were histories of crime, kinship, social structure, urbanization, literacy, population change, household relations, sexual behaviour, riot, witchcraft and moral regulation (amongst other subjects) to be written. These histories produced unexpected revelations. It became clear that the early modern economy and social structures had gone through rapid, convulsive change. Those changes bred important local conflicts which, since so few strayed into the public world of state-centred elite politics, the 'new' social history could claim as its territory.[13] Occasions of organized disorder were regarded as especially important. It was shown that many disputes occurred between lord and tenant, or between different sections of the local population, over custom and common right. These sometimes exploded into riot. Alternatively, riots occurred as a result of high food prices. Moreover, the sixteenth century saw a number of important rebellions and near-rebellions, from which important conclusions concerning relations between ruler and ruled could be drawn. Fascinating though such occasions of disorder were, they none the less presented a conceptual problem: some historians felt that they could detect a spirit of 'class antagonism', even of 'class hatred' amongst rioters and rebels.[14] Others remained certain that the localism of such disturbances

---

[12] For the influence of structuralist anthropology, see especially K. Thomas, *Religion and the decline of magic: studies in popular beliefs in sixteenth and seventeenth century England* (London, 1971); for the liminal influence of Weber in historical understandings of social change in the period, see especially P. Laslett, *The world we have lost: further explored* (London, 1965; 3rd edn, 1983); K.E. Wrightson, *English society, 1580–1680* (London, 1982).

[13] B. Sharp, *In contempt of all authority: rural artisans and riot in the west of England, 1586–1660* (Berkeley, 1980); J.D. Walter, 'A "rising of the people"? The Oxfordshire rising of 1596', *P&P*, 107 (1985), 90–143; *idem*, 'Grain riots and popular attitudes to the law: Maldon and the crisis of 1629', in J. Brewer and J. Styles (eds.), *An ungovernable people: the English and their law in the seventeenth and eighteenth centuries* (London, 1980), 47–84; J.D. Walter and K.E. Wrightson 'Dearth and the social order in early modern England', *P&P*, 71 (1976), 22–42.

[14] J.A. Sharpe, *Crime in early modern England, 1550–1750* (London, 1984), 135–6; Sharp,

meant that they were pre-class, even pre-politics.[15] The archival evidence therefore embedded a strange contradiction at the heart of the 'new' social history. On the one hand, rioters and rebels seemed sometimes to speak about early modern society in class terms. On the other, modern social historians were insistent that class society only arrived with industrial modernity and the fully formed nation-state.[16]

If the pattern of social relations in the period raised problems, so too did the emerging picture of English social structure.[17] Sixteenth- and seventeenth-century society was starting to appear as much more diverse, complex and dynamic than the 'traditional' societies imagined in classical sociology and structural anthropology, and with which it has sometimes been compared.[18] In many respects, the picture which the early modern social historians were drawing of their subject was coming to look rather more like a Weberian 'modern' society than its near-static 'traditional' precursor. And yet, it still *felt* so different from the industrial modernity of the mid-nineteenth century. For here, as every early modern social historian had been trained to recall, stood an obvious class structure and real, true class consciousness in all its fully formed, mid-nineteenth century, masculine, urban, conscious, organized forms. Most importantly, here was the *word* class, and here could be found its organized political expression.

Real class, it was decided, lay beyond early modernity. Historians came

---

In contempt, 7–8, 33; J. Samaha, 'Gleanings from local criminal-court records: sedition amongst the "inarticulate" in Elizabethan Essex', *Journal of Social History*, 8 (1975), 61–79.

[15] R.B. Manning, *Village revolts: social protest and popular disturbance in England, 1509–1640* (Oxford, 1988); K. Lindley, *Fenland riots and the English Revolution* (London, 1982).

[16] See for instance H. Perkin, *Origins of modern English society* (London, 1969); J. Foster, *Class struggle and the Industrial Revolution: early capitalism in three English towns* (London, 1974). For a dissenting view, see R.S. Neale, *Class in English history 1680–1850* (Oxford, 1981).

[17] For important case-studies, see K.E. Wrightson and D. Levine, *Poverty and piety in an English village: Terling, 1525–1700* (1979; 2nd edn, Oxford, 1995); M. Spufford, *Contrasting communities: English villagers in the sixteenth and seventeenth centuries* (Cambridge, 1979). For migration, see P. Clark, 'Migration in England during the late seventeenth and early eighteenth centuries', in P. Clark and D. Souden (eds.), *Migration and society in early modern England* (London, 1987), 213–52. For urbanization, see P. Clark and P. Slack (eds.), *Crisis and order in English towns, 1500–1700: essays in urban history* (London, 1972). For population, see E. A. Wrigley and R. S. Schofield, *The population history of England, 1541–1871: a reconstruction* (1981; 2nd edn, Cambridge, 1989). For the implications of demographic change, see D. Levine, *Family formation in an age of nascent capitalism* (New York, 1977).

[18] For the comparison, see J.C. Davis, 'Radicalism in a traditional society: the evaluation of radical thought in the English commonwealth, 1649–60', *History of Political Thought*, 3, 2 (1982), 193–213. Peter Laslett, while producing some pioneering studies of the dynamics which underwrote early modern social structure, none the less persisted in regarding early modern society as 'traditional': *World we have lost*, esp. chs. 1–3, 8–9, 11.

to see that claim as so obvious and commonsensical as to require simple reassertion rather than demonstration. Thus, Anthony Fletcher and John Stevenson found the case against the presence of class in early modern society so overwhelming that their bald statement that 'a class society had not in our period yet arrived' was thought sufficient discussion of the topic. The concept of class was regarded as alien to the period, and conceptual barriers erected against its infiltration: John Morrill found the 'importation of notions of class' to be 'highly dubious'. David Underdown advised 'great . . . caution' in the use of the term. For Perez Zagorin, 'early modern society was [simply] not a class society'.[19] Working from such assumptions, J.C.D. Clark could therefore discover a hierarchical, paternalist 'ancien regime' which endured until the end of the eighteenth century.[20] Despite all the advances in the social history of the period, and with certain notable exceptions, it therefore seems that H.N. Brailsford's comment of almost forty years ago that 'historians are as shy in confronting the fact of class as were novelists of the last century in facing the fact of sex' still holds true.[21]

Borrowing from Thompson, it was decided that class stirred into life from the late eighteenth century, to achieve its mature dominance in politics, material life and discourse by the middle of the nineteenth century. For all that social historians found that the peasants were revolting in early modern England, their plebeian culture could not be a class culture. And thus, in spite of the curious structural precocity of early modern society, it was in the very absence of class that early modernity found its peculiar and unique identity. In a highly influential formulation, Keith Wrightson summed up the matter:

The broad structural characteristics of local society were common. It was not a society dominated by class affiliation; for however strong the awareness of status within a specific local context, broader class consciousness was inhibited for those below the level of the gentry by their lack of alternative conceptions of the social order; their envelopment in relationships of communality and deference, by the localism which gave those ties force and meaning, and by the lack of institutions which might organize and express a horizontal group consciousness of a broader kind. It was perhaps a society which possessed an incipient class dimension in its distribution of wealth, productive relations and market situation, and in which antagonisms between social strata undoubtedly existed. But these were too limited to a specific social situation and too temporary an element in cognitive experience

---

[19] Fletcher and Stevenson, 'Introduction', 4; see also p. 19 for a reiteration of the point; J.S. Morrill, *Seventeenth century Britain 1603–1714* (Folkestone, 1980), 108–9; Underdown, *Revel, riot and rebellion*, 168; P. Zagorin, *Rebels and rulers 1500–1660*, I: *Society, states and early modern revolution – agrarian and urban rebellions* (Cambridge, 1982), 61.

[20] J.C.D. Clark, *English society, 1688–1832* (Cambridge, 1985).

[21] H.N. Brailsford, *The Levellers and the English Revolution* (London, 1961), 6.

to allow us to speak of class as a dominant principle in social relations. That was to come.[22]

In this important discussion, a series of claims are made. The language of both Marx and Weber are heard, but neither are fully articulated, nor admitted. A modernization paradigm is immediately apparent: early modern society was on its way to somewhere else. On that journey, 'an incipient class dimension' is to be observed, standing at the gateway to modernity. That incipient class dimension existed within what Marxists used to call the objective world of economics: not only is exploitation perceived to exist, but (crucially) it is seen to be organized through market mechanisms. None the less, within the subjective world of social relations and power politics, the early modern lower orders, enveloped 'in relationships of communality and deference' lacked 'alternative conceptions of the social order'. If not exclusive, these were at least hegemonic; their 'localism' dovetailed with a lack of class-based 'institutions'. Antagonisms between social groups existed, but were temporary and local. From this series of negativities which illuminate what early modern society was *not*, we can discern the positive definition of class which motivates Wrightson's account. A real class, a class-for-itself, is seen as possessing permanent and nationally organized political institutions which articulate its own vision of how society should be organized, and as striving towards such a condition. Class is presented as dependent upon objective, material circumstances. These form the combustible material which is ignited by experience and agency into national political struggle. It is inferred that in the modern, industrial society of mid-nineteenth-century Britain, a working class could be positively identified in all these respects. It is explicitly stated that in 'pre-industrial', early modern England a working class could not be so identified. The periodization depends upon Weber; the internal theorization of nineteenth-century class formation upon the culturalist Marxism of Edward Thompson.

All of this made sense within a social history paradigm which saw the end-point of early modernity at the close of the eighteenth century, where class was being formed. It makes rather less sense if that end-point were to be removed. That removal is currently being effected. Yet we need not assume that the destruction of the modernization model renders the concept of class useless. Ironically, the postmodernists' claim that social identities in modern Britain were more contingent and less homogeneous

---

[22] Wrightson, *English society*, 65. For a very similar formulation, see Underdown, *Revel, riot and rebellion*, 115. See also Wrightson's highly suggestive but ultimately frustrating 'The social order of early modern England', in L. Bonfield, R.M. Smith, K.E. Wrightson (eds.), *The world we have gained: histories of population and social structure* (Oxford, 1986),177–202.

than had first been thought, and that they were primarily constructed through discourse rather than produced out of economics, can prove positively useful in the re-evaluation of early modern social relations.[23] Rather than seeing in the early modern period a protracted transition from one condition of social relations to another, we are freed to assess the historical content of those relations on their own terms. Instead of measuring early modern social formations and identities against a reified category of class deriving from nineteenth-century experience, we can develop more flexible, sensitive and historicized understandings of class identity and conflict.[24] In the next section, I will sketch some of what I see as the salient features of class identity, illuminated by examples taken from the early modern Peak Country. The list is not exhaustive or proscriptive. Theorists and purists may be offended by the strange assemblage of authorities who stand behind some of my claims.[25] I can only say in my defence that I have tried to suggest a series of categories by which social relations and conflict might be understood historically. This is not an attempt to construct yet another universal model. We will begin with the most materialist of statements about class conflict, class formation and class identity.

RETHINKING CLASS IN EARLY MODERN ENGLAND

Class exists as a structural, economic fact, embedded in material life. Perceptions of social inequality, immiseration and exploitation are struc-

---

[23] I imagine that the leading proponent of postmodernist practice within nineteenth-century social history would not find himself in sympathy with this. After performing ritual postures concerning the 'untenable' nature of 'linear notions of class development', Patrick Joyce announces that 'there is no denying that class was a child of the nineteenth century': *Visions of the people*, 3, 1.

[24] The point has been made elsewhere. See for instance Thompson, 'Eighteenth century English society', 149–50, 151; W.M. Reddy, 'The concept of class', in M.L. Bush (ed.), *Social orders and social classes in Europe since 1500: studies in social stratification* (London, 1992), 23; and most recently G. Rosser, 'Crafts, guilds and the negotiation of work in the medieval town', *P&P*, 154 (1997), 9.

[25] Recent debates over the nature of class identity and the future of the 'social history' project have been very polarized. Protagonists have tended to work from stereotypes of one another's positions, while ignoring those areas of practical and conceptual overlap which might exist between materialist and post-structuralist approaches. I am thinking here of the recent debate over the legacy of E.P. Thompson and the purported 'death' of social history in the pages of *Social History* in the years 1992 to 1996. For what it matters, I tend to feel that much of the work of the early Marx does not lie a million miles away from the post-structuralist emphasis upon language, agency and ideology. For more on this, see especially P. Curry, 'Towards a post-Marxist social history: Thompson, Clark and beyond', in Wilson (ed.), *Rethinking social history*, 158–200; M.W. Steinberg, 'Culturally speaking: finding a commons between post-structuralism and the Thompsonian perspective', *Social History*, 21, 2 (1996), 193–214.

tured by and expressed through discourse, but remain built upon (if not always reducible to) a material reality. Dominant forms of production and exploitation inherently produce discontents and conflicts, and differences in the social distribution of wealth and power form the bedrock of all class societies. It therefore matters intensely to the history of social relations in the mid-seventeenth-century Peak Country that in 1658 the Earl of Rutland could spend £1,146 on 'Jewells' and some £4,000 on the wedding of his son, Lord Roos, while that same year a landless skilled miner working for wages in the Earl's mines could expect a yearly cash income of perhaps £18.[26] We are dealing here with extremes, of course. In other parts of England in 1658, it may well be that a largish, relatively affluent middling group existed between these two polarities.[27] But not in the Peak, which throughout the course of our period remained one of the poorest regions in England. Indeed, as we shall see in Part I, our hypothetical skilled miner stood near to the broad apex of village society in the mid-seventeenth-century Peak. As a means of demarcating blunt, harsh, cruel social facts, class therefore lives and breathes beyond discourse, just as differences in the distribution of wealth and power bleed into the discursive fabric of class identities.

Economic power could be very visibly centred. And in the early modern period, just as today, economic power meant political power. The location of that power in the manor house or the mine-owner's account book remains brutally obvious, and can be historically retrieved. But power was not the unmediated product of economics. Rather, the maintenance of social inequalities and exploitation depended upon politics. The power of dominant social groups could be accepted by their subordinates. It could also be negotiated, undermined, ignored, contradicted and overtly contested. Social conflict in the Peak possessed an inherent politics (the nature of which is explicitly discussed in Chapter 11) which took a public, collective form. In contesting the authority of lords, gentlemen, priests and employers, the miners and peasants of the Peak de-centred power from its traditional locations. Thereby, they helped to construct and renew a new set of exclusions and oppressions, in which women and unskilled men were locked out from political participation. Women's attempts to contest that exclusion complete the conceptual loop within local plebeian political culture.

Class is therefore about power in at least two important respects: as a means of defining the practice of social relations in the interest of ruling

[26] NAO, DJFM/83/1; miners' earnings calculated from PRO, RGO 33 and PRO, DL41/17/19.
[27] See most recently J. Barry and C. Brooks (eds.), *The middling sort of people: culture, society and politics in England, 1550–1800* (Basingstoke, 1994).

groups; and as a source of conflict over that practice. Both matters bear heavily upon the issue of social deference. Insofar as any debate exists over the nature of early modern social relations, it usually takes the form of a dispute over the extent to which social relations were conducted according to rules of deference and reciprocity, or to notions of class conflict.[28] Yet strong senses of class solidarity and dominant languages of social deference have been seen to co-exist in other historical contexts.[29] Rather than seeing class and deference as mutually exclusive, plebeian spirits of class antagonism and public faces of lower-class deference should be seen as two sides of the same coin.[30] Class societies consistently breed situations in which members of subordinated social groups are rendered visibly powerless. Those situations are themselves produced out of preceding periods of conflict, and can be intended to restate the threatened authority of a ruling group. Nowhere was this more apparent than in the matter of punishment. In the 1630s, the powerful gentleman Sir William Armyn prevented the inhabitants of Wirksworth from exercising their customary right to take timber from Cromford wood. Two 'poor men' whom Armyn caught 'stealing' timber there were flogged through the streets of their home town. When George Vallence and his brother John were also caught in Cromford wood in 1636, they therefore made public submission to Armyn, coming to the gentleman 'to humble themselves for such their trespass & to make their composicion wth him that they might not be sued for their offence soe made'. The event was still remembered with bitterness by the women and men of Wirksworth in the 1660s.[31] The mask of deference which the Vallence brothers wore stated their lack of power in the situation in which they found themselves. That lack of power took

---

[28] See for instance J.A. Sharpe, *Early modern England: a social history, 1550–1760* (London, 1987), 120–3, 223–4; Underdown, *Revel, riot and rebellion,* 168–74. On the foundations of the 'deference' model in functionalist sociology, see A. Arriaza, 'Mounsier and Barber: the theoretical underpinning of the "society of orders" in early modern Europe', *P&P,* 89 (1980), 39–57.

[29] Deference has seen as a by-product of the harsh class relations of post-Chartist south-east Lancashire: see P. Joyce, *Work, society and politics: the culture of the factory in later Victorian England* (London, 1980).

[30] I try to deal with the matter more fully in A. Wood, '"Poore men woll speke one daye": plebeian languages of deference and defiance in England, c. 1520–1640', in T. Harris (ed.), *The politics of the excluded in early modern England* (Basingstoke, forthcoming). For an important historical study of the subtleties of deference, see K.D.M. Snell, 'Deferential bitterness: the social outlook of the rural proletariat in the eighteenth and nineteenth centuries', in Bush (ed.) *Social orders and social classes,* 158–84. For an anthropological perspective, see J.C. Scott, *Domination and the arts of resistance: hidden transcripts* (Yale, 1990). For the classic sociological statement, see H. Newby, *The deferential worker: a study of farm workers in East Anglia* (London, 1977).

[31] PRO, DL4/109/8.

the form of a ritual act of submission, but was produced out of social conflict.

The language of deference held a real force within early modern society. Founded upon the unequal distribution of power, it required constant maintenance through displays of coercion and contempt on the part of elites. But it also fed into ritualized exchanges between social groups which might mask a real friendship. By the late seventeenth century, for instance, a dole of ale was traditionally given by mine overseers to their workforce upon striking through into new veins. Such relations cut both ways: in the late sixteenth century, free miners in Wirksworth chose not to exercise their controversial right of free mining in one local gentleman's fields because he was 'a very good housekeep[er] & generally beloved of all the miners'.[32] But the language of deference could cover over a more complex and political interplay of social relationships. In 1659, the miners of Youlgreave thanked the Earl of Devonshire for the 'clemency' he displayed in not prosecuting them for their trespass on to Meadowplecke Grange, on which they and their ancestors had long claimed a customary right of free mining. In the same document, the Earl granted the miners the rights over the Grange which they had long sought. Represented as a grant from a gracious lord to a recalcitrant plebeian group, in fact an agreement had been reached over Meadowplecke Grange in which Devonshire came out the loser. Shortly before 1659, the Earl of Rutland had defeated the last of a protracted series of attempts by the Youlgreave miners to claim a right of free mining on his nearby Haddon estate. In granting the Youlgreave miners free mining rights in Meadowplecke Grange, Devonshire avoided the disruption and expenses to which Rutland had been put. The document in which the new customs were agreed was worded so as to save the Earl's face.[33] Displays of deference and hierarchy were always, therefore, extremely political.

When representing their grievances or answering complaints before courts, plebeians spoke of themselves in a submissive language which was belied by their actions. In the *c.* 1590–1640 period, the Peak miners fought protracted disputes with their superiors over their claimed right of free mining, resulting in a series of legal actions, riots and organized invasions of gentry estates. Yet in representing their grievances to the Westminster courts which adjudicated in those disputes, the miners described themselves as submissive and powerless, arguing that since they were 'poore men', they should be 'suffered and supported to digge and searche for lead'.[34]

---

[32] PRO, RGO 33; PRO, DL4/72/31.

[33] BL, Add. MSS 6678, fols. 1–13. For the Haddon disputes, see Chapters 10 and 12 below.

[34] S.R. Gardiner (ed.), *Reports of cases in the Star Chamber and High Commission*, Camden Society, new ser., 39 (1886), 106; PRO, DL4/72/31.

Claims to poverty and powerlessness were seen to guarantee rights.[35] Appeals to elite authorities could flatter, cajole or threaten. Around 1650, the inhabitants of Litton made petition to the Earl of Rutland, requesting his intervention in their dispute with their lord, who sought to enclose their commons. The petitioners asked for 'pittie' and 'compassion' from the Earl, and then went on:

Farre bee it from us to censure, who rather desire to pray for your Honour: yet as we cannot be insensible of that imm[in]ent danger which threatens us & our posteritie, so are wee very sensible of the mouths which will bee opened against & that vaile of disgrace which would be drawn over that Ancient and Hoble. house of Hadden if this should be written of her & recorded to future generations that she deserted tenants & sold them over into the hands of a merciless man.[36]

The petitioners were moved more by tactics than deference. Many of the named petitioners had themselves run into trouble with the House of Hadden. Although their plea to the Earl was couched in the classical language of deference, its sting is still apparent: for England's gentry and nobility were taught to place great weight upon reciprocity and reputation. The Litton inhabitants were here attempting to exploit that system of thought, arguing that if the Earl should be seen to desert his tenants, then the credit of the House of Hadden could only suffer.

The dominant discourse which assumed a reciprocal exchange of patronage and deference could therefore be contested, exploited and undermined. In so doing, lower-class individuals and groups could unbalance local systems of power, if only for a moment. The long-running disputes over customary law which gave the politics of social conflict its peculiar flavour within the Peak Country provided the experiential basis upon which plebeians could reimagine the local social order in highly conflictual and polarized terms. In describing social conflict, plebeians sometimes fell reflexively into a language of class. The idiomatic quality of that language persisted through the sixteenth, seventeenth and eighteenth centuries, and defined an opposition of material interest between 'Rich and Powerful men' and 'Poor men' over the matter of custom in particular.[37] In that encounter, 'Rich men' held a series of structural advantages. Most obviously, miners and cottagers could be physically coerced by mounted and armed gentlemen and their retainers using 'Terrer & Feare' and 'grette force & stronge hand'. Plebeians conceived of the 'power and commaunde' of 'Rich

[35] For other examples, see *APC, 1615–16*, 224; HLRO, MP 9 April 1624; PRO, C2/JasI/G2/48; PRO, DL1/352, answer of Anthony Harding *et al.*; LPL, Shrewsbury MS 705, fol. 110.
[36] SA, Bag C 2094.
[37] Quotations are from: PRO, DL4/43/24, /27/26, /53/59, /72/31, /144/1746/1; PRO, C21/F11/10, /C11/10, /D1/13; PRO, REQ2/3/301; PRO, E178/611. Examples are dated anywhere between 1518 and 1746.

men' as socially produced. The bonds of blood, marriage and interest which linked gentry and noble families together were known to early modern plebeians long before historians identified the existence of gentry 'county communities'. Peak miners and peasants knew that 'rich men' held 'greate power & commaunde' as part of a network with other 'rich men'. Thus 'men of great power & substance' could threaten 'pore men' 'wth [their] own greatnes and the greatnes of [their] freinds', and 'Powerful men . . . [held] great Comande . . . by themselves their kindred and alleyances.' The exercise of that social and political power was built upon and driven by economics: 'Great rich men . . . keepe great score of sheepe'. 'Men of welthe & estate' denied poor men their right through the overstocking of the commons, and thereby increased their own profits. Most importantly, 'powerful men . . . by violence [have] holden the myners down by their own combynacion', to deny the right of free mining in their own interest. All of this bred a close awareness of the basic inequalities of wealth and power which ran through class society. 'Great men could do great things', but 'poor men' could not.

Yet this did not mean that 'poor men' had no voice in the contest. It was known that the legal system could be biased in favour of the rich. In the early seventeenth century, tithe proprietors threatened the miners with their 'Orders and Decrees' and 'threats, imprisonments [and] punishments'. John Gell in particular was known as a 'powerfull man' who did not hesitate to 'undoe' those miners who opposed him. Similarly, the mid-seventeenth century miners' 'rich and powerful . . . oppressor' the Earl of Rutland was able to manipulate the legal system through 'niceities at law', and enjoyed privileged access to the 'power of the lord's house'.[38] But in order to secure its authority, the law had to give 'poor men' a voice. Collective litigation before central law courts engendered organizational skills and legal knowledge in local cultures, and built within them a tradition of resistance. That tradition became most visible in the instances of riot and demonstration which went together with popular collective litigation in the Peak Country during the *c.* 1590–1660 period. The miners of the Peak were at the forefront of this movement.

Classes are identified in relationship to other classes through systems of difference. Class identities are thereby built into the proscription of gender difference.[39] In identifying 'rich men' as the opponents of free mining

[38] PRO, E112/75/165, /294/31; N. Kirkham, 'Lead miners and royalists', *Derbyshire Miscellany*, 2, 5 (1961), 294; *The case of a publique business*, (1649?) DCL; BL, Add. MS 6677, fol. 49.

[39] G.M. Sider, *Culture and class in anthropology and history: a Newfoundland illustration* (Cambridge, 1986), 5–9; Thompson, *Making*, 12; J.W. Scott, 'On language, gender and working-class history', in her *Gender and the politics of history* (New York, 1988), 62, 66.

custom, Peak miners drew an upper limit to their social identity. By *c.* 1600, to be a Peak miner was to be a member of a community of skilled, knowledgeable, adult, plebeian men who respected custom and tradition, and who were prepared to fight (legally, politically and perhaps physically) in defence of their rights. Built into that identity were a series of inclusions, enabling 'poor men' to claim 'rights' which stood in opposition to the interests of 'rich men'. And at the hard edges of that identity lay a series of exclusions. In this instance as in so many others, conscious class identity therefore appears as relational, differential, and profoundly normative. It was also historically specific. The elucidation of the historical process whereby that construction was established is the central concern of Part II of this book, but should be noted here.

In 1581, the customs by which the lead industry had been governed were in a state of flux, imperilling the hitherto dominant position of the free miners. On some manors, lords were preventing the miners from digging in their estates, and were employing waged labourers to dig the deposits in their place. Elsewhere, thousands of poor, semi-vagrant 'cavers' were undercutting the free miners by flooding local markets with the scraps of lead ore they had taken from ancient rubbish tips. Yet within a generation, the miners had regained control, and had established themselves as a key interest group in local politics. Their new collective agency was bound up with the simultaneous redefinition of their identity, as miners came to see themselves as markedly different both from lords and from women and the unskilled. The coincidence of the specification of class and gender difference was not accidental. In 1581, some High Peak miners provided the fullest and one of the earliest statements of those interconnected exclusions.[40] They condemned the 'comon disorder' which resulted from the employment of 'men women and children that have little skill' in the mines by 'riche men', and presented in this the failure of the barmaster to uphold the customs of the industry. Defining themselves as the 'auncient and skilful miners', they presented themselves as the protectors of the 'auncient orders' of their industry and their communities against the combined threat of 'riche men' and 'unskilfull folke'. Both custom and skill were thereby taken as a male possession, at the same time as a social opposition was imagined between 'riche men' and 'skilful miners'. When male plebeians spoke of social conflict, they did so in highly gendered terms: 'rich men' opposed 'poor men'. The claim was fictional, but universal. In reality, many of the noble and gentry opponents of the plebeian interest were women. The names of Bess of Hardwick, Christiana the dowager Countess of Devonshire, Lady Grace Manners, Mrs Jennet Carrier and Lady Isabel Bowes will

---

[40] PRO, E178/611, more fully discussed in Chapter 7 below.

feature prominently in our discussion of the twists and turns of the politics of social conflict. Similarly, plebeian women had a real interest in the exercise of common rights and the maintenance of key aspects of customary law. As we shall see in Chapter 11, the public plebeian political culture of the early modern Peak Country allowed relatively little formal space to women. Part II of this book is partly concerned with how that exclusion was attempted, and with the nature of plebeian women's contestation of authority.

Class identities therefore emerge as contingent, unstable, relational and dynamic. Like gender, class is of necessity always being defined.[41] The comparison is more than rhetorical: for early modern conceptions of social order and disorder were highly gendered. Albeit in different contexts, the gendered sectionalism of the male working-class politics of the 1780–1832 period was shared by its predecessors. Following recent studies of that later period, class and gender will here be seen as intimately connected.[42] This study will reach forwards in time to connect with the rich social history of the early Industrial Revolution. Certain key similarities will be observed. But in Chapter 14 a key discontinuity will be noted, as the plebeian political tradition *of* the Peak Country is seen to twist into a working-class political tradition *in* the Peak Country. We will observe a different kind of class formation in which the fabric of early modern solidarities was partially unravelled and reworked. Yet we should not suppose that the regional specification of plebeian culture prior to 1780 ensures the absence of class identity. Studies of class formation have long been hampered by modern social historians' strange obsession with the nation-state. Ever since late nineteenth- and early twentieth-century European socialists linked their political project to the transformed national identities of that period, social historians have been mesmerized by that single definition of class identity.[43] The assumption that 'true' class consciousness can only be manifest on the level of the nation-state has led historians to find in the closely felt local and regional plebeian identities of the early modern period one of the main barriers to the

---

[41] Here paraphrasing L. Gowing, *Domestic dangers: women, words and sex in early modern London* (Oxford, 1996), 28.

[42] Most especially L. Davidoff and C. Hall, *Family fortunes: men and women of the English middle class 1780–1850* (London, 1987), and A. Clark, *The struggle for the breeches: gender and the making of the British working class* (London, 1995). It is unfortunate that early modern social historians have often tended to consider gender identities as a discrete field of inquiry, without relationship to social identities. For an attempt at unravelling the complexities of that relationship, see S.D. Amussen, *An ordered society: gender and class in early modern England* (Oxford, 1988).

[43] The subject perhaps needs its own historian, but see the very suggestive remarks in D. Sassoon, *One hundred years of socialism: the West European Left in the twentieth century* (London, 1996), 5–8.

operation of class.[44] The reductive connection between nation and class reaches its logical dead end in the argument that the gentry and nobility comprised the only 'real' class in early modern England, since they were the only social collectivity that was organized on a national level.[45] Yet the history of modern European working-class political culture has often been the history of regions and localities. Whether historians are describing the insurrectionists of the Paris Commune, the mining communities of the Rhondda valley or the Anarchists of Catalonia, class and local identity have in many contexts been historically inseparable.

Class identities are therefore inscribed in space, and frequently depend upon strong local and regional cultures.[46] Peculiarities of local social structure can help to maintain the junction of social identity in particular places. Hence, the domination of a particular industry within a discrete territory can ground social identities within a specific site; similarly, the sudden collapse of that industry can break the collectivities and fracture the communities inhabited by class solidarities. Culturally, senses of local history can be written into the material environment, encoding memories of past struggles or lost liberties. Rather than requiring a national focus, the imagination of class identity can proceed from a reading of local history. The control of local histories by a subordinate social group can therefore become an empowering force, legitimizing the public political practice of a class as the defence of a community or a tradition.[47] In all these respects, local histories can become rather less antiquarian and rather more political. One way of approaching the historical study of social identities is therefore through an appreciation of local culture. In the early modern period, this should be especially appropriate, for it was within the locality or the small region such as the Peak Country that plebeian social identities were imagined.

LOCAL CULTURES AND POPULAR CULTURES

All social history should try to be comparative, moved by a sensitivity to difference and similarity across space and time.[48] Yet at the same time, social history must describe and analyse historical situations within contexts which were meaningful to their subject. These impulses conflict with

---

[44] Hence Underdown draws a distinction between 'localism' and 'class antagonism': *Revel, riot and rebellion*, 110.

[45] Laslett, *World we have lost*, ch. 2. But see also C. Hill, 'A one-class society?', in his *Change and continuity*, 205–18.

[46] M. Savage, 'Space, networks and class formation', in N. Kirk (ed.), *Social class and Marxism: defences and challenges* (Aldershot, 1996), 58–86.

[47] See J. Fentress and C. Whickham, *Social memory* (Oxford, 1992), 114–26.

[48] P. Abrams, *Historical sociology* (Shepton Mallet, 1982).

one another, generating a creative tension which has helped to drive this book. We will see that the story told here has a broad historical relevance. Early modern historians will find that the description of economic processes and social structures within the Peak Country adds to the limited literature concerning the history of English industrial regions.[49] The discussion of popular politics connects to current debates over the nature of early modern social relations and conflict, and to popular allegiances during the English Revolution. The account of custom, community and popular culture is addressed to the larger social history of the period. At the same time, historians of different periods should discern other strains in our story. The history of the Peak Country between 1520 and 1770 bears upon historical understandings of economics and social structure, industrialization and early capitalism, gender and class identities, literacy and popular culture, magic and official belief, state formation, law and custom, subordination, contestation and rebellion.

But this book is not simply a case-study of bigger issues. For us, 'the local' is a 'substantive' rather than a 'methodological' focus.[50] We approach the Peak Country as a place possessed of a historically important meaning in its own right. Its topography and mineral resources gave the region a distinct physical appearance, and helped to generate social structures and local identities within which the construction of cultural difference was articulated. Most importantly, that regional identity had a special force within early modern popular culture. Rather than seeing the Peak as the unproblematic backdrop to the history of larger processes, we will see it as central to popular culture. To that end, 'local culture' will be seen as interchangeable with 'popular culture'.[51] This, of course, represents a large simplification. Boundaries between 'elite/gentry' and 'plebeian/ popular' culture were not fixed. Members of the gentry could partake of aspects of local culture at times – on Wakes days, or on perambulations of the bounds, for instance. Neither was popular culture homogeneous. Differences of religion, literacy, gender, place, social status and age ran through early modern English popular culture, whether studied from the

---

[49] For which, see especially Levine and Wrightson, *Making of an industrial society*; M. Zell, *Industry in the countryside: Wealden society in the sixteenth century* (Cambridge, 1994); V.H.T. Skipp, *Crisis and development: an ecological case study of the Forest of Arden, 1570–1674* (Cambridge, 1978); D. Hey, *The fiery blades of Hallamshire: Sheffield and its neighbourhood, 1660–1740* (Leicester, 1991).

[50] Savage, 'Space', 71.

[51] D.E. Underdown, 'Regional cultures? Local variations in popular culture during the early modern period', in T. Harris (ed.), *Popular culture in England, 1500–1850* (Basingstoke, 1995), 28–47. For an evocative reconstruction of popular culture in one region, see Rollison, *Local origins*.

macro- or micro-perspective.[52] Yet members of the gentry were at best only occasional participants in local culture: they could chose to partake of or to withdraw from the rough-and-tumble of village life. Plebeian men and women, old and young, or richer and poorer inhabitants might frequently perceive of one another as culturally distinct. Yet all made claims within the language of local, popular culture, and most of all upon the legitimizing grounds of custom and neighbourliness. Village disputes, while calling the historians' attention to discontents and divisions within local culture, at the same time reaffirmed its existence.

We begin, then, with the Peak Country. Bounded on the east, west and north by dark gritstone moors, the lead mining area of the early modern Peak sat in a wide limestone plateau, watered by the rivers Derwent and Wye and their tributaries (see Map 1). It is with the affairs of the human population of that limestone plateau that we are here concerned. The scattered inhabitants of the area which is today known as the Dark Peak – that is, those large tracts of gritstone moor which lay to the north of the lead field – must find their own historian. Devoid of lead deposits, and possessed of scant cultivable land, the history of the Dark Peak's inhabitants was quite different from that of their neighbours in the hills and valleys of the lead mining area. Like David Underdown's study of the West Country, we will develop an intimate knowledge of the geology and geography of the Peak Country. We will observe the importance of landscape and material environment in conditioning local conflicts, cultures and social structures within the Peak.[53] Yet structural and cultural differences were not the simple, unmediated product of ecology and economy. The peculiarities of administrative boundaries within the Peak were at least as important to the construction of local difference as was the material environment. From time to time, this study will therefore dwell in perverse detail upon the significance of changes in the legal, cultural and political meanings given to administrative boundaries. Those meanings were far from unproblematic, for they gave a concrete definition to abstract demands to rights or authority. In establishing that a particular custom operated within a specific place, or that a certain form of lordship pertained somewhere, local meanings were subject to change. We have seen in the preceding section how social identities depended upon the creation and maintenance of cultural boundaries. Those boundaries were often conceived in spatial terms, and drawn upon the material environment. Hence the village, the manor or the 'Country' could be reimagined as the

---

[52] See most recently T. Harris, 'Problematising popular culture', in Harris (ed.), *Popular culture*, 1–27.

[53] Underdown, *Revel, riot and rebellion, passim.*

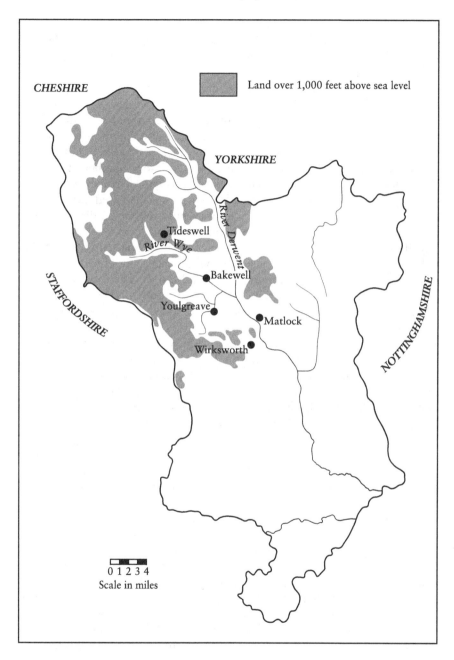

Map 1   The topography of the Peak Country

possession of one group to the exclusion of another. Boundaries and the places they demarcated 'thus became a key battleground – a key field – in which different social and cultural interests were played out'.[54] If they are to do justice to their subject, neither the social nor the cultural historian can therefore afford to ignore the history of jurisdictional change in the Peak.

The lead mining area of the Peak Country covered about a quarter of the county of Derbyshire, and some twenty-one parishes fell within its bounds (see Maps 2 and 3). Some of these parishes, such as Bakewell and Wirksworth, were extremely large, and were divided into a number of smaller chapelries. None the less, the sheer size of the typical parish within the Peak meant that local identity tended to be village-based rather than parochial. The parish enters into our story only insofar as disputes over parochial tithes defined it as an important arena of local conflict. Day-to-day life was focused rather more upon the village or the small town. Most individual settlements fell into a single civil township, of which there were some fifty-seven within the mining area (see Map 4). The townships were the basis of civil administration within the county of Derbyshire as a whole, and were divided into six agglomerates, called Hundreds (see Map 3). Most of the lead mining area fell into two of these Hundreds: the Wapentake of Wirksworth in the south of the lead field, and the Hundred of High Peak in the centre and north. Township boundaries were ordered within the manorial structure of the Peak Country (see Map 5). Every township formed a constituent part of a manor. A manor might contain only one such township, but typically spanned a number of coterminous townships. Most land within the Peak Country was held by the Crown, through the Duchy of Lancaster. The Duchy owned four very large manors within the Peak: namely, the manors of High Peak, Castleton, Hartingdon and Wirksworth. What remained fell into a variety of estates, the most important of which were the lordships of Ashford and Haddon. Like the Peak's parochial structure, the manor matters more as a focus of social conflict than as a unit of day-to-day life. The boundaries of manors and lordships expressed the limits within which manorial custom operated. At the beginning of our period, such boundaries were vague and flexible. But between c. 1570 and 1660, the nature of lordship and the whereabouts of manorial boundaries were given much sharper specifications. This legal and spatial clarification of manorial difference was produced out of conflict over the ownership and control of resources. Of special importance was the miners' claim to a right of free mining which transcended manorial difference. Arguing that they enjoyed the right to dig for lead ore wherever

[54] M. Johnson, *An archaeology of capitalism* (Oxford, 1996), 71.

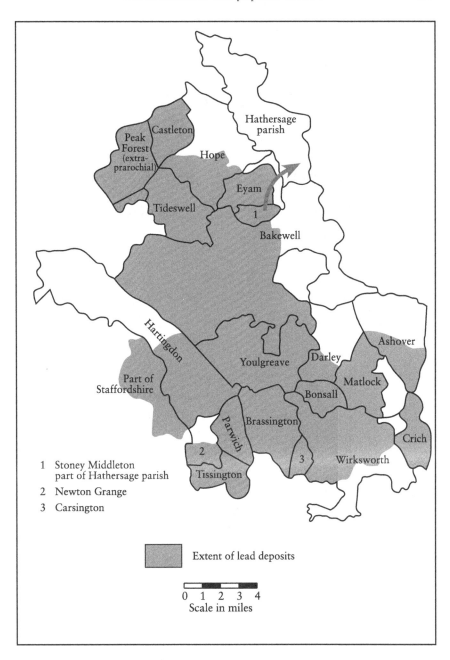

Map 2   The parishes of the Peak lead field

Map 3   The administrative divisions of Derbyshire

it was to be found, the miners arrived at a radically different definition of the Peak Country from that of their social superiors. Social conflict therefore entailed a reimagination of local identity, as the Peak Country became not merely the site of dispute, but its conceptual subject.

The clarification of jurisdictional difference represented more than the simple statement of where one manor ended and another began. Like the large-scale enclosure of commons, it wrote the defeat of the free mining interest on to the landscape. Miners barred from access to a manor in which they had hitherto exercised free mining rights understandably came to a different perception of space than that which prevailed prior to their ejection. So too the enclosure of common land reordered both the material environment and senses of community. Yet in spite of the bifurcation of local identities within the Peak Country, both the place and its plebeian inhabitants continued to be conceived of as distinct. In seeing the so-called 'Peakrills' as an undifferentiated mass of industrial workers, writers like Defoe and Cotton obscured the social, cultural and local differences through which the place's inhabitants understood one another. Save for when the miners spoke of their desire to extend their customs across all the lead-bearing parts of the county, Peak plebeians tended to refer to exclusive, local identities which cut into any homogeneous spatial identity within the region. Yet in the miners' political project, as much as in their tactics and organization, lay a wider sense of community. That wider community was negatively implicit in the off-hand remarks of some plebeian men who gave evidence to the Court of the Duchy of Lancaster in the early seventeenth century.

Giving evidence in 1640, some of the men of Wirksworth referred to the county town of Derby, lying only eight miles from their home town, as a 'Remote place'. One of the limits on migration patterns within the Peak seems to have been the boundaries of the lead field. This affected broader perceptions of community and regionality. While Brassington miners were pulled into disputes concerning the mining rights of other manors within the lead field, the eighty-year-old John Land of that town could say in 1615 that while he 'hath knowen the mannor of Wirkesworth threescore yeares . . . [he] doth not know the mannor of Ashburne [lying four miles distant], becuaes he hath had little to do there'. John Land, like other miners, seems to have centred his movements and attentions upon the orefield. The Peak Country appears only rarely to have been imagined by its own inhabitants as a composite whole. Asked in 1625 to give an account of his Wapentake of Wirksworth to Duchy commissioners, Robert Shawe of Elton explained that 'the townes of Ashbourne & Wirkesworth . . . doe lye in the outside of the said weapontake & southward in respect of the hundred of the high peake . . . the said townes are called Ashbourne in the peake, & Wirkes-

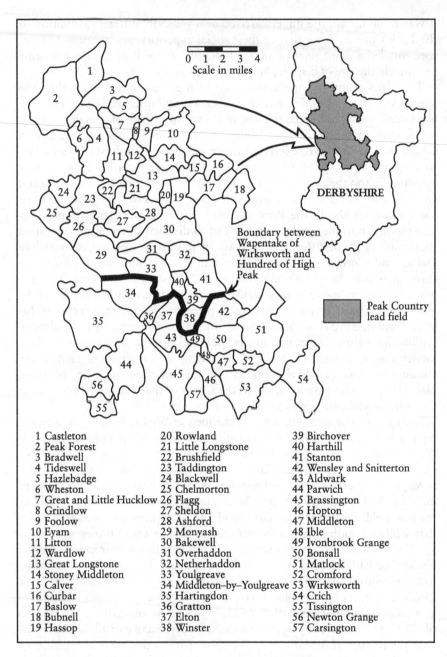

0 1 2 3 4
Scale in miles

DERBYSHIRE

Boundary between
Wapentake of
Wirksworth and
Hundred of High
Peak

Peak Country
lead field

1 Castleton	20 Rowland	39 Birchover
2 Peak Forest	21 Little Longstone	40 Harthill
3 Bradwell	22 Brushfield	41 Stanton
4 Tideswell	23 Taddington	42 Wensley and Snitterton
5 Hazlebadge	24 Blackwell	43 Aldwark
6 Wheston	25 Chelmorton	44 Parwich
7 Great and Little Hucklow	26 Flagg	45 Brassington
8 Grindlow	27 Sheldon	46 Hopton
9 Foolow	28 Ashford	47 Middleton
10 Eyam	29 Monyash	48 Ible
11 Litton	30 Bakewell	49 Ivonbrook Grange
12 Wardlow	31 Overhaddon	50 Bonsall
13 Great Longstone	32 Netherhaddon	51 Matlock
14 Stoney Middleton	33 Youlgreave	52 Cromford
15 Calver	34 Middleton–by–Youlgreave	53 Wirksworth
16 Curbar	35 Hartingdon	54 Crich
17 Baslow	36 Gratton	55 Tissington
18 Bubnell	37 Elton	56 Newton Grange
19 Hassop	38 Winster	57 Carsington

Map 4   The township boundaries of the Peak Country lead field

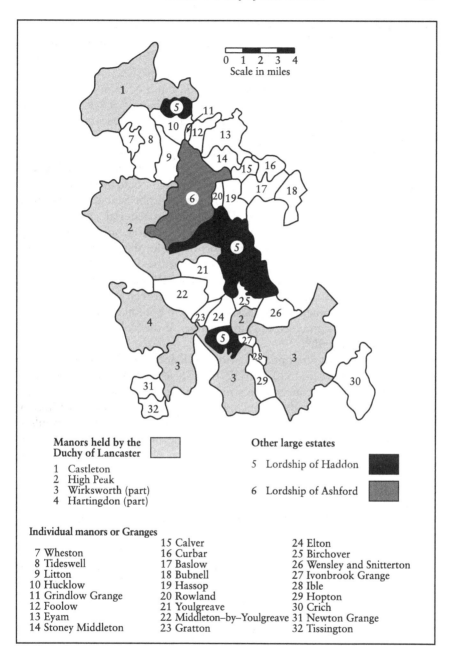

Map 5   The manorial structure of the Peak lead field, *c.* 1640

worth in the peake by southern men'.[55] Writing a memorandum of 'the Great Snow' of 1615, the parish clerk of Youlgreave called into his mind an image of the region he inhabited. In that year, the snow had covered 'this peake c[ou]ntry' and 'these mountaynes' about his parish. The bad weather had touched the 'south ptes' beyond the Peak, but a quite different pattern had prevailed in 'Lankshyre & Cheshyre' that winter.[56] It was only upon leaving or entering the Peak Country that its identity became apparent. Enfolded within that place, what mattered to its plebeian inhabitants were the spatial, social and cultural differences they felt between one another. Yet its regional identity was, and remains, obvious. Its geography marked the place as distinct. In the winter time, people could easily die while crossing the moors which separated the region from Scarsdale Hundred, Staffordshire and the north-west. The dominant material culture of the Peak remained vernacular and local. First the gentry, and by the early eighteenth century the small middling sort of the local market towns, aped the fashionable building styles of the south. But the 'Peakrills' remained in their huts, cottages and caves. The 'Peak-wheat' and oat-cakes they ate, like the thick dialect they spoke and the poverty of their condition, marked them as men and women of the Peak Country. In both material and cultural terms, the Peak was amongst the most distinct of the 'cultural provinces' of early modern England.[57]

This book will not attempt to provide a full account of the history of the Peak Country between 1520 and 1770. Instead, it tells a series of overlapping stories which concentrate strictly on some key themes: the origins of capitalism in early modern England; the sources of social conflict in that society; and the nature of plebeian political culture. One of the impulses which has driven the production of this book has been the desire to write as full an account as possible of an early modern plebeian political culture. That culture will be shown to have been riven with and moved by contradiction. In some respects it was far from inclusive, yet was capable of transcending its own limitations. At one moment mean-spirited and cold, at another moment the plebeian politics of the Peak could articulate a social opposition or speak to a vision of different possibilities with an authority which remains moving. In their encounters with the 'Great men' and 'Powerful men' of early modern England, the miners and smallholders of the Peak seemed possessed of few material, cultural or political resources. Yet for three generations before 1660 they fought a long,

---

[55] PRO, DL4/94/56, 64/14, 75/10; A. Wood, 'Migration and local identity in early modern England' (forthcoming).

[56] DRO, D3644/42/1, p. 73.

[57] On 'cultural provinces', see C. Phythian-Adams, *Re-thinking English local history* (University of Leicester, Dept of English Local History, Occasional Papers, 4th ser., no. 1, 1987).

protracted conflict with their would-be rulers. The historical fact of that conflict gives the lie to the supposition that early modern plebeians were not possessed of a politics. By the Restoration, that politics was exhausted, and the miners settled down to a long, painful defence of established freedoms. Those freedoms, given the name of custom, were won by the poor, illiterate and apparently powerless ancestors of the 'subterranean wretches' whom Defoe encountered in 1717. The circumstances in which the miners of the Derbyshire Peak Country created their politics were not of their own choosing. But in their encounters with established authority they made their own history.

Part I

THE STRUCTURES OF INEQUALITY

2

Economy and society in the Peak Country, c. 1520–1570

TECHNOLOGY AND INDUSTRY

The responses of educated Augustan visitors to the Peak Country may have been scripted, and their views of the Peak's inhabitants patronizing or dismissive. But at least their writings provide some contemporary sense of the region and its people. The further the historian's reach extends back in time, the more elusive becomes the world of the 'Peakrills'. Even the most comprehensive accounts of sixteenth-century England shed little light upon the region. Camden understood Derbyshire's division into a pastoral, industrial north and an agrarian south, and knew that in the 'mountains, lead stones are daily digged up in great abundance', but his account of the lead industry was well out of date at the time of its publication.[1] In his journeys of 1535–43, John Leland missed the Peak. His only mention of the area noted its two market towns, the 'Castel of the hy Peke longging to the King', and sketched the routes of its major rivers, the Derwent and the Wye. He intended to discuss the boundaries, forests, monastic houses, the 'Notable Places of Gentilmen' and the 'Frutefulnes of the Shire', but never completed the task. The Peak lay upon the margins of his journeys, his writings and his England.[2]

In the absence of colourful travel writings, the historian of the sixteenth century Peak Country must rely upon the archive, and here too the record is uneven. The economic history of the late medieval region has been reconstructed in some detail.[3] But of the social structures of the Peak in the early sixteenth century, very little is known. In this chapter, we shall begin

---

[1] W. Camden, *Britannia* (1596; Eng. trans., London, 1610), 556.
[2] L. Toulmin Smith (ed.), *The itinerary of John Leland in or about the years 1535–43*, 5 vols. (London, 1964), V, 31–2.
[3] D. Kiernan, *The Derbyshire lead industry in the sixteenth century*, DRS, 14 (Chesterfield, 1989); I.S.W. Blanchard, 'Economic change in Derbyshire in the late middle ages, 1262–1540', PhD thesis, University of London, 1967.

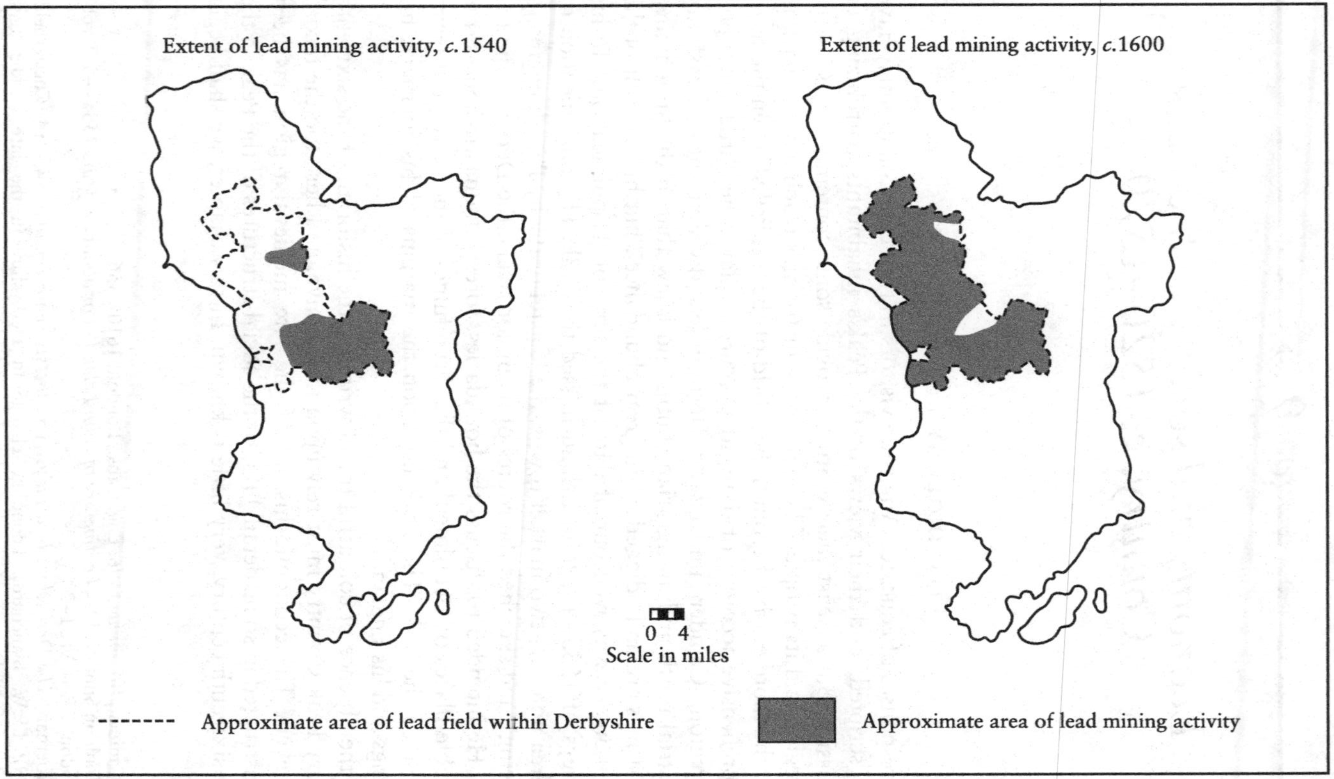

Extent of lead mining activity, c.1540

Extent of lead mining activity, c.1600

Scale in miles

0   4

------- Approximate area of lead field within Derbyshire

Approximate area of lead mining activity

Map 6   The growth of the Peak lead field, c. 1540–1660

with what is already known: that is, with the history of the relatively well-documented lead industry. Close attention will then be given to the social structures of the mining town of Wirksworth and its adjacent villages in the early sixteenth century. The broad characteristics of the region's farming economy will receive attention, followed by a discussion of population distribution in 1563.

The Derbyshire lead industry's medieval history was one of long-term booms and slumps, pushed by shorter-term fluctuations. At the beginning of the sixteenth century, the industry was recovering from the latest depression, which had lasted for the preceding hundred years. Lead mining activity had been reduced into the south-east corner of the lead field, within the Wapentake of Wirksworth (see Map Six). Within this area recovery from fifteenth-century depression was swift. Production of lead ore within the Wapentake increased roughly threefold between *c.* 1480 and 1520, reaching a yearly output of around 1,400 loads. By the early 1540s, ore production had doubled again.[4] For all that this recovery was locally specific, important changes in the scale and character of the Wirksworth industry are implied in the approximate sixfold increase of ore production which occurred between *c.* 1480 and 1540.[5]

The mining workforce of the *c.* 1480–1540 period remained dominated by the key group of the medieval industry: the free miners. Working in gangs of two or three, perhaps supplemented by a labourer who carried ore to the surface and cleaned it, free mining groups claimed a universal right to dig for lead ore wherever it was found. This right of free mining extended across the Duchy of Lancaster's Peak estates, an area known collectively as the 'King's (or Queen's) Field'. Within the hierarchy of the mining workforce, the free miners stood above a second category of workers, the 'cavers' or 'purcasers', who dug over the miners' rubbish tips for scraps of ore. For all that they affected to despise the cavers, the source of the free miners' independence lay more in their customs than in their economic circumstances. Most miners owed money to wealthier orebuyers who operated on the behalf of powerful smelters and lead merchants. Drawn from the wealthiest of the yeomanry and the gentry, these smelters and merchants were known as the 'brenners'. Many had cannily purchased

---

[4] I.S.W. Blanchard, 'Derbyshire lead production, 1195–1505', *DAJ*, 2nd ser., 91 (1971), 125–9; Kiernan, *Lead industry*, 36–7. A dish was the basic unit by which lead production was measured. A standard dish, known as the 'King's dish', had been established within the Duchy's King's Field by 1512. This measured about 14 Winchester pints, or 60–5 lb of ore. Nine dishes made up a load, or approximately 5 cwt of ore. The 'King's dish' soon became the universal measure across the whole of the lead field.
[5] For the moribund High Peak mining industry, see PRO, DL1/29/F9; Kiernan, *Lead industry*, 3, 6.

the leases of the Duchy of Lancaster's tolls on the lead industry. [6] Most important of all leases was that to the 'lot' and 'cope' of the industry. The 'lot' duty was raised from the miners and consisted of a one thirteenth of their production, while the 'cope' was levied upon the purchaser in any ore sale, who was obliged to pay four pence (later raised to six pence) upon every load purchased. The lessee of the Duchy's lot and cope was also entitled to a 'lord's meer' on newly discovered lead veins. Stakes upon the lead deposits were known as meers, each meer being a stretch of territory varying between twenty-seven and thirty-two yards. Upon the discovery of a new vein, the finder took the first two meers, and the lord or their lessee took the third ('lord's') meer. Finally, after the 1530s the lessee of the Duchy's lot and cope also occupied the important office of barmaster. The barmaster was responsible for calling the barmote courts which regulated mining activity, for collecting dues, and for maintaining the customs of the industry. The political potential of the office was obvious to its holders who increasingly extended their claims at the expense of the miners and cavers (see Chapters 6 and 9). Moreover, after the 1480s, brenners bought or seized mineworkings, employing wage labourers to dig the lead. This process was gradual, and was to take over a century to achieve domination over other forms of ore production. But in the brenners' acquisition of mineshares is found the first organizational separation of labour from capital, and a challenge to the hegemony of the free miner within the political economy of the lead field. [7]

No contemporary description exists of early sixteenth-century mining.[8] Most mines were probably very small, and typically took the form of open cast quarries which followed lead veins along the surface of the land. Early sixteenth-century miners referred to their workings as 'hooles' rather than (as they were to later in the century), 'mines' and 'groves'. Above the mines, the cavers dug over rubbish tips and hunted for scraps of lead, knocking rubbish from the ore with their caving hammers.[9] By the 1540s, the extractive workforce numbered around 400, implying that some 2,000 people were dependent upon mining. The large majority of these workers did not only labour upon the mines. Production was affected by the demands of lambing and harvest and by the flooding of the lead deposits in

[6] S.M. Wright, *The Derbyshire gentry in the fifteenth century*, DRS, 8 (Chesterfield, 1983), 21–2.

[7] For examples of brenner-owned workings, 1480–1550, see PRO, DL1/29/F1a, /11/B6, /25/ D1. For a fuller discussion, see Blanchard, 'Economic change', 299–300.

[8] While recognizing its anachronisms, Kiernan relies on a description of mining methods from 1630: *Lead industry*, 11–13.

[9] Based on BL, Add. MSS 6685, fols. 56, 58, 32465, fols. 2–4; NAO, DD.P7/2; I.S.W. Blanchard, 'Rejoinder: Stannator Fabulosus', *AgHR*, 22 (1974), 65–7. A surviving example of a worked out opencast lead rake is to be found at Dirtlow rake, near Castleton.

the winter months. Only a small number of workers laboured through all or most of the year, as wage labourers or as full-time free miners.[10]

The nature of smelting technology also enforced a seasonal pattern upon lead production. Until the 1570s, Derbyshire ore was smelted in 'boles' which consisted of bonfires built into a three-sided structure, within which large amounts of lead ore were placed. Boles were sited at the tops of hills to catch the south-west winds of spring, so that powerful winds would stoke the flames, thereby increasing the temperature to the point at which the lead ore would melt. The ore would run down channels to be caught in trammels where it would set in an ingot form. The process required high-grade ore which, by the middle of the sixteenth century, only the remaining deposits of the Wapentake of Wirksworth could supply. Its dependence upon wind power rendered the yearly fortunes of the lead industry reliant upon a few weeks' smelting campaign, and upon the vagaries of the weather. In terms of ore supply, the problem was twofold: sufficient high-quality ore existed to pose no problems, but almost all of it lay beneath the water table. Above the water table, large amounts of ore remained to be dug either from old rubbish tips, or from unexploited veins and rakes. But the quality of the ore was too poor to be smelted by the bole. Thus, in spite of rising demand, by the mid-sixteenth century the industry was becoming incapable of further expansion. Following smelting, the ingots were transported by packhorse to Bawtry on the Trent, from where it was shipped to Hull, and then to London or the continental markets. Alternatively, Derbyshire lead found a regional market within the North Midlands and south Yorkshire. On the national and international markets, lead was used for large prestige projects; on the regional market, it found buyers further down the social scale. But it was by no means the consumer durable or the staple product of England's export trade that it was to become by the end of the sixteenth century. [11]

LAND, WEALTH AND COMMUNITY

So much for what is known of the lead industry. As to the social history of the mining workforce, less has so far been revealed. Historians are divided as to how closely the medieval mining workforce was integrated into the broader village community.[12] None the less, some sense can be made of the social structures of mining villages through the cross-reference of a

---

[10] PRO, DL1/34/L6; Kiernan, *Lead industry*, 28–9, 22, 32, 13–14.

[11] Discussion based on Kiernan, *Lead industry*, chs. 2 and 3.

[12] I. Blanchard, 'Labour productivity and work psychology in the English mining industry, 1400–1600', *EcHR*, 2nd ser., 31, 1 (1978), 5, 9; *idem*, 'Rejoinder', 68–9; *idem*, 'The miner and the agricultural community in late medieval England', *AgHR*, 20 (1970), 97; J.

sequence of sources dated between 1520 and 1543. Linking this data enables us to form islands of relative certainty at two points in time: between 1520 and 1528, and between 1541 and 1543. In 1520, the Court of Star Chamber heard the complaint of Sir Godfrey Foljamb, the lessee of the Duchy of Lancaster's duties of lot and cope in the Wapentake of Wirksworth concerning his right to a lord's meer upon every newly discovered lead vein. On 26 September, a commission took verbal evidence from 'the most ptye of All the brenners byers and Sellars of oare' in the Wapentake. The buyers also presented their accounts of recent ore purchases from the miners and the cavers. These papers provide a partial list of the names of the miners of the towns of Matlock and Wirksworth, and their adjacent villages of Bonsall, Wensley, Snitterton, Cromford and Middleton.[13] The dispute did not end with the 1520 litigation at Star Chamber, but stretched into the 1530s.[14] In 1528, further evidence was taken by the Court of the Duchy of Lancaster, again including a list of ore sales in the Matlock, Bonsall, Wensley and Snitterton area. Like the 1520 list, the 1528 record listed those miners who had sold ore in those villages, or on the adjacent moors and fields.[15]

The combined list of 1520 and 1528 ore sales names some 122 individuals who made ore sales. Of these ore sellers, 98 were men. Although less numerous than a subsequent list taken in 1541–2, these lists were more socially comprehensive of the extractive workforce as a whole.[16] The 1541–2 list, which recorded payments of lot dues from miners, and cope payments from orebuyers, covered the whole of the Wirksworth Wapentake lead field over almost a full year. Yet unlike the 1520s lists, it refrained from naming the women cavers from whom small purchases had been named, and instead relegated the cavers' production to anonymous statistics. Hence, while women made up some 20 per cent of ore producers listed in the 1520s, in the 1541–2 list they comprised a mere 7 per cent. The comparison is instructive, for it points up the extent to which the 1541–2 list (and subsequent lot and cope records) concealed a larger number of extractive workers who were not considered miners, and yet none the less remained dependent upon the extraction of lead for all or a part of their income.

The composite list of the 1520s and the 1541–2 return can be cross-referenced with taxation returns, in the form of Lay Subsidy returns taken

---

Hatcher, 'Myths, miners and agricultural communities', *AgHR*, 22 (1974), 61; Kiernan, *Lead industry*, 35, 13.

[13] PRO, STAC2/15/141–9.   [14] For a full discussion, see Chapter 9.

[15] PRO, DL3/18/F2a.

[16] For Kiernan's alphabeticized list of the 1541–2 lot and cope receipts, see *Lead industry*, 271–7. For the original, see PRO, SP1/244, fols. 28–75.

Table 2.1 *Comparison of the 1524–5 Lay Subsidy with lists of miners of the 1520s*

Town	Estate on which assessed				
	£1	£2	£3–£5	£6+	Total
Wirksworth					
Miners	0	1	0	1*	2
Total	3	9	6	5	23
Matlock					
Miners	0	1	0	0	1
Total	3	11	1	1	16
Bonsall					
Miners	1	5	1	0	7
Total	1	20	0	0	21
Middleton and Cromford					
Miners	0	1	0	1*	2
Total	0	11	2	1	14
Total					
Miners	1	8	1	2	12
Total	7	51	9	7	75

* Although listed as an ore producer, this was a wealthy yeoman or gentleman mine-owner, possessing interests in lead merchanting and smelting.
Sources: PRO, STAC2/15/141–9; PRO, DL3/18/F2a; PRO, E179/91/105.

in 1524–5 and 1543. These returns named all the male householders who paid the Lay Subsidies in those years. Survival of both is fragmentary, and we are fortunate in that those for Wirksworth Wapentake have survived nearly intact. Comparison between the lists of extractive workers and the Lay Subsidies is instructive, providing us for the first time with a glimpse of how the male mining workforce of the early sixteenth century fitted into the social structures of their settlements (see Tables 2.1 and 2.2).

Turning first to the general distribution of wealth, we see that all of the mining settlements within the Peak appear as unusually poor, with the large majority of those assessed in both the 1524–5 and 1543 returns falling into the first two categories of taxpayers: those bands classified elsewhere as representing landless labourers and poorer husbandmen and craftsmen.[17] In the 1524–5 return, 77 per cent of the total were assessed upon estates valued at £2 or less, while in the more detailed return of 1543, that figure

[17] Following classification adopted by Wrightson and Levine, *Poverty and piety*, 34.

The structures of inequality

Table 2.2 *Comparison of the 1543 Lay Subsidy with the 1541–2 list of miners*

Town	Estate on which assessed				
	£1	£2	£3–£5	£6+	Total
Wirksworth					
Miners	2	1	1	0	4
Total	18	16	10	6	50
Matlock					
Miners	6	3	1	0	10
Total	17	10	2	2	31
Bonsall					
Miners	0	1	1	0	2
Total	6	4	11	0	21
Wensley and Snitterton					
Miners	0	3	0	0	3
Total	12	6	5	2	25
Middleton and Cromford					
Miners	3	1	2	1*	7
Total	5	2	5	1	13
Total					
Miners	11	9	5	1	26
Total	58	38	33	11	140

* Although listed as an ore producer, this was a wealthy yeoman or gentleman mine-owner, possessing interests in lead merchanting and smelting.
Sources: PRO, E179/91/145; Kiernan, *Lead industry*, 271–7.

stood at 68 per cent. The next two tax bands represent the wealthier yeomen farmers and lesser gentry. Of the wealthier gentry to be found in similar tax returns elsewhere in early sixteenth-century England, there were none. If we are to accept the Lay Subsidy returns of 1524–5 as reliable indicators of the distribution of wealth within the whole of a settlement's population, we are therefore given the impression of the mining area of the southern Peak as thinly settled.[18]

[18] On the use of 1524–5 and Lay Subsidy returns as reliable indicators of overall population and wealth distribution, see C. Husbands, 'Regional change in a pre-industrial economy: wealth and population in the sixteenth and seventeenth centuries', *Journal of Historical Geography*, 13, 4 (1987), 345–59; B.M.S. Campbell, 'The population of early Tudor England: a re-evaluation of the 1522 muster returns and the 1524 and 1525 Lay Subsidies', *Journal of Historical Geography*, 7, 2 (1981), 145–54; Wrightson and Levine, *Poverty and piety*, 31–4. J. Sheail, 'The distribution of taxable population and wealth in England during

Such an impression is deceptive. Comparing the names of taxpayers in 1524–5 and 1543 with our lists of ore producers from the 1520s and 1541–2, a rather different picture of the mining villages emerges. Of the 122 men and women who appeared in the 1520s lists of ore producers, only 12 (10 per cent) were listed in the 1524–5 Lay Subsidy. A similar figure presents itself two decades later: of the 212 miners listed in the 1541–2 lot and cope records, 26 (12 per cent) were listed in the 1543 Lay Subsidy return. It might be argued that this disparity is to be explained by some staggeringly rapid population turnover amongst the mining workforce. But so many of those miners of the 1520s and 1541–2 appear in sources other than the Lay Subsidies as to render such an argument untenable. The Lay Subsidy records, hitherto accepted by historians as representing close to a full list of a place's householders, actually concealed a substantial proportion considered too poor to be assessed. We must therefore amend our picture of the early sixteenth-century social structures of the mining area. The mining towns and villages still appear as lacking any significant gentry presence; a very small group of lesser gentry holding freehold land and combining lead smelting with marketing and very limited direct investment in extraction are to be found in Wirksworth and Matlock. A larger group of relatively wealthy yeomen, those assessed on estates valued at between £3 and £5, emerges. A small number of this group can be shown to have been miners. Amongst the still larger group of the poorest taxpayers, only a small fraction appear as miners or ore producers. Both in 1524–5 and 1543, the large majority of the extractive workforce lay beyond the social range of the tax returns. The people of the mining area of the early sixteenth century therefore appear as rather more numerous, and as very much poorer, than at first glance.

Important spatial distinctions in the distribution of wealth and occupation, and in economic function, also reveal themselves. The town of Wirksworth emerges as wealthier, more socially variegated and less industrial than its poorer and apparently less populous neighbours, which take on the appearance of dependent, semi-industrial satellite settlements. Ore produced in these villages was sold to lead merchants and smelters who lived in Wirksworth. Disputes over mining rights were settled in the barmote court, which sat in the moothall in Wirksworth, as were those village disputes heard by the Court Leet of the Duchy manor of Wirksworth. In its administrative, legal and economic functions, as much as in its social structure, early sixteenth-century Wirksworth emerges as qualitatively different.

the early sixteenth century', *Transactions of the Institute of British Geographers*, 55 (1972), 111–26, sounds a cautionary note.

While revealing generalizations can be made from the study of tax data, the poorer inhabitants of the mining area remain indistinct. Local court records enable us to study more closely the poor mining population of the early sixteenth century. The records of the Court Leet of the Duchy of Lancaster's manor of Wirksworth, and the jury lists of the attendant Courts Baron of Wirksworth, Bonsall and Matlock for the period between 1509 and 1553 have been compiled to produce partial lists of tenants within the lead mining villages.[19] Freeholders from across the whole manor sat on the Court Leet of Wirksworth, while the juries of the Courts Baron of Wirksworth, Bonsall and Matlock were comprised of copyholders of those settlements. Linkage with our other data yields important results. Freeholders were more likely to pay Lay Subsidies than were copyholders, typically paid larger amounts, and scarcely engaged in extractive work. Miners were more common amongst the poorer copyholders: in total, whereas only 15 identified miners can be shown to have held freehold land between 1509 and 1553, at least 72 were copyholders.

Of the 325 copyholders who sat on the Courts Baron of Wirksworth, Matlock and Bonsall between 1509 and 1553, 14 sat for the Courts Baron of two settlements, and only one sat on all three. This implies an unusual degree of association on the part of tenants with their settlement, suggesting that the land market was perhaps not as fluid as elsewhere in early sixteenth-century England, with individuals holding land in only one settlement rather than a number of different villages. Some individuals and families dominated the membership of the court juries. In Bonsall, 21 men occupied exactly half of the 505 recorded places as jurors. Of those 21 men, 10 can be identified as miners. A similar pattern is evident in the distribution of the office of headborough. Headboroughs from each settlement within the Duchy manor of Wirksworth made presentments of their neighbours (and sometimes of one another) to the Court Leet for minor offences. Between 1525 and 1553, some 60 men from Wirksworth and its adjacent mining villages held office as headborough more than once. Of these men, at least 30 (50 per cent) can be identified as miners. In terms of their wealth and social position, these individuals can scarcely be considered any kind of a parochial elite. Yet they did form some part of the hard bed on which social structures and local culture were built and renewed. Oliver Stone, for instance, appeared twelve times on the Court Baron of Bonsall between 1514 and 1550. He sat on two Great Barmote courts in 1549 and 1550, and appears in the 1528 mining records, making three ore sales. He was unusual amongst the mining workforce in that he was

---

[19] PRO, DL30/49/588–598, /50/600, /603, /606–7, /609–10, /614–16. Coverage is incomplete, in particular for the 1530s.

assessed upon his estate of £2 in the 1524–5 Lay Subsidy return, but was less unusual in that he appeared three times between 1531 and 1543 as a headborough for Bonsall, making presentments of minor offences to the Court Leet.[20] While wealthy enough to be assessed upon his estate, he was, by any standards, still extremely poor. He was a typical example of those who made frequent appearances as jurors: a copyholder who produced small amounts of ore and who also sat upon the juries of those manorial institutions which maintained both agricultural and mining custom.

As a free miner who was also closely bound up with local communal life and agricultural production, Oliver Stone was far from unusual. There may have been a large corpus of such men in the mining villages: poor but independent, some holding both land and mineshares and staying in the place of birth for all or most of their lives. William Roper of Matlock was located further down the social scale than Oliver Stone. He does not seem to have owned land in Matlock or elsewhere, and was not assessed for the Lay Subsidies. But in spite of his poverty, he too had an investment in local laws and communal responsibilities, appearing three times as a headborough before the Court Leet between 1543 and 1553. He made four ore sales in the 1541–2 records, and was still describing himself as a miner when, aged eighty, he told the commissioners of the Court of Exchequer in 1592 that he had known the township of Matlock and nearby Snitterton since his youth.[21]

Others amongst the mining workforce were less settled. For them, the structures of local society and community were something through which they moved rather than actively constructed. Out of the total of 264 men who made ore sales listed in our sources, 129 (49 per cent) do not appear in any other source. Some of these 129 men may well have been settled in a mining village, but were so poor as to have escaped further historical observation. But others were not. They were drawn to the Peak by the opportunities afforded by the open laws of the lead field. Registering a single sale of ore in our surviving records, they simply moved on. The social structures of the mining villages through which they passed were determined by others: the jurors of Courts Leet and Baron, the headborough, the Great Barmote. They benefited from those communal structures insofar as they were entitled to free mining rights, and to extensive common rights upon the commons. But they cannot be considered to have formed any lasting association which defined them as of a community. For some who went on to work in other mines, their spatial identity may have been located on the lead field as a whole, rather than any individual settlement.

[20] This assumes, of course, that we are dealing with the same Oliver Stone of Bonsall.
[21] PRO, E134/32&33Eliz/Mich28.

For many others, who passed through and out of the Peak, they probably did not.

Some of these transient individuals may have been regarded as free miners, insofar as they paid lot duties upon the ore which they sold. But most would probably have fallen into the category of cavers. Of the 2,899 loads of ore sold within the Wirksworth Wapentake lead field in the year following Michaelmas 1541, only 6 per cent was produced by cavers. Yet the 234 sales of ore recorded by cavers made up some 25 per cent of the total of 921 sales recorded for that year.[22] The free miners, many holding copyhold land, appear as rather more settled, even as bound into their communities. They dominated the industry, both numerically and in terms of combined output in the early sixteenth century, accounting for 88 per cent of sales in the 1541–2 returns. Finally, the 1541–2 returns name some thirteen mineworkings which were owned by brenner families and worked by wage labourers. These were responsible for 6 per cent of recorded production in that year. It would be tempting to see the work-force of such mines as the precursors of an alienated nineteenth-century proletariat. But this seems to have been far from the case. Where the names of wage labourers have been left to the historical record, they can almost always be shown to have been settled free miners, combining wage labour with work in their own mines and in some cases on their own land.

The freedoms of barmote custom allowed the free miner to dominate the early sixteenth-century industry, fostering and protecting the small-scale industrial producer. In the same way, agricultural custom and common right enabled an early sixteenth-century peasantry to maintain its hold upon the land. Settled villagers exercised extensive rights upon the large commons where they dug for turf and coal, pastured beasts, and collected firewood and foodstuffs. Together with smallholdings, and perhaps supplemented by waged labour in the fields of larger farmers, in smelting and its attendant trades, in mineworkings, or by occasional forays into free mining, the commons and the existence of common rights enabled the 'ubiquitous small peasant proprietor' to survive across the Peak.[23] Customary law enabled economic independence and encouraged a plebeian community of interest in agriculture as much as in industry. But just as in lead mining, that was not the whole story.

[22] Kiernan, *Lead industry*, 16.
[23] I.S.W. Blanchard, *The Duchy of Lancaster's estates in Derbyshire, 1485–1540*, DRS, 3 (Chesterfield, 1971), 14.

LANDSCAPE AND POPULATION

The semi-autarchy engendered by common right grew alongside trade connections with areas beyond the Peak. Large sheep flocks, owned by powerful gentry families or by the monastic granges which prior to the Dissolution still studded the Peak, roamed the commons together with herds owned by commercial beef farmers. Both were felt by many Peak villagers to strain the collective resources guaranteed by local custom. Similarly, attempts by larger farmers to increase the size of their holdings at the expense of the commons also caused conflict.[24] Yet conflict in the early sixteenth-century Peak was muted, certainly by comparison with later developments. One reason for the relative quietude of the region lay in its lack of population. The distribution of human settlement within the region can be glimpsed from study of a census taken in 1563 (see Map 7).[25] This listed the number of communicant households in each parish of the county. Without knowing more about differences in household structure and size within the Peak at this time, it can only be used to suggest general patterns. But combined with our knowledge of the mining industry and of the dominant agricultural regime, the census provides us with an opportunity to paint a broad brush picture of the social and economic topography of the region. [26]

The main lead deposits lay embedded in the limestone plateau which nestled between three connecting ranges of gritstone upland (see Maps 1 and 3). Ecologically, the Peak was defined by this broad limestone plateau, and by the lead it carried. The limestone plateau begins in the south at Wirksworth, rising steadily to the north and west. It is cut through by the river Derwent, running along a long, flat-bottomed valley within which lay the best agricultural land of the early modern region. The Derwent is fed by smaller rivers which have sliced dramatic gorges through the lead bearing

---

[24] PRO, DL3/8/F1, /54/F2, /49/C1, /22/J2, /36/R8, /79/H1; PRO, DL5/8, fol. 119; PRO, DL5/3, fol. 82; Blanchard, 'Economic change', 17–19, 22, 40, 42, 176–8, 180; *idem*, *Duchy of Lancaster's estates*, 1–16; PRO, STAC2/19/270, /17/138, /26/142, /32/25, /25/162, /29/18, /29/13, /31/65, /34/33; PRO, STAC3/3/33, /8/9, /5/60; PRO, STAC4/8/9; PRO, C21/F11/10.

[25] Bl, Harl. MS 594; analysed in P. Riden, 'The population of Derbyshire in 1563', *DAJ*, 2nd ser., 98 (1978), 61–71.

[26] Subsequent discussion is based on J. Barnatt and K. Smith, *The Peak District: landscapes through time* (London, 1997); P. Stafford, *The East Midlands in the early middle ages* (Leicester, 1985); R. Millward and A. Robinson, *The Peak District* (London, 1975); D.G. Hey, *Packmen, carriers and packhorse roads: trade and communications in north Derbyshire and south Yorkshire* (Leicester, 1980); T.D. Ford and J.H. Rieuwerts, *Lead mining in the Peak District* (1968, 3rd edn, Matlock Bath, 1983); R. Hodges, *Wall-to-wall history: the story of Roystone Grange* (London, 1991); C.R. Hart, *The north Derbyshire archaeological survey to A.D. 1500* (Chesterfield, 1981); W.E. Wightman, 'Open field agriculture in the Peak District', *DAJ*, 2nd ser., 81 (1961), 111–25.

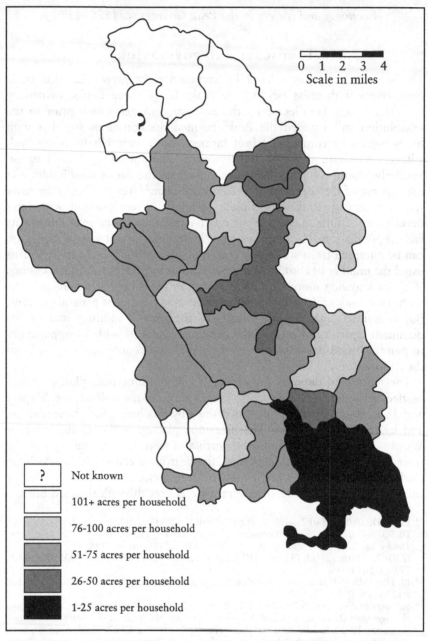

?	Not known
	101+ acres per household
	76-100 acres per household
	51-75 acres per household
	26-50 acres per household
	1-25 acres per household

Map 7   The population of the Peak Country in 1563: the distribution of acres per household

The 1563 census was based upon parishes, not townships. This map therefore does not accurately reflect the extent of the lead field.

Source: BL, Harl. MS 594.

54

limestone, the most important of which is the Wye, running from the high land to the west to join the Derwent just below Bakewell. Matlock, Bakewell and Wirksworth comprised the major towns of the sixteenth-century Peak Country. Scattered around these towns, in decreasing number as one moved north and west, lay smaller villages. On the high northern and western peripheries of the limestone plateau, human settlement was formed into hamlets and large, isolated farmsteads. Finally, the Dark Peak and the Staffordshire moorlands closed the Peak Country off from Cheshire, Staffordshire and the north-west, while the eastern moors rising above the Derwent valley threw up a barrier against close concourse with south Yorkshire and the Scarsdale Hundred of north-east Derbyshire. Such barriers were not insuperable. Two Roman roads ran over the Staffordshire moorlands, converging on Buxton, and through Hartingdon, to connect the north and south ends of the Peak with Staffordshire and Cheshire. Track-ways connected the Peak to Chesterfield and Sheffield. A dense network of very ancient tracks and paths drew the mining villages and towns together, and provided a means of communication with the tiny hamlets and farms on the margins and beyond the lead field. But the most important highway of communication remained the natural feature of the Derwent valley and its tributaries.

The history of the distribution of population within the Peak observes some basic continuities over the millennia which preceded the end of the sixteenth century. The topographical closure of the area by the gritstone uplands also closed the spatial identity of its inhabitants. The *Pecsaete*, the 'People of the Peak' were defined as a separate entity within the Mercian kingdom of the seventh century, and from that point onwards the Peak and its people were seen as distinct. From the first point at which finer distinctions can be made, in 1086 with the compilation of the Domesday Book, through to the 1563 census, the Peak's population remained concentrated into the valleys of the lead field. The Derwent and its tributaries had given passage to invaders into the Peak from the first century to the eleventh; but they also gave shelter and succour to a large proportion of its inhabitants. In 1563, the most populous part of the Peak was the lead mining industry's last redoubt around Wirksworth and Matlock. To the east, the human population of the higher parishes of Carsington and Brassington was much smaller. Moving north along the Derwent valley from Matlock, the large parish of Bakewell appeared as the next most populated area, due in large part to the market town which gave the parish its name. But on every side of Bakewell, in the upland parishes which lay on the limestone plateau, population fell away. As the eye of the 1563 census moved north, so population diminished. In 1563, the clerk of the parish of Castleton, sitting below the empty wastes of the Dark Peak, recorded the existence of 97 households there. These households sat within some 9,985 acres of land, providing a ratio of one household to every 103 acres; in the neighbouring parish of Hope, that ratio stood at some 133 acres per household. By way of contrast, for every of the 470 households in the parish of Wirksworth in the south-east of the lead field, there were 28 acres of land.

In the south of the lead field, then, the population was heavily dependent upon lead mining, smelting and related trades. Here a large section of the region's total population was cramped into settlements separated by broad, flat moors and commons, and bonded by trackways along which flowed trade and capital. The lead industry of the west of Wirksworth Wapentake and the whole of the High Peak was virtually moribund. Here, with the exception of Bakewell town, population was scattered into those tiny villages which had escaped late medieval depopulation. Fragments of buildings, overgrown mounds and grassy ridged fields remained to testify that humans had once lived upon the deserted sites of villages such as Netherhaddon. A thriving settlement at the end of the fourteenth century, by 1465 the village was deserted, its chapel incorporated into the fabric of Haddon Hall, the family seat of the lords of Netherhaddon, the powerful Vernon family.[27]

The marks which lay upon the land spoke of the end of community and the death of industry. Deserted fulling mills along the Derwent and its tributaries called attention to the passage of the short-lived textile industry.[28] Rounded hollows and worked out rakes showed where 'old wurcks had ben in old tyme', but were now 'quite ovrgrowne wth grasse', and testified to the extinction of mining in the High Peak lead field.[29] Yet in the early sixteenth century the fortunes of what remained of the mining industry were beginning to improve. The production of lead from the Wapentake of Wirksworth's lead field increased throughout the 1480–1570 period, in tune with expanding demand. But given the productive constraints imposed by bole smelting methods and the absence of effective drainage technology to unwater the rich lead deposits known to exist below the water table, that increase could not be sustained by demand alone. The informed observer of the Derbyshire lead industry in 1570 could have been forgiven for imagining that lead mining and smelting, and the communities sustained by those industries, were reaching the end of their natural lives.

[27] On the desertion of Netherhaddon, see I.S.W. Blanchard, 'Industrial employment and the rural land market, 1380–1520', in R.M. Smith (ed.), *Land, kinship and life cycle* (Cambridge, 1984), 227–75.
[28] For long memories of this industry, see PRO, DL4/133/1712, /33/25, /94/56.
[29] PRO, DL4/67/59; for other examples, see PRO, DL3/79/H1t; PRO, E134/32&33Eliz/Mich28.

3

Industrialization and social change, c. 1570–1660

POPULATION CHANGE AND TECHNOLOGICAL INNOVATION

If the demise of the lead industry of Derbyshire seemed imminent in the mid-sixteenth century, in the lead mining districts of the Somerset Mendips 200 miles to the south, the future seemed rosy. Here, the constraints imposed on the industry by bole smelting methods had been removed. At some point in the 1540s, lead ore started to be smelted according to a new method: a foot-powered bellows heated burning charcoal, under which lead ore was placed. This 'footblast' was soon superseded by a further development upon the principle: the ore hearth smelting mill. Smelting houses were built alongside fast-running streams, which provided the motive force for a water wheel. This drove powerful bellows, forcing air into a furnace containing lead ore, which was then smelted at high temperatures. Unlike the bole, the ore hearth mill did not depend upon the vagaries of the weather, could produce ore throughout the year and was capable of smelting a low grade of ore.[1]

The first such mill was introduced into Derbyshire in 1552, but met with little success. Around 1569, a second ore hearth mill was established at Beauchief by William Humphrey, who had acquired the monopoly on its operation in 1564. The success of Humphrey's mill encouraged imitators amongst the local brenners, gentry and nobility. Running legal and political battles ensued over the subsequent decade, but by the late 1570s Humphrey was forced to recognize that his attempt to monopolize the ore hearth mill had failed.[2] By the 1580s, the bole was virtually extinct.

The significance of the ore hearth mill was twofold. First, the smelting side of the industry was freed from the seasonal and productive constraints of the bole, and its productive capacity was hugely increased. Secondly,

---

[1] A full account of the operation of the ore hearth mill is to be found in Kiernan, *Lead industry*, ch. 4; for contemporary accounts, see PRO, E134/24Eliz/Hil4, /Trin4; PRO, E178/611.

[2] See Kiernan, *Lead industry*, 164–91, for an account of the dispute over the monopoly.

mining activity burst into life, as poorer ore deposits and waste from old mines were dug over. In particular, this led to the expansion of those parts of the lead field under exploitation (see Map 6). In both these respects, the introduction of new smelting technology 'revolutionized' the lead industry. Between 1569 and 1584, as Kiernan has put it, 'a small-scale localised industry wedded to a primitive smelting technology and producing small quantities of a high quality product mainly for the domestic market was transformed into a major overseas trade'.[3]

The immediate beneficiaries of this transformation lay at extreme ends of the social spectrum. The sudden expansion of the mining industry meant that thousands of poor people flocked into the lead field, in particular on to the deserted High Peak deposits; while the defeat of Humphrey's monopoly allowed the main noble and gentry families to build their own mills and make quick profits. Chief amongst these, and best placed to exploit the new situation, was George Talbot, the sixth Earl of Shrewsbury. As owner of a number of large manors within the High Peak lead field, lessee of the Duchy's lot and cope rights and the office of barmaster in the King's Field in the High Peak and the Wapentake of Wirksworth, and as the most powerful political figure within the region, he cut a commanding figure. By the early 1579s he dominated the institutions and trade of the lead industry. On his death in 1590, smelting started to pass from the major gentry to a larger number of minor gentry with diversified interests in lead marketing, and mining.[4] Although the greater gentry continued to hold an important place in the industry, as we shall see this typically took a parasitic form. As lords of manors, owners of former monastic granges and as lessees of Duchy rights of lot and cope, such families extracted seigneurial tolls upon miners' production and orebuyers' sales. Manorial profits combined with the purchase of controversial leases of tithe rights upon the miners' output. Some, such as the Gell family, added investments in mineshares to a continuing interest in smelting and marketing, but by the early seventeenth century such direct involvement was more the preserve of the mercantile lesser gentry.

Humphrey's monopolistic claims of the 1570s extended to another important innovation: the sieve. This prosaic instrument enabled the cavers to turn swift profits as they turned over the deserted workings of the High Peak in search of discarded ore. One miner described in 1582 how the introduction of the sieve had changed working practices. Prior to its introduction, he explained, the cavers had dug laboriously over old works with picks or 'caving' hammers. Using such instruments, they received little for their work: in a day, a man and a boy could earn four pence. In contrast,

---

[3] *Ibid.*, 126, 1.   [4] *Ibid.*, 177, 209, 211.

by 1582 a caver who took lead scraps from the earth '& fylled yt into a sive sett in a Tubbe of water whereby the lose of earthe doth ryse to the toppe of the water and the owre doth fall to the bothom of the syve', if accompanied with a boy to get water, could earn up to two shillings in a day.[5] Again, it seems that the sieve originated in the Somerset Mendips. Humphrey employed waged labourers to use the sieve in Tideswell and Elton around 1568, and within a short period the miners and cavers of the 'Country' had copied him. He claimed a monopoly, or pre-emption, of all the miners' and cavers' sales of ore got with the sieve, and at unfavourable prices, but by the late 1570s had to recognize defeat in this as in other matters.[6]

The introduction of Humphrey's innovations began a long-term increase in population which would only falter in the later seventeenth century, and an even longer cycle of growth in the lead mining industry which would not be checked until the end of the eighteenth century. From the early 1570s, 'Poore cuntrye people' flocked into the rejuvenated lead field, working the remains of the deserted lead mines in what the free miners regarded as 'comon disorder'. By 1583, mining was recognized as the 'onelie livings' of 'ma[n]y poor people'. Those dependent upon caving and sieving had been estimated at some 2,000 two years earlier. In 1593, there were said to be 3,000 people dependent upon lead mining within Wirksworth Wapentake alone.[7] In 1616, aged inhabitants of the High Peak well remembered the arrival of immigrants in the area during the 1580s and 1590s. In that year, the experienced miner William Furness suggested that a fortyfold increase in mining activity in the High Peak had occurred since the introduction of the sieve.[8]

The changing population of the mining area at this time can be sketched from the registers of four parishes within the lead field (see Map 2). Crude decadal totals have been compiled, and averaged for missing years (see Fig. 3.1). Total decadal baptisms have then been compared against burials, in order to arrive at a figure for surpluses or deficits of baptisms over burials (see Fig. 3.2). Youlgreave, lying in the south of the Hundred of High Peak, and in the centre of the lead field, is the only parish whose registers predate the introduction of Humphrey's innovations, beginning as they do at 1558. Those of the large parish of Hope, at the far north of the lead field, and ranging into the near-empty gritstone Dark Peak, begin in 1598. Entirely located within the lead field, the register of the nearby parish of Eyam begins in 1630; while that for the large parish of Wirksworth straddling the southern borders of the lead field begins in 1614. Our description of

---

[5] PRO, E134/24Eliz/Hil4.   [6] See Chapter 9 below.

[7] PRO, E134/24Eliz/Hil4; Kiernan, *Lead industry*, 183, 192; PRO, DL4/34/22.

[8] PRO, E134/13JasI/Mich3; PRO, DL4/64/12/4, /62/19, /64/11, /67/59, /67/61, /69/51, /71/39.

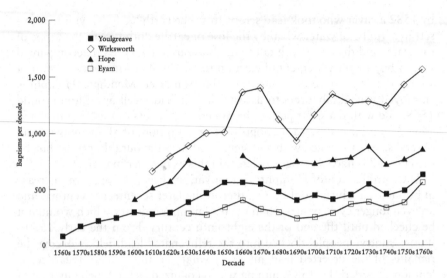

Figure 3.1   Total baptisms per decade, four parishes, 1560–1769
Sources: DRO, D3644/1/1–6; DRO, D3105A/PI/1/1–6; DRO, D1828A/PI/1/1–3;
DRO, D2602A/PI/1/1, 3.

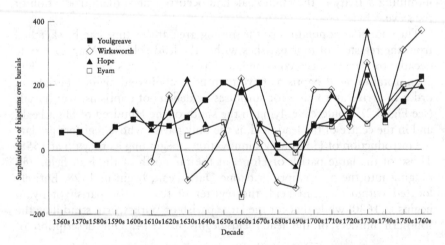

Figure 3.2   Surplus/deficit of baptisms over burials, four parishes, 1560–1769
Sources: DRO, D3644/1/1–6; DRO, D3105A/PI/1/1–6; DRO, D1828A/PI/1/1–3;
DRO, D2602A/PI/1/1, 3.

Table 3.1 *Occupational ascriptions in Youlgreave burial register,*
1558–1604

Title	Year			
	1558–69	1570–9	1580–9	1590–1604
Husbandman	6	15	13	23
Yeoman	2	5	6	3
Labourer	9	15	34	23
Cottager	1	—	—	—
Gentry	1	1	1	2
Clerk vicar	—	—	—	1
Servant	—	5	9	7
Unknown	—	1	—	—
Tradesman*	—	1	5	8
Miner	—	—	1	3
Poor**	—	—	—	12

*Tradesman: miller, victualler, butcher, joiner, thatcher, tailor, blacksmith, shearman.
**Poor: poor man, poor widow, poor woman, poor labourer, poor miner, beggar.
Source: DRO, D3644/1/1.

population change in the last decades of the sixteenth century is therefore dependent upon the Youlgreave records alone. This shows that the number of baptisms recorded in the 1570s, the decade following upon the introduction of new technology, almost doubled the decadal total for the 1560s. This increase was offset by high mortality, as burials in the 1570s increased by nearly fourfold on the 1560s total, but none the less over succeeding decades baptisms managed to outstrip the decadal total of burials. By the turn of the century, Youlgreave's parish clerk was recording average yearly baptisms which stood at three times those of the 1560s. The recollections of the aged witnesses of 1616 therefore appear as quite accurate.

Between 1558 and 1604, the parish clerks of Youlgreave were in the habit of recording the occupation or perceived social place of those entered in the burial registers. Save for five references to 'poor widows' or a 'poor woman', burials of women were recorded according to the place of the deceased within the household. The occupations given to deceased men are more revealing, as are the changes in such ascriptions over time, suggestive as they are of changes in the definition of social place engendered by population increase and industrialization (see Table 3.1).

The burial registers for 1558–69 define Youlgreave as a pastoral, rural society, albeit one comprised primarily of the poorer classes of husbandmen and labourers. As the century moved to its close, these two groups increased in number, at the expense of the richer yeomanry. As with Wirksworth in the early sixteenth century, the gentry of Youlgreave appear as numerically insignificant. The small number of miners recorded in the register should not surprise us. As we shall see in Chapter 7, the term was little used before the last decade of the sixteenth century. Most importantly, the proportion and definition of those at the base of the parochial social structure underwent important change. The term 'cottager', denoting the poor, landless household, was used only once, at the beginning of the period under observation. By the 1590s, the definition of that group had changed to a range of more exclusive terminology: 'poore man'; 'poore widow'; 'poore mynor; 'poore laborer'; 'beggar'.

Returning to population change, we see that growth continued apace into the early and mid-seventeenth century. With the exception of the parishes of Hope and Eyam in the decade of the first and second civil war, and a slight decrease in Youlgreave during the 1610s, the number of registered baptisms in all four parishes under observation increased every decade. In some cases, such increases could be quite extreme: baptisms in Hope increased by 33 per cent in the 1630s over the preceding decade; in the same decade, those in Youlgreave increased by 32 per cent over the 1620s total. Sustained population growth is also apparent in the decadal surpluses of baptisms over burials. With the exception of Wirksworth in the 1610s, 1630s and 1640s, all four parishes registered surpluses over the early seventeenth century. Again, these could be quite extreme: Hope enjoyed a surplus of 219 baptisms over burials in the 1630s, Youlgreave a dramatic rise in both the 1630s and 1640s. The composite evidence of the parish registers allows us to establish a rough chronology in the population history of the Peak in the 1570–1660 period. Important relative increases occurred in the decade following the introduction of new technology which were given an added boost at the turn of the century. Individual parishes, of course, experienced crisis years, such as Wirksworth's difficult times in the 1630s and 1640s, or the arrival in 1636 of 'the childrens pocks' in Hope, which caused 'the great death of many children & others by Contageous disease'. None the less, following more gradual increases in the 1610s and 1620s, the four decades which followed saw dramatic population expansion.

Other sources allow us to develop a bird's-eye view of the changing distribution of population within the Peak. Once again, these point to very dramatic increases in population within the High Peak in particular. In Chapter 2, we saw that the 1563 census revealed the concentration of the Peak's population into the last redoubt of the mining industry around Wirksworth and Matlock, with a lesser concentration in those parishes lying along the fertile Derwent valley. Just over a century later, assessors for the Hearth Tax listed all the heads of household in the county by name and township, distinguishing between those who were too poor to be able to pay the tax, and listing for the remainder the number of hearths on which they paid. The Hearth Tax has been used by historians as a crude means of assessing the distribution of income in a given area, and is so used in Chapter 4 below. It is here deployed as a source of information concerning the geographical distribution of population. Moreover, because the 1563 census and the 1664 Hearth Tax were based upon the same unit of calculation – that of the household – they can be compared, and the results mapped. From this can be drawn information concerning changes in the distribution of population over the intervening century.[9] Finally, the distribution of population within the lead field suggested by the 1664 Hearth Tax accounts is confirmed by a militia roll of 1638 for the whole county, listing all those able-bodied men by township and hundred (see Maps 8 and 9).[10]

Between 1563 and 1664, Derbyshire's population probably increased by around a half. Such growth was most obvious in the lead mining area of the north-west. The redistribution of population into the industrial and pastoral north of the county was a part of a general trend manifest across the whole country, as population was drawn to upland, pastoral and industrializing areas.[11] In 1563, some 22 per cent of the county's households were located in parishes within the lead field. By 1664, that figure stood at 27 per cent. That increase was locally uneven. Starting at the south of the lead field in the parish of Wirksworth, the total rise in the number of households between 1563 and 1664 was only 30 per cent. This large parish included a number of townships which lay outside the lead field, and the figure obscures real increases within the mining townships of the parish. Hence, the number of households in the neighbouring mining parish of Carsington increased by 361 per cent. Moving along the Derwent valley to Matlock parish, the households listed there rose by 220 per cent. Entering the parishes at the south of the Hundred of High Peak, in areas where population had been rather higher than the rest of the Hundred in 1563, increases in total households were less dramatic: Bakewell parish increased by 54 per cent; Darley parish's household increase was mostly made up by expansion into the mining townships of Wensley and Snitterton, raising the

---

[9] For such a map, see A. Wood, 'Social conflict and change in the mining communities of north-west Derbyshire, *c.* 1600–1700', *International Review of Social History*, 38, 1 (1993), 58.

[10] For a statistical breakdown of this source, see *ibid.*, 52–4; for its representation in map form, see A. Wood, 'Industrial development, social change and popular politics in the mining area of north west Derbyshire, *c.* 1600–1700', PhD thesis, University of Cambridge, 1994, map 7.

[11] Husbands, 'Regional change', 353, 355.

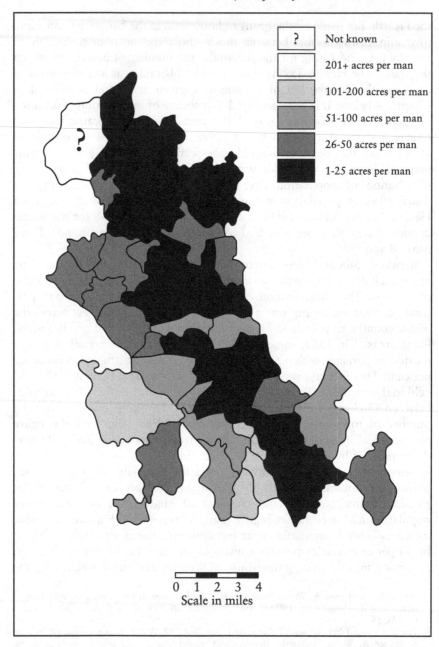

Map 8   The population of the Peak Country in 1638: the distribution of acres per
able-bodied man
Source: PRO, SP16/405 Pt 2.

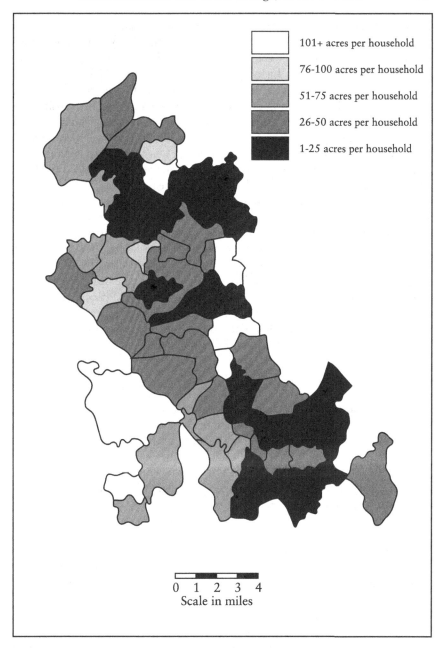

Map 9   The population of the Peak Country in 1664: the distribution of acres per
household
Source: PRO, E179/94/401–3.

number of households by 80 per cent within the parish as a whole. In Ashford and Sheldon chapelries, further up the valley, the number of households rose by 129 per cent, and to the west within Youlgreave parish by 123 per cent. Moving further west, population increases on the limestone uplands again showed dramatic increases until the very large and remote parish of Hartingdon is reached: here the slight lead deposits and thin soils did not prove a sufficient attraction for human population and the parish actually experienced net population loss between 1563 and 1664. Over the same period, every other High Peak township expanded its population. This pattern was most noticeable in the northern lead field, on the limestone plateau. The parish of Eyam increased its number of households by 398 per cent; neighbouring Stoney Middleton increased by 297 per cent.

Simply put, between 1563 and 1664 the spatial patterning of human settlement within the Peak Country was turned on its head. While almost every mining township increased its overall population, in the High Peak what had been thinly settled hamlets in 1563 had become heavily populated industrial villages by 1664. While Wirksworth and Matlock retained a sizeable proportion of the mining area's overall population in the mid-seventeenth century, the Derwent valley had ceased to be the main container of human population within the High Peak.

ENCLOSURE AND COMMON RIGHT

If the distribution of inhabitants upon the land changed significantly between 1570 and 1660, so did the use they made of it. Senses of space and related definitions of community and customary law underwent important alterations as conflicts over use rights within and between settlements became more frequent. In 1652, the ninety-four-year-old Adam Woolley of Bonsall recalled how fifty years ago his neighbours had felt that 'the inhabitants of Bonsall [were] streatned for Roome about their houses . . . [and] were necessitated to putt theire cattle uppon Masson' moor in neighbouring Matlock, leading to their prosecution for trespass. Similarly, legal definitions of landholding underwent change: in Ashford, as in the Duchy of Lancaster's manors of High Peak and Castleton, land was taken from the commons and redefined as copyhold.[12] The availability of large tracts of open waste and moorland in the High Peak, together with the loose lordship exercised by the Duchy of Lancaster, allowed large numbers of squatters to establish illegal smallholdings. These holdings were subsequently ratified by lessees of Duchy manorial rights, eager to claim rents

---

[12] PRO, DL4/103/12, /72/5, /56/6; PRO, C2/ChasI/A51/87; PRO, DL44/810.

upon their occupants. It is not always possible to see what proportion of a village's population were landless and dependent upon the commons for their survival. In the case of the parish of Hope in 1658, firmer conclusions can be drawn than elsewhere. In that year, it was shown that in the township of Abney 73 per cent of households were landless; in Bradwell that figure was 50 per cent; in Little Hucklow 76 per cent had no land; and in Wardlow some 77 per cent. In all of these townships, there were still large open fields on which the landless exercised limited common rights, and broader expanses of common.[13] Such cottagers tended to be of the poorest and most marginal sections of society.[14] The point was illustrated dramatically in the complaint made by 360 poor cottagers from the Tideswell area against the Earl of Shrewsbury in 1576. They argued that his enclosures in the Peak Forest had deprived them of pasture for their beasts, which for many were their only source of livelihood.[15]

The Earl of Shrewsbury was not the only prominent figure of the late Elizabethan period to be earning the hostility of the recently expanded population of the Peak's mining villages. The greater gentry and nobility leap out of the sources as the greatest enclosers of the commons. The long-standing interest of lords in expanding their demesne and increasing their rents was given an added push with the enlarged population of their manors. References to manorial attempts at large-scale enclosure are not difficult to find for the Elizabethan, Jacobean and Caroline periods. On the Duchy's manors, lessees of manorial rights were also attempting to cut into the commons. In this, they were initially backed by the Duchy Court, and with greater consistency by the studied disinterest of the county bench in enforcing legislation against enclosures.[16] The acquisition of former monastic granges by noble and gentry families gave 'Rich men' another opportunity to press their priorities upon the commons, as their attorneys searched the scattered archives of dissolved monasteries for proof that the

---

[13] J.P. Carr, 'Open field agriculture in mid-Derbyshire', *DAJ*, 2nd ser., 83 (1963), 66–81.

[14] PRO, DL42/50, fols. 29–32; PRO, DL42/51, fols. 304–16, 340–51, 353–363, 417–439; PRO, DL42/53, fols. 25–53; PRO, DL42/55, fols. 96–102; PRO, DL42/58, fol. 249; PRO, DL42/59, fols. 36–40, 79–83; PRO, DL42/61, fols. 6–11; 115–121; PRO, DL43/1/27; CHT unlisted Book of Surveys, 1634–8; PRO, DL4/109/8; PRO, C21/S63/18. On the transience of cottagers in Cromford and Wirksworth in the 1650s, see Wood, 'Industrial development', 70–4.

[15] PRO, DL4/18/20.

[16] On opposition to late Elizabethan enclosures, see PRO, DL4/11/45, /10/23, /19/7, /38/17, /21/31, /26/4, /26/28, /27/67, /27/87, /27/49, /28/6, /37/4, /41/51; PRO, STAC5/E12/14. On opposition to Jacobean and Caroline enclosures, see PRO, STAC8/64/4, /51/15, /212/28, /103/6; PRO, DL4/54/36, /56/17, /60/16, /69/56, /72/5, /77/3, /78/13, /80/3. On John Carpenter's attempts at enclosure in Wirksworth and Parwich, see PRO, E308/43/426. On the county bench's attitude to enclosure in 1630, see PRO, PC2/40, fol. 385, and *VCH*, II, 173.

ownership of a grange carried with it entitlement to a sheepwalk, or
pasture on the commons for a further thousand sheep.[17]

But the gentry and nobility were not the only group accused of
overstocking the commons, denying common rights, or of enclosing.[18]
Wealthier yeomen farmers and lesser gentry, typically men and women
who also held mineshares and sometimes operated lead marketing busi-
nesses, were also indicted by village opinion. The scale of such incursions
was smaller and less threatening; the unanimity of communal resistance
less apparent; therefore the sources speak with less volume.[19] None the
less, a combined process of agrarian change was underway. Stinting
agreements amongst landed inhabitants of manors, under which the landless or near landless were restricted from exercising significant grazing
rights on the commons, become more widespread in the documentation
from the 1570s.[20] Enclosure by the agreement of landed inhabitants, and
the consolidation of scattered landholdings by exchange into composite
fields 'for the better Division of the Lordship', may seem like processes of
rationalization to modern economic historians, and were justified by those
who carried them out as improvements.[21] But as their contemporary
opponents made clear, they also represented the gradual marginalization
and eventual obliteration of use rights on which hundreds of people had
come to depend. This process was local and uneven. Most of Stanton
common, for instance, had been enclosed by 1622. But the landless
inhabitants of neighbouring Winster still held pasture rights over their wide
commons.[22]

We must set such disputes in their proper historical context. Disputes
between one Peak village and another, and between one set of inhabitants
and another, over customs, use rights and boundaries had a long history in
the region. But after the 1570s, such conflicts became driven by new motive
forces. Sudden population growth in an area of hitherto low population
and wide agricultural resources forced distinct changes in the nature and
organization of agricultural production. Evidence for the existence of open-
field systems, rotated annually, worked communally and according to

---

[17] PRO, E134/9JasI/Mich5; PRO, DL4/40/18, /37/4, /32/26.
[18] On yeoman sheep flocks, see for instance PRO, E134/12ChasI/Mich42; LJRO, B/C/5/1626, Carsington.
[19] For examples, see PRO, DL4/68/55; PRO, DL30/54/664.
[20] DRO, D258M/60/81; PRO, DL4/19/7, /28/22, /23/9, /27/83, /27/49.
[21] On the exchange of holdings in Litton, see SA, Bag C 2066, 2068, 2070–1, 2098–105. For the same in Brassington, see R. Slack, *Lands and lead-miners: a history of Brassington, in Derbyshire* (Nottingham, 1991), 61. On copyholders' enclosures in Ashford, Great Long-stone and Sheldon, see SA, Bar D 44. On the improvement of Ashbourne's common fields after 1625, lying just outside the lead field, see PRO, DL4/113/4; PRO, C21/C11/10.
[22] PRO, DL4/71/39, /73/26, /74/12.

locally decided custom, available to all as pasture in the winter months and overseen by elected officers, can be found in the Peak villages of the late sixteenth and early seventeenth centuries. But for the most part, that evidence existed only within the memories of aged men and women. In 1616, Thomas Longden could still remember keeping the town cattle of Stoney Middleton on the common in summertime during the 1560s; at that time, as he explained, there were only two mines in operation there.[23] By 1616, Stoney Middleton had become a heavily populated industrial village. Such reports tell of dead or dying systems of communal agriculture within the lead field. In those Peak villages which lay close to the lead field but did not themselves include lead deposits, and hence were not experiencing the same pressures on resources brought about through industrialization and population increase, this communal system died more slowly.[24] But within the lead field of the early seventeenth century, agricultural production and subsistence were becoming driven by imperatives which lay outside the economy of the village community. Such processes were, at first, incremental. None the less, the rationalization of holdings, enclosure of common land, imposition of stints upon commons, denial of common right and decline of communal regulation represented novel orderings of production and society. They amounted to local, political processes of exclusion, whereby the small-scale privatization of land and the individualization of production in the patriarchal household became central features of a dominant mode of agrarian production within the mining area by the mid-seventeenth century. At that point, and at every point thereafter, such dominance was never absolute; for in most manors, the smallholder and the landless still enjoyed some form of access to common land and common right. But neither was that domination challenged effectively.

A coincidence of records between 1610 and 1641 enables the examination of landholding patterns within the six townships in the large lordship of Ashford (see Table 3.2). This administrative unit was held by the Cavendish family when surveys were taken between 1610 and 1617, and again between 1634 and 1638. The former list is particularly revealing, as it details the acreage as well as the character of holdings in the six townships.[25] Comparisons of the two lists show that the number and

---

[23] PRO, DL4/64/12/4, /56/6.

[24] PRO, DL4/28/6, /11/30. For an account of the communal system in its intact form, see PRO, DL3/49/C1. In Beeley, on the eastern border of the lead field, communal agriculture died out after the Restoration. V.S. Doe, 'The common fields of Beeley in the seventeenth century', *DAJ*, 2nd ser., 93 (1973), 49.

[25] D.V. Fowkes and G.R. Potter (eds.), *William Senior's survey of the estates of the first and second Earls of Devonshire, c. 1600–28*, DRS, 13 (Chesterfield, 1988); CHT, unlisted Book of Surveys, 1634–8.

Table 3.2 *Landholding on Cavendish estates, 1610–17*

Acreage	Miners' landholdings	Total landholdings
Less than 10	26	60
10–30	23	50
31+	17	39
Total	66	149

Source: Wood, 'Industrial development', 76.

character of landholdings changed little between 1610 and 1638. The lists have also been compared with names of local miners taken from a variety of sources: depositions given by miners and placed before the Courts of Exchequer and the Duchy of Lancaster; a petition of some 1,912 named miners, listed by township, from 1641 and analysed more fully below; and lists of miners who refused payment of lead tithes in the parishes of Bakewell, Hope and Tideswell, into which the six townships here considered fell, between 1615 and 1632.[26]

Within Ashford lordship, about one quarter of landholders between 1610 and 1617 held more than thirty acres of land. Most of these were established copyholders or lessees of demesne land, and were drawn from the yeomanry. By the standards of downland, arable England, such a holding could hardly be considered substantial. In her study of fenland farming in the same period, Joan Thirsk defines a holding of up to thirty acres as that of a subsistence farmer. But in the conditions prevailing in these industrial northern villages, a thirty-acre farm was large indeed.[27] Sizeable groups of landholders occupying ten to thirty acres were also recorded in most of the six townships; but the largest group of landholders, in particular in the poor villages of Sheldon and Wardlow, were those smallholders who occupied less than ten acres of land. Mining households do not stand out from this pattern. Known mining households comprised roughly 40 per cent of each section of landed society, from the large holdings of over thirty acres down to the poor smallholders. Both in terms of the integration of miners into landed society, and in the distribution of

---

[26] For the 1641 petition, see PRO, E101/280/18. Lists of lead tithe non-payers, of which the first listed is the most extensive, are in PRO, E112/75/129, /75/128; PRO, E126/2, fol. 122. Sources for miners' depositions from these townships are taken from the PRO classes DL4 and E134.

[27] J. Thirsk, *English peasant farming: the agrarian history of Lincolnshire from Tudor to recent times* (London, 1957), chs. 1–4. Compare Table 3.2 with M. Spufford's study of landholding in sixteenth- and seventeenth-century Cambridgeshire villages: *Contrasting communities*, esp. 166–7.

land within the villages, these places appear as considerably less polarized and differentiated than in downland England. But a note of caution needs to be sounded. Comparison of the 1634–8 surveys with the militia list of 1638 shows that the number of holdings in each of these townships bore little relationship to the number of adult men. In the wealthier and more differentiated of the six townships, there were four times as many men as landholdings; in the poorer villages there were half as many men as landholdings. But in all the villages, we can assume that a large section of the total population – probably larger than a majority – were landless.

Study of landholding patterns in other early and mid-seventeenth-century Peak villages and towns confirms the picture derived from the Ashford case-study. In each settlement, the largest number of landholders were those in occupation of small or very small plots of land (often less than an acre). A substantial group of middling landholders also emerges, followed by a much smaller group of large landholders. Importantly, in richer, downland villages and towns, in particular within Wirksworth Wapentake, miners were represented at all levels of landed society. In poorer, upland villages within the High Peak, they were integrated into landholding society amongst smallholders and middling sized landholders, but scarcely appeared at all amongst the largest landholders. Finally, comparing the lists of landholders with population lists, high levels of landlessness can be detected.[28]

A false barrier between the smallholder and the landless should not be erected. A household possessed of a smallholding of two acres was scarcely better off than the landless, unless access to the commons were stinted; even then, stinting discriminated against the smallholder almost as much as the landless. The real potential for intra-village conflict over land use lay between the larger landed households on the one side, and the smallholders and landless on the other. The largest group in Peak village society at this time comprised the composite bloc of landless and near-landless. It is of central importance to our understanding of the conflicts of the late sixteenth and early seventeenth centuries that members of this composite group were much more dependent upon the commons and mining employment than were their wealthier neighbours. As the miners emphasized in 1616, many of their number were landless, having but 'a cowe or twoe apeece to give them milke'.[29] Both in agriculture and in industry, the fragile domestic economy of such households therefore depended upon the protection of custom.

[28] For a fuller discussion, see Wood, 'Industrial development', 77–81.
[29] PRO, E134/13JasI/Mich3.

THE MINING INDUSTRY AND ITS WORKFORCE

We must now turn to consider the changing structure of the mining industry between the introduction of Humphrey's innovations and the Restoration. Like its smaller British competitors in the Mendips, Yorkshire, North Wales, Lancashire, Staffordshire and County Durham, the Derbyshire lead industry of the mid-sixteenth century had served a primarily regional market. By a century later the scale of that market had expanded, as had the productive capacity of the industry. Demand came from a series of connected sectors. Internally, the rising wealth of early modern England's 'middling sort' expressed itself in increased demand for pewter tableware. The growth of urban centres, in particular of London, required lead for roofing and piping. The same was true of the 'great rebuilding' of the houses of the rural 'middling sort', the gentry and, of course, the nobility. The production of paint, glass and (earlier in the period) silver extraction all consumed Derbyshire lead. Finally, the establishment of large European standing armies provided a vital source of demand.[30] Due as much to lengthy periods of warfare as to the collapse of central European lead mining, continental markets for British lead therefore expanded.[31] Between the middle of the sixteenth century and the last decade of the eighteenth century, thanks to the geological accident of the richness and size of its lead deposits, the Derbyshire industry was the pre-eminent international supplier of lead.[32] By 1600, lengthy tendrils of trade and capital connected the remote mining villages to the heart of an international trading system. After smelting, Derbyshire lead followed the traditional route overland to Bawtry, and then by river to Hull. From there, it could be exported to the Amsterdam markets, or shipped on to London or Bristol. It might then pass across Europe to the Mediterranean; to 'the Indies'; to the Americas; or to trading ports on the African coast. The Derbyshire lead mining

---

[30] Kiernan, *Lead industry*, 88–92; Clay, *Economic expansion* , II, 23, 57–8; R. Burt, 'The transformation of the non-ferrous metals industries in the seventeenth and eighteenth centuries', *EcHR*, 2nd ser., 48, 1 (1995), 32–5; Wrightson, *English society*, 135–7; Slack, *Lands and lead-miners*, 72–7.

[31] See Kiernan, *Lead industry*, 268, and I.S.W. Blanchard, 'English lead and the international bullion crisis of the 1550s', in D.C. Coleman and A.H. John (eds.), *Trade, government and economy in pre-industrial England: essays presented to F.J. Fisher*, (London, 1976), 21–44. For signs of an early seventeenth-century revival in some European lead mines, see PRO SP14/109/165.

[32] I.S.W. Blanchard, *Russia's 'age of silver': precious-metal production and economic growth in the eighteenth century* (London, 1989), 43–9; W.J. Lewis, 'Some aspects of lead mining in Cardiganshire in the sixteenth and seventeenth centuries', *Ceredigion*, 1 (1950–1), 177–92; J.W. Gough, *The mines of Mendip* (Newton Abbot, 1957), 112, 157; PRO, E134/19ChasII/East3, /34ChasII/Mich37, /34ChasII/Mich25, /17ChasII/East24, /36ChasII/Mich47; PRO, SP16/341/130; BL, Lansdowne MS 31, fol. 164.

industry, located in the landlocked hills and valleys of the southern Pennines, had become a leading element in the integration of England's economy into a developing system of global exchange, exploitation and empire.

The success of the Derbyshire industry received unwelcome confirmation through the attentions of Jacobean and Caroline courtiers and entrepreneurs, anxious to acquire patents, feefarms or licences upon the mines, as also in the attention of the Privy Council in mining, smelting and the export trade as a source of revenue.[33] Clearer indications of rising demand can be drawn from surviving lot and cope accounts, inferred from the productive capacity of known smelting mills, and from the port books of Hull, the main outlet of Derbyshire lead on to national and international markets. In the early 1540s Derbyshire's mines produced a yearly total of about 3,000 loads. By 1600, production had increased to about 34,000 loads of ore every year. Thirty-six years later, that total stood at around 95,000 loads. The highest level of output in the 1540–1660 period was reached in the latter years of the first civil war, when production may have stood at around 120,000 loads every year. Thereafter, total production fell off in the 1650s, only to begin to increase again in the following decade.[34] Crudely put, the lead mining industry increased its output elevenfold between 1560 and 1600, and by a further factor of three on its 1600 total by 1636. Even given the low base at which the industry started in the mid-sixteenth century, rates of growth within the lead field in the 1540–1640 period were clearly phenomenal.

During the late sixteenth and early seventeenth centuries, the free miners were favoured by a contradiction in the lead industry's history. Over this period, rising demand coincided with a general rise in the price of lead.[35] Importantly, this coincidence was maintained in spite of the large growth in the output of both lead ore and smelted lead (see Fig. 3.3). Following the disastrous years of the 1540s, which saw the artificial depression of lead prices as the market was flooded with high-quality lead stripped from the roofs of dissolved monastic houses, prices climbed again to reach nine

---

[33] For evidence of periodic attempts by the Privy Council or a number of courtiers to raise revenue from tolls, increased customs duties and pre-emption on the industry, see BL, Add. MSS 6681, fols. 201–5, 6686, fols. 57–8, 160; PRO, E112/75/165; W. Waller, *An essay on the value of mines* (London, 1698); Kiernan, *Lead industry*, 221–2; PRO, SP16/14/35, / 341/129–30, /431/32, /78/20, /310/11; PRO, SP14/109/94, /111/36, /109/164, /10/165, / 14/35; PRO, PC2/44, fols. 614–20; PRO, DL44/390; DRO, D258M/31/10w.

[34] Wood, 'Industrial development', 35–6; D. Kiernan, 'Lawrence Oxley's accounts, 1672–81', in J.V. Beckett, J.P. Polack, D.M. Riden and D. Kiernan (eds.), *A seventeenth century Scarsdale miscellany*, DRS, 20 (Chesterfield, 1993), 123; Kiernan, *Lead industry*, 196, 202; SA, BFM2/76, 78; LPL, Shrewsbury MS 705, fol. 148.

[35] For lead prices on the London market, see Blanchard, *Age of silver*, 46.

shillings per load by the 1560s. They may have continued to rise over the following decade, only to fall back again in the 1580s. This fall was probably a consequence of the introduction of Humphrey's innovations, and the sudden increase in production from the High Peak. Prices remained stable at between nine and ten shillings per load until the turn of the century. Given the static price of ore in the 1590s, and the price inflation of that decade, mining households may have been forced to work the easily accessible deposits with increased intensity.[36] By 1610 however, prices had increased to around sixteen shillings per load. Thereafter they continued to increase, reaching a peak of twenty-four shillings in the mid-1630s. This rise roughly followed the general course of prices over the 1610–35 period. Depression followed in the years leading to the civil war, and again coincided with increasing inflation. Once more, this must have brought on a crisis in many mining households, which was likely to have been felt most sharply amongst the growing number of landless or near-landless workers who had become most heavily dependent upon industrial employment. The years of the civil war caused severe dislocation in both the extractive and distributive sides of the industry. But military demand lifted lead prices once again. By 1653, ore was being sold at twenty-eight shillings per load, climbing to a peak of between thirty and thirty-four shillings by 1661. With inflation stabilizing and even falling in the 1650s, and as the price of lead ore increased to its all-century high, a free mining group with access to a good vein could make substantial profits. This rise in the price of lead may have been caused by the continuing effects of the wars, but is more likely to have been the result of the capital and technological difficulties faced by the industry in developing productive deep works, a theme explored more fully below.

Such basic facts of economic life, charted in the laconic form of Figure 3.3, are pivotal to any historical understanding of the material, political and cultural worlds inhabited by the Peak's plebeian inhabitants in the late sixteenth and early seventeenth centuries. When set against the general pattern of inflation, such short-term fluctuations in the price of lead ore could bring poverty or prosperity to the thousands of households dependent upon the mining industry. The getting of ore had become a central concern to the people of what, by the middle of the seventeenth century, had become an industrial region.

Contemporary estimates of the mining workforce are far from reliable. In 1616, for instance, the High Peak workforce was placed at anywhere between 900 and 12,000. The mining population was often presented as an

---

[36] Following on Blanchard's suggestion in 'Labour productivity', 14.

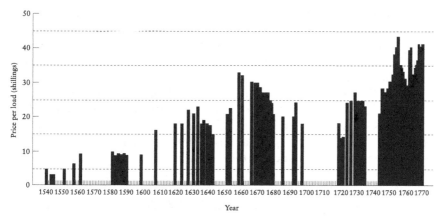

Figure 3.3. Price of lead ore per load, 1540–1770
Sources: Kiernan, *Lead industry*, 38; PRO, E134/11ChasI/Mich20, /12ChasI/
Mich3, /18ChasI/East12, /1658/Mich15; PRO, E178/611; PRO, DL4/40/34, /68/50,
/68/52, /72/31, /81/6, /103/18, /112/13, /117/8, /127/1693/6; PRO, DL41/17/19;
BL, Add. MS 6676, fols. 42–3; PRO, RGO 33; CHT, High Peak lot and cope
accounts, 1679; CHT, Ashford lot and cope accounts, 1697; CHT, Odin mine
accounts, 1730; PRO, STAC8/201/19; LJRO, B/C/5/1636, Eyam; LPL, Shrewsbury
Ms. 705, fol. 148; SA, BFM2/76; SA, Bag C 549 (1), fol. 3, 549 (3), 702 (1a), 702
(3)-22, 704 (11–13); SA, WHC 34; SA, BD 189; DRO, 504B/L55, L71; DRO,
D258M/28/20g, /28/20da, /31/55; DRO, D1288M/L252–80; DRO, D3105/A/PI9/
1–3; H. Lawrance, 'The will of Lionel Tylney, lead-miner and merchant: died 19
November 1653', *DAJ*, 2nd ser., 5 (1931), 14.

undifferentiated 'great multitude' of 'many thousands'.[37] Such accounts
obscure important but subtle distinctions amongst the extractive workforce. These were both structural and cultural in character. For one frozen
moment we are able to illuminate the spatial, cultural and economic
qualities of those distinctions. In 1641, as a part of the petitioning movement which provided the background noise to the debates occurring in
parliament in that year, some 1,912 miners signed a petition which was
placed before the House of Commons.[38] The petition demanded the
lowering of the Crown's duties upon exported lead which, it explained, had

---

[37] PRO, E134/13JasI/Mich 3; PRO, STAC8/226/27, 73/4; PRO, E112/168/11; PRO, DL4/90/
24; DRO, D258M/31/10da; PRO, SP16/193/29, /293/115; PRO, SP16/185/93. For similar
descriptions of mining population expansion in the northern coalfield, see Levine and
Wrightson, *Making of an industrial society*, 173.

[38] The political context to the production of this petition is discussed in Chapter 12; its
cultural significance in Chapter 8. For the petition itself, see PRO, E101/280/18. This is a
clerk's copy.

damaged the export trade, and therefore the miners' livelihood. A clerk's copy of that petition, together with its signatories has survived. This unique source allows the observation of fine distinctions within the mining work-force through a bird's-eye view of the distribution and structure of mining households across almost the whole lead field.

The leading signatory to the petition was Lionel Tynley, a yeoman of Holmesfield who was also a minor lead merchant and mine investor.[39] The petitioners included a scattering of such merchants and orebuyers, but case-studies show that the large majority were indeed miners.[40] Far from exaggerating the importance of the industry, the petition underestimated the number of miners in 1641.[41] The number of the miners' 'dependants' are also listed against each name, and in the case of most townships, the nature of that dependency is indicated, thereby describing the constituency of individual households.[42] Beneath most township's list of miners, the number of 'hirelings and cavers' and their families follows. 'Hirelings' here refers to the waged labourers. 'Cavers', of course, refers to the very poor individuals who made a tenuous living from turning over rubbish tips for scraps of ore. Three major works are included in the list: the operations at the large Dovegang mine, where a drainage channel or 'sough' was being constructed, which 'when it is in worke' was said to support 1,000 people, indicating an overall workforce of perhaps 200; the Cromford moor works, employing around sixty men, and Ball Eye mine, providing work for about forty men. Finally, crude statistics of the number of people employed in various ancillary trades supported by the mining industry were included: transport, rope making, wood cutting, chandling, smelting and metal working. These last, unverifiable figures appear as round numbers, and are probably unreliable.

The contents of the 1641 petition have been linked with other sources to provide a snapshot of the place of the mining workforce within Peak society. In order to indicate the proportion of adult men involved in free mining activity, the names of the miners given in 1641 have been compared with those of the able-bodied men of 1638. This is represented in Map 10.

[39] See H. Lawrance, 'The will of Lionel Tylney, lead-miner and merchant: died 19 Nov., 1653', *DAJ*, 2nd ser., 5 (1931), 1–26.

[40] Based on cross-reference of names in the list for Wirksworth, Middleton and Cromford with lot and cope and mine accounts for those places, 1639–45. See DRO, D258M/58/18j, /24a–d, 60/11.

[41] Of a list of 99 miners, mostly from Youlgreave, operating in Harthill in 1647, only 27 are included in the 1641 petition: BL, Add. MS 6682, fols. 80–5. Similarly, a sample of one in every eight weeks of production records for Wirksworth township between 1639 and 1645 reveals that of the 137 individual miners listed, only 55 appeared on the 1641 petition: DRO, D258M/60/11.

[42] Household structures as revealed from this source are discussed in Chapter 8 below.

The distribution of 'cavers and hirelings', taken together with the numbers employed upon named large mining operations, has been expressed as a percentage of the overall mining workforce, and is depicted in Map 11. This is here taken to indicate the extent of wage dependency. Finally, the local importance of mining employment is indicated by comparing the total workforce (including the 'cavers and hirelings', the workforces of named workings and the miners) with the number of able-bodied men in each township. The results are represented in Map 12.[43]

The results of this record linkage exercise enable us to tour the lead field in 1641, observing local difference in the extent of mining activity and the structure of the workforce. We begin once more at the southern boundaries of the lead field, in the ancient heart of the lead industry. Here we can observe important changes in the organization and intensity of mining activity from that of 1541–2, but a continuity in the spatial distribution of the industry around Wirksworth town. The town itself appears as less dependent upon mining activity than its satellite villages: in Wirksworth, 22 per cent of the adult male population was listed on the 1641 petition; in nearby Middleton and Cromford that figure stood at 43 per cent. 'Cavers and hirelings' made up only 3 per cent of the total extractive workforce. However, the vast majority of that workforce were employed upon the large Cromford moor and Dovegang works. In total, comparison of the 1641 petition and 1638 militia roll suggests that some 90 per cent of Wirksworth, Cromford and Middleton's male population was involved in some form of mining activity. Within the neighbouring parishes of Brassington and Carsington a less extreme picture is drawn. One third of the adult male population was involved in mining, of whom 30 per cent were 'cavers and hirelings'. Moving east and north along the Derwent valley to Matlock, Bonsall and Wensley, our survey is hampered by the lack of statistics for cavers and hirelings. That waged labour was becoming increasingly important is apparent from the prominence of the large Ball Eye mine near Bonsall in the 1641 petition.[44] None the less, 34 per cent of the able-bodied men in Bonsall defined themselves as miners. In total, 77 per cent of that township's population was partially or wholly dependent upon mining.

Moving north along the valley, we enter the southern parishes of High Peak Hundred at Netherhaddon. Our statistical survey is blind to the disputes raging over the Earl of Rutland's estates in the year of the miners'

---

[43] Methods of calculation and full results are given in Wood, 'Social conflict', 52–5. Since the totals of cavers, hirelings and the workforce of the three large mines are given as composite figures with their 'dependants', but are compared alongside lists of adult men, they have been divided by the household multiplier of 4.496 suggested by the petition.

[44] See for instance PRO, DL1/352, answer of Grace Columbell *et al.*

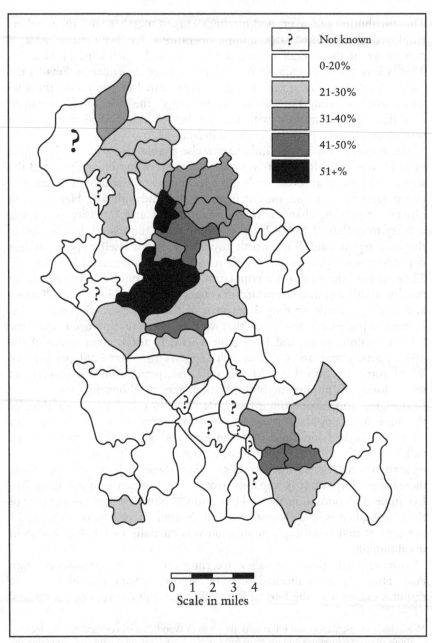

Map 10   Free mining as an employer: free miners as a percentage of the adult male
population, 1641
Sources: PRO, E101/280/18; PRO, SP16/405 Pt 2; BL, Add. MS 6682, fols. 80–5

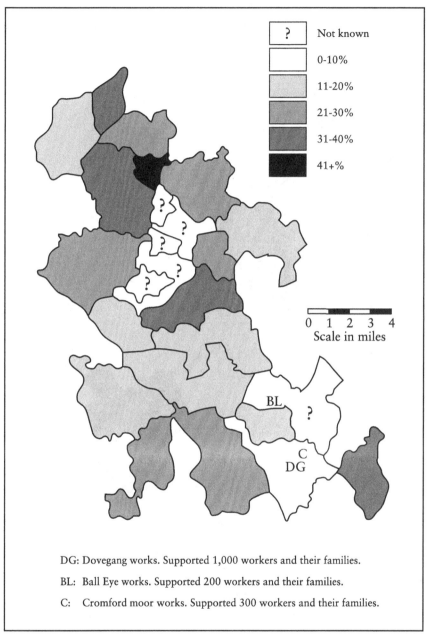

DG: Dovegang works. Supported 1,000 workers and their families.

BL: Ball Eye works. Supported 200 workers and their families.

C: Cromford moor works. Supported 300 workers and their families.

Map 11   Wage dependency and marginality: percentage of the mining workforce
described as 'cavers and hirelings' in 1641
Source: PRO, E101/280/18.

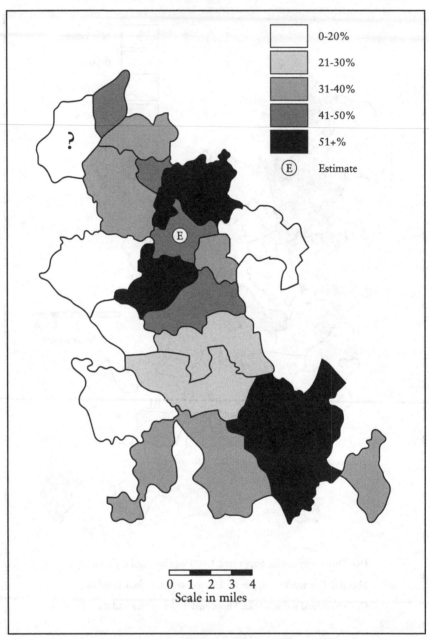

	0-20%
	21-30%
	31-40%
	41-50%
	51+%
(E)	Estimate

0 1 2 3 4
Scale in miles

Map 12   Industry and society: total percentage of the population dependent upon
mining, 1638–1641
Sources: PRO, E101/280/18; PRO, SP16/405 Pt 2.

petition. But we can note the large preponderance of free miners in the area: in both Bakewell and Youlgreave, one quarter of the adult men were free miners in 1641. Clustered on the hills above Youlgreave and Bakewell were smaller industrial villages where the proportion of miners was larger, such as in Overhaddon where 45 per cent of the men were miners. Continuing north and west along the Wye valley, we reach Ashford, where 60 per cent of the able-bodied men of 1638 signed the miners' petition in 1641. Nearby, the smaller, poorer upland settlements of Wardlow and Sheldon registered almost identical proportions of miners. In these villages we find the heart of free mining territory in 1641: not yet undercut by the cavers and hirelings or by the large, capitalized works to be found to the south. Reaching the western fringe of the lead field, miners comprised a mere 5 per cent of the male population of Hartingdon. In this large parish, population was scattered, ore deposits poor and the soil thin.

On entering the northern reaches of the lead field, where population had expanded most dramatically in the late sixteenth century, the mining workforce appears as heavily wage dependent. Within the townships of Castleton and Bradwell, the free miners remained socially significant. But even here the 'cavers and hirelings' made up one quarter of the mining workforce. Similarly, in nearby Tideswell and Litton free mining still formed an important source of employment for 27 per cent of the adult men. In Eyam and its adjacent villages, mining activity employed over half of the adult men, but one third of the workforce were defined as 'cavers and hirelings'. The starkest statistics present themselves in the small, populous townships of Great and Little Hucklow, where an unusually wage-dependent mining workforce shows itself. Some 59 per cent of the total population were engaged in mining, almost half of whom were 'hirelings and cavers'.

In 1641, the free miners remained the most numerically important group within the industry. But that domination was illusory. They were being challenged by two connected forces: the large preponderance of 'cavers', and 'hirelings', and the establishment of the first large, complex, heavily capitalized mines. Important correspondences should be observed in the relationship between industrial employment, landholding and population growth. Where population had grown most sensationally between 1563 and 1664, high levels of landlessness, industrial employment and wage dependency were observable. In the year in which the miners' petition was compiled, we therefore find the free miner in a precarious position. Clinging to shares in his small workings, he found occasional paid work in the larger mines gradually blossoming across the lead field. The fragile domestic economy of the free miner was buttressed by access to common rights and common land, and built upon the long-term rise in lead prices which had occurred over the first four decades of the seventeenth century. That price rise had occurred in the face of important changes in the structure, scale and technology of mining.

Early sixteenth-century lead miners were only beginning to develop underground mining methods, with most ore extracted from long, deep-surface trenches, called rakes. By the 1580s, that was no longer the case. In 1581, free miners gave revealing evidence to an Exchequer commission looking into the organization of the High Peak industry. They criticized the easy, disorderly work of the cavers, and grumbled about their own technological difficulties. Whereas the cavers had only to dig over the multitudinous 'old wurckes' and 'ancient rakes' left by the decline of the late medieval industry, and then to sift the ore with Humphrey's sieves, the miners explained that in their search for underground ore they had 'firste [to] sinke a pytt wherein they firste digge sometimes iii fadome in stone'. Upon discovering ore, they had then to sink a further forty or even sixty fathoms. The methods of underground working were therefore already known by 1581. So too were the dangers: miners were 'in p[er]ill of theire lives for lacke of timber and sometimes men loste or spoiled in the pytts'.[45]

The typical lead mining operation of the late sixteenth century was organized around the relationship between three workers.[46] Foremost in control of the circumstances of his labour was the miner, who typically owned a share within the mine, and who cut the ore from the lead vein at the 'forefield'. A 'carrier' transported the ore from the forefield to the foot of a shaft which allowed access to the mine, and up which the ore was wound to the surface. At the surface a 'winder' operated the windlass, and would chip and sieve earth and stone from the ore. The key unit of production in this system was the household. Both the underground carrier and the winder were likely to be subordinate members of a household headed by the free miner: in the case of the carrier, an older son or servant; in the case of the winder, the miner's wife, adult daughter or female servant. Late sixteenth-century mines were shallower than those of a generation later. The example given above of a sixty-fathom mine was unusual; most references suggest a depth of about twenty fathoms, or 120 feet. Changes in the organization of underground work and the size of the underground labour force can be drawn from a report presented to the Duchy of Lancaster in 1630 by Roger Kenyon, which described mining methods and customs in the Peak. This was produced in the course of the Duchy's inquiries into the working of the lead deposits at Thieveley in

---

[45] PRO, E178/611; PRO, DL4/64/11, /71/39; PRO, DL44/390.
[46] The social and cultural implications of changes in relations of production and divisions of labour are discussed in Chapter 8.

Lancashire, a matter in which the costs and benefits of the free mining customs of the Derbyshire King's Field loomed large.[47] Kenyon's account has been supplemented with other contemporary sources which cast light on the operation of a typical lead mine of 1630.

At the forefield laboured the key skilled worker: the 'pickman or myner'. Kenyon highlighted the miners' sense of skill: 'The myner ever tymbers the worke as hee goes . . . and none are accompted . . . myners, unles they can do the whole worke aswell tymber as myne.' If the miner did not own a share in the work, he was paid on piece rates 'according to the goodnes of the workmen', with wages ranging between four shillings and six shillings and sixpence per week. In contrast, both the carriers and winders were paid flat weekly rates. The latter were mostly 'woemen or lads', but if a man did the job, he earned more. The deepest mines which Kenyon saw sank forty fathoms deep, or 240 feet. He noted that 'According to the depth of the worke more or lesse workmen are employed.' A forty-fathom mine ran 'by severall stories', each stepped gallery ten fathoms deeper than the last. Kenyon was describing mines which had developed organically over generations, starting as a simple ten-fathom working which employed a workforce of three, and consisting simply of a single shaft and gallery. By 1630, such a working might have grown into a forty-fathom mine, of three galleries, three shafts and requiring a workforce of at least five, as each 'pickman or hewer' at the forefield needed a supporting workforce of three underground carriers and one surface winder. A single vein could support many such workings. Legal papers describe how mines were broken into one another, and detail their growing complexity by the death of James I.[48]

The miners' proximity to one another in the honeycombed deposits was inherently dangerous. So too was their habit of softening limestone rock by lighting fires against it. This could result in neighbouring works becoming 'filled with suffocating smoke'.[49] In the narrow underground galleries, miners were frequently overcome due to lack of oxygen, or the 'damps'. The concentration of methane could lead to 'firedamp', in which gas was ignited into an explosion. Kenyon observed that in order to prevent the 'damps', 'they have ever a wynde shaft about 6, 8 or 10 yards from that they work at'. Chambers and shafts could collapse due to poor timbering or earth movements, burying the workers alive. Mines were flooded by heavy rains, or due to miners breaking into underground streams. Miners

---

[47] R. Sharpe France (ed.), *The Thieveley lead mines, 1629–35*, Lancashire and Cheshire Record Society, 52 (Preston, 1947), 6–9, 25–8, 74–6, 90–6, 158–64, 183–5. Kenyon's report is reproduced in *ibid.*, 81–4; for the original, see PRO, DL41/17/19.

[48] See for instance PRO, DL4/68/52.

[49] SA, Bag C 587 (95). For a description, see N. Kirkham, 'The tumultuous course of the Dovegang', *DAJ*, 2nd ser., 73 (1953), 5.

often found themselves working deposits down to the water table, 'though they stood sometymes in water up to the knees and sometymes legges', while carriers scooped the water out in leather bags.[50] The deeper the miners descended, the more such problems multiplied. Giving evidence in 1615, miners presented uniformly grim accounts of their work. William Greaves recalled that he was over eleven fathoms down in Mandale rake near Bakewell when 'a load of Earth fall uppon him . . . whereby he hardlie escaped wth his life'. Henry Hancocke had lost two brothers and a servant twenty years earlier 'wth the fall of earth'. Robert Greaves, 'being a near neighboure hath knowne eight severall psons killed outright' in the mines. Another man remembered seeing 'dyvers dead bodies . . . so killed drawne upp out of the said groves'. Some had been killed by rockfalls, others by 'dampe'.[51]

Gradually, technological solutions were developed which offered the possibility of at least lessening such dangers. 'Wind pumps' could be installed, operated by bellows which pressed air along pipes into the deeper galleries. 'Horse gins' and rag-and-chain pumps were positioned within or on top of the mines to drain inundated deposits. Ventilation shafts were dug at regular intervals, connecting directly to 'the daye'. But all of this cost money. As we have seen, even without the employment of such technology the miner of the 1630s was reliant upon a larger number of ancillary workers than had been his predecessor of the 1580s. This fact alone required an escalating reliance upon labour drawn from outside of the household, thereby increasing costs. The introduction of ventilation and drainage technology, or the fuller timbering of underground works, proved costly. But the miners simply had no alternative: for many, their smallholdings and access to the commons were insufficient to sustain their households without the income derived from industrial employment. They therefore turned in gathering numbers, and with deepening need, to gentry smelters and lead merchants for advances of capital.

Free mining groups of the early sixteenth century had depended upon the lesser gentry for credit. But their successors experienced qualitative and quantitative changes in that dependence. In 1615, miners complained that after payment of their growing wages bills, together with lot and cope duties and (where applicable) the hated lead tithe, they were lucky to make a 10 per cent profit. Even after all their costs and dangers, miners knew that theirs was a chancy business: some might hit it lucky on one vein, while others found nothing but earth. The cannier miners therefore spread

[50] PRO, DL4/91/16.
[51] PRO, E134/13JasI/Mich3. See also PRO, STAC8/201/19; PRO, E134/4ChasI/Mich33; PRO, DL4/72/31; LJRO, B/C/5/1628, 1629 Wirksworth. For later examples of such descriptions, see PRO, E134/2JasII/Mich21.

their risks and bought shares in a variety of small workings.[52] Yet the knowledge 'That the lead mines are decayed . . . Charge more, and perill greater than formerly' forced the free miners into ever more exploitative relationships with the mercantile gentry.[53] Gentlemen liked to cast themselves in the role of paternal benefactors to the 'poore myners'. But merchants did not lend money merely out of a sense of Christian charity. Loans were secured against miners' smallholdings or mineshares. Since many miners operated a dual household economy, the failure of their mining activities could bring creditors to seize their land. Alternatively, creditors might take the miners' share in his working as compensation. Either way the economic independence of the free miner was subject to continual erosion.[54]

In connection to the growing dependence of the free miner upon outside capital, but at the same time becoming gradually distinct from that development, from the early seventeenth century a new generation of deep, sophisticated mining operations owned largely or exclusively by mine investors was established. The separation of labour from capital here took a pristine form. Some works had been bought from free miners, or taken from them upon their descent into debt.[55] Others were newly established. Tearsall rake mine, operating in Wensley in the 1630s, was one such. Owned by a coalition of gentlemen, rag-and-chain pumps were used to lift water from deep, rich, inundated deposits. Between August and December 1634, Tearsall produced some 644 loads of ore.[56] In this early stage in the development of larger, gentry-owned works, their organizational characteristics were diverse. Some, such as Tearsall, were worked on six-hour shifts 'by night as day', by groups of waged labourers; the miners were paid on piece rates, the rest of the workforce on day rates. It was a single, coherent enterprise, owned by a coalition of wealthy individuals. Nearby Paddock Torr rake differed in that it comprised a series of individually owned workings, held by lead merchants, who had combined to fund the drainage of the whole deposits. Elsewhere, as the gentleman Richard Wigley explained to the Duchy Court, it was 'usuall amongst the mynrs . . . to give a pte thereof' to lead merchants in return for credit, making them co-partners in the enterprise. In such circumstances, the degree of control exercised by gentry investors was less absolute, yet it is likely that such arrangements were far more common before the Restoration than 'rationa-

[52] For later examples of this, see PRO, DL4/127/1693/6, /127/1694/6.
[53] PRO, E134/13JasI/Mich3, /22JasI/East30, /4ChasI/Mich33; BL, Add. MS 6682, fol. 38.
[54] PRO, DL4/112/10, /64/12/4; PRO, C2/JasI/M13/61; PRO, C2/Eliz/B6/12; DRO, D258M/42/15, unlisted receipt; SA, Bag C 358, 1514, 1368A.
[55] For examples from 1634, see PRO, DL4/84/24.
[56] PRO, E134/11ChasI/Mich20.

lized' works like Tearsall rake. [57] Between c. 1630 and c. 1660, as we shall see in Chapter 4, such joint arrangements grew organically into something rather different: gentry-owned mines, in which the miners worked under collective contracts for high piece rates.

Through such innovations in organization, ownership and control, the mercantile lesser gentry extended a gradual and tentative hold over the mining industry which allowed investment in the ventilation and drainage technology necessary to exploit the deep lead deposits. Such technology, still in its infancy, was often unsuccessful and as the free miners knew to their cost, upon the 'unwatering' of deposits their yield could be poor.[58] Mining remained a business constricted by growing labour costs and high risks. Due as much to such factors as to their limited reserves of capital, mine investors tended to combine together as shareholders. The typical scale of such workings was not vast: at the vein a workforce of perhaps three or four miners was supported by eight or ten carriers and surface workers, who could produce perhaps fifty loads of ore in a week.[59]

It was in the 1650s that the capacity of a small number of deep, heavily capitalized mines to dominate lead ore production was first demonstrated. In 1629, the famous Dutch engineer Sir Cornelius Vermuyden began work on a long drainage channel, or sough, the purpose of which was to drain the rich, deep Dovegang deposits near Wirksworth.[60] After many technological, legal and political difficulties, the Vermuyden sough finally reached its objective in 1652. An unforeseen consequence of the Dovegang operation was the unwatering of the neighbouring deposits on Cromford moor. Their drainage led to a dramatic, if temporary, increase in production. The scattered survival of lot and cope records covering some years between 1639 and 1660 for Wirksworth and four adjacent towns, together with estimates of the Dovegang's production in 1652, allow us to observe the impact of this successful drainage operation (see Table 3.3).

Records from 1639 to 1645 point to the continued domination of free mining in all five townships. Despite the presence of some small gentry-owned mineworkings, and the shadowy presence of large numbers of cavers, the free miners were responsible for the large bulk of ore extracted. By 1653, the lot and cope records tell a different story. In this year, the Cromford moor deposits had been drained by the Dovegang sough. Full records of ore production from the Dovegang circuit do not survive for the 1650s; but between May and December 1652, some 8,036 loads were

---

[57] PRO, DL4/81/6, /85/58.

[58] For miners' memories of the financial dangers of large-scale drainage, in the 1630s, see PRO, E134/2JasII/Mich21.

[59] For mid-century examples from Winster, see PRO, E134/1658/Mich15; SA, TC 366(3).

[60] This set off a protracted dispute with the free miners of the area. See Chapter 10.

Table 3.3 *1653 production totals for five townships, expressed in loads and dishes*

Category	Wirksworth	Cromford	Middleton	Brassington and Carsington	Total
Free miner	263–8	286–0	273–8	582–2	1,406–0
Cavers	895–6	1,285–0	89–5	119–6	2,389–8
Gentry-owned mining operations					
Major works	—	6,354–6	—	—	6,354–6
Minor works	68–1	197–2	4–0	27–7	297–1
Total	1,227–6	8,122–8	367–4	729–6	10,447–6

Note: categorization of gentry-owned mining operations: major workings: those works making five or more sales and producing an average of six or more loads each sale. Minor works: all those operations known to employ only waged labour which do not fit into the preceding category.
Measurements given in *loads-dishes*. Nine dishes make up a load.
Source: DRO, D258M/28/20c.

extracted from them.[61] The following year, the adjacent Cromford moor works produced 6,354 loads. If we assume that in 1653 the Dovegang mines produced a similar output as in 1652, and add that output to the known production from the five townships covered in Table 3.3, this suggests that within Wirksworth and its immediate satellite settlements, a total of 22,500 loads of ore were extracted. Of this total, some 83 per cent was extracted from gentry-owned works, and a further 11 per cent by cavers, leaving the hitherto dominant free mining groups with a miserable 6 per cent of total production. The combined extractive force employed on the Cromford moor and Dovegang works probably stood at around 154 in 1653, implying a total labour force of at least 462.[62] Taken together with the large production of caved ore, this points to a very heavy wage dependency amongst the industrial workforce of the Wirksworth area in 1653.

Comparison of the 1653 returns with those for the Wirksworth area in 1541–2 is instructive, highlighting long-term changes in the structure, organization and productive capacity of the mining industry. In 1541–2, some 1,674 loads of ore were extracted from within the five townships here considered. In 1653, that amount had increased by a factor of thirteen. If the scale of production had undergone seismic change, so too had the

[61] PRO, DL4/103/18.
[62] For method of calculation, see Wood, 'Industrial development', 41.

organization of the industry. The free miners of 1541–2 had been the key producers of ore. By 1653, the hitherto dominant free miners of the Wirksworth area had been suddenly levered aside by the huge productive capacity of the deep works on Cromford moor and the Dovegang, and by the scavenging activities of hundreds of semi-vagrant cavers. There is no more eloquent testimony to the decline of the free miner. Although the seasonal pattern of productivity of the free miners of 1653 suggests that, like their forebears of 1541–2, they alternated work in their mines, on their smallholdings or paid work for larger farmers, the production of the large works demonstrates no such seasonal pattern. Work of the deposits continued on a shift system, unaffected by the passage of the seasons as by that of day and night.[63]

The early 1650s were unusual years. The structure of the industry in most Peak mining villages probably retained a similar profile as that suggested by the returns for Brassington or Middleton (see Table 3.3). Here, the free miners remained the most important group of ore producers. A large presence of cavers can be detected, as can a few small-scale gentry-owned works. Moreover, by 1660, the large works on Cromford moor and the Dovegang had declined, and free mining resumed its traditional domination of the area. Viewed from the perspective of the 1630s and 1640s, the transformation of the mining industry around Wirksworth seemed a temporary aberration. But with the historian's advantage of hindsight, these large works heralded the future of the lead mining industry.

[63] For a full discussion of the 1653 returns, see *ibid.*, 38–47.

4

The Peak Country as an industrial region, c. 1660–1770

THE ECONOMICS OF REGIONAL IDENTITY

In the year of the restoration of the Stuart monarchy, the Derbyshire lead mining industry stood upon the turning crest of rapid change. The deep mines near Wirksworth whose production had faded out in 1658 presaged the growing domination of large-scale capitalism within the industry. Coincidences of source material between 1639 and 1664 have allowed us to map long-term changes in population, together with the distribution of mining households and the significance of industrial activity within the Peak in the early 1640s. The Hearth Tax records of 1664 have already been deployed as a source of information about the distribution of population. The full survival of the Hearth Tax returns also sheds light on the forms assumed by the social structures of the mining area at the point at which long-emergent capitalist relations of production began to acquire local domination within the mining industry.

Economic and social historians have used Hearth Tax returns as a rough indicator of local patterns of wealth and poverty in mid-seventeenth-century England. The Hearth Tax assessed named heads of households upon the number of hearths within their dwelling. A general and consistent correspondence has been observed between the number of hearths on which a householder was assessed, and their discernible wealth as drawn from other sources. Importantly, those regarded as unable to pay on the grounds of 'poverty or smallness of estate' were exempted from payment. On some assessments, such as those for Derbyshire for 1664, these exempted householders are also named.[1] Taken as a whole, the Hearth Tax returns from the Peak mining townships therefore provide a statistical

---

[1] The Derbyshire Hearth Tax assessments for 1670, which do not include returns of exempted households, have been published. See D.G. Edwards, *Derbyshire Hearth Tax assessments, 1662–70*, DRS, 7 (Chesterfield, 1982). The 1664 assessments are at PRO, E179/94/401–3. A full statistical breakdown of the 1664 assessments for the mining townships is provided in Wood, 'Industrial development', 84.

expression of local social structure, sketched in the 'frozen moment' of
their assessment.[2] As with the earlier discussion of population change and
industrial employment, that picture is here given a spatial expression. Of
particular importance is Map 13, which records the overall percentage of a
township's households that were exempted from the Hearth Tax. Again,
the results enable us to take a mental journey of the Peak, this time in 1664,
focusing upon the relative wealth of settlements as we pass.

We shall begin once more at the ancient heart of the mining industry,
around Wirksworth. Although other market towns such as Bakewell had
grown in importance as centres of trade and capital, the town of Wirksworth retained this important function. The 1664 assessments therefore
observe the relatively large number of multiple hearth households, comprising 16 per cent, headed by men and women identifiable as lesser gentry
merchants, or as yeoman farmers. At the other end of the social spectrum,
49 per cent of the town's householders were exempted from the tax.
Wirksworth emerges as more socially variegated than the surrounding
mining villages, which were comprised almost exclusively of exempted or
single hearth households.[3] Moving east to Matlock, we find that, like
Wirksworth, this valley settlement contained a larger proportion of multiple hearth households than its immediate upland neighbours: again, 16
per cent of households were assessed on two or more hearths. Again, the
town's role as a marketing centre is revealed. The same, familiar pattern
asserts itself as we move north and west along the valleys formed by the
Derwent and its major tributary, the Wye. Bakewell, Ashford and Youlgreave all appear as more socially differentiated than the poorer, more
homogenous upland mining villages. Yet even the valley townships included
significant proportions of single hearth and exempted households; in 1641,
all had included large numbers of mining households. By the standards of
urban and downland, arable England, these villages and small towns
appear as desperately poor. Given the conditions of the industrial Peak,
however, they were comparatively rich. Once we move upland, away from
the valleys, the real extent of the relative poverty of the mining villages

---

[2] For a survey of the source, see C. Husbands, 'Hearths, wealth and occupations: an
exploration of the Hearth Tax in the later seventeenth century', in K. Schurer and T. Arkell
(eds.), *Surveying the people: the interpretation and use of document sources for the study of
population in the late seventeenth century* (Oxford, 1992), 65–77. For the correspondence
of the distribution of hearths with levels of wealth as detected from other sources, see Wood,
'Industrial development', 92–105; Wrightson and Levine, *Poverty and piety*, 34–5; Levine
and Wrightson, *Making of an industrial society*, 153–72; Spufford, *Contrasting communities*, 39–41.

[3] For a closer study of the relationship between occupational structures, landholding and the
distribution of wealth in Wirksworth and its adjacent settlements, see Wood, 'Industrial
development', 92–7. For a similar study of the parish of Youlgreave, see *ibid.*, 98–100.

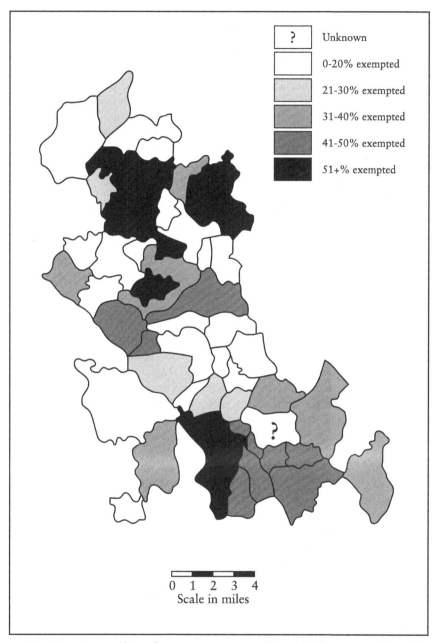

Map 13   Topographies of poverty: percentage of households exempted from the
Hearth Tax, 1664
Source: PRO, E179/94/401–3

reveals itself. Only two of Sheldon's fifty-three householders dwelt in houses with two or more hearths. In nearby Wardlow, thirty-eight of the thirty-nine householders were either exempted from the tax or paid for only one hearth.

The far north of the mining field was locked into poverty. In Stoney Middleton, 59 per cent of the households were exempted and a further 31 per cent paid only for a single hearth. In Castleton, 98 of the 106 householders lived in single hearth or exempted households. In neighbouring Bradwell, some eighty of the eighty-five households were so classified. The townships of Great and Little Hucklow were unfortunate in recording the highest exemption rates of the whole county. In Little Hucklow, 74 per cent of the households were exempted; in Great Hucklow that figure stood at 84 per cent. Within Eyam, which was to be famously afflicted by the plague within two years, the population seems almost as impoverished: 63 per cent of householders were exempted; of the charge payers, fifty-three of the fifty-nine households paid for one hearth. These statistics represent a remarkable concentration of both relative and absolute poverty into the northern part of the lead field.

The spatial distribution of wealth in 1664 follows a strikingly similar pattern to our preceding discussion of the distribution of mining activity, waged labour and landholding in the 1638–41 period, and of the uneven pace of population increase across the lead field between 1563 and 1664. A close correspondence is apparent between these key indicators of the structures of inequality, pointing towards the continuing effects of the great wave of immigration of the late sixteenth century. In those townships where the population had expanded most dramatically, such as the mining villages of Hope parish in the north of the lead field, the large majority of the population was marked by landlessness, dependence upon waged labour, and the heavy predominance of the mining as an employer. Conversely, within those areas where population increase was less impressive, such as in Wirksworth, there was less landlessness, a lower percentage of 'cavers and hirelings' in the mining workforce and a more varied distribution of hearths. As we shall see in Part III, the differing structural characteristics of these towns and villages were centrally important in understanding local patterns of social conflict.

We have seen that in the early sixteenth century much of the population of the Wirksworth area was already unusually poor and dependent upon industrial employment. The spatial patterning of social structure and economic relationships within the much smaller lead mining area of that time was not inherently dissimilar to that which can be observed in 1664. In 1541–2, poorer mining villages were seen to cluster around a valley settlement which functioned as a centre of trade and capital. As the area subject to mining activity expanded, this pattern replicated itself across the whole lead field. Unique in their functions in 1541–2, by the mid-seventeenth century the towns of Matlock and Wirksworth ranked along-side Tideswell, Youlgreave and Bakewell. Over the same period, the number of mining households in the Peak increased, and the extent of their dependence upon industry deepened. By 1664, the lead mining area of the Peak Country had become an industrial region. It qualifies as such on a series of criteria. The importance of the lead industry as an employer, the distinct character of local social structures, the nature of agricultural production, the basis of exchange with adjacent agrarian regions and the changing character of its landscape all announced the Peak as a small but discrete industrial region. During and after the population increases of the late sixteenth century, the economic and social structures of the Peak were warped and twisted into novel and distinct forms. As we have seen from the evidence of the Hearth Tax and landholding records, by 1664 much of the population of the Peak was unusually poor and prone to landlessness. By 1641, the mining industry had become either the prime or the only source of income for a majority of the Peak's households. An industrializa-tion process possessed of an unusual rapidity and intensity, and which stands at odds to conventional assumptions concerning growth in the early modern economy, was moving through the Peak.

One consequence of social and economic change between 1570 and 1660 was a radical shift in the relationship between the Peak and adjacent regions. Just as the textile areas of the West Riding became dependent upon grain produced in the East Riding, so the industrialization of north-west Derbyshire should be seen against attendant processes of economic change in south Derbyshire and the East Midlands. As the Peak industrialized, so adjacent areas developed into agrarian regions. In the same way, the fuel needs of the Peak were fed from nearby coalfields. Semi-autarchic Peak settlements of the early sixteenth century, which had produced at least a proportion of their grain from within the region, were replaced by the seventeenth century by pastoral-industrial villages dependent for supplies of food and fuel from beyond the region. Arable production within the mining villages seems to have declined over the 1570–1660 period, in favour of mining, sheep farming, dairying and in the southern part of the lead field, beef fattening. Viewed with hindsight, there was nothing excep-tional about the Peak: it was merely an early example of a general process. Within the rest of mid-seventeenth-century England, industrial regions were also being forged, attached umbilically to attendant agrarian areas. The spatial rearticulation of the English economy along relatively defined regional lines was thus one consequence of early industrialization. Such demarcations between regions were not fixed for all time; but they were real none the less. Thus, even in the richer farming land of the southern part of the Peak, in 1640 it was said that 'the greatest pte of the inhabts of the towne & towneship of Wirkesworth doe Buy a great pte of their Corne ... and ... Malt ... from Derbie, Mansfield, Nottingham & other Remote places'. By way of contrast, it was reported from the villages of Shottle and Postern in 1618, only five miles to the south of Wirksworth, that the number of households there had grown from nine households around 1580, to some sixty-six. Almost all of these households engaged in 'husbandry' with such success that they were able to sell corn on the market and maintain great families. In years of successful harvests, there were few problems in this spatial order. But in times of dearth, when agrarian regions found it difficult to produce sufficient grain to serve their own needs, industrial areas fared badly.[4]

We are able to chart the progress of agrarian change from the changing seasonal pattern of marriage over two centuries in the three parishes of Youlgreave, Wirksworth and Eyam (see Table 4.1). In their study of English demographic history, Wrigley and Schofield demonstrated that the timing of marriage depended upon the dominant farming regime of the locality.[5] In arable areas, the large majority of marriages were conducted after the harvest in October and November. In areas of pastoral farming, marriages were more likely to be conducted in the months following on the lambing season, in April, May and June, with a lesser but still significant number of marriages occurring after the harvest. Very few marriages were conducted in parishes of either farming type in other months.

The three parishes under scrutiny here do not exhibit the characteristics of either farming regime. Save for the months of March and December, which prior to the eighteenth century saw few marriages across England due to the presence of the festivals of Christmas and Lent, there is no obvious pattern that would enable us to categorize these parishes as part of an arable or a pastoral farming region. The lack of a pattern implies that within the Peak the rhythms of the farming year were of less importance than elsewhere, suggesting that its population was more dependent upon non-agricultural sources of employment than in idealized 'farming' regions. None the less, although the pattern does not match that of Wrigley and Schofield's 'ideal type', subtler long-term changes are suggestive of changes in farming within the Peak. The growing proportion of marriages which occurred in the three months following the lambing season point to the shift in farming practice towards the pastoral type. In particular, this trend

---

[4] PRO, SP14/113/17, /145/16; PRO, SP16/185/93, /193/29, /293/115; PRO, DL4/122/1683/1; PRO, DL4/94/56, /96/29; PRO, C21/D1/13.

[5] Wrigley and Schofield, *Population history*, esp. 298–305; see also A. Kussmaul, *A general view of the rural economy of England, 1538–1840* (Cambridge, 1990).

Table 4.1 *Seasonality of marriage in three parishes, 1560–1770 (%)*

	Month											
Year	Jan.	Feb.	Mar.	Apr.	May	Jun.	Jul.	Aug.	Sep.	Oct.	Nov.	Dec.
1560–79*	10	11	5	1	4	10	7	8	11	10	16	7
1580–99*	12	11	0	5	14	9	11	9	5	6	13	6
1600–19**	8	10	3	7	12	16	10	7	7	12	12	3
1620–39	7	6	1	9	15	12	7	7	9	12	13	2
1640–59	8	9	3	7	14	10	9	7	13	7	10	4
1660–79	10	5	1	10	11	15	8	8	11	7	10	3
1680–99	11	6	2	11	11	13	8	7	9	7	12	2
1700–19	11	5	3	12	11	9	6	9	9	10	10	5
1720–39	7	9	4	11	12	9	7	8	9	5	9	10
1740–59	10	9	7	9	10	7	8	8	8	9	9	8
1760–70	9	7	6	9	9	10	6	6	12	9	10	7

* Youlgreave marriages only.
** Youlgreave and Wirksworth marriages only.
Thereafter, marriages for Youlgreave, Eyam and Wirksworth.
Sources: DRO, D2602A/PI/1/1–3; DRO, D3105A/PI/1/1–6; DRO, D3644/1/1–6, /3/1.

is observable in the 1600–1739 period, when marriages occurring within the April–June period constituted between 31 and 36 per cent of the total marriages conducted. The study of seasonal marriage patterns therefore corresponds with other evidence pointing to the pastoral-industrial nature of the Peak's economy at this time. Such crops as were grown were produced to satisfy some element of subsistence need, or as feed for animals. Most references to crops mention pease, rye, barley, beans, hay and in particular oats. It was this last crop which contributed so importantly to the diet of the poor labourers and miners, in the form of 'sour oat cake', eaten with 'vegetables, milk and cheese'.[6]

A final opportunity exists to survey the outlines of the social structures of the mining villages at the end of our period. Between 1754 and 1770, the marriage registers of Wirksworth, Eyam and Hope recorded the occupations and parish of residence of grooms, and are here tabulated (see Table 4.2). Grooms from outside the parish have been omitted. The registers for Wirksworth are unusually detailed and record the townships of residence of grooms living within this large multi-chapel parish. Grooms residing

[6] PRO, E112/294/47, /382/24; LJRO, B/C/5/1602, Wirksworth, 1637, Eyam, 1590, Baslow; VCH, II, 180; C. Whetstone, *Truths No. 1, or the memoirs of Charles Whetstone, or an exposition of the oppression and cruelty exercised in the trades and manufactures of Great Britain* (London, 1807), 17.

Table 4.2 *Occupations of grooms in three parishes, 1754–70*

	Parish			
Occupation	Wirksworth	Hope	Eyam	Total
Manufacturing and mining				
miners	196	147	79	422
textiles	40	13	3	56
tailors, clothing	21	6	1	28
shoemakers	21	5	1	27
Agriculture				
farmers	20	35	2	57
yeomen	0	3	2	5
husbandmen	7	7	4	18
labourer	11	1	0	12
Professions, gentry	3	1	1	5
Commerce				
merchants	2	0	1	3
innkeepers	2	0	0	2
bakers	6	3	2	11
butchers	7	1	3	11
other	4	0	0	4
Tradesmen				
mason	6	2	1	9
blacksmith	7	5	2	14
cordwainer	10	4	1	15
other	23	14	4	41
Others	2	3	1	6
Unknown	0	80	33	113
Total	388	330	141	859

within chapelries lying outside the lead field have therefore also been excluded. Eyam parish lay wholly within the lead field; but the least populated parts of Hope parish did not. The definition of the social structures of the mining townships of the parish have been blurred by the inclusion of the non-mining townships in the total, therefore understating the extent of industrial employment within the mining area of the parish. The parish clerks of Eyam and Hope failed to give occupational ascriptions for some months, but those for Wirksworth are complete. The results are further skewed by age and gender factors. Since brides were defined in the register by their marital status, as spinsters or as widows, their occupations were not recorded. Furthermore, grooms were likely to have been disproportionately concentrated amongst younger men. None the less, the results are revealing.

Taking the results as a whole, the most immediate conclusion is that mining remained the dominant form of employment of the younger men of all three parishes in the 1754–70 period, making up some 61 per cent of known occupations. The young men of Eyam appear as especially dependent upon mining. The familiar absence of wealthier men in the mining area reasserts itself: yet again, gentlemen and the professions made up less than 1 per cent of total known occupations. Within Wirksworth, a higher proportion of grooms were engaged in commerce, highlighting its relative wealth and importance as a marketing centre. Agricultural employment in the three parishes made up only 13 per cent of total known occupations. Of course, many miners held some form of land, as did some of the artisans, textile workers and craftsmen who made up a combined total of 27 per cent of known occupations. Such occupational ascriptions can also be slightly misleading: as in the late seventeenth century, a man may have been recorded in one source as a miner, yet appear a few years later in another as a tailor or shoemaker. But since such occasions were relatively rare in the late seventeenth century, we can reasonably assume a similar pattern for 1754–70. It is important that so many grooms chose to define themselves as miners rather than according to any less significant by-employment.

Structural and cultural factors combined to delineate the post-Restoration Peak as a discrete industrial region. After crossing the moors to the north, east and west, or on entering the valleys to the south, visitors to the Peak Country knew that they had entered a special land. This region was marked out in their recollections by the curious customs, appearance and dialect of the inhabitants, and by the strange geological 'wonders' they encountered. But most witnesses also recognized the importance of mining as an employer, just as they noted the deep poverty of the region's inhabitants. The constitution of the Peak Country as an industrial region has here been rendered visible through the manipulation of abstract statistics. But its industrial identity meant more than this: it was inscribed upon the physical form of the land and upon the cultural identity of its people. By 1650, most of the Peak's woods had been 'putt downe and destroyed', torn up for fuel in the ore hearth mills, or timbering for the miners' pits. Much of the land along streams and rivers was 'bellanded' by lead pollution, as were the tops of the hills on which boles had been located. Rubbish tips lay scattered about the surface of mineworkings; medieval lead rakes lay exposed to the daylight, continuously turned over by cavers still scratching for a little ore.[7] In terms of its economy, social structure, material culture and physical appearance, the Peak had become

---

[7] PRO, E134/2JasII/Mich21; PRO, C21/P42/9; SA, BFM2/75; PRO, DL4/54/36.

an industrial region some century or more before the beginning of the classic period of the Industrial Revolution.

We are able to chart the changing fortunes of that industrial region in the period between the Restoration and the establishment of Arkwright's mill at Cromford in 1771 with reference to the interplay of lead prices and population indicators (see Figs. 3.1, 3.2 and 3.3). If nothing else, their relationship demonstrates how directly intertwined the fortunes of thousands of the Peak's people had become with international fluctuations in the price of lead. By 1661, the price of lead had reached an all-century high. Over the subsequent four decades a general decline in prices occurred, with devastating consequences for the free miners. By the mid-1660s, the price of a load of lead ore had fallen slightly to around twenty-eight shillings per load. Fluctuations in lead prices followed in the late 1660s and early 1670s, but with a general downward trend maintained throughout. It was in the late 1670s and the 1680s that the greatest fall occurred, as prices plunged from twenty-seven shillings per load to sixteen shillings by 1692. Prices within the economy as a whole declined slightly over the same period, but at nothing like the dramatic fall in lead. Slight increases in lead prices during the 1690s brought little comfort to the miners, as inflation once again climbed, this time to an all-century high.

After the Restoration, population indicators moved in close correspondence with the price of lead. Baptisms in all four parishes under observation peaked in the 1660s, only to fall back continuously down to the 1690s. The parishes of Hope and Eyam experienced their first deficits in the number of baptisms recorded over burials in these years. That recorded for Eyam in the 1660s was the consequence of its devastating plague in 1666, but the same cannot be said of the 1690s. Wirksworth's parish register also showed a similar deficit in the 1680s and 1690s, with Youlgreave registering only a very slight surplus. The early eighteenth century saw a stabilization in population indicators in all four parishes, as lead prices troughed until 1720. Thereafter, prices began a gradual upward rise. Population indicators increased in tune with lead prices once more down to 1770, save for during the 1740s, in which decade both population indicators and lead prices fell.

These patterns represent significant discontinuities in the history of the industry. For the first time since the introduction of Humphrey's innovations in the late sixteenth century, population in the four parishes under observation fell in the 1670–1700 period. For the first time since the depression of the 1540s, long-term lead prices simultaneously declined. There was a further important change in the relationship between different indicators. Total lead production, as inferred from shipments of smelted lead from Hull, continued to rise over the two decades following the Restoration, peaking in the late 1670s. Only thereafter did production decline, reaching a nadir in the mid-1690s. Recovery set in during the early eighteenth century, and despite short-term fluctuations, established itself over the period down to 1770 at a level similar to that of the 1660s.[8] Lead production after the 1680s followed roughly the same pattern as the price of lead ore and smelted lead. There should be no surprise here. It is the relationship between prices and production in the decades of the 1660s and 1670s which should concern us. Here, we see the inversion of the usual relationship: spectacular increases in output are registered at a time of falling prices.

This changed equation in the relationship between prices and production was the consequence of the increased productive capacity of the large mines which after the 1650s blossomed across the lead field. Drained by expensive soughs, worked by shifts of wage labourers, their production easily outstripped both that of the free miners and of the smaller gentry-owned works which had hitherto constituted the outriders of industrial capitalism. Given the costs of deep mining, the depth of capital investment in such works could be considerable: between 1663 and 1669 the excavation of a sough at Odin mine cost investors some £1,259. While production of lead ore from the mine increased considerably, with 4,137 loads extracted in the same period, the initial rate of return on the investment was slight. Investment in the lead industry therefore involved patience, and a degree of risk.[9]

Investors in the mining industry of the post-Restoration period were demarcated both spatially and socially. Following the final ejection of free miners from his manor of Netherhaddon in 1658, the Earl of Rutland invested large sums of money in drainage equipment for his new mines at Haddonfields. Worked by wage labourers, these mines continued to produce large amounts of ore into the early eighteenth century.[10] But like his neighbour the Earl of Devonshire, he and his successors rarely invested

[8] L. Willies, 'Technical and organisational development of the Derbyshire lead mining industries in the eighteenth and nineteenth centuries', PhD thesis, University of Leicester, 1980, 34–9; R. Burt, 'Lead production in England and Wales, 1700–1770', *EcHR*, 2nd ser., 22, 2 (1969), 267; Kiernan, 'Lawrence Oxley's accounts', 123.

[9] PRO, DL4/112/10. For deep mining and soughing operations in the 1660–1700 period, see also PRO, DL4/112/12, /112/13, /121/1680/9, /125/1689/2, /126/1692/2, /127/1694/6; J.H. Rieuwerts, 'A technological history of the drainage of the Derbyshire lead mines', PhD thesis, University of Leicester, 1981.

[10] O.R.F. Davies, 'The Dukes of Devonshire, Newcastle and Rutland, 1688–1714. A study in wealth and political influence', DPhil thesis, University of Oxford, 1971, 139–40, 142, 189–91.

in mining operations outside their own estates. By the Restoration, the most powerful noble and gentry families had withdrawn from direct contact with the lead industry, remaining content in their parasitic exaction of manorial tolls as lords or lessees of Duchy rights in the King's Field, or as the owners of parochial tithes. The elite social group which contributed most capital to the post-Restoration industry, and which took the closest interest in it, was the mercantile lesser gentry. It has been estimated that by the Restoration some 70 per cent of the gentry families of north and west Derbyshire possessed some interest in mining. At that time, a surprisingly large number of wealthier artisans, farmers and even a scattering of free miners also held shares in large mines, or became partners in drainage operations. The significance of this last group of investors declined over the course of the eighteenth century, as the industry as a whole became increasingly concentrated into the hands of the mercantile gentry. Integrated control of mining, smelting, transport and marketing, always implicit from the late fifteenth century, by the middle of the eighteenth century was a reality.[11] Few investors came from beyond the Peak, and intense local connections between capital and industry can be observed.[12] Unlike other British lead mining areas of the eighteenth century, nationally organized mining companies made little progress within the Peak. Finance continued to be provided through semi-formalized contracts between groups of investors, who contracted with miners to work the deposits upon agreed piece rates, and employed surface workers on day wages. Investors spread their risks by buying small shares in a variety of mines within their immediate local area, together with scattered interests elsewhere within the lead field.[13] Individual control thus remained diffuse, and regulated by contract and custom.

If individual mercantile gentlemen and women did not dominate the post-Restoration industry, they did so as a class. The capital they made available to the extractive side of the industry, derived from successes as mine investors, smelters, landholders and merchants, enabled spectacular increases in production from individual operations. Changes in the design of 'wind shafts' allowed easier ventilation of deep works. Deposits could be drained by 'second generation' soughs which connected to older drainage

---

[11] S.C. Newton, 'The gentry of Derbyshire in the seventeenth century', *DAJ*, 2nd ser., 86 (1966), 3; Wood, 'Industrial development', 13–15; K. Honeyman, *Origins of enterprise: business leadership in the Industrial Revolution* (Manchester, 1982), 20–56; L. Willies, 'The Barker family and the eighteenth century lead business', *DAJ*, 2nd ser., 93 (1973), 55–74; A. Raistrick and B. Jennings, *A history of lead mining in the Pennines* (London, 1969), 255.

[12] Willies, 'Technical and organisational development', 299. See for instance DRO, 504B/ L221.

[13] For examples, see DRO, D258M/54/19p, 28/20g.

channels, or which struck out on ever longer and deeper journeys of their own. Improvements in construction methods and geological knowledge resulted in greater efficiency savings. The first sough in Derbyshire, that designed by Sir Cornelius Vermuyden in the 1630s, was 1,000 feet long. By the late eighteenth century, some of its descendants reached for over a mile. Drainage could also be effected using waterwheels. The ninth Earl of Rutland was the first to make use of this method, employing five wheels to lift water from deep deposits at Haddonfields in 1680. While steam power was rarely deployed in drainage operations, the results could be impressive. Between 1717 and the early 1740s, the employment of Newcomen engines in Yatestoop mine near Winster led to dramatic increases in production. This was an example of technological innovation extending the life of an already heavily capitalized and complex work. Yatestoop mine had produced some 25,000 loads of ore in 1702 after the construction of a sough; continuing use of the Newcomen engines in the 1730s resulted in yearly production totals of around 10,000 loads of ore. A similar story is apparent from the surviving mine accounts, lot and cope receipts and tithe books from across the ore field.[14]

Some historical perspective is required to make sense of such statistics. In one uniquely 'glorious' week during the local boom of the 1740s, a single mine in Eyam produced one third of the yearly output of the entire Derbyshire lead field of the mid-sixteenth century. The average yearly output of the Yatestoop mine near Winster during the 1730s represented something like the total output of the whole lead field in 1580.[15] Technological innovation also arrived in the smelting side of the industry in 1735, with the introduction of the coal-fired reverbatory furnace or cupola smelter. Since the cupola relied for its energy source upon fossil fuel rather than the motive force of rivers, it could be sited anywhere. Its energy efficiencies allowed lower grades of ore to be smelted than the ore hearth mill. In a less dramatic rerun of the 1570s, the introduction of this new technology again revitalized the mining industry as ore deposits hitherto rejected as useless became suddenly profitable. By the 1780s, the cupola had largely replaced the ore hearth smelting mill.[16]

These large increases in the production of individual mines have to be read alongside our earlier discussion of industry-wide output which,

---

[14] Rieuwerts, 'Technological history', 41, 202–4, 207, 285–6; Willies, 'Technical and organisational development', 74, 94–7, 285–6; DRO, 504B/L12.

[15] For the Eyam area, see G.G. Hopkinson, 'Lead mining in the Eyam district in the 18th century', *DAJ*, 2nd ser., 80 (1960), 92–3; DRO, D2270/1; SA, OD 1501; SA, BD 189. On production from Odin mine in Castleton, see CHT, Odin mine, unlisted accounts; SA, OD 1149; DRO, 504B/L71. On the 1580 production, see Kiernan, *Lead industry*, 208.

[16] For an account of the operation of the cupola, see Willies, 'Technical and organisational development', 186–203.

despite periodic fluctuations, remained relatively stable between the 1690s and the 1770s. Sources of demand did not alter significantly from those identified earlier: Derbyshire lead continued to feed national and international demand for building, consumer durables and ammunition. Similarly, although river communications with Derby were finally improved after 1719, the most important transport route remained that to Bawtry and Hull. The roads down which this traffic passed were not turnpiked until after 1756. Moreover, although Derbyshire remained the most productive British lead field up to 1770, its domination was being eroded by the North Wales and north Pennine fields.[17] Stable demand, declining real prices and increased internal competition engendered structural and organizational change within the industry. From the Restoration onwards, and in particular after 1700, technological innovation and capital became concentrated in a small number of highly productive deep mines. While free mining continued over the whole period, its contribution to total output was declining in 1660, and negligible by 1770. This remained the case in spite of free mining works remaining, in numerical terms, by far the most typical of eighteenth-century mining operations.

POVERTY AND LABOUR

The fall in lead prices from the mid-1660s was partly the consequence of the expanding output of large mining operations, both in Derbyshire and elsewhere. The inflated lead prices of the 1650s soon fell off, hitting free miners much harder than the new large gentry-owned operations. Continuing increases in production from the large mines, combined with diminishing returns on their own works, pushed free miners into crisis. Moreover, the fall in prices occurred at the same time as rising land rents, and the large-scale enclosure of wastes and commons on the Duchy's High Peak estates. Trapped in this vice, it was no wonder that miners of the 1690s should look back upon the 1650s as the Indian summer of free mining. Every qualitative source concerning the miners' post-Restoration living standards conveys a real sense of hardship. In 1687, the Exchequer Court heard that if the miners of Darley parish were forced to pay a tithe on their lead production 'very many of the Myners would hardly bee able to gett bread for the generality of them are growne very poore already'. The miners of Hartingdon made a similar point in the 1690s.[18] When the ratepayers of Wirksworth petitioned the Quarter Sessions for the continuation of the House of Correction there, they described their town as 'a very

---

[17] Burt, 'Lead production', 251, 254, 258–63.
[18] PRO, E134/3JasII/East15, /4&5Wm&Mar/Hil15.

populous place & greatly oppressed with poore by reason of the Mines now in decay'. In his report to the Duchy of Lancaster in 1673, Richard Shalcrosse remarked upon the 'thousands of poore mynors' in the High Peak 'wch by reason of the decay of the mynes there doe surcharge the said Hundred wth poore'. He proposed that they be employed in the enclosure of the wastes and commons on which many of them depended. In 1699 it was even proposed that in order to provide 'relief' to the free miners, the Crown should take their workings, and employ them as labourers.[19]

Yet in spite of their growing immiseration, as a social group the free miners survived this crisis. After the 1650s, the establishment of a large mining operation invariably resulted in an immediate fall in the number of local free mining operations. Such works typically remained few, only to increase upon the exhaustion of the large mine. The history of the industry after the Restoration was not, therefore, one of the simple replacement of independent, small-scale producers by large-scale capitalism. No such single, unitary transition occurred. Instead, while free mining was marginalized in terms of its contribution to total ore production, it remained an essential part of the domestic economy of thousands of plebeian households.[20] Of equal or greater importance were the work opportunities afforded by the new, deep mines. The introduction in 1655 by the Wirksworth Great Barmote of regulations governing waged labour points towards two related facets of the organization of the labour force within the new deep mines.[21] Most obviously, they point to the growing importance of wage labour within the workforce as a whole; but they also point towards the regulation of the circumstances of that labour by custom and contract. As we shall see in Chapter 6, eighteenth-century barmote court juries remained dominated by free miners, many of whom also worked for wages within larger mining enterprises. Thus, even though increasing numbers of free miners were relying on wage labour, they maintained a large amount of control over the circumstances and contractual basis of their labour.

The miners' petition of 1641 had discriminated between miners, who were listed by name, and 'hirelings' who were lumped together in a composite category with the cavers. In working for wages, the miners were in danger of falling into the very pejorative category they had invented. Yet they managed to maintain the difference between themselves and

---

[19] PRO, DL41/19/4; DRO, QAB/1/6/3; M. Stringer, *English and Welsh mines and minerals discovered* (London, 1699), 21.

[20] Willies, 'Technical and organisational development', 281. For examples, see DRO, 504B/L12; DRO, D258M/42/21.

[21] G. Steer, *Compleat mineral laws of Derbyshire* (London, 1734), 117–18; DRO, D258M/28/20w; SA, TC 366 (6).

'hirelings'. As we saw in Kenyon's account of 1630, a distinction was already drawn between the 'myner' of ore, who either worked for piece rates or who held a stake in the mine, and the carriers and surface workers, who were paid upon flat rates. This distinction, based upon age, skill and gender, maintained itself into the eighteenth century in the form of the 'coping' system.[22] Under this system, a group of skilled miners would be invited to contract with the owners of a large mine to work at the lead vein. After examining the vein concerned, the miners then negotiated their piece rate 'upon a cope' with the owners. The meaning and derivation of the term is important. By the eighteenth century, the 'cope' specified the relationship between employers and skilled workers. It derived from a contraction of the term 'co-partner'. The first reference to the term comes from the 1630s, when Thomas Allen and his partners were said to have worked Tearsall rake near Wensley 'uppon a Coape'. In the 1650s, Winster miners can be found selling their ore to merchants at preferential rates 'upon a cope'. A distinction was made between them and other workers, who were paid 'wages'.[23] At this point, the 'cope' represented a further development in the long-existent credit relationship between miners and merchants. Informal credit agreements whereby the miner agreed to sell ore at preferential rates to a merchant in return for guaranteed advances of capital gradually mutated into a semi-formal arrangement in which the merchant became a 'co-partner' with the skilled miners.[24] Alternatively, 'coping' grew out of earlier agreements made between free miners and combinations of gentlemen to drain inundated deposits. In the earliest agreements, the ownership of the mines remained with the miners, and the drainers took a composition of a quarter or a third of ore production. By the later seventeenth century, such agreements were becoming increasingly exploitative, as drainage technology became more expensive and the miners' bargaining power diminished. Here, too, the miners and drainers therefore exchanged formal positions: the drainers took possession of a mine, with the miners working it as 'copers' upon a piece rate.[25]

Thus, strict lines of division between labour and capital were blurred.

---

[22] The implications of the 'coping' system for labour processes and work and gender identities are discussed in Chapter 8. For a full discussion of the eighteenth-century coping system, see L. Willies, 'Management and workers at miners engine mine, Eyam, in the mid-eighteenth century', *BPDMHS*, 11, 5 (1992), 146–60.

[23] PRO, DL4/91/16; PRO, E134/1658/Mich15. John Downes remembered working 'upon a cope' in the 1650s: see PRO, E134/2JasII/Mich21. See also PRO, DL4/117/8.

[24] For a description of one such arrangement in 1653, see Wood, 'Industrial development', 11–12.

[25] See for instance SA, TC 366(4); DRO, D258M/28/20h; PRO, DL4/112/12; CHT unlisted articles between Godfrey Haslehurst and the miners and owners of Ashton rake, 7 June 1683; SA, SpSt 60450.

Losing part of his economic independence, the free miner retained control over the circumstances of his work and in the negotiation of wages enjoyed recourse to contract and custom. In return, labour discipline was ensured. 'Coping' miners did not require any 'diligent and watchful overlooking of them'. Moreover, they could be expected to act as the 'overseers' of other underground workers.[26] The gradual evolution of the coping system blunted the sharp edge of capitalist relations of production and exploitation. The establishment of piece rates as the measure of labour allowed miners a degree of flexibility in their waged work. Miners were able to alternate daily or weekly waged labour with the maintenance of smallholdings and with work in their own free mining operations. The free miner of the seventeenth century thus retained his artisanal mentality, and seemed to show every sign of developing into an early aristocrat of labour.

Mining methods underwent important changes in tune with alterations in the organization of labour and its relationship to capital. Yet the sexual division of labour was preserved intact. On the surface of the mine, women, children and old men operated jigging machines which cleansed the ore of earth and stone, and then dressed it into smaller lumps with caving hammers. In some cases, horses operated crushing wheels, or provided power for engines which lifted ore and water to the surface. In rare instances, as at Yatestoop, a steam engine was to be seen in operation. Passing down a mine-shaft, the miner at first entered galleries cut by his predecessors in the sixteenth and seventeenth centuries. In the eighteenth century, new lead veins were rare discoveries: instead, the miners worked the known deposits with improved technology and greater intensity by 'night & day'. On the older shallow workings, ventilation pumps and engines were in operation, lifting water from the deep works to deposit it into 'sink holes', some of which were so deep as to have no known bottom, or into older, redundant soughs. Alternatively, a new sough may have reached its source, to carry away an underground stream. Shafts had widened and deepened. Much haulage of ore was still conducted by hand, but by the later eighteenth century, wooden rails were lain, along which wheeled carts were pushed by carriers operating in stages. As mines expanded, and tunnels connected, broader meeting places were cut at the junction, allowing the carts to pass.

Wearing the leather 'grove clothes' described by Defoe, the miner carried a burning turf for warmth. Celia Fiennes wrote that the turves 'gave off an unpleasant smell, it makes one smell as if smoaked like Bacon'. Other smells greeted the miner's descent: burning gunpowder, melting tallow, smoke, dust, or the sudden absence of air which presaged the dreaded

[26] Sharpe France, *Thieveley*, 75; PRO, E134/3JasII/East15.

'damps'. William Hooson, a free miner writing in 1747, likened the scent of the damps to 'resembling something of an Onion . . . all the signs we know of it being there', he explained, was 'a blue Circle invironing . . . the faint Light of the Candle'. Leigh reported a discussion with a miner who had avoided 'suffocation' from the damps in 1700:

he told me he perceiv'd a sudden Coldness to strike to his heart, as he term'd it, and an extraordinary sweetness in his mouth, that he lay like a person in a swooning Fit, and not sensible of any pain or sickness, nor could he remember any thing farther, save that he drew his breath short as he recovr'd and was drowsy for some time afterwards.

Miners tried to escape the damps by 'digging an hole in the earth, and lieing in it upon their faces'; or, in the case of methane, by igniting it with a long, burning brand. On descending levels of the deep deposits, illuminated by tallow candles, in each gallery miners worked in groups of up to four, while carriers conveyed away the ore and rubble. In some cases, the workings reverberated to the sound of explosions, as gunpowder blasted through rock. Its use was 'sometymes hazardous to the people and destroys them at work', as Fiennes noted. Hooson agreed:

Men very often [are] killed, or at least bruised or maimed, all their Days after, or if they escaped with their limbs whole, they are often times burnt Blind by the Force of Gunpowder . . . there are men now living, that have been thus hurt Twenty years ago, whose Faces have been discolor'd by the Powder by such mischances, that it is not yet worn out, nor perhaps never will while they live.

Yet the use of gunpowder increased the productivity of a miner by threefold. Introduced to Derbyshire in the 1670s, its use had become common by the eighteenth century. In wet or dangerous conditions, a 'superior class of miner' was required to carry out such work. One 'very good and Experienced miner' of Hooson's acquaintance was able to blast gunpowder while under water. Growing complexity engendered specialization and the separation of labour processes in other respects; most mines employed a carpenter to timber workings and repair pit props in existent galleries. References to 'skilful Engeneers' who maintained the engines and to 'Plummer dyallers' who were skilled in underground surveying can first be found in the 1620s. At the lead vein, there were more dangers. Hooson describes the effects of 'bellanding', or lead poisoning: 'in Working upon hard Ore, the Dust whereof arises from [the miner's] pick-point, being a very Sulpherous Smell, gets into his Bowells, and causes strange Costiveness, with Intolerable Pain for many Days together'. After a time, miners could be identified by the grey pallor of their skin, 'pale as a dead corps' as Defoe put it, acquired from prolonged exposure to toxic lead in a confined environment. The mercury content of the lead could, in the final stages of lead poisoning, induce psychotic disturbances in the sufferer. Cotton described the effects of a 'distemp'red brain' as 'A fault'ring tongue, and a wild staring look' followed by death. In heavy rains, even deep soughs could fail to draw away the water. In 1791, one mine agent wrote that 'At present the workmen are afraid to go into the level as two of them were catched & forced to lye on the Pipes for many hours in perpetual danger of being drowned which must have been the case if the water had risen 8 inches more.' Parish registers bear laconic testimony to the hazards of deep mining. May 1690 saw the burial in Eyam of John Daniel and Robert Berry, 'damp'd in a groove in Middleton Dale'. In January 1698 Francis Gregory of Eyam was buried; 'he was killed in a grove' noted the parish clerk. In June of the following year Edward Torre met the same fate: 'killed in a plugg in a groove over against the Parsonage Fold'.[27] These were the 'bitter fruits' of early industrial capitalism. How the miners understood, explained and coped with the dangers of their work is addressed in Chapter 8.

In 1698, Celia Fiennes marvelled at her lump of lead ore, a souvenir from the Peak: 'I have some which looks full of silver its so bright just brought up out of one of the mines.' As she recognized, the ore had been won at great danger. Once cut from the vein, such ore went on to be smelted, transported and sold on the markets of what has been identified as the 'first consumer society'. Turned into tableware, roofing for fine mansions and churches, or guttering for the houses of the nation's middling and better sort of people, its presence as a consumer durable contributed to a contemporary and historiographical perception of the post-Restoration period as prosperous and benign. If England did indeed experience rising living standards and a 'consumer revolution' in the late seventeenth and eighteenth centuries, as we shall see in the rest of this chapter, many of the plebeian inhabitants of the Peak saw little of it. For the miners and workers of the lead industry were, in Edward Thompson's memorable phrase, being consumed by the first consumer society.

We saw in Chapter 3 that by 1660 many of the wealthier inhabitants of the mining towns and villages of the Peak were enclosing parts of the commons, moors and wastes. We also saw that in some manors, access to the commons had been restricted in favour of the landed. This went

---

[27] This discussion has been based on Ford and Rieuwerts, *Lead mining*; SA, Bag C 206 (3); PRO, DL4/129/1699/5, /127/1694/6, /90/24, /66/6; C. Morris (ed.), *The journeys of Celia Fiennes* (London, 1947), 258, 102–3; Willies, 'Technical and organisational development', 75, 84–6; Leigh, *Natural history*, 79; Hooson, *Miner's dictionary*, 20, 23, 11, 49–55; Cotton, *Wonders of the Peak*, 34; Waller, *An essay*, 6; J.H. Rieuwerts, 'The earliest lead mine soughs in Derbyshire', *BPDMHS*, 7, 5 (1980), 277; *idem*, 'Technological history', 47; MCL, Carill Worsley MS M35/2/44/4, 32; J.G. Clifford and F. Clifford (eds.), *Eyam parish register, 1630–1700*, DRS, 21 (Chesterfield, 1993), 64, 159, 178, 181, 182.

together with the redefinition of community and neighbourliness, as wealthier inhabitants drew finer linguistic distinctions between themselves and the 'poorer sort'. Yet in spite of such developments, and for all that most of the common fields had gone, at the time of the Restoration large tracts of common land remained. In particular this was the case within the Duchy of Lancaster's large manors of High Peak and Castleton, often referred to collectively as the 'Lordship' of High Peak. Much of the territory of these manors lay within the lead field, and encompassed very poor villages such as Castleton, Overhaddon, Bradwell, Taddington, Chelmorton and Monyash. In 1641, all of these towns were heavily dependent on the mining industry; many contained a large number of 'cavers and hirelings'; and the majority of the population was either landless or possessed only minor smallholdings. Between 1639 and 1642, the Duchy made abortive attempts to enclose the large commons on which these townships enjoyed open and mostly unstinted common rights. These attempts were greeted by the combined opposition of landed and landless alike. The changing social alignments and legal manoeuvres are more fully discussed in Part III, but between the outbreak of the civil war and the death of Charles II, this local alliance of landed, near-landless and landless faded away.[28] The social and economic profiles of these villages became drawn around the twin structures of poverty and capitalism. In the village of Castleton, large sheep flocks owned by the wealthiest yeomanry grazed the moors in the summer, reducing the sustainability of this common resource. In 1681 the village was said to be 'scant of comon', the land being 'badd and barren'. None the less, the 'poorer sort of people' depended upon the commons. Rights of turbary were important: 'beareing burthens of Turfes on their backes [they] get some livelyhood', together with 'keeping of a horse or cow or other small goods upon the sd comons'. Yet the poor themselves contributed to the destruction of the resources on which they depended: in that year, there were forty-one cottages on the common. Deep works, in which the wealthiest yeomanry, together with the local mercantile lesser gentry, were important investors, were established at Odin mine.[29]

From 1673 onwards, the Duchy of Lancaster set in motion the legal and administrative machinery leading to the enclosure of much of the commons of the manors of High Peak and Castleton. The process was contested by

---

[28] On legal and administrative aspects of the enclosure of the manor and lordship of High Peak, see R. Somerville, 'Commons and wastes in north-west Derbyshire: the High Peak "new lands"', *DAJ*, 2nd ser., 97 (1977), 16–22.

[29] D.W. Shimwell, 'Sheep grazing in Edale, Derbyshire, 1692–1747, and its effect on blanket peat erosion', *DAJ*, 2nd ser., 94 (1974), 35–40; PRO, DL4/121/1681/6, /123/1684/12, /122/1683/1, /128/1695/3.

the poorer inhabitants, with the backing of some of the yeomanry and lesser gentry. But the Duchy's decision to grant a proportion of the commons to the freeholders in compensation for their loss of common rights persuaded many others of that social group that their interests were better served by enclosure. The commons were divided into two sections: the 'Tenants' Part', granted in severalty to the freeholders; and the 'King's Part', which passed to the Duchy, and was leased to the farmers of large sheep flocks. Most communal rights over the old commons were suppressed upon enclosure.[30] At the same time as the Duchy was pursuing the enclosure of commons and wastes on its High Peak manors, it was also closely scrutinizing and leasing out its possessions and rights. Post-Restoration leases were less restrictive of the lessee. Rents on cottages, smallholdings and 'incroachments latelie discovered' were increased; popular rights to important resources such as lime, turves, coal and fishing removed and granted as parts of feefarms.[31] Similar policies were followed on other large estates, in particular those of the Earls of Devonshire and Rutland.[32]

By the mid-seventeenth century, many plebeian households depended upon a combination of free mining, occasional wage labour, the resources of the commons and the possession of a smallholding. Combined with the catastrophic fall in lead prices after 1670, post-Restoration changes in estate policies cast many such households into deeper poverty. Declining returns on free mining, falling wages in deep mines, increased rents, the enclosure of commons and the removal of common rights hit poorer households very hard. These factors are more than sufficient to explain the falling population of the 1670–1700 period. They also provide the context within which signs of increasing concern about the poor of the post-Restoration Peak must be judged.

As elsewhere in Restoration England, parish officers and the magistracy responded to the immiseration of the poor and the landless with blunt severity. The poor came to be viewed not as a threatening mass, but as a fixed, certain social fact. That social fact required discipline, but could be made useful. In line with the contemporary mercantilist theory, 'manufac-

[30] PRO, DL4/121/1681/6, /122/1683/1, /123/1684/12, /124/1686/9, /124/1686/14, /124/1687/7, /126/1691/3, /127/1693/8, /128/1695/3, /128/1696/7, /129/1698/3, /129/1698/5, /129/1698/6.

[31] PRO, DL42/57, fol. 189, /58, fols. 248–9, /59, fols. 36–40, 79–83, /60, fols. 2–3, 6, 10, 23–4, 35–6, 62–3, 77–8, /61, fols. 6–11, 38, 81–83, 115–121, 157–8, 159–162, /62, fols. 312–5, /64, pp. 57–9, fols. 284–6, 277–9, /65, fols. 34–48, /66, fols. 3–6, /67, fols. 166–89, 313–17, /68, fols. 1–67; PRO, DL41/30/9; PRO, DL43/20/9B; PRO, E317/9/12, 20.

[32] Davies, 'The Earls of Devonshire, Newcastle and Rutland', 144–6; C.E.B. Bowles, 'Agreement of the freeholders of Eyam to the award for dividing Eyam pasture, 12th November 1702', *DAJ*, 1st ser., 20 (1898), 1–11.

tures' were introduced for the parish poor. The object was to set the
paupers to useful work, while providing a disincentive to obtaining parish
relief. Attempts at industrial diversification within the Peak were specifically directed towards the poor. In Wirksworth, the poor were set to
'manufactures'; in the High Peak to building walls which enclosed the
commons on which they had so recently depended. With the decrease in
lead prices in the 1740s, the habit was renewed. In Winster, suffering from
the results of the temporary closure of the Yatestoop works, the poor were
employed in weaving. Neighbouring Youlgreave had already brought in a
similar form of out-door relief. A tradition of incarcerating the dependent
poor had already been established with the creation of a house of correction
for the poor of the Wapentake of Wirksworth in Ashbourne by 1631.
Another had been set up at Wirksworth town by the time of the civil wars,
but was suppressed after the Restoration, only to be re-established in 1727.
A similar institution was established for the Hundred of High Peak at
Bakewell by 1683, and others at Tideswell in 1711, and at Tissington in
1753. All were constructed with the primary purpose of housing the poor,
along the lines of the workhouse at Winster, set up in 1744. This was
intended to hold the poor in one place: a rule provided that 'no persons
shall be allowed any relief out of the house, unless in sickness, or on some
very extraordinary occasion'.[33]

The desire to control the movement of the poor grew out of disputes over
parochial responsibility for the growing class of landless paupers. The
parish of Crich announced itself to be 'overcharged wth poore' in 1683. In
the same year, the townships of Hope and Bradwell were in dispute over
their relative contributions to the parish's poor relief. In 1711 the freeholders of Bradwell declared that 'The hamlett of Bradwell . . . is so
overcharged with the multitude of the poore tht are therin tht the
inhabitants . . . thereof are not able to relieve them , but they are forced in
great numbers to wander about from towne to towne to ask for relief
contrary to the lawes of this Nation' and promised to provide meals for the
township's poor. Yet it is possible to detect a sharper parochial hostility to
the poor than before the Restoration.[34] Mary Machant of Youlgreave told
the bench in 1684 that since her husband 'beinge foran' was 'driven away',
she had to care for their 'little girle', and had become destitute. By the
consent of the town she was put into a tenement, but her landlord had

[33] J.O. Appleby, *Economic thought and ideology in seventeenth century England* (Princeton,
1978), 138, 142, 152; PRO, DL41/19/4; DRO, QAB/1/6/3; DRO, Q/SO/1/1, fols. 11, 90;
DRO, D776A/PO 804, 805; DRO, D3644/43/1; *VCH*, II, 189.
[34] Study of the manorial rolls of Wirksworth for the Jacobean and Caroline periods, for
instance, turns up few instances of prosecutions of inhabitants to housing 'strangers'. See
PRO, DL30/54/666–76. For an exception, see PRO, DL30/54/666.

expelled her. By the late seventeenth century, such hostility could extend surprisingly far down the social scale of the settled inhabitants of a place. In 1689, Robert Holmes, a miner of Wensley, gave evidence to the Court of the Duchy of Lancaster. In that year, he and his fellows were experiencing great difficulties in maintaining free mining, and many were leaving off their works. He explained that thirty years before the poor assessments were 'much lesse than now'. During the free miners' Indian summer of the 1650s, the yearly poor rate stood at about £5 or £6; in 1689, it was £50. Holmes was himself such a ratepayer, '& Conceives the reason of the Increase of such charge is occasioned by the mines there, people comeing thither to worke and gaineing settlement and becomeing poore'.[35]

Settled inhabitants, whether elite or plebeian, therefore sought to prevent the easy movement of the poor. Peter Clark has detected a general decrease in the geographical range of plebeian migrants after the Restoration, and has related this to the Settlement Act, and to the increased provision of parochial provision for the poor. He has cited the Derbyshire bench as a notable example of how Justices attempted to ensure that proper relief was provided for the poor by parish authorities.[36] That concern showed itself in the provision of useful employment for the poor within a limiting, disciplinary regime. It was also apparent in the willingness of mining parishes to find indentured employment for the youthful poor within the parish, and in their keenness to prevent settlement by paupers from other parishes.[37] The poor of the Peak, just as those lucky enough to find waged labour in industry or on the enclosed fields, had become a permanent part of the social topography of the region.

The economic and social structures of the Peak were, if not unique, certainly unusual for mid-seventeenth-century England. Large sections of its population were landless or near-landless industrial labourers, working in an industry which was already heavily capitalized, and was becoming more so. By 1770, these basic statements still remained accurate; but the structures of exploitation and production in the Peak's economy had undergone significant change. Lead production was concentrated into a small number of large, labour- and capital-intensive workings. While overall output did not stand significantly higher than in the 1670s, the individual production of large mines would have seemed incredible to a

---

[35] DRO, 1038A/PO261; DRO, Q/SO/1/1, fols. 23, 10; DRO, Q/SB/2/386; PRO, DL4/125/ 1689/2; on the difficulties of the free miners of Wensley in the 1680s, see PRO, E134/3JasII/ East15.

[36] Clark, 'Migration', 240–1.

[37] DRO, D253A/PO5/1–97, /PO6/1–133, /PO11/1; DRO, D776A/PO343–424, 380, 446–77, 513–75, 656–744; DRO, D2057A/PO7/3–90, /PO11/1–4, /PO12/1–14; DRO, D3578/7/2/1–9; DRO, D3644/43/1; DRO, D747/PO1/1–34, /PO2/1–7, /PO3/1–6.

mid-seventeenth-century miner or investor. In 1770, the free miners, still clinging tenaciously to their independence, continued to labour in their small workings. Large, unenclosed tracts of commons remained, in spite of centuries of encroachment and enclosure. But the structural profile of the region was now dominated by large-scale industrial capitalism. Yet in spite of the changes of the 1660–1770 period, the Peak's economy and social structure no longer seemed so unusual. Over the same period, other regions had industrialized, breeding similar patterns of landlessness, poverty and proletarianization as those in which so many of the Peak's inhabitants had become trapped. In 1771, as Arkwright's mill rose in Cromford, the Peak Country seemed set to take its place alongside areas such as the West Riding, the northern coalfield or the nexus of textile production that was developing around Manchester as another formed industrial region of late eighteenth-century Britain. But this was not to be its fate.

5

Social conflict and early capitalism

THE PEAK COUNTRY AND THE INDUSTRIAL REVOLUTION

The study of economic and social history does not always benefit from the identification of clear moments of discontinuity. Such moments are often inventions of historians, keen to find disjunctures where the sources imply only seamless continuity. None the less, such moments do occur. We have seen how the introduction of Humphrey's new technology in the 1570s forced one such transformation. A more protracted, but still visible, period of decisive change started to take form at around 1770. And just as with the moment of technological breakthrough some two centuries earlier, its implications were only to be only realized some two decades later. After 1763, enclosure acts concerning the Peak Country started to pass through parliament. Slowly at first, but with gathering force in the years of the French Wars, what survived of the Peak's commons were enclosed, and remaining common rights extinguished. In spite of long-standing piecemeal enclosure by tenants and cottagers, and the much larger post-Restoration enclosures, many commons still provided vital resources to poor inhabitants in the form of pasture, foodstuffs, fuel and building materials. But with parliamentary enclosure, the long movement towards the privatization of communal land and the commodification of collective rights was completed. As always, the local chronology of enclosure was subject to variation. But taken as a whole, the period of parliamentary enclosure spanned some two generations, and gathered in intensity over time. In legislation of the 1760s, cottages of less than twenty years were removed. By the turn of the century cottagers had to demonstrate that their dwellings had stood for thirty or even forty years. The physical extent of the commons which fell victim to parliamentary enclosure grew from a few hundred acres in the acts of the 1760s to up to the 4,000 acres enclosed in Tideswell in 1807.[1] Most of the land passed into the hands

---

[1] DRO, D160A/PZ1; DRO, 504B/I1, 3, 5, 6, 8–13, 15, 17, 18, 20, 23, 24, 26; DRO, D3029/ Z25; JRL, Bagshawe Muniments, 13/3/35–6.

of wealthy farmers, and manorial authorities. Smallholders were compensated for their loss of common rights with modest grants of enclosed land. But the wage-dependent landless poor received nothing. Thus a central part of the poor mining household's economic independence was ended in the years after 1770.

Just as parliamentary enclosure reworked the Peak's landscape, so it remodelled society and plebeian culture. It did so in tune with the simultaneous decline of the lead industry. The industry's peak production of the mid-eighteenth century was never surpassed. In episodes between 1760 and 1770, and again after 1800, the number of mineworkings in the field reduced dramatically. The old problems of diminishing returns and increasing technological difficulties cut into the industry after 1770. At the same time, the international predominance of Derbyshire's lead field was overcome by internal and external competition. By 1799, the miners of Wirksworth were vainly begging for capital investment in their industry. Three years earlier, the Duke of Rutland's agent wrote of the inhabitants of the mining village of Foolow that 'the poor people in this neighbourhood never suffr'd as they now do'. The decline of industry led to the loss of population, and to increasing poverty amongst those who remained. In Ashover, the poor rate doubled between 1790 and 1808, and doubled again between 1808 and 1815. By 1820, the figure was seven times that of 1790. Some moved to the expanding coalfields of Staffordshire and County Durham; others found employment in the textile mills of Lancashire and Cheshire. The Derbyshire lead industry was, however, a long time in dying. Every so often over the succeeding 130 years, a large mine was established for a few years. Some, such as Millclose in the 1930s, for a brief time produced spectacular outputs. A few free miners clung tenaciously to the independent traditions of their ancestors. The Assistant Poor Law Commissioner noted in 1832 that many smallholding miners were in poverty, but would not apply for relief, knowing that they would lose their cottages. Ten years later, the Children's Employment Commission found 'acute poverty' on their visit to the Peak. One thirteen-year-old boy told the commissioners that he wished to return to the service of a farmer, for 'you are then sure of something to eat'. The free miners were reduced to 'scraping the old workings and poorer veins for a miserable living'. Yet somehow, free mining continued to afford some form of an independent living.[2]

---

[2] Willies, 'Technical and organisational development', 285–6, 457–62; SA, Bag C 587 (71), 578 (10); G.G. Hopkinson, 'Lead mining in 18th century Ashover', *DAJ*, 2nd ser., 72 (1952), 20–1; *idem*, 'Lead mining in the Eyam district', 96; Raistrick and Jennings, *Lead mining*, 302, 325, 316, 304, 277. On the loss of population in many mining villages in the early nineteenth century, see BL, Add. MS 6671, fols. 314–18.

In 1771, drawn by the fast-flowing rivers of the Pennines as a source of motive power and by the already proletarianized workforce, Arkwright established his first mill at Cromford. Hitherto, Cromford's population had been dependent upon the mines. Now, a new and apparently revolutionary form of industry had arrived. In the four decades which followed, such cotton mills became a familiar part of the landscape and economy of the Peak. As the lead industry bled away, it seemed as if a new, heavily capitalized, labour-intensive industry had arrived to supplement the cottage industries of the region: ribbon making, stocking weaving, jersey combing, spinning and picking cotton. Yet the cotton industry of the Peak lasted little more than two generations.[3] A few mills survived through the nineteenth century but most closed in the face of the transport costs which doomed them in their competition with the textile industry of the north-west. By the middle of the nineteenth century, sitting on the margins of the British economy, the Derbyshire Peak had returned to its strange isolation. Contradictions abound in the economic history of the early modern Peak Country. At the middle of the sixteenth century, the lead industry appeared on the point of extinction. By a century later, it had experienced a rate of growth which compared favourably with that of leading sectors of the British economy in the nineteenth century. Yet by 1770, at the time at which the traditional periodization of economic history tells us that the British economy was about to be reworked in the Industrial Revolution, the Derbyshire lead industry was poised to enter the long, terminal stage of its history.

Cast in the shadow of the Industrial Revolution, the economy and social structures of early modern England have been conventionally described as pre-industrial. Stageist, evolutionary accounts of economic change have suggested that following gradual accumulation over two preceding centuries, capital was released in the mid-eighteenth century, creating an industrial revolution which transformed the economy and thereby modernized society, politics and culture. Since the 1970s, such accounts have found less favour amongst economic historians. Following a gloomy period of self-scrutiny in the 1980s, in which the very applicability of the term 'industrial revolution' was called into question, historians of the Industrial Revolution have recently returned to a more historicized view of industrialization and economic change. Current approaches to the history of industrialization have seen economics as interconnected with culture, society and politics within close regional contexts. Furthermore, they have been founded on a fuller appreciation of the significance of structural

---

[3] J. Aikin, *A description of the country from thirty to forty miles round Manchester* (London, 1795), 483–508; R.S. Fitton, *The Arkwrights: spinners of fortune* (Manchester, 1989).

change in the early modern period for later eighteenth-century industriali-zation.[4]

Within such a context, the economic history of the Peak Country between 1520 and 1770 starts to make a little more sense. It was not some freakish 'industrial region in a pre-industrial world'.[5] Other parts of mid-seventeenth-century England shared analogous structural characteristics. In the metalware-producing area of the West Midlands, the textile region of the West Riding, the lead fields of the northern Pennines and Yorkshire and the booming northern coalfield around Newcastle, similar processes of change had moved through local economies, embedding distinct social structures which marked them as industrial regions. Between the late sixteenth and the mid-seventeenth centuries, all these areas had experienced rapid bursts of population growth; all became heavily dependent on nearby agrarian regions or upon the long-distance transport of grain for their supplies of food; all saw an increase in landlessness and waged dependency upon industrial employment; most witnessed the creation of larger units of production and the growing separation of labour from capital.[6] While the cultural and structural characteristics of mid-seventeenth-century England differed markedly from those of mid-nineteenth, the appellation 'pre-industrial' is clearly an inaccurate descriptor of the early modern economy. The structural changes through which the English economy was dragged after 1550 do not constitute merely the opening drumroll to a more dramatic story of industrial growth in the nineteenth century. It has its own relevance, as a distinct period in English economic history.

CUSTOM AND ECONOMIC CHANGE

For much of Part I of this book, processes of economic change have been addressed as if the motive forces driving those processes lay beyond human agency. In describing changes in the organization and control of the mining industry, shifts in markets, as reflected in lead prices, have been given primacy. The interrelated discussion of population change and price move-

---

[4] See, in particular, M. Berg and P. Hudson, 'Rehabilitating the Industrial Revolution', *EcHR*, 2nd ser., 45, 1 (1992), 24–50; P. Hudson, *The Industrial Revolution* (London, 1992); idem, 'The regional perspective', in idem (ed.), *Regions and industries: a perspective on the Industrial Revolution in Britain* (Cambridge, 1989), 5–40; E.A. Wrigley, *Continuity, chance and change: the character of the Industrial Revolution in England* (Cambridge, 1988).

[5] I am here paraphrasing Levine and Wrightson, *Making of an industrial society*, 76.

[6] P. Hudson, 'Proto-industrialisation: the case of the West Riding', *History Workshop*, 12 (1981), 34–61; Levine and Wrightson, *Making of an industrial society*; C.J. Hunt, *The lead miners of the northern Pennines in the eighteenth and nineteenth centuries* (Manchester, 1970); M.B. Rowlands, 'Continuity and change in an industrializing society: the case of the West Midlands industries', in Hudson (ed.), *Regions and industries*, 105; Skipp, *Crisis and development*.

ment has been presented as if human beings were iron filings, drawn into and out of the lead field by the magnetic force of price indices. Although I have used the term capitalism, it has been in a loose, descriptive sense. In describing shifts in ownership and control, I have avoided ascribing any conscious strategic intent to the mercantile lesser gentry, the greater gentry or the nobility. It has almost been implied that changes in organization, ownership and control within the mining industry were produced mechanistically out of market demand. Such impersonal, apolitical assumptions will not drive the rest of this book.

We have seen that from the middle of the seventeenth century, the productive capacity of large, sophisticated, labour-intensive, highly capitalized mines marginalized free mining activity in the Derbyshire lead field. Roger Burt has argued the contrary. He has stated that in the British non-ferrous metal mining industries of the early modern period,

Large-scale working was rare and the great expansion of production of tin, and particularly lead, between the late fifteenth and early eighteenth centuries, was achieved principally by the multiplication of traditional small units of production. These small mines continued to be worked mainly by semi-independent part-time miner/farmers, albeit with a greater degree of application and intensity, and little progress was made in the proletarianization of the labour force.[7]

This stands in contradiction to the archival evidence of change in early modern Britain's largest lead field. But the assumption from which Burt's argument proceeds is more interesting. He states that the customary laws and institutions which governed the mining industry, and which allowed for the continuation of free mining, created 'constrictions and frustrations for more modern, large-scale mining'. This leads Burt to claim that if 'the early modern period saw significant and general changes in practice, [such organizational change] would have been reflected either in an increased restlessness with the customary systems, or in major changes with their provisions'. Since Burt finds 'no evidence of either development', he therefore assumes 'stability and continuity' in the organization, control and ownership of early modern Derbyshire lead mining.[8]

If Burt's claim that the organization and control of Derbyshire's lead mining industry remained fundamentally unchanged before *c.* 1700 stands in opposition to the evidence, his logic proceeds from at least a partial

---

[7] R. Burt, 'The international diffusion of technology in the early modern period: the case of the British non-ferrous mining industry', *EcHR*, 2nd ser., 44, 2 (1991), 249.

[8] *Ibid.*, 263–4; Burt mysteriously reverses key elements of his argument in a later piece: *idem*, 'Transformation', 23, 29, 31–2, 35, 42. For criticism of Burt's 1991 article, see D. Kiernan, 'Twenty thousand miners can't be wrong!', *BPDMHS*, 11, 5 (1992), 249–53; R. Slack, 'Free men or wage-slaves? The miners of the Wirksworth area in the 1650s', *BPDMHS*, 11, 6 (1992), 272–4; Wood, 'Industrial development', 51–2.

truth. We shall see in Part III that intense social conflict developed over the customs and laws which governed the mining industry. This was especially true of the period between *c.* 1590 and 1660, in which the Peak's free miners became pitched against a coalition of aristocrats, gentry and entrepreneurs. Like all customary legal systems in early modern England, free mining law was inherently local. Social conflict therefore expressed itself in a small-scale and limited form. But taken together, local conflicts formed a larger confrontation. The outcome of each individual struggle possessed its own chronology and outcome. But a broad unity of purpose on both sides of this social conflict can none the less be detected. The outcome of local disputes over mining custom fundamentally affected the economic history of the Peak Country. For it was in these struggles over the meaning of custom and property that the control of the lead industry was decided.

This point bears heavily upon a central debate in Marxist historical sociology, and a coincidentally similar argument developed within neo-classical economics by D.C. North.[9] Both in North's work, and in that of Brenner, Martin and Lachmann, the development of capitalism is seen in the context of the prior establishment of institutional and legal frameworks which favoured the interests of capital. For both schools of thought, it was the successful resolution of political and class conflicts in the interests of early agrarian capitalism which allowed for its free development in England. From North's neo-classical perspective, post-Restoration changes in English land law and the formation of an incorporative, mercantilist state created a stable politico-legal framework within which capitalism was free to develop. 'Feudal' forms of expropriation were replaced by capitalist relations of production which operated in a rational manner to maximize the productive potential of the English economy, whereby unproductive and parasitic lower-class 'free riders' were removed from the economic

[9] R. Lachmann, *From manor to market: structural change in England, 1536–1640* (Madison, 1987); J.E. Martin, *Feudalism to capitalism: peasant and landlord in English agrarian capitalism* (Basingstoke, 1983); R. Brenner, 'Agrarian class structure and economic development in pre-industrial Europe', in T.H. Aston and C.H.E. Philpin (eds.), *The Brenner debate: agrarian class structure and economic development in pre-industrial Europe* (Cambridge, 1985). See also M. Dobb, *Studies in the development of capitalism* (London, 1948); R. Hilton (ed.), *The transition from feudalism to capitalism* (London, 1976). For a differing account within Marxist historical sociology of the origins of capitalism, which places greater weight upon changes in the structure of markets, see I. Wallerstein, *The modern world-system, I: Capitalist agriculture and the origins of the European world-economy in the sixteenth century* (New York, 1974), and *idem, The modern world-system, II: Mercantilism and the consolidation of the European world-economy, 1600–1750* (New York, 1980). For North, see D.C. North and R.P. Thomas, *The rise of the western world: a new economic history* (Cambridge, 1973), 146–56; D.C. North, *Structure and change in economic history* (New York, 1981), 143–57.

equation. In spite of the curiously Marxian periodization, North's interpretation appears as conflict-free. The possibility that North's 'free riders'
might have resisted their removal, or that clear distinctions between
feudalism and capitalism may be difficult to draw, does not impede his
account.

In the work of the Marxist historical sociologists, the establishment of
capitalist relations of production in agriculture is seen as the product of
earlier class struggles between lord and peasant. Assaults on common
rights and the enclosure of common land followed upon the successful
resolution of such social struggles in the interests of the dominant class.
Productive increases in agriculture resulted, thereby releasing labour and
capital into industry and leading to the first stirrings of a nascent capitalist
world economy. The argument is inherently schematic. As with North's
formulation, too sharp a distinction is drawn between feudal and capitalist
relations of production. But for all that the argument often proceeds from a
series of abstracted ideal types, it at least takes the study of early modern
English economic history away from the arid particularism practised by the
conventional economic historians of the period, and places social and
political struggles at the heart of accounts of economic change. Especially
welcome is the attention paid to what Lachmann calls 'local level class
struggles'. Brenner's concern with the importance of 'communal village
institutions' as foci of peasant resistance to new forms of seigneurial
expropriation mirrors that interest in the local history of social conflict and
early capitalism. This work should have forced early modern social
historians into a closer scrutiny of the implications of growing rural
industry, proletarianization and landlessness. For as Pat Hudson has noted,
'What is at issue [in the work of the Marxist historical sociologists] . . . is
whether the proletariat was a "natural" or a social creation.' That question,
first raised by R.H. Tawney in 1912, has since become marginal to many
social historians. Yet in spite of historiographical neglect, the issue festers
at the heart of early modern English social history.[10]

North, Tawney and the Marxist historical sociologists were attempting
to explain what they saw as the early establishment of capitalism in English
agriculture, especially within commercial grain-producing areas. But in
spite of their agrarian bent, they have a relevance to the social conflicts
over mining custom within the Peak and elsewhere.[11] We are now in a

---

[10] Lachmann, *From manor to market*, 100–27; Brenner, 'Agrarian class structure', 12;
Hudson, *Industrial Revolution*, 71; R.H. Tawney, *The agrarian problem in the sixteenth
century* (London, 1912).

[11] For a very perceptive study of the implications of contests over custom for local social
relations, see C.E. Searle, 'Custom, class conflict and agrarian capitalism: the Cumbrian
customary economy in the eighteenth century', *P&P*, 110 (1986), 106–33.

position to sketch a chronology of the changing relationship between local social conflict and early capitalism within the Peak. We should not see in the early sixteenth-century disputes over cope payments and lord's meers any innovations in the extraction of surplus value from the mining work-force. Rather, they constituted the intensification of traditional seigneurial demands. Neither did renewed conflict between lord and free miner over mining custom in the High Peak up to *c.* 1590 represent a significant historical discontinuity. Much of the newly profitable lead deposits of the Hundred of High Peak lay outside the Duchy of Lancaster's King's Field. Within a few years of the sudden expansion of the High Peak industry, the lords of such manors therefore attempted to lay claim to rights over the lead deposits on their estates. In most cases, lords did not curtail free mining activity. Rather, both lords and miners came to see the King's Field as the model on which the organization of mining within non-Duchy manors should be based. Thus, lords allowed free mining as a custom or a privilege on most manors within the High Peak, in return for the payment of lot duties from the miners' ore production. Within some manors, lords also followed the practice of the Duchy in taking cope payments from orebuyers in return for waiving their right of pre-emption of ore sales. In allowing a free market in lead trading, lords were therefore compensated by the payment of four pence upon every load sold.

Initially, this practice was not followed by the sixth Earl of Shrewsbury, the most powerful magnate within the late sixteenth-century Peak Country. Shrewsbury held the leases of the Duchy's rights of lot and cope in the King's Field within both the Wapentake of Wirksworth and the Hundred of High Peak. In his own right, he also owned the bundle of manors in the High Peak which made up Ashford lordship. The orebuyers' right to free ore sales upon their payment of a cope of six pence was too long established within the Wapentake of Wirksworth to be challenged effectively. But the recent re-establishment of the mining industry within the Hundred of High Peak left the customs there rather more uncertain. Shrewsbury therefore followed a policy, inherited by his immediate successors, and followed by other lords within the High Peak, of forcing the miners to sell all of their ore to him. Moreover, Shrewsbury and other lords set such ore sales at below the free market price pertaining within the Wapentake of Wirksworth. The policy was, of course, opposed by both miners and orebuyers alike.[12] By the early seventeenth century, this opposition had forced most

---

[12] On pre-emption in the Duchy's High Peak manors, see SA, BFM2/78; for Ashford lordship, see PRO, DL4/67/59; for Little Hucklow, see PRO, DL4/62/19; for Grindlow, see PRO, DL4/64/11; for Meadowplecke Grange, see PRO, DL4/68/50; for Calver, see PRO, C2/Eliz/ S12/18. For attempts by lords to impose pre-emption on various manors and granges in Wirksworth Wapentake in 1623, see PRO, DL4/72/31.

lords to waive their claim to a manorial pre-emption in return for the orebuyers' payment of a four pence cope upon every load they bought. By 1630, only the powerful Manners family of Haddon Hall continued to insist upon the direct sale of all ore produced within their manors to themselves, at prices set well below the market rate.[13]

Between *c.* 1590 and 1660, the forms by which lords attempted to increase their revenue from the mining industry underwent important change. Gradually, some lords began to appreciate that the industry offered more than a simple opportunity to increase their traditional seigneurial dues. After *c.* 1590, the seigneurial system under which miners and orebuyers were guaranteed rights in return for the payment of dues began gradually to mutate into something rather different. Some lords recognized that ambiguities in local custom allowed them to gain direct control over the mining industry on their estates. Thus, for instance, the lord's right to lot and cope dues could be so twisted as to reduce free miners to the status of poor wage labourers. In 1630, John Manners took all ore sales on his manor of Hazelbadge into his hands, and set the price of such sales at nine shillings per load. At that time, the market price for a load of ore stood at twenty-two shillings. The cost of that decision was renewed conflict with the assertive free miners of the neighbouring villages, backed by the wealthier orebuyers. If lords wished to avoid confronting such a potentially powerful coalition, they could increase their entitlement to lot dues upon the miners' ore production. Following the practice in the King's Field, most late sixteenth-century lords had agreed with local miners to take one thirteenth of the miners' production as a lot payment. In theory, this payment guaranteed the miners' custom or privilege of free mining, and also gave them the right to take timber from the lord's woods. In the early seventeenth century, the Manners of Haddon chose to set such payments on the manors of Netherhaddon and Harthill at one seventh of the miners' production. The owner of Newton Grange took one fifth of the miners' ore as lot payments at that time, as did the owner of Steeple Grange. The exaction of such high rates of lot payment effectively reduced the miners to the status of wage labourers. Hence, free miners from the King's Field described the workforce in such manors as 'labourers' or 'servants'. No formal right of free mining existed within these 'arbitrary jurisdictions'. The lord appointed the barmaster, whose actions went unregulated by any barmote. Rates of lot and cope were not fixed by custom, but were variable and determined by the lord.[14]

---

[13] See especially PRO, DL1/323, Att.-Gen. v. John Manners.
[14] Willies, 'Technical and organisational development', 27; PRO, DL4/105/1661/22, /72/31, / 71/39.

In some cases, lords formalized the marginalization of free mining within their manors by banning the custom altogether, and employed wage labourers to exploit the lead deposits. This could lead to the formal integration of the lead industry around the manorial system. After Sir Francis Foljamb banned free mining in the manor of Elton in the 1590s, the lead deposits were worked by his tenants and servants. The lead ore was then transported by paid labourers to his smelting mill at Walton, where it was processed and sold.[15]

The legal changes which resulted from the intense period of conflict between *c.* 1590 and 1660 conditioned the pattern of capitalist development into the eighteenth century. In the manor of Eyam, the lord and the freeholders had combined to marginalize free mining custom by the 1660s. Under the custom of the manor of Eyam, free miners had to pay high compositions to freeholders for digging in their land, and could be ejected by the lord if required. Their mines could then be granted *en masse* as 'consolidated titles' to groups of entrepreneurs. This formulation of custom allowed for the establishment of the big works on Eyam Edge whose productivity proved so impressive in the 1740s. Similar definitions of mining custom in Netherhaddon after 1658, Harthill after 1748 and in Ashover by the 1640s also allowed lords or freeholders to eject free miners by 'force majeure' and to introduce consolidated titles in the eighteenth century.[16] This construction of mining custom had the advantage of flexibility. Upon the exhaustion of the deep deposits worked by a large mine, the lord could grant what remained to the free miners, while remaining assured of continued revenue from the high rates of lot duties exacted from them. Nor were the miners of the King's Field exempt from such pressure. The large-scale drainage and subsequent profitable working of the Dovegang deposits in the 1650s was made possible by the Court of the Duchy of Lancaster's decision to override customary law and ban free mining activity there. The matter was given a legal gloss with the alteration of mining custom by a rigged jury in 1655, which allowed free miners' inundated works in the Wapentake of Wirksworth to be seized by entrepreneurs. But such instances were relatively rare. Overall, the right of free mining within the Duchy's King's Field remained much more secure than in other lordships.

Thus, at least within some jurisdictions, the establishment of deep works

[15] PRO, DL4/75/10; see also PRO, DL4/72/31 for similar developments elsewhere.
[16] Davies, 'The Dukes of Devonshire, Newcastle and Rutland', 139–42, 188–90; Hopkinson, 'Lead mining in the Eyam district', 93–4; L. Willies, 'The working of the Derbyshire lead mining customs in the eighteenth and nineteenth centuries', *BPDMHS*, 10, 3 (1988), 151–2; *idem*, 'Technical and organisational development', 296; Raistrick and Jennings, *Lead mining*, 187–8.

and the creation of an industrial wage labour force was not a natural process. Rather, proletarianization resulted from social conflict and the suppression of custom.[17] Within those parts of the lead field where free mining was successfully extended or defended, large-scale capitalist works developed in a more organic fashion. Within such jurisdictions, their emergence bears superficial similarities to the gradual marginalization of cottage industries by market relations and larger units of production described by proto-industrialization theory.[18] Yet the proto-industrialization model does not easily fit with the history of industrialization in the Peak. Proto-industrialization theory has ignored social conflict as a factor in local and regional patterns of industrialization. Free mining custom created difficulties for entrepreneurs who hoped to establish large, deep mines. Whereas in manors such as Netherhaddon entrepreneurs could appeal to the lord to have free miners ejected from their works, within the King's Field investors had to create large units by buying the free miners out, or by becoming their partners. As we have seen, the coping system, which allowed for the continuation of the skilled miners' tradition of independence, resulted from such developments.

The weight of market forces was not sufficient to crush free mining. Even after small-scale, independent production became but a small contributor to the overall output of the industry, the tradition continued in those manors where the right had been defended. In part, this can be attributed to a stubborn bloody-mindedness amongst the miners. Partly, its continuation was due to the enduring importance of free mining to the mining household. But the retention of the tradition also had much to do with the legal and contractual apparatus which attached to free mining, or which devolved from it: the powers of the barmote, the relative independence guaranteed by the coping system, the actual independence of small-scale production. Where the custom of free mining was defended successfully, an uneven and contradictory pattern of industrial development resulted, in which even into the nineteenth and twentieth centuries large, complex, labour- and capital-intensive deep mines sat uncomfortably alongside the small workings of the free miners. Where the custom was defeated, the story was rather different. But in each case, the local history of industrial

---

[17] For examples of the suppression of free mining codes elsewhere, see C.J. Williams, 'The mining laws in Flintshire and Denbighshire', *BPDMHS*, 12, 3 (1994), 66–7; Wood, 'Custom, identity and resistance', 263–6.

[18] Burt, 'International diffusion', 268–9; M. Gill, 'Mining and proto-industrialisation', *British Mining*, 41 (1990), 99–110. For the original proto-industrialization model, see F.F. Mendels, 'Proto-industrialization: the first phase of the industrialization process', *Journal of Economic History*, 32, 1 (1972), 241–61. For a fuller critique of its application to the early modern Derbyshire lead industry, see Wood, 'Industrial development', 47–52.

development and economic change was founded upon social conflict over custom.

The legal framework within which the lead mining industry developed after 1660 was therefore a hybrid. In some places, capitalist relations of production were imposed consequent upon the defeat of free mining. In others, they grew incrementally out of conflict, accommodation and compromise. There was no single, unitary road to industrial capitalism in the Peak. We cannot reduce the history of its economic development to a neat formula, or construct from it an abstract model. Yet a basic truth is apparent: at the heart of the local difference in the development of capitalism within the Peak lay the forms assumed by custom. The point has a broader relevance. Maxine Berg and Adrian Randall have both suggested that patterns of industrial growth in eighteenth-century Britain were partially decided by the efficacy of workers' resistance to new forms of exploitation.[19] The issue extends through time, and over space. The creation of large-scale, labour-intensive, capitalist mines in the nineteenth century in Lanarkshire and Ayrshire, Decazeville, Real del Monte, Colorado and California, as in Nigeria in the century which followed, all depended upon the legal and physical suppression of earlier traditions of free mining.[20] And in each case, as in the Peak, there was resistance. The economic history of the early modern Peak Country starts to look less curious; for here as elsewhere, the advent of capitalism was as much a political event as it was an economic process.

[19] M. Berg, 'Workers and machinery in eighteenth-century England', in J. Rule (ed.), *British trade unionism, 1750–1850: the formative years* (London, 1988), 52 73; Randall, *Before the Luddites*, 7, 26–7.

[20] D. Reid, *The miners of Decazeville: a genealogy of deindustrialization* (Cambridge, Mass., 1985), 11–14; C. Velasco Avila, 'Labour relations in mining: Real del Monte and Pachuca, 1824–1874', in T. Greaves and W. Culver (eds.), *Miners and mining in the Americas* (Manchester, 1985), 55–9; M. Neuschatz, *The golden sword: the coming of capitalism to the Colorado mining frontier* (New York, 1986), 9–23; A. Campbell and D. Reid, 'The independent collier in Scotland', in R. Harrison (ed.), *Independent collier: the coal miner as an archetypal proletarian reconsidered* (Hassocks, 1978), 54–74; B. Freund, *Capital and labour in the Nigerian tin mines* (London, 1981), 8–72.

Part II

THE CONDITIONS OF COMMUNITY

— ✦ 6 ✦ —

'The memory of the people': custom, law and popular culture

If social conflict helped to produce economic change in the Derbyshire Peak Country, customary law formed the terrain over which that conflict was fought. Custom defined property, and thereby underwrote social relations and cultural practice. It developed 'at the interface between law and agrarian practice' within local junctions of law, culture, economics and politics. As Thompson characterized it, 'custom itself *is* the interface, since it may be considered both as praxis and as law.'[1] As such, custom was not the possession of a single social group. Rather, it represented the codification of negotiation and conflict over long periods of time. As local law, custom regulated production within village economies, defining and inter-meshing forms of subordination and exploitation. Its norms and rules could be invoked by lord against tenant, rich against poor, and landed against landless. Hence, early modern social conflicts were often reducible to confrontations over the control of customary offices and institutions, or over the authentication of the local memory.

The early control acquired by miners and tenants over the language and institutions of custom in the Peak therefore represented a major achievement of local plebeian politics. That control was never total. Neither was it unproblematic. The public world of plebeian politics came to be defined as that of the settled, adult male. Those on the margins of that world – women, the unskilled, the transient – had to fight to gain a place within it. Yet where miners and tenants controlled custom, they denied the nobility and gentry access to its legitimizing language and organizing force. In many legal disputes, the region's ruling elite were therefore forced to mount frontal

---

[1] Thompson, *Customs in common*, 97. On this, see also *idem*, 'The grid of inheritance: a comment', in J. Goody, J. Thirsk and E.P. Thompson (eds.), *Family and inheritance: rural society in western Europe, 1200–1800* (Cambridge, 1976), 328–60.

attacks upon the organized force of local memory. Hence, the law became 'a place, not of consensus, but of conflict', and custom the location of 'class conflict, at the interface between agrarian practice and political power'.[2]

Disputes in the Peak over customary law in general, and free mining law in particular, did not occur in isolation from one another, but rather collectively constituted a larger social conflict. Fought out through the law courts of Westminster and in the mines and fields of the Peak, this conflict reshaped custom in important respects: custom became increasingly standardized and dependent upon written documentation; social conflict fostered a politicized and conflictual sense of local history; and it strengthened the authority of custom within local culture. In all these respects, custom acquired an unusually powerful force within the popular culture of the Peak. The complexities and nuances which moved within notions of custom are best appreciated within a long chronology and a local context. Much of the best work on custom has concerned the eighteenth and early nineteenth centuries, and has presented custom as a relatively static component of a 'clearly defined conservative plebeian culture'.[3] In contrast, we will here stress the contextual ambivalences and dynamism which underwrote custom. The language of custom was mutable in its meaning and application. It might at one moment call into existence a wide social solidarity, but the next be used to validate the exclusion by richer villagers of the poor, by the landed against the landless, or by established villagers against newcomers.[4] Class, gender, age and residence could interlock within custom to produce a concept of place which defined a location as the possession of its settled, male inhabitants.[5] Similarly, the customs of a trade could be so constituted as to define the public honour and reputation of the skilled man in opposition to the dishonourable, de-skilled labour of the woman.

The meanings given to custom were therefore locally and historically specific. In the early modern Peak, custom continued to define the use of resources; but as we shall see, it did so in ways that were novel. It came to prescribe community and collective identity. At the same time, custom provided a hegemonic space and a legitimate discourse within which

[2] Thompson, *Customs in common*, 110; idem, *Whigs and hunters: the origins of the Black Act* (London, 1975), 241, 245–69.
[3] Randall, *Before the Luddities*, 48–9. See also B. Bushaway, *By rite: custom, ceremony and community in England, 1700–1880* (London, 1982); J. Neeson, *Commoners: common right, enclosure and social change in England, 1700–1820* (Cambridge, 1993).
[4] Thompson, *Customs in common*, 123, 132; S. Hindle, 'Persuasion and protest in the Caddington common enclosure dispute, 1635–1639', *P&P*, 158 (1998), 37–78.
[5] For an exception, see T. Stretton, 'Women, custom and equity in the court of requests', in J. Kermode and G. Walker (eds.), *Women, crime and the courts in early modern England* (London, 1994), 170–89.

plebeians could develop a critique of the established order. The authority of custom drew from its legal meaning. Presented as ancient and immutable, customary rights were in reality both contested and changeable. Yet the appeal to the past gave custom an ideological potential which was legitimated by its meaning within contemporary legal thought. The most obvious role of customary law lay in its mediation and definition of the use, control and ownership of resources. In law, the sale, inheritance or lease of land could be circumscribed by manorial or borough custom, as could the use of land. Individual property in land often ran parallel to collective common rights to (for example) access, pasture, gleaning, building materials, fuel, food or minerals. Across England, custom defined local authority and codified relations of exploitation and subordination. Parochial custom might specify the form of election or appointment of churchwardens or other local offices, and borough custom stipulate the extent of the franchise. Manorial custom might identify the nature and weight of manorial duties, just as parochial custom defined the minister's right to tithes. In every case, custom operated as *lex loci* within specific geographical boundaries. Just how rigidly such boundaries were defined varied from one place to another, and over time. But it is important that jurists presented the common law as the only general, national custom. In contrast, the operation of a local custom had to be established within a distinct and legally meaningful area: as the customs of a manor, a parish, a borough, a lordship (that is, a collection of sub-manors) or, in the case of Derbyshire free miners' claim to a general custom of free mining, within the King's Field.

Precise definitions of local custom varied from one legal authority to another at any given moment, and changed in important respects over our period. None the less, both in 1520 and in 1770, law courts assessed the validity of a custom according to certain basic criteria. A custom had to be reasonable, certain, 'according to common right', 'to his profit that claimeth the same', and must have its basis in the laws of God, nature and of man. Its operation had to be confined to a specific jurisdiction; and it must have grown out of continuous common usage originating in ancient time. Law courts set that point in ancient time at 1189. In terms of much contemporary legal practice, proof that a custom had been exercised continuously and beyond living memory, or 'time whereof the memory of man is not to the contrary', and so long as documentary evidence did not contradict such living tradition, was accepted as sufficient. It therefore became a convenient legal fiction that 'Customs, and prescriptions, resteth onely in the memory of man.'[6] These legal principles became internalized within social practice.

---

[6] Quotations from C. Calthorpe, *A relation between the lord of a manor and the coppyholder*

On 9 May 1666, the copyholders of the manor of Matlock gathered to agree upon a full account of their customs. They stated in their preamble their knowledge that 'Custome is law for coppiehold estates & the chief basis upon wch stands the whole fabrick of our Coppihold estates', that they had examined both witnesses and ancient records, and that it was from that evidence that their understanding of custom had proceeded.[7] The document was prepared on the assumption that its authenticity was likely to be challenged, and its authors therefore made a point of citing their sources. Whatever the intention of those who drew up the document, the 1666 customary did not constitute a simple, descriptive statement of what was already 'known' of the customs. Rather, the document defined a moment at which custom became more certain and solid, but at the same time more codified and restrictive. Finally, the customary simultaneously played upon and exposed the fiction that custom 'resteth onely in the memory of man'. Ostensibly a genuine product of oral tradition, in fact the Matlock customary relied upon a synthesis of written and oral evidence. At the same time as the 1666 customary reified a constructed oral tradition, the act of writing itself denied that tradition an authority in the future. Thereafter, at least in the minds of the tenants who drew up the document, the customs of Matlock would proceed according to written rules.

Orality and literacy intertwined in many plebeians' knowledge of custom. The depositions placed before Westminster central courts in the course of disputes over custom enable us to reach beyond the evidence of the customary and to observe the interplay of speech and writing in local culture. At a certain stage in legal proceedings, central courts empowered commissions of local gentlemen to take depositions from witnesses for both sides. These commissioners proceeded to meet with all who wished to give evidence in the matter at a specified place and time. The witnesses, or deponents, gave verbal accounts of their knowledge of the customs of a place, produced in answer to written interrogatories.[8] For the purposes of this study, we will largely concern ourselves with depositions heard by commissions operating in the name of two central courts: the Court of the Duchy of Lancaster, and the Court of Exchequer.[9] Both courts were heavily

---

his tenant (London, 1635), 18–22. For a useful summary of the legal basis of custom, see A. Kiralfy, 'Custom in medieval English law', *Journal of Legal History*, 9, 1 (1988), 26–39.

[7] BL, Add. MS 6669, fol. 217. The tenants of Matlock bought the manor in 1629. On the division of the new rents, see BL, Add. MS 6689, fols. 480–505.

[8] For the practice of the Court of Exchequer, see W.H. Bryson, *The equity side of the Exchequer: its jurisdiction, administration, procedures and records* (Cambridge, 1975), 138–43.

[9] The existence of good finding aids and the full run of records for both courts over the period covered by this book enable us to make firm conclusions concerning depositions presented to the Exchequer and Duchy Courts in Peak Country cases.

engaged in legal disputes concerning the Peak. The Duchy Court had a peculiar interest in the Peak Country due to the large estates held by the Duchy of Lancaster within the region (see Map 5). Disputes over the boundaries of those estates and the rights, and over the manorial tolls and offices within them, generated much litigation up to the early eighteenth century. In contrast, the Court of Exchequer had no such local interest in the region. Instead, it heard matters concerning Crown and church revenue from across the country. It therefore formed an obvious forum for litigation concerning the contentious lead tithes in particular, together with more standard parochial tithe disputes within the Peak. The records of these courts have been supplemented by the less consistent use of depositions presented to other central courts – Chancery and Star Chamber in particular – and by the records of the Consistory Court of the diocese of Coventry and Lichfield. This court enjoyed a jurisdiction over church revenue within its diocese, together with (amongst other things) defamation cases and religious dissidence. The records of diocesan Consistory Courts have therefore often been deployed by historians of sexuality, the family and of popular religion.[10] Yet the Consistory Court of Coventry and Lichfield heard surprisingly few cases from the Peak, resulting in a mere 136 depositions concerning cases from within the mining area being placed before that court, dated between 1591 and 1663. Most of these concerned tithe disputes. Much more impressive (and rather less frequently studied) are the records of depositions given to the Exchequer and Duchy Courts. Between 1517 and 1754, some 3,779 depositions were given to commissions of these two courts in the course of legal cases concerning the Wapentake of Wirksworth or the Hundred of High Peak (see Table 6.1).

Taken as a whole, the 3,915 depositions given by Peak Country people to the Duchy, Exchequer and Consistory Courts between 1517 and 1754 constitute a remarkable, if deliberately selective and often contradictory, body of evidence concerning custom and local culture. In particular, the deponents' answers to the interrogatories, and their still more illuminating asides, reveal something of the texture and structure of local memory. At their most extreme, such memories could reach back in time by up to a century and a half.[11] Richard Buxton, for instance, was aged sixty-four

---

[10] For example, see Gowing, *Domestic dangers*; R. Houlbrooke, *Church courts and the people during the English Reformation, 1520–1570* (Oxford, 1979); J.A. Sharpe, *Defamation and sexual slander in early modern England: the church courts at York*, Borthwick Papers, 58 (York, 1980); M.J. Ingram, *Church courts, sex and marriage in England, 1570–1640* (Oxford, 1987).

[11] For examples, see PRO, DL4/128/1696/7, /55/46, /56/17.

Table 6.1 *Number and gender of deponents to Consistory, Exchequer and Duchy of Lancaster Courts, 1517–1754*

Date	Women	Men
1517–49	0	241
1550–99	13 (2%)	703 (98%)
1600–49	39 (3%)	1170 (97%)
1650–99	63 (4%)	1397 (96%)
1700–54	48 (17%)	241 (83%)
Total	163 (4%)	3752 (96%)

when he gave evidence in 1712 to a commission of the Court of the Duchy of Lancaster in Wirksworth concerning the manorial monopoly of milling there.[12] He recalled conversations with Joan Sowter, with whom 'hee this deponent hath severall times had discourse . . . concerning diverse Antient things about Wirkeworth'. Those conversations began about fifty years earlier, when Joan Sowter was aged about eighty, and concerned local knowledge she had acquired as a child. Buxton's recollec-tions of Sowter's conversation *might* therefore carry us back from 1712 into the Wirksworth of the 1590s. Such memories were part of a close, detailed sense of place carried by the bearers of local culture. In Richard Buxton's memory, Joan Sowter possessed sufficient local knowledge to identify the corn mill of 1712 as a former fulling mill – part of an industry which died out in the last decades of the fifteenth century. That historical fact was written into the landscape by a remembered place-name. By 1712, the alley which ran beside the mill had become St John's Lane; but Joan Sowter had known that it had once been called Walkmill Lane, in remembrance of its role in the old fulling industry. In its long historical reach, as in the close attention given to local place, Buxton's deposition was an ideal type of the structured memories contained in depositional evidence. But in recalling the words of his female neighbour, Joan Sowter, Buxton strayed from the norm.

Depositional evidence was strongly gendered. Some 96 per cent of the deponents who gave evidence to the Courts of the Duchy of Lancaster and Exchequer and to the Consistory Court between 1517 and 1754 were men (see Table 6.1). On the rare occasions on which women gave depositions, they tended to justify their evidence with reference to the words and actions of aged male and female neighbours and kin in roughly equal measure. In

12 PRO, DL4/133/1712/1.

contrast, men scarcely ever referred to the actions or words of women as a source of information about custom or local history. Such depositions were not, therefore, neutral descriptions of an individual's knowledge of a place. Deponents' responses could be shaped by the interrogatories which they were obliged to answer, and by the prompting of attorney. They were also ordered by the public, communal, male interests which defined custom. In 1581, Bakewell manor court drew up a new list of by-laws. These specified a series of injunctions directed to 'every ma[n]' of the manor. The only deviation from this formula came in the new rules established for every 'ma[n] or woma[n]' concerning the washing of clothes at St Mary's well.[13] We can assume that the women of Bakewell did more than the washing. They were as likely to be tending to their cattle upon the common, or working in the fields, as the men.[14] Yet within the customary, if not in social reality, the women of Bakewell were closed out of this public assertion of custom. Save only for that single area conceived of as falling into the supposedly private, domestic and thereby feminine sphere, the official language of local custom in Bakewell in 1581 was exclusively masculine.

Custom could be conceived of in bodily terms, as lying in 'the breaste of the coppiehoulders', or as the 'common voice' of a place. It claimed a special place within communal discourse, lying within 'comon talke and speeche'. As common knowledge, custom occupied a normative position within local society, simultaneously defining a place as a legal and communal unit. The very obviousness of custom gave it a special authority. Hugh Wright of Bowden could not remember which of his esteemed ancestors had broken down illegal enclosures upon the commons any more than he could recall which 'neighbour' told him that the inhabitants of Bowden had rights upon the common. Indeed, he seemed almost irritated at the question: after all, that the community possessed rights upon the common 'was thought [so] amongst the neighbours', and was a part of the 'generall reputacon' of the area. There is a seductive charm to such claims. We can all too easily validate the claim made by the 'common voice' to universality and thereby ignore the exclusions which gave that voice its special tenor. As we have seen, women were largely absent from accounts of custom. Deponents were usually selected from amongst the settled, older male inhabitants. Their evidence could present rapidly changing

---

[13] DRO, D258M/61/9.
[14] On women's earnings from the assertion of common rights, see P. King, 'Customary rights and women's earnings: the importance of gleaning to the rural labouring poor, 1750–1850', *EcHR*, 2nd ser., 44, 3 (1991), 461–76; J. Humphries, 'Enclosures, common rights and women: the proletarianization of families in the late eighteenth and early nineteenth centuries', *Journal of Economic History*, 50, 1 (1990), 17–42.

industrial villages as cosy, traditional communities. Edward Johnson's claim to have known 'most part of the then Inhabitants of Wirksworth' in 1674 should not therefore be accepted at face value: at that time the town had a population of around 2,300 people and the local mining industry was changing rapidly. Where the 'common voice' of a place spoke in unanimity, it often did so against a deafening silence. Equally, on other occasions there might be no 'common voice', but only a babble of conflicting opinions.[15]

Yet in spite of such qualifications, the depositions given by Peak Country plebeians to central courts allow us to reach further down the scale of local society than does any other large body of source material. In particular, they illuminate the place of custom in popular culture. Custom drew upon the peculiar character of the Peak's social structure. Wide common rights and the easy availability of free mining opportunities persuaded many people to remain in or near the place of their birth, producing unusually limited migration patterns.[16] In consequence, a profound sense of local place developed within the protective embrace of custom. Miners were able to name previous owners of their groves going back generations, partly because mineshares often passed down from father to son. Passage over moors or labour in the fields by succeeding generations deepened familial associations with localities.[17] Drawn-out customary conflicts, extending over several centuries, generated a still deeper sense of local place: witness the protracted contest between the owner of Wigwell Grange and the inhabitants of nearby Wirksworth concerning common rights on the adjacent moors, which stretched between the 1550s and the 1730s.[18]

Young people learnt custom through the instruction of their elders. Being shown the bounds of the parish or manor, or the limits of a common, marked an important point of transition into adolescence. For miners, further instruction proceeded at early adulthood. The instructor was typically an aged authority figure within the locality, usually joined to the instructed by ties of blood. Thus, Robert Buxton knew that the boundaries of Chelmorton started from 'twoe lenyinge mearstones' because it was there that his grandfather had started the young Robert's tour of the

---

[15] Manning, *Village revolts*, 139–40; LJRO, B/C/5/1623, Youlgreave; PRO, DL4/40/29, /58/7, /133/1712/1.

[16] Wood, 'Migration and local identity'.

[17] For detailed examples, see PRO, DL4/120/1678/1, /133/1712/1; PRO, E134/10Geol/Mich 11.

[18] PRO, DL4/11/45, /12/10, /54/36; BL, Add. MSS 6667, fol. 235, 6682, fol. 168; PRO, E134/10Geol/Mich11, /9Geol/East6, /1GeoII/East2, /2GeoII/East7, /32GeoII/Trin1.

bounds some seventy years before. Robert Buxton's memory of his grandfather's words joined in his imagination with his subsequent use of the
commons: 'the reasons that move him to knowe the [bounds] are because
he hath ev[er] synce he was able contynually keepte cattle there and that his
grandfather . . . brought this depont to the said meares, and shewed him
the same'.[19] The apparently seamless continuity of custom and memory
helped to confirm the authority of the aged male voice within local society,
reinforcing their claims to the ownership of custom, and thereby community.[20] As an ideological claim, it was a powerful one. Yet that claim was
both contested and partly fictitious.

Despite insistence that customs were ancient, continuously exercised and
lay nowhere but 'in the memory of the people', in actuality many were
relatively recent, subject to continuous alteration, and known through
written documentation. Local inhabitants were highly sensitive to outside
alterations to custom partly because they themselves were so often changing their customs. In the 1620s, the powerful Foljamb family created a
sheepwalk upon land which they claimed as part of their manor of Elton.
The neighbouring villagers of Brassington, who believed the land to lie
within their commons, 'began to murmer at the Foljambs man and said
that in tyme they [the Foljambs] would gett in more shepe And soe create A
custome to keep sheepe there'.[21] The sensitivity to changes in landscape
and land use again suggest how deeply enmeshed were senses of local law
within the material environment. Similarly, the knowledge that custom
could be 'created' points to the sophisticated knowledge of legal principle
and precedent possessed by many early modern plebeians.

Social historians have begun to appreciate the extent to which early
modern popular culture was deeply influenced by the operation of the
criminal law.[22] The increasing intrusion of Westminster courts into local
law should be seen in the same light. While the gentry and nobility enjoyed
a basic advantage in legal proceedings concerning local custom, plebeian
claimants to custom none the less became deeply involved in such disputes,
and could emerge victorious.[23] Like the inhabitants of the Cambridgeshire

---

[19] PRO, DL4/56/17.
[20] For a fuller discussion of the theme, see K.V. Thomas, 'Age and authority in early modern
England', *Proceedings of the British Academy*, 62 (1976), 205–48.
[21] PRO, DL4/123/1685/2.
[22] See especially J.A. Sharpe, 'The people and the law', in B. Reay (ed.), *Popular culture in
seventeenth century England* (London, 1985), 244–70.
[23] On the even-handed attitude of central courts in Elizabethan and Jacobean disputes over
tenant right in the northern border counties, see R.W. Hoyle, 'An ancient and laudable
custom: the definition and development of tenant right in north-western England in the
sixteenth century', *P&P*, 116 (1987), 24–55; *idem*, 'Lords, tenants and tenant right in the
sixteenth century: four studies', *Northern History*, 20 (1984), 38–63.

fens, the litigiousness of the Peak's inhabitants was well known. In 1618, difficulties arose between the Rowland Eyre, lord of Hassop, and the inhabitants of the neighbouring village of Ashford over the right to the commons which separated the two settlements. Two poor miners of Ashford met with Eyre to discuss the case. The record of their conversation reveals something of popular attitudes to and knowledge of the law. Eyre insisted to them that he possessed written proof of his rights, to which the miners 'said it is verie strange that you have such a deed & never before claymed nor occupyed the same accordinge to your deed . . . yt is likelie if there had been anye such deed the same would have been shewed before now'. The miners' truculent scepticism produced Eyre's condescending advice that 'If you be wronged the lawe is open for you.' The Ashford men scarcely needed the encouragement. As we shall see in Chapter 10, by 1618 the inhabitants of that village had established a strong tradition of collective litigiousness.[24]

Custom was not inherently plebeian. Elsewhere in early modern England, lords and employers were able to make arguments through custom which undercut popular rights. Within elite political discourse, opponents of the pretensions of the early Stuarts drew upon the language of custom to define the rights of the subject. But in the Peak, the conceptual and organizational apparatus of custom became the contested possession of miners, tenants and cottagers. Although such people possessed a considerable knowledge of the operation of common law and central Westminster courts, and were more than willing to take cases to them, it is important that many exhibited a wariness towards such legal fora. Similarly, the Peak's gentry and nobility tended to see local custom as a primarily plebeian preserve. When Thomas Bagshawe of Ridge Hall bought the manor of Litton 'beinge desirous to informe himselfe of the meares & boundaries of the said mannor' he asked the advice of 'divs ancient inhabitants thereabouts'. Clearly, Bagshawe paid insufficient attention to his tenants' advice, for lord and tenant were soon at one another's throats over Bagshawe's attempted enclosure of Litton's commons. The close sense of space which custom engendered was held to by settled plebeians, and occasionally revealed to their social betters. In the 1680s, when the gentleman Adam Eyre told his shepherd Thomas Stone to put sheep upon a sheepwalk established by the Foljambs some sixty years earlier, Stone advised him against such a course of action, pointing out that the litigious inhabitants of Brassington still claimed the land as part of their common, and were certain to sue.[25]

[24] W. Cunningham, 'Common rights at Cottenham and Stretham in Cambridgeshire', *Camden Miscellany*, new ser., 12 (1910), 177; PRO, C21/D1/13.
[25] PRO, C21/D1/13; PRO, STAC8/64/4, 271/3, 51/15; PRO, DL4/123/1685/2.

Yet the gentry and nobility could have a most dramatic effect upon local custom. In enclosing land, they could dissolve the system of boundaries and markers by which the defenders of custom wrote their rights upon the landscape. By breaking or undermining local systems of courts and offices, they could annihilate the organizational focus for local memory. More positively, through negotiation and compromise with their tenants, they could take part in the constant redefinition of living custom. Agreements between lord and tenant, lists of manorial by-laws, proceedings of Great Barmote sessions or codified undertakings before the Court of Chancery all formed new layers in the crust of custom.[26] Customaries tend to present themselves in a deliberately prosaic format, clothing themselves in the consensual fabric of common-sense in order to claim an immemorial authority. But as every claim to common sense will tend to, they thereby conceal their ideological quality. In reality, accounts of local custom often covered over simmering conflict, lauding manorial authority as the gracious grantor of customs which had in fact been won through protracted dispute.

Custom therefore codified relations of subordination and exploitation, drawing a 'line of right', which continued to shift in tune with balances of power. Custom helped to establish local social identities, and maintained rules for the proper conduct of social relations. Thus in 1747, the miner William Hooson lauded the miners' barmote court as 'the only bulwark that preserves the miner in his privileges, and the lord in his right'.[27] Just as the relationship between miner and lord was charged with conflict, so the place of the barmote court and of mining custom itself came to form the key terrain over which the character of that relationship, and thereby the ownership and control of one of early modern England's most important industries, was decided.

'TIME OUT OF MEMORIE OF MAN': MINING CUSTOM IN THE EARLY SIXTEENTH CENTURY

Like so many other systems of customary law, that upon which Derbyshire's free miners founded their unusual rights was born out of conflict and accommodation. The origins of the right of free mining were, and remain, shrouded in mystery. The lawyer, antiquarian and opponent of free mining George Hopkinson wrote in 1644 that the miners' customs originated with the Druids. In 1735, Richard Spenser argued that the barmote court had its

---

[26] For a contextualized example, see M. Zell, 'Fixing the custom of the manor: Slindon, West Sussex, 1568', *Sussex Archaeological Collections*, 122 (1984), 101–6.

[27] Hooson, *Miner's dictionary*, 9.

origins in the Roman period. Both Spenser and Hopkinson pointed to the Saxon origins of so many mining terms as evidence of an important later influence. Most modern historians link the peculiar freedoms allowed under barmote custom to the introduction of Viking Danelaw within the Peak in the ninth century.[28] Whatever their origins, the earliest surviving law code dealing with mining custom was that which resulted from the Quo Warranto proceedings of 1288. In the course of these proceedings, which initially concerned a dispute between the High Peak miners and a lord over the right of free mining in Mandale rake near Youlgreave, the miners' customs received official sanction for the first time. As such, the provisions of the 1288 Quo Warranto represent a significant moment in the development of mining custom. They are also important in understanding changes in early modern attitudes to custom in the Peak, as they were taken throughout the 1520–1770 period to form the legal core of the miners' customs. Most importantly, the Quo Warranto proceedings did not grant rights to the miners: rather, they codified existent practice established 'time out of memorie of man'.[29] The fourteen regulations of the Quo Warranto implicitly allowed the miners to dig for ore wherever it was to be found within the lead field, regardless of the tenure of the land, but only with the lord's permission. In return for this right, and for the right to take timber from the lord's woods, the miner paid a lot duty of one thirteenth of his lead production. The buyer of ore also paid a cope duty of four pence per load. The 1288 proceedings formed part of a broader process across the Peak in the late thirteenth century, in which lords sought to define their powers and dues more closely.[30] The object of the proceedings was not, therefore, to define popular freedoms, but rather to describe the extent and character of dues which flowed to the lord from the miner. None the less, the Quo Warranto came to form an important legal bulwark to the miners' rights.

The provisions of the 1288 Quo Warranto were modified and extended over succeeding centuries, such that the Duchy of Lancaster ordered the

[28] G. Hopkinson, *The laws and customs of the mines within the Wapentake of Wirksworth* (1644, repr. Nottingham, 1948), 1, 3; BL, Add. MSS 6668, fols. 506–7, 6681, fols. 201–5; Raistrick and Jennings, *Lead mining*, 93; R.R. Pennington, *Stannary law: a history of the mining law of Devon and Cornwall* (Newton Abbot, 1973), 12–13; M. Daniel, 'The origin of the Barmote court system: a new theory', *BPDMHS*, 8, 3 (1982), 168–70; *idem*, 'The early lead industry and the ancient demesne of the Peak', *BPDMHS*, 8, 3 (1982), 166–7; E. Miller and J. Hatcher, *Medieval England: rural society and economic change, 1086–1348* (London, 1978), 120.

[29] On the background to the 1288 Quo Warranto, see J.H. Rieuwerts, 'The Inquisition or Quo Warranto of 1288', *BPDMHS*, 7, 1 (1978), 41–9; A. Henstock, 'The Ashbourne inquiry of 1288: a reply', *BPDMHS*, 7, 2 (1978), 96–9.

[30] PRO, DL41/6/9, /18/20; DRO, D258M/38/19.

creation of further customaries at some point in the 1490s,[31] and again in 1525.[32] Comparison of their provisions is instructive. As with the 1288 proceedings, those of the 1490s and 1525 followed protracted conflict: in the 1490s, over the physical extent of the Duchy's manor of Wirksworth, and in the 1520s over the level at which cope payments should be set.[33] Both followed the basic principles of the 1288 Quo Warranto, specifying in greater detail the frequency of barmote meetings and the duties of the barmaster. But there were important changes. Included amongst the twenty-eight regulations laid down in the 1490s customary was an injunction that 'First att the tyme that myne was founde of new in the Feyld the marchandes & the myners chussyn a Berthemast.' The customary of 1525 echoed this reflection upon the past, stating that by ancient custom the miners and merchants ought to elect the barmaster, but that the right had been lost. Both customaries agreed a novel and harsh punishment for the third act of theft of ore from a mine, by which the right hand of any thief 'shalbe putt threw owte the Ball of the hand wt a knyf so he shalbe stykke in the stows [that is, crucified upon the timber stows which marked possession of the mine] to the haft of the knyfe & shall remaine ther tyll he be ded or elss tyll he have put hym selve from the knyfe'. The customaries therefore assumed that the maintenance of the criminal law 'upon the myne' was the unambiguous responsibility of the barmaster. Of the right of free mining, the customaries stated simply that the miner may 'sorche whether he may fynd owre'.

The 1525 customary went on to ordain that the lord should keep a standard measuring dish by which the measurement of all ore sales had to be conducted. Such a dish had already been granted to the Wirksworth miners in 1512 by Henry VIII in his right as Duke of Lancaster, with a written statement of its authority running around its sides. Known as the

---

[31] The original is at PRO, DL41/11/27, and is described as a customary of the mines 'in the peeke'. For an early seventeenth-century transcription of the customary, see BL, Add. MS 6704, fols. 115–16. Blanchard, in 'Rejoinder', 70, claims that the attribution of the customary to Derbyshire is mistaken, and that it in fact describes the customs of the Flintshire lead mines. But see aged Wirksworth miners' recollections in the 1520s of a visit by the Chancellor of the Duchy, Sir Reginald Bray, to inquire into their customs, when they produced 'a copye of their Chartr', which Sir Reginald took to London: PRO, STAC2/15/141–9. Bray was Chancellor between 1485 and 1504, and was given the 'rule and reform' of the Honour of Tutbury, which included the Duchy's Derbyshire estates, on 16 March 1493. See R. Somerville, *History of the Duchy of Lancaster*, I: *1265–1603* (London, 1953), 260–95, 392. Furthermore, many of the provisions of the *c.* 1490s customary were repeated by the Great Barmote of 1525.

[32] BL, Add. MS 32465, fols. 2–4. This is a transcript of 1620, and was probably drawn up by Duchy commissioners searching into the mining customs at that time. See PRO, DL5/27, pp. 704, 720, 733, /28, fol. 468.

[33] See Chapter 9.

'King's dish', like the 1288 Quo Warranto it became a powerful symbol of the royal authority which underwrote the miners' customs. A further change came with the unusual claim that all miners held rights of pasture upon the commons. Taken together, the customs of 1525 and the 1490s therefore stated the means by which this bounded industrial democracy of small producers ordered themselves and their industry. In some clauses, the customaries seemed to describe everyday practice. In others, such as the claimed right of election over the office of barmaster, or in the right of all miners to pasture upon the commons, they recounted the ideal at which the miners aimed. Yet compared to the barmote by-laws of the later seventeenth and eighteenth centuries, those of the 1490s and 1525 seem rudimentary, laying down general principles rather than specific rights and firm practice. It was only as the miners became increasingly enmeshed in disputes before Westminster courts over their laws that firmer and more exclusive rights became specified.

In spite of the continuing claim that the body of free mining custom was of ancient origin and subject to continuous use, important changes occurred in its operation and definition in the mid-sixteenth century. These changes were to lay the cultural and legal basis for the emergence of the miners as a collective political agent in the early seventeenth century. For all their contemporary importance in defining the state of mining law, the 1490s and 1525 customaries contributed little to the future development of customary law, or to the free miners' collective identity. Both customaries were collectively forgotten by the miners after the mid-sixteenth century, to be replaced by fuller recodifications of custom initiated by the Great Barmote of Wirksworth in 1549 and 1557.[34] As with the earlier customaries, the recodification of mining law which occurred between 1549 and 1557 was the consequence of local conflict. Continuing dispute over the barmasters' right to take lot and cope payments resulted in the first cases concerning Peak mining custom being heard before the Court of the Duchy of Lancaster in Westminster. Some miners and orebuyers resented the intrusion of the Duchy Court into their affairs, and declared against its authority to adjudicate in the matter, claiming that the Great Barmote was the proper court to hear all mineral disputes.[35] At the same time, a long-running dispute between powerful rival Brenner families over Dale mine, coupled with the vaguely specified limits of the Duchy's manor of Wirks-

---

[34] Printed copies of both the 1549 and 1557 laws are to be found in BL, Add. MS 6682, fols. 72–75. For the original of the 1549 laws, see DRO, D258M/38/1. For a manuscript copy of the 1549 laws, see BL, Add. MS 32,465, fols. 4–7. The 1557 laws were repeated verbatim in the customs of 1566. See Nottingham UL, Middleton MS., 4/126/11.

[35] PRO, DL1/28/B10a, /11/B6a.

worth, also raised doubts over aspects of the mining code.[36] It is important to bear in mind that at this point the lead field under exploitation had been reduced to a small area within the Wapentake of Wirksworth which was almost coterminous with the Duchy's manor of Wirksworth. Within the High Peak, where the majority of lead deposits lay within non-Duchy manors, the industry was extinct.

Coupled with important judgements of the Duchy Court in the 1530s and 1540s, the 1549 and 1557 customs established the Duchy Court as a superior body over the Great Barmote. For the next century, the Duchy Court was the final court of appeal in Peak Country mining matters. In itself, this was an important step in the local, piecemeal process of English state formation, and should be linked to the growing importance of the Duchy Court in other respects.[37] Deletions from the earlier body of mining custom were as significant as additions. The 1549 and 1557 Great Barmotes made no claim to elect the barmaster. The barmaster's authority upon the mine was more closely defined, and the punishment of any felony upon the mines including the theft of ore was transferred to the local common law. Henceforward, the punishments available to the barmaster and barmote were restricted to the imposition of fines or the use of the stocks. Again, this represented a significant extension of the authority of the common law. The barmote jurors compensated themselves by taking new powers. The barmaster was to choose four jurors to cross the lead field and indict offenders against custom. A clearer distinction emerged between Great Barmotes, which were to meet twice a year to hear major cases and to initiate new by-laws, and small barmotes which dealt with the day-to-day running of the industry. Furthermore, the 1549 and 1557 Great Barmotes drew sharper distinctions between the miners and both their social superiors and inferiors. New by-laws prevented merchants from touching the King's dish or approaching the miners' works without permission. A further by-law instructed gentry mine-owners to keep their works in proper order. Three new by-laws were directed against the 'cavers' and 'purcassers' who dug the miners' rubbish tips for scraps of ore. Like the merchants, they were prevented from approaching the miners' works, and under an order that 'noe psone or psones shall from hensforth cave in any

---

[36] BL, Add. MS. 6669, fol. 27, 6678, fols. 35–8; DRO, D258M/64/48; PRO, STAC2/23/307; PRO, DL3/2/F3; PRO, DL1/29/G2, /28/B10a, /34/L6; Blanchard, 'Derbyshire lead production', 121. Kiernan has claimed that an act of parliament of 1554 recodified mining custom within the Wapentake of Wirksworth. See his *Lead industry*, 9. I can find no evidence of parliamentary involvement in the matter, either in the sources cited in support of this claim, or elsewhere. I was earlier led into error on the matter: see Wood, 'Custom, identity and resistance', 269–70. On the background to the recodification of the customs, see Chapter 9.

[37] R. Somerville, 'The Duchy of Lancaster Council and the Court of the Duchy Chamber', *Transactions of the Royal Historical Society*, 4th ser., 23 (1941), 159–77.

mynrs groundes or ells whear upon paine to forfett the oar to them that will take the same from the cavers', any support for the cavers from wealthier orebuyers was closed off. Most importantly, the 13th injunction of the 1557 Great Barmote specified

that yt is Lawfull for all the King and Quenes Liege people to digg, delve, serch, subvert, & turn up all mannr of groundes, Landes medowes Closures pastures Mores & Marsh for Oer myne wthin the said wapentag of wirkesworth of whose soev. inheritance or possessions the same.

This 13th injunction came to occupy as important a position in the miners' legal defence of their customs as the 1288 Quo Warranto. In undercutting the rights of the landowner, it amounted to the clearest expression of the principle of free mining. This right was unequivocally stated to operate across the whole of the Wapentake of Wirksworth, regardless of manorial distinction. Upon the revitalization of the High Peak lead industry, the 13th injunction became the basis of the miners' claim that their rights extended across the whole lead field.

Analysis of the jury lists of the 1549 and 1557 Great Barmotes shows that they were made up of the same class of men who dominated the lead mining industry in the mid-sixteenth century: established free miners, possessing close links with other villagers who sat on courts baron and acted as Headboroughs. Many held copyhold land, though freeholders were unusual. Such relatively poor but independent men formed the core of barmote juries into the seventeenth and eighteenth centuries.[38] The customs of 1549 and 1557 became the basis for subsequent mining law within the King's Field, and were widely copied during the codification of the mining customs of non-Duchy manors in the late sixteenth and early seventeenth centuries. Typically, the Great Barmote of a manor, comprised of twenty-four jurors, met every year to restate existing custom, and to consider the introduction of new by-laws. Small barmotes of twelve jurors met more often to decide cases concerning debt, trespass or other aspects of the day-to-day running of the industry.[39] Jurors were selected by the barmaster, who in non-Duchy manors was appointed by the lord. On the Duchy's estates, after the 1530s the lease of the lot and cope of the King's Field in the High Peak or Wirksworth Wapentake carried with it the right of appointment of the barmaster. Due to the size of the Duchy's King's Fields, the barmaster was assisted by deputy barmasters who were responsible for the collection of lot and cope and for the maintenance of mineral law within an individual village. Deputy barmasters were typically free miners themselves. The system was open to abuse. Allegations of corrup-

---

[38] Wood, 'Industrial development', 162–4; for the eighteenth century, see DRO, D504/L24.
[39] For business conducted in small barmotes, see SA, Bag C 702 (1).

tion against barmote jurors were not uncommon.[40] It was possible for the barmaster to ensure the passage of controversial by-laws by packing barmote juries.[41] Similarly, the barmaster could use the office to intimidate the mining workforce; but as we shall see in Chapters 9 and 10, the barmasters' success in such ventures was far from guaranteed. None the less, the miners grew to dislike the power concentrated in the hands of the gentry through their control of the office of barmaster, and by the middle of the seventeenth century, encouraged by the discovery of the forgotten customaries of 1525 and *c*. 1490, were demanding the right to elect the barmaster from amongst their own number.

In origin and spirit, Derbyshire mining law was egalitarian and democratic. For all its antiquity, it was no anachronism. Rather, mining custom developed into a flexible system which allowed miners both individual and collective agency. By 1557, the mining laws of the King's Field granted unusual freedoms to men of comparatively low rank. Those freedoms defined the miners as an identifiable collectivity in local society. Free mining liberated the miners from the discipline of an agrarian manorialism while barmote law institutionalized and legitimated their collective independence. Over the succeeding two centuries, the free mining code changed in important respects. But its basic function as a means of legitimating and organizing the free miners' rights and collective identity did not alter. It should not, therefore, be surprising to find that almost all of the Peak Country's gentry and nobility remained consistently hostile to the custom of free mining over the whole of our period.

'A KIND OF LEVELLING CUSTOM': THE OPPONENTS OF FREE MINING

We have seen in Chapter 5 that the provisions and principles of free mining custom stood in opposition to the interests of many lords and investors. Attacks upon free mining took a variety of forms. Lords sought to raise dues upon the miners and, in the earlier part of our period, upon orebuyers as well. Alternatively, lords resurrected old rights of pre-emption on ore sales, then imposed such low prices upon the miners' ore as to reduce them to the status of wage labourers. Many lords banned free mining activity altogether, and employed wage labourers to work the mines. In some manors after the middle of the seventeenth century, wealthy freeholders defeated the miners' claims to mineral rights on their land, and leased the

---

[40] See for instance DRO, D258M/42/29e; PRO, DL4/105/1661/22, /66/6; BL, Add. MS 6678, fols. 83–130; PRO, STAC8/286/19.
[41] For an example, see Wood, 'Industrial development', 173–4.

land to mine investors. Elite hostility to mining custom was therefore partly driven by a desire for profit.

That hostility drew upon a second, deepening source. From the early seventeenth century, a blunt prejudice against custom showed itself amongst England's nobility and gentry. Gentlemen who had been taught to see commons, forests, moors and fens as the loci of rebellious and libertarian local cultures instinctively saw free mining in threatening terms.[42] This was as true of the free mining customs of the Forest of Dean and the Somerset Mendips as it was of the Peak Country. Here too free mining had secured a firm legal basis and a strong hold on male plebeian culture. Senses of rights and liberties grew from participation in mining courts which bore close similarities to the Derbyshire barmotes, and from collective political engagement against social superiors in defence of custom. In response, the opponents of free mining sought to excise custom from 'the myndes of the vulgar sort' through legal action in which free miners were likened to 'Robin Hoods' for their defence of such 'dangerous' customs.[43] Implicit before the civil war, these prejudices were given full voice in the late 1640s, when a section of the High Peak miners, in pressing their claim to free mining rights within the Earl of Rutland's Lordship of Haddon, allied themselves to the Leveller movement. The print debate which developed over the issue actively reflected the anxieties generated by the English Revolution. Just as Leveller and Independent had disagreed at Putney church in 1647 over the threat posed by democracy to property, so the conflict between miner and lord over the fields of Haddon in the autumn of 1649 seemed a microcosm of larger struggles over property, democracy, liberty and rights.

The miners were accused of attempting to 'destroy all property, the right of every Englishman' in their attempts to extend the King's Field on to the Earl's estates.[44] The laws of free mining were denounced as 'a strange custome, and sure inconsistent with property, that another should force the owner to doe what he conceives prejudiciall in his house or upon his ground, and deserves to be null'd'.[45] A petition of the major landowners in the High Peak explained how the free mining law threatened social stability, arguing that if 'all men . . . at their free wills against the lawe' be allowed to 'dig for lead mynes in any lands' then the result would be to 'increase the number of poore there, uppon pretence of being mynors and

[42] B. Sharp, 'Common rights, charities and the disorderly poor', in G. Eley and W. Hunt (eds.), *Reviving the English Revolution: reflections and elaborations on the work of Christopher Hill* (London, 1988), 107–38.
[43] Wood, 'Custom, identity and resistance', 254, 264.
[44] *A Modest Narrative*, 1–8 Sept. 1649, BL, TT E. 572 (28).
[45] *The Modest Intelligencer*, 30 Aug.–6 Sept. 1649, BL, TT E. 572 (26).

of searching for lead oare'.[46] Should the principle of free mining be extended to other industries, then the Many Headed Monster would seek the destruction of all property and order:

what can be more unjust than that mens estates should be taken from them and given to others. And why not mines of other nature, as Stone Coal and Iron stone be also claimed by the workemen and colliers to be divided amongst them as well as for Lead Oare; and so likewise for Allom, Fullers Earth or any other commodity which is in the hands of a few that many could willingly be made rich by them; though against the will of the owners, and why may not these serve as a leading case to divide even the land itself all the Kingdom over amongst the multitude who are far more in number and power, than the proprietors and owners of the land.[47]

The fount of this anarchy was the 'pretended' right of free mining which allowed 'many dissolute vagrant idle psons' to destroy lands 'where they have no just custome' to mine. Furthermore, a 'great confluence of idle and criminall psons' had been attracted by the free mining laws, 'by means whereof the said Countie swarmeth with infinite numbers of poore and idle vagrant people & groaneth under the burthen thereof'.[48] Barmote law was presented as illegitimate and the precedents on which it depended as irrelevant to proper legal process: 'the Barm(aste)r and myners cannot be indifferent and impartiall judges and jurors to trye their owne title and clayme in another mans soyle in their Barmote Court'. Similarly, the proofs on which mining custom rested were merely 'presentments of the miners themselves . . . which in judgment cannot prejudice much less conclude others rights'.[49] The connection established in the elite mind between free mining and levelling communism proved an enduring one, persisting into the Restoration and beyond, provoking one Attorney-General to remark that 'it was a kind of levelling custom thus to enter into a man's land and dig'.[50]

Yet for all the rage directed by early modern England's governing class against free mining custom, the social and ideological contract upon which government rested required that custom had to be disproven at law, rather than simply swept away. Attempts by lords or others at coercing miners into abandoning their customs generally proved fruitless. Moreover, since free mining custom was a form of manorial law, courts could not simply declare against the applicability of the custom within the Peak Country as a whole.[51]

---

[46] BL, Add. MS 6682, fol. 33.   [47] BL, Add. MS 6677, fol. 50.
[48] SA, Bag C 3438.   [49] BL, Add. MS 6677, fol. 51.
[50] Middle Temple Library, Treby's MS Reports 22–4 Chas II, fol. 744; I am grateful to Alan Cromartie for this reference. For further hostile legal comment on free mining, see BL, Add. MS 6681, fols. 1–6.
[51] In the same respect, litigation over tenant right in the late sixteenth century, or over gleaning in the late eighteenth century, concerned individual jurisdictions. See Hoyle, 'An ancient and laudable custom'; P. King, 'Gleaners, farmers and the failure of legal sanctions in England, 1750–1850', *P&P*, 125 (1989), 116–50.

The legal attack upon free mining was therefore piecemeal and protracted. Attempts to transfer jurisdiction over 'mineral cases' to courts other than the barmote formed a key element of the attack upon the miners' rights. As we have seen, by the middle of the sixteenth century the miners had been persuaded to accept the authority of the Duchy Court over the barmote. As a result, the Duchy Court became more familiar with free mining custom than other central courts. Indeed, by the early seventeenth century the Duchy Court had developed a protective policy towards mining custom, and had come to resent encroachment upon its jurisdiction over the matter just as much as the barmote had earlier in the century.[52] In their turn, miners became keen to defend the Duchy's authority over the barmote and mining custom.[53]

Thoroughly aware of how free mining custom was perceived by common law jurists to stand in opposition to property, opponents of the right sought to have cases heard before courts which were less familiar with the matter than was the Duchy Court.[54] In particular, the common law was favoured by many of the greater gentry who were either themselves Justices of the Peace, and thus were able to imprison or bind over miners for trespass on their estates, or who enjoyed personal friendships with members of the bench.[55] Certain Westminster courts, especially the Courts of Exchequer, King's Bench and Star Chamber, also proved popular with lords whose estates were threatened by free miners.[56] During the civil wars and Interregnum, central government also assumed the right to intervene in mining cases, and in every known case sided with the local elite.[57]

Very few miners could bear the costs of expensive action at common law and the Westminster courts, and for that reason in the early seventeenth century they collected 'common purses' to defend their customs at law. But after the decline of this tradition of collective organization, the mere threat of litigation on the part of the lord of a manor could be sufficient to frighten off potential claimants to the right of free mining.[58] For a poor miner, the effects of having a suit filed against him could be devastating. Non-appearance at court in London might result in imprisonment, and the

---

[52] For examples of the Duchy Court ordering a halt to proceedings in other courts, see PRO, DL5/33, fols. 516–17, /29, fol. 166.

[53] See for instance, BL, Add. MSS 6677, fol. 49, 6682, fol. 212.

[54] Hopkinson, *Laws and customs*, 4, 8.

[55] PRO, DL1/366, complaint of William Goodwin *et al.*, /293, complaint of Att.-Gen. v. Sir Fras. Foljamb *et al.*; PRO, DL4/123/1684/4, /84/24; PRO, DL5/33, fols. 516–17; BL, Add. MS 6681, fols. 139–45; PRO, E112/294/31; PRO, STAC8/73/4; PRO, C3/416/95; PRO, E134/17Chas I/Mich 4, /13Jas I/Mich 3.

[56] See for example PRO, E112/75/160; Kiernan, *Lead industry*, 27–8; PRO, REQ2/291/35; PRO, DL4/34/22.

[57] Willies, 'The working of Derbyshire lead mining customs', 151, and Chapter 12 below.

[58] PRO, DL1/293, complaint of Att.-Gen. v. Sir Fras. Foljamb *et al.*

costs of a legal defence could drag a man into debt. Many miners therefore decided to make a composition with their persecutors rather than face the courts.[59] The miners were quite aware that the law was being used as a coercive tool against them, to 'terrify' them into silence. The miners of the parishes of Bakewell, Hope and Tideswell believed that John Gell sought to defeat their opposition to his claim for the tithe of lead 'by terrifying the . . . poore myners by multiplicitie of suites & intollerable charges to so poore men (and thereby) obtain some order in this honorable court which might tend to the p(re)judice of all of the . . . myners'.[60] Conflicting plebeian and elite interests over mining custom therefore expressed differing attitudes to the law. In particular, the miners perceived the real disparity of power between themselves and their rulers as most visibly manifest in the law. Miners who were fighting the Earl of Rutland through the courts over the matter of free mining rights in Haddon lordship recognized his 'great power', adding that they 'shall not bee able to defend themselves in any trial here to bee brought'.[61] This was no pretended supplication designed to draw a reciprocal, sympathetic response from the Exchequer Court, but rather a hard-headed recognition of reality. The Earl and his powerful supporters had been able to prosecute and jail their opponents at King's Bench, Assizes, Quarter Sessions and the House of Commons through the greater power granted to them by their class position as lords, Justices of the Peace and 'rich and powerful' men.[62]

In the course of the English Revolution, the opponents of free mining secured an accidental but important victory. The authority of the Duchy Court, hitherto an important supporter of the miners' cause, was severely impaired by the events of the 1640s and 50s. As we shall see in Chapter 10, aside from those cases such as the Dovegang dispute of the 1630s in which the distorting influence of a powerful courtier made itself felt, prior to 1642 the Duchy Court had been relatively sympathetic towards the miners' customs, even going so far as to sanction the miners' collection of common purses to fund legal action against their enemies.[63] However, over the early seventeenth century, the Court had become associated with the perceived

---

[59] PRO, DL4/124/1686/7.
[60] PRO, C2/Jas I/G2/48. For other examples, see PRO, DL4/90/24; PRO, DL1/366, complaint of William Goodwin et al.
[61] PRO, E112/294/31.
[62] BL, Add. MS 6677, fol. 49. For examples of the Manners family using their positions as Justices to defend the Eyres' interests, see R. Meredith, 'The Eyres of Hassop, 1470–1640: I', DAJ, 2nd ser., 84 (1964), 26; idem, 'The Eyres of Hassop, 1470–1640: II', DAJ, 2nd ser., 85 (1965), 75; PRO, STAC8/128/12.
[63] PRO, DL5/30, fol. 100, /26, fols. 164, 388.

arbitrary pretensions of Charles I and his father. Within Derbyshire, as elsewhere, it had been used to extort new payments from tenants, and to crush those local customs which were judged to stand in the way of the interests of powerful courtiers. Parliamentarians therefore came to see the Duchy Court as an arm of prerogative power, and it was abolished in the course of the English Revolution. Although it was re-established in 1657, the volume of business with which it dealt was a mere shadow of that prior to 1640.[64] Coupled to this, in an important ruling concerning free mining in the Wapentake of Wirksworth in July 1642, the Duchy Court decided to follow the precedent of the Court of Exchequer rather than its own practice and founded its support for free mining custom upon the King's interest as lord of the manor of Wirksworth, rather than upon 'prescripcion' as hitherto.[65] The difference may seem obscure, but the effect was to remove the Duchy's capacity to support the miners' claim to a general custom of free mining across the whole of the lead field. The effects were felt in post-Restoration litigation, as lords whose territories within Wirksworth Wapentake had been subsumed into the Duchy's King's Field in the 1620s renewed legal opposition to the right of free mining. In every case heard by the Duchy Court concerning the right of free mining after 1660, the free miners were defeated, as the Court overturned its verdicts of the 1620s without explanation.[66] The effect of the legal change was seriously to impair the miners' ability to sustain their customs before the law.[67]

Despite Lord Hardwick's declaration in Chancery in 1743 that 'the mineral laws and customs [of Derbyshire] were as old as and part of the common law of England', the eighteenth century saw the removal of further legal supports to the right of free mining. Although central courts still operated on the principle that 'Immemorial custom, not contrary to express statute, is law', the expanding boundaries of statute law were increasingly redrawing the limits of accepted custom. Free mining law was criticized for its general nature, in allowing the right to 'be claimed by all the inhabitants of England . . . Customs must in their nature be confined to individuals of a particular description, & what is common to all mankind can never be claimed as a custom.' The eighteenth-century legal mind

---

[64] More research is needed on the Duchy Court in the sixteenth and seventeenth centuries. For litigation patterns, see PRO, IND1/16918–21.

[65] PRO, DL5/34, fols. 57, 64, 194–5. Contrast this verdict to that of seven years earlier, in the same case: PRO, DL5/32, fols. 94, 105.

[66] PRO, DL5/40, fols. 269–70; see also fols. 181, 387–8, 393, 428–30, /35, fol. 54, /37, fols. 129, 130, 159, 201, 205, 216, 218, 227; PRO, DL4/109/8, /123/1684/4, /124/1686/7, /120/ 1678/1.

[67] In his 1795 notes on the legal history of mining custom, the Derbyshire antiquary and lawyer William Woolley arrived at the same conclusion as that expressed here. See BL, Add. MS 6676, fols. 132–6.

which thought 'coincident use-rights to be untidy' saw in the 'loose' custom of free mining 'a heterogeneous mass of matter, valid and illegal, sensible and imperfect' which formed the antithesis of the dominant rationalizing, improving spirit of the age.[68]

The growing contradiction which occurred in the eighteenth century between the assumptions and values of equity and common law on the one hand and custom on the other found its fullest expression in protracted litigation which occurred between 1750 and 1776 over the rights of the cavers.[69] Since at least the 1530s, the small scraps of ore known as smitham which the poor cavers dug from rubbish tips had been exempt from payment of lot and cope duties. In 1750, claiming that the owners of the large Yatestoop mine in Winster had instructed their employees to break ore into small lumps of smitham so as to avoid payment of duties, the Duke of Devonshire initiated action at Chancery. Devonshire claimed that the exemption of smitham ore did not constitute a custom, but was instead an indulgence, or privilege, allowed by earlier lessees. The mine-owners and miners, united by their mutual opposition to the extension of lot and cope duties, combined in hostility to the Devonshires' case. Citing the Quo Warranto proceedings of 1288 as the ancient basis of their customs, the miners in their depositions, like the mine-owners in their written answers to Chancery, argued that the cavers' exemption originated beyond time out of mind. The case at Chancery lasted until 1760, when the Masters, influenced by the provisions of the Quo Warranto proceedings, issued an inconclusive judgement. Devonshire's attorney recognized that the case rested upon the 'Validity Authenticity etc.' of the 1288 Quo Warranto, and concluded that 'if we can shake that we destroy their Magna Charta & the basis of all their reasoning'. Devonshire therefore appealed to the House of Lords, who in a key ruling cast doubt upon the legal validity of the 1288 proceedings, and thereby upon the whole body of free mining law. The most important outcome of the 'smitham case' was to deal a body blow to the subsequent defence of mining custom before central law courts. By the early nineteenth century, the rights of the free miner were prejudiced at law by the privileged position occupied by the interests of the landholder and the mine investor, who as holders of definable, individualized property held a greater authority before law courts. Calls were heard for 'a speedy revisal and alteration of these Mining Laws', so that the 'free-booting practices' of the free miners which had 'become in numerous instances injurious to the progress of improvement' could be disposed with in the

---

[68] BL, Add. MSS 6681, fols. 1–6, 6685, fol. 180, 6676, fol. 132.; Thompson, *Customs in common*, 106.

[69] BL, Add. MSS 6682, fols 1–37, 6686, fols. 82–104, 6676, fols. 1–41, 44–49, 96–131.

interests of the 'enlarged System of Mining' practised by the mining companies.[70]

The attack on free mining law represented an important event in the long process of English state formation. As that conflict developed, contending notions of property and order came to blows, ultimately resulting in the marginalization of mining custom. The struggle for control of Derbyshire's lead mining industry was as much a clash between formal and informal legal systems, and between different senses of the law, as it was a jurisdictional dispute. The miners' customs were designed to maintain order amongst a community of small producers; the barmote court itself represented the institutionalization of a culturally bounded notion of industrial communalism. The gradual replacement of that mining code with a centrally organized legal system, evidentially founded upon written documentation, operated by and in the interests of the wealthy, mirrored the economic marginalization of the free miner. Changing senses of writing and speech in popular culture and legal process became intimately interwoven with that wider contest.

THE USES OF LITERACY: SPEECH, WRITING AND CUSTOM

Whereas in the seventeenth century the Peak Country's nobility and gentry regarded free mining as a levelling threat to private property and social order, in the eighteenth century they tended to see it as an irritating anachronism. Sir John Stathom of Wigwell Grange provides an extreme example. Obsessed with his own authority and lineage, he regarded the miners and their customs with distaste, describing them as 'clownes' and placing them 'amongst the dregs of mankind'. Stathom fancied himself an expert on mineral law, and in 1727 penned a series of biased and inaccurate notes on the subject. For Stathom, the oral basis of mining custom invalidated its authority and produced the miners' degenerate, backward and barbarous culture. Since the miners' customs were founded upon oral tradition, this meant that 'no record or footsteps remain . . . other than what occurs to everyone's memory'. Hence mining custom was 'all pompous pretence' without any real basis in law: 'the miners suck [their laws] up with their mother's milk . . . [they] look upon them as primary laws of nature, and cannot abide innovations . . . the [memory of the] oldest miner has superintendancy'.[71] Antiquity, community and orality, the

---

[70] J. Farey, *A general view of the agriculture and minerals of Derbyshire*, 3 vols. (London, 1815), II, 363–4, 357, 337–8; S. Glover, *The history and gazetteer of the county of Derby*, 2 vols. (Derby, 1829), I, 75.

[71] BL, Add. MS 6667, fol. 235, 6682, fol. 168; Scottish Record Office, GD 345/824: microfilm held in DRO, D2270/1.

very forces which held custom at the heart of local custom, seemed here to doom it.

In associating custom with oral tradition, Stathom merely reiterated a contemporary cliché. Eighteenth-century radicals who saw in free mining law the survival of a democratic, Saxon culture also regarded custom as dependent upon an authentic oral tradition. Robert Spenser's claim that 'The mineral laws in the times of our Saxon Ancestors were oral, certain and uncontroverted' allowed him to construct an opposition between the 'judgement of the plain-dealing miner' and the corrupt, class-based authority of the central legal system:

Antiently the English laws were made by Kings and their Privy Councils, and lately by Parliaments, which laws are imposed on the subject before any probation or trial whether they are beneficial to the nation, or agreeable to the nature and humour of the People, but Customes bind not the People, till they have been approved and tried time out of mind.

For Spenser, the superiority of custom drew from its uncorrupted basis, lying 'nowhere but in the memory of the People'.[72] Starting at quite different ideological positions, both Spenser and Stathom arrived at the same simplistic, idealized interpretation of the relationship between custom, speech and writing.

Back in 1644, William Hopkinson had also connected mining custom to oral tradition, stating that 'our Miners . . . have learned the Laws by Tradition and practice from one Generation to another, and have not learned the same out of any Books'. But he contradicted himself in his next breath, noting the miners' readership of 'some Articles . . . of Later times which every Miner hath Ready almost at his finger ends'.[73] The perception of custom as inherently antique and based solely upon 'the memory of the people' does not do justice to the constant dynamics within that system of local law. We have already seen how despite rapid change in the provisions of mining law in the early and mid-sixteenth century, it continued to be presented as ancient, immutable, and based upon oral tradition. Yet even at the beginning of our period, miners who spoke of an oral tradition which reached back to 'tyme out of mynde' in the next breath mentioned their knowledge of 'the charter of the myne'.[74] From the late sixteenth century, most aspects of customary law within the Peak became increasingly interwoven with writing.

---

[72] BL, Add. MSS 6668, fols. 506–7, 6681, fols. 189–5. On early modern idealizations of the Saxon past, see C. Hill 'The Norman yoke', in his *Puritanism and revolution: studies in interpretation of the English Revolution of the seventeenth century* (London, 1958), 58–125.

[73] Hopkinson, *Laws and customs*, 1.

[74] PRO, STAC2/15/141–9; PRO, DL1/10/F2c, /22/T2, /34/L6.

Over the course of the sixteenth and seventeenth centuries, central Westminster courts demanded more exact definitions of customary law. Where courts were unhappy with the amount or quality of written and depositional evidence supplied to them by litigants, they ordered searches of local and national archives.[75] As a result, a greater burden of evidence came to be placed upon writing in legal process. A flourishing trade in forged customaries was further stimulated, and allegations of the theft or destruction of key documents were not uncommon. This change in the evidential priorities of central courts gave the advantage to the gentry and nobility. The need for litigants to produce written evidence in bulk meant that the muniments rooms of great houses and the document chests of wealthier gentry families became sources of legal authority and thereby of cultural power. By the middle of the seventeenth century, many gentlemen within the Peak possessed some degree of legal training, and were in the habit of searching out and transcribing or preserving ancient documents which concerned local custom.[76] Chief amongst their concerns was the matter of free mining rights.

We might, therefore, be tempted to see writing as an agency of ruling-class power, providing both legal sanction and cultural authority to the appropriation of the collective resources. Were we to accept Sir John Stathom's description of custom as entirely oral, it would certainly seem that writing was synonymous with the interests of the nobility and gentry. But in fact, writing had been intimately intertwined with popular senses of custom from a very early date. We should rather see writing, like custom, as a contested category in the period. In that contest, the Peak's gentry possessed important advantages, one of which was related to the growing significance of the written word within legal process. Ownership of muniments provided the opponents of free mining rights with access to a larger body of written evidence. Furthermore, literacy played a considerably greater role within the culture of the Peak's gentry and nobility than it did within popular culture. Before we can comprehend the role played by writing in custom, we must therefore turn first to the changing distribution of literacy within the Peak, and to its meaning within popular culture.

If the ability to sign one's name can be taken as a rough indicator of literacy, the Peak Country's plebeian population in the late sixteenth and early seventeenth centuries appears as less touched by the general increase in literacy levels exhibited elsewhere within the period (see Table 6.2). Statistics for women's literacy are based on too small a sample to be

---

[75] For examples, see PRO, DL5/27, pp. 527, 630.
[76] Anthony Bradshawe, John Fern, and the Hopkinsons of Ible are outstanding examples. For the importance of estate stewards in preserving written documents, see PRO, DL4/56/12.

meaningful. But important geographical and occupational distinctions in the distribution of literacy are apparent amongst the Peak's male inhabitants in 1641–2 (see Table 6.3). The male householders of six mining villages set their marks or signatures to a petition in support of the Protestant religion which was sent to parliament in February 1642. The names of the householders of a further two mining villages who signed or marked their names in subscription to the Protestation of 1641 have also survived. These have been compared with the names of the miners in those villages as were listed in the miners' petition of 1641. The results enable us to discuss the distribution of literacy amongst miners and non-miners in 1641. Whereas about one third of male householders were able to sign their names across England as a whole in 1641–2, the average within the Peak's mining villages stood at only 19 per cent.[77] Closer scrutiny of local variations reveals that the householders of poorer, upland and more wage-dependent villages were considerably less likely to sign their names than were the householders of the more socially variegated, richer valley settlements. Similarly, with the exception of Ashford, miners were consistently less likely to sign their names than were other householders. If nothing else, the evidence of Table 6.3 suggests that one of the more accurate stereotypes applied to seventeenth-century Peak miners was that they were 'illiterate'.[78]

Writing was distant from the everyday lives of the people of the Peak Country before the civil wars. Qualitative evidence suggests that the only person likely to be able to read or write in the typical Peak village of the early and mid-sixteenth century was the priest, and it was to him that the inhabitants turned when they wanted a letter written or read. The larger market towns included lesser gentry with some legal training, who might find employment as clerks of court, but many transactions of property and rulings by local courts went unrecorded.[79] Indeed, it was the custom of the barmote that mineshares could be transacted 'by word of mouth' so as to avoid unnecessary expense.[80]

The miners' culture and the nature of their work gave a particular authority to speech. In spite of gentry opinion that 'The miner's Tearms are like to heathen Greek, Both strange and uncouth', their trade dialect was exact and functional.[81] Terminology existed for tools, types of deposits,

---

[77] D. Cressy, *Literacy and the social order: reading and writing in Tudor and Stuart England* (Cambridge, 1980), 73. See also R.A. Houston, *Scottish literacy and Scottish identity: illiteracy and society in Scotland and northern England, 1600–1800* (Cambridge, 1985).

[78] Hopkinson, *Laws and customs*, 7.

[79] On the role of priests, see PRO, DL3/54/F2, PRO, DL4/27/54, /32/25; DRO, D258M/59/14r, /64/48; on attorneys, see PRO, DL4/5/17.

[80] PRO, DL4/105/1661/22, /112/10; BL, Add. MS 6677, fols.177–90.

[81] E. Manlove, 'The liberties and customs of the lead mines within the Wapentake of Wirksworth', 1653, reprinted in W.W. Skeat (ed.) *Reprinted glossaries* (London, 1873), 19.

Table 6.2 *Literacy of Peak Country deponents at the Consistory Court of the Diocese of Coventry and Lichfield, 1593–1638*

	Men	Women	Total
Sign name	32 (25%)	0	32 (24%)
Mark name	94 (75%)	5 (100%)	99 (76%)
Total	126	5	131

Table 6.3 *Literacy in eight mining townships, 1641–2*

	Miners		Non-miners		Total	
Township	Sign	Mark	Sign	Mark	Sign	Mark
Ashford	15 (31%)	33 (69%)	16 (15%)	91 (85%)	31 (20%)	124 (80%)
Bakewell	7 (29%)	24 (71%)	46 (45%)	57 (55%)	53 (40%)	81 (60%)
Castleton	0	34 (100%)	30 (25%)	89 (75%)	30 (20%)	123 (80%)
Elton	1 (5%)	19 (95%)	9 (18%)	40 (82%)	10 (15%)	59 (85%)
Overhaddon	0	16 (100%)	1 (4%)	27 (96%)	1 (2%)	44 (98%)
Sheldon	4 (15%)	23 (85%)	4 (12%)	29 (88%)	8 (14%)	52 (86%)
Taddington	0	10 (100%)	5 (11%)	42 (89%)	5 (9%)	52 (91%)
Ashover	?	?	?	?	60 (20%)	239 (80%)
Total	27 (15%)	159 (85%)	111(23%)	375 (77%)	198 (20%)	774 (80%)

Sources: DRO, D2537/PI/1/1; DRO, D258/60/6; HLRO, MP 26 February 1642; PRO, E101/280/18.

mining operations, legal processes and for the huge variety of lead ores. Although many of these 'Miners Terms of Art' were Saxon in origin, developments in trade dialect suggested an underlying mutability to the miners' collective identity. That dialect allowed the miners to maintain and develop their highly sophisticated technical and geological knowledge. It possessed a dynamic which grew from the ever-increasing body of mining knowledge, expanding its range with the miners' finds.[82] The realization that lead deposits lay under shale surface cover, that distinct types of lead ore could be encountered, that the deposits followed particular courses through the rock, all occurred as a result of the miners' observations.[83] As

---

[82] Hooson's 1747 account lists a complex range of types of lead ore, earth, rock and other minerals such as Brassil ('a hard substance, and Fiery, and somewhat resembles Brass in colour') or Brown-Hen ('a hard kind of soil, of a brown colour, sticking hard to the ore'): Hooson, *Miners' dictionary*, 23.

[83] J.H. Rieuwerts, 'Derbyshire lead mining and early geological concepts', *BPDMHS*, 9, 2 (1984), 51–100.

we shall see in Chapter 8, many of the miners' early conceptions of geology were at least semi-magical. But their ideas served the practical purposes of the miner well, and were communicated through a trade dialect which gave the lie to claims that the miners lacked 'Elocution'.[84]

Unlike other parts of the country, the Peak did not experience an organized drive towards moral reformation in the early seventeenth century. None the less, a growing concern on the part of the few godly ministers of the area can be discerned with the education of the 'yonge'. The first grammar school to be established within the Peak was founded at Ashbourne in 1560, but it was not until the 1620s that such institutions flourished across the region. These catered for the sons of the lesser gentry and more prosperous yeomanry, and no doubt were responsible for the higher literacy rates apparent in the wealthier mining settlements in 1641–2. But it was not until after the Restoration that 'freeschools' catering 'for the better education of poor children' increased in number.[85] By the middle of the eighteenth century, the ability of Peak Country brides and grooms to sign the marriage registers of sampled parishes corresponded to the national average.[86] Furthermore, significant local and occupational differences had been abolished (see Table 6.4).

There was no educational revolution in the Peak Country during the seventeenth century. Instead, literate skills were gradually extended across key sections of the population. As Tables 6.2, 6.3 and 6.4 remind us, that process was coloured by gender, location, occupation and class. None the less, by the later seventeenth century the cumulative effect was to expand the place occupied by writing within local culture, and to increase the number of written documents in circulation within the Peak. The growing separation of labour from capital within the mining industry, together with its expanding size and output, generated increasing documentation such that by the last decades of the century many mines employed an 'accomptant'. From the middle of the seventeenth century, barmote courts started to record not only their customs but also their verdicts, jury lists and fines with greater regularity, and barmasters made a point of preserving notes of their decisions. Even free miners sometimes took to keeping detailed accounts of their small works.[87] A generational gap in understandings of local culture may have started to emerge. In 1614, five men gave evidence to the Duchy Court concerning the inheritance customs of Castleton. The

---

[84] Hopkinson, *Laws and customs*, 4.

[85] D. Robson, 'Some aspects of education in Derbyshire in the eighteenth century', PhD thesis, University of Sheffield, 1972, 22–3, 32, appendix.

[86] R.S. Schofield, 'Dimensions of illiteracy in England, 1750–1850', in H. Graff (ed.), *Literacy and social development in the West* (Cambridge, 1981), 201–13.

[87] PRO, DL4/112/10, /112/12, /121/1680/9, /120/1678/1, /120/1679/2, /117/8, /125/1689/2.

Table 6.4 *Literacy in three mining parishes, 1754–70*

(Showing ability of brides and grooms marrying in parishes of Wirksworth, Hope and Eyam to sign their own name.)

	Sign	Mark	Total
Brides	278 (26%)	778 (74%)	1,056
Grooms			
Manufacturing and mining			
lead miners	248 (59%)	174 (41%)	422
textiles	38 (68%)	18 (32%)	56
tailors, clothing	23 (82%)	5 (18%)	28
shoemakers	17 (63%)	10 (37%)	27
Agriculture			
farmers	52 (80%)	13 (20%)	65
yeomen	4 (80%)	1 (20%)	5
husbandmen	13 (43%)	17 (57%)	30
Professions, gentry	5 (100%)	0	5
Commerce			
merchants	3 (100%)	0	3
innkeepers	2 (100%)	0	2
bakers	11 (100%)	0	11
butchers	10 (83%)	2 (17%)	12
other	6 (75%)	2 (25%)	8
Tradesmen			
mason	9 (90%)	1 (10%)	10
blacksmith	13 (93%)	1 (7%)	14
chandler	3 (100%)	0	3
cordwainer	10 (55%)	8 (45%)	18
other	33 (81%)	8 (19%)	41
Others			
others	3 (38%)	5 (62%)	8
labourer	5 (42%)	7 (58%)	12
Unknown	62 (55%)	51 (45%)	113
Total	570 (64%)	323 (36%)	893

Note: brides and grooms whose place of habitation lay outside the parish or (in the case of Wirksworth) in chapelries beyond the lead field have not been included.
Sources: DRO, D2602A/PI/1/1, 3; DRO, D3105A/PI/1/5–6; DRO, D1828A/PI/1/3.

four oldest men, aged between fifty-one and seventy, all founded their knowledge of custom upon its ancient character, remembered time out of mind. The fifth deponent, aged twenty-five, also referred to an ancient custom proved time out of mind, but added that he was further induced to believe that custom to be true 'for that he hath seene and read dyvers copies of court roll' on the matter.[88] By 1735, not only did freeschools exist in many mining villages, but most of the main towns within the Peak actually possessed bookshops.[89]

In positing too sharp a distinction between literacy and illiteracy, historians may be guilty of anachronism. Modern conceptualizations of reading as an individualized and silent moment of intellectual revelation may not be readily transferable into the early modern past. A more sensual feel for literacy is revealed in the depositions of literate Peak plebeians, who spoke of having heard and seen a document in very similar terms as did their illiterate neighbours. Furthermore, there existed different levels of literacy. Some men, and rather fewer women, were fully literate in that they were able to write and to read both the written and printed word. Others could comprehend only printed text, whereas others still could make no sense of any writing. Yet the illiterate were also touched by the growing importance of writing within popular culture. One deputy barmaster overcame his illiteracy by employing his teenage son to write his accounts.[90] An orebuyer kept a record of his purchases and calculations upon a tallying stick.[91] The documentation is replete with examples of documents being read to illiterate men and women by their literate neighbours.

A slow transition was underway over the course of our period, in which literacy shifted from a position which touched tangentially upon cultural practice, to occupy, instead, a key site within local popular culture. As a consequence of that process, written documents changed from being unusual, prized objects, to become everyday, functional tools. Yet while literacy changed popular culture in general, and ideas about custom in particular, it did not overwhelm oral tradition. Literacy did not displace orality, nor was there any necessary conflict between the two within popular culture. Instead, writing and speech acted together to sustain custom and local memory. That written documents were referred to as 'remembrances' was no accident, for writing was conceived of within plebeian culture 'an adjunct to memory', rather than its 'replacement'.[92] In the clearest instance of how orality and literacy could be drawn together in the maintenance of collective memory, in 1653 Edward Manlove, a Wirks-

---

[88] PRO, DL4/62/21.   [89] BL, Add. MS 6668, fol. 507.
[90] LJRO, B/C/5/1623 Bonsall.   [91] PRO, C3/416/95.
[92] Fentress and Whickham *Social memory*, 9–10.

worth gentleman, produced a printed account of the mining laws. The laws were laid out in verse so as to aid their memorization by literate and illiterate alike, and provided a description of the customs and their historical and legal bases. By the eighteenth century, the rhyming customs were being cited as preambles to barmote by-laws, and were reprinted as late as 1809.[93]

The growing importance of writing in the articulation of custom was paralleled by its increasing significance within local culture. Down to the 1590s, the defenders of free mining custom made only fleeting and vague reference to the written evidence which supported their laws. There seems to have been a general awareness that the 'Myne Charter' gave legal sanction to free mining, but its exact provisions were unclear to miners, who instead tried to legitimize their customs with reference to their ancient usage. Where miners referred to the Quo Warranto proceedings, or to the recodified customs of the 1490s, 1549 or 1557, it was on the basis of their sight of such documents in the possession of the barmaster. Anxious to find proof of the longevity of custom, miners could point only to 'old hooles and grooves' which had been worked 'in ancient tyme'.[94] By a generation later, all that had changed. Between the late 1580s and the middle of King James' reign, the miners arrived at a close, specific and legally meaningful definition of their existent customs. As we will see in Chapters 9 and 10, this development formed an important part of the miners' growing political assertiveness. At the core of the assertion of the miners' new collective identity of the early seventeenth century sat a popularized reading of two documents: the 1288 Quo Warranto proceedings, and the provisions of the Great Barmote of Wirksworth of 1557. The former was the earliest written expression of the miners' laws, the latter the tightest statement of their claim to universal free mining rights across the whole of the Peak Country.

In the years before the civil war, manuscript copies of the 1557 by-laws and the 1288 Quo Warranto proceedings circulated amongst the mining workforce, passed from one miner to another and read aloud at barmote sessions.[95] Duchy commissioners inquiring into the legal basis of mining custom were led immediately to the Quo Warranto proceedings by the miners.[96] Knowledge of the Quo Warranto and the 1557 Great Barmote's laws formed the rich soil of customary consciousness from which the

---

[93] Manlove, 'Customs'; BL, Add. MS 6674, fols. 126–30; Hooson, *Miners' dictionary*, 9; SA, TC 366(6). For Manlove, see Newton, 'Gentry', 24.

[94] PRO, DL1/34/L6, /22/T2, /11/B6a, /10/F2, /2/F3i; PRO, E134/32&33Eliz/Mich 28; PRO, E178/611.

[95] PRO, DL4/72/31; for seventeenth-century manuscript copies of the 1288 Quo Warranto, see DRO, D258M/38/1; BL, Add. MS 32465, fols. 1–2.

[96] PRO, DL44/390; PRO, DL41/17/19.

miners' political assertion grew. Raphe Oldfield of Litton, who for over thirty years stood at the forefront of resistance to lords, tithes and enclosures in the High Peak, knew the customs of the King's Field by heart from having 'hard the Quowarranto read touchinge the lead mynes & the liberties therof'. To Martin Hallom of Bradwell, the Quo Warranto was 'the most ancient record for the customes of the mynes that this deponent ev[er] did see', and from them he had 'credibly hard . . . the ancient customes'.[97] On the basis of his reading of the provisions of the 1557 Great Barmote, Hallom developed an argument in favour of the extension of free mining rights across the whole of the lead field. Other miners followed Hallom in defining a general 'Custome of the *myne*' which took precedence over a particular 'Custome of the mannor'.[98] The difference was important, for it enabled the miners to transcend the localism typically inherent to the politics of custom.

The codification of custom therefore represented rather more than its simple transcription. It had the potential to provide custom with a solidity and uniformity which was important to the miners' collective political project. The extensive circulation of hand-written copies of the Quo Warranto and the 1557 Great Barmote by-laws, and their regular reiteration at barmote meetings, had the effect of forming key reference points which unified demands for free mining rights. After the mid-1590s, commissioners for depositions recorded the reflexive, standardized responses of miners who had been asked to state the basis of their claim to free mining rights. Their answers amounted to near-exact reiterations of the provisions of the 13th by-law of the 1557 Great Barmote which had provided the first full statement of the claim to free mining rights.[99] Of equal importance, the provisions of the 13th by-law of 1557 were repeated by Great Barmote courts empanelled to draw up mining customs for High Peak manors in the early seventeenth century.[100] Such repetitions helped to provide the miners' claims to 'ancient' customs with a spurious authenticity.[101]

The standardizing effects of the written word upon custom were given a powerful boost by the publication of the first printed version of the mining customs in 1645. Entitled *The liberties and customs of the miners*, it was written and published by William Debankes, a wealthy free miner and orebuyer of Cromford. He jointly operated a working in Elton with John Lowe, a prominent opponent of the lead tithe in the High Peak, and had

[97] PRO, E134/4ChasI/Mich33; PRO, DL4/64/11, /64/12/4.
[98] PRO, DL4/67/62, /71/36, /69/51.
[99] See for instance PRO, DL4/75/10.
[100] J. Mander, *The Derbyshire miners' glossary* (Bakewell, 1824), 119–20; BL, Add. MS 6676, fol. 144; SA, TC 366(6).
[101] BL, Add. MS 6678, fols. 149–52; PRO, DL4/66/6.

himself been prosecuted at the Court of Chancery in 1629 as a leader of tithe resisters in Wirksworth. The knowledge of mining law which Debankes exhibited in his pamphlet was strengthened by his service as a barmote juror.[102] The *Liberties and customs* was produced in the course of the long-running dispute between the High Peak miners and the Earl of Rutland, and due to its wide circulation was reprinted in 1649. Its object was to demonstrate that the custom of free mining had applied 'time out of memorie of man in all the territories and liberties of the High Peake' and to further knowledge of custom by supplying the miners with printed versions of the most important documents concerning mining law. It therefore included transcriptions of the 1288 Quo Warranto and the Wirksworth customs of 1549 and 1557. In spite of attacks upon its authenticity, the popularity of the pamphlet was undiminished years later, as over the course of the later seventeenth and eighteenth centuries miners produced the printed pamphlet in defence of their rights, explaining how they had 'oft read' its contents.[103] Later printed versions of the laws followed, breeding a still more standardized knowledge of local law.

As a means of propagandizing its audience, printed versions of mining custom were superior to the earlier hand-written customs. The limited literacy of many miners had prevented them from making sense of the hand-written laws: William Booth explained in 1623 that although he possessed a copy of the 1557 customs, he could not decipher it since 'he cannot read written hand'. Clearly his memory was superior to his reading, since he was able to confirm all thirty-one points of the customs.[104] It was to benefit men such as Booth that Debankes printed his pamphlet, 'beinge a Grand Juryman & willing to pleasure many myners that could not write or read Written hand'.[105] Yet we should not overstate the standardizing effects of print, nor come to see its force as overriding local identity and difference.[106] Published accounts of mining custom allowed the miners to develop firmer definitions of local custom as it operated *within* the Peak Country. The effects of print upon local culture were to homogenize its internal content, while hardening the spatial boundaries within which local identity was defined.

The effects of writing and print upon local identity were therefore ambiguous. So, too, was the relationship between the miners and their legal

---

[102] For a copy of the 1645 pamphlet, see BL, Add. MS 6682, fols. 65–75. On Debankes, see PRO, E101/280/18; DRO, D258M/28/20a, /48/36; PRO, DL4/112/13, /109/8; PRO, DL30/54/669; BL, Add. MS 6677, fols. 1–8.

[103] BL, Add. MSS 6677, fol. 51, 6682, fols. 65–75; PRO, DL4/117/8, /125/1689/2, /123/1684/4, /112/10.

[104] PRO, DL4/72/31.   [105] PRO, DL4/117/8.

[106] As some historians have been prone to: see for instance Johnson, *Archaeology of capitalism*, 196; Rollison, *Local origins*, 14.

advisers. By the early seventeenth century a powerful sense of rights and legality constituted the centre of the miners' political culture and collective identity. We will see in Chapter 10 that local attorneys could be very important in guiding the miners towards fuller knowledge of their customs. Bluntly posed, we must therefore ask to what extent the miners' legalism was handed to them by better schooled local gentry. It is possible to answer that question with close reference to the discussion of mining law provided by one leading gentry expert on mining law, John Ferne of Hopton.

John Ferne enjoyed close, warm relations with many miners in Wirksworth, and sided with them in a number of important legal disputes. He was possessed of some legal knowledge and made a habit of collecting and transcribing historical documents. He seems to have built up a small archive, to which he would refer in the construction of legal arguments. In a protracted and rambling deposition to a Commission of the Court of the Duchy of Lancaster in 1623, Ferne provided the most influential reading of mining custom in the early modern period. In this evidence, he demonstrated that the right of free mining predated the 1288 Quo Warranto proceedings, and that it had at one time extended across the whole lead field.[107] Like the miners, he saw the Quo Warranto proceedings of 1288 as central to his case, and from a close textual study of its contents argued that since free mining had been practised 'in the beginning . . . before any deeds or charters were made', so 'yt ought to be so still to this day'. Ferne's reading of the Quo Warranto was presented as part of the miners' attempt to extend the right of free mining across the whole of the Wapentake of Wirksworth. In this, they encountered the vigorous and organized hostility of the greater gentry and nobility of the area. The matter is more fully discussed in Chapter 10, but it is important to note here that Ferne saw the contest over mining rights in stark class terms, as an attempt by 'great men' and 'powerful men' in 'combynacion' and through 'violence . . . Terrer & Feare' to prevent 'poore men' from exercising 'their right'. Ferne saw a polarization of class interest over the matter of mining custom which he conceived of in the same language as his poorer neighbours, the miners.

Ferne's reading of the origins of mining custom appears to have been his own. The opinions of this educated and impassioned lesser gentleman entered into popular culture. But the interaction was not one-way. In his deposition, Ferne described the sources on which he based his knowledge of mining custom. These included medieval manuscripts from his own collection, his sight of the material remains of earlier mining activity, what 'he hath heard' from his neighbours concerning local history, and copies of mining customaries which he had borrowed from a miner called Raphe

---

[107] PRO, DL4/72/31.

Cadman. As he explained, like 'others of the cheife mynors' in Wirksworth, Cadman kept manuscript copies of the mining laws. Perhaps like his neighbour William Booth, Raphe Cadman was unable to read the important documents he held in his collection. But also like William Booth who, as we have seen, knew all thirty-one articles of the customs, he was quite capable of recalling their contents, and of placing an interpretative burden upon them. In 1609, Cadman had given evidence to the Duchy Court concerning the mining customs, in which he referred to his possession of the 'aunceint wrytinge' which he later lent to Ferne, which showed that cope payments used to be lower than the level at which they were set in that year, and that the miners had once enjoyed a right to take wood.[108]

Neither John Ferne nor any other lawyer empowered the miners' political culture with its authoritative legalism. Ferne added to that culture with his reading of the 1288 Quo Warranto. But then, he also borrowed from it. The example points to the permeability and mutability of popular culture. In the 1590s, the miners of Wirksworth had been confused as to the legal sources of their liberties. By 1623, they were not. John Ferne had some responsibility for this; but so too did the miners themselves.[109] Through their growing involvement with central law courts, the Peak miners were made forcefully aware of the importance of written documentation in the sustenance of their peculiar rights and liberties. Examples can easily be found from across the Peak Country of tenants keeping old leases of their property in the case of legal challenge.[110] Men of surprisingly low social status acquired reputations for their knowledge of law and custom and for their possession of archives of historical documents and transcriptions, which they loaned to neighbours who found themselves involved in legal action.[111] What made the Peak miners unusual in this respect was that their customs provided them with an institutional focus for the collection of documents and for the maintenance of local memory. That institution was the barmote, and around it gathered the cultural forces which allowed the miners of the early seventeenth century to define themselves as a collective political force.

[108] PRO, DL4/44/46.
[109] Compare PRO, DL4/34/22, and PRO, DL4/72/31.
[110] See for instance PRO, DL4/56/22, /58/7.
[111] PRO, DL4/122/1683/1, /124/1686/14, /67/59, /27/83; PRO, C21/B72/13.

7

The politics of custom

Contemporaries well understood the politics of custom in the early seventeenth century. Its legal and ideological authority masked the multiplicity of contending claims made through the language of custom. Within the parameters of elite politics, critics of arbitrary government identified a fictional ancient constitution, based upon custom, which guaranteed inviolable political and legal rights to the subject.[1] Plebeians used a similar terminology to articulate a vision of the proper ordering of society which often jarred with that of their rulers. Yet modern social historians are only starting to appreciate the political qualities of custom.[2] The language of custom held a discursive hegemony within many local plebeian cultures. Its institutions could provide an organizing focus for resistance, just as its basis in law granted legitimacy to its defence. Custom defined the values upon which the public world of local plebeian politics was built. Nowhere was this more obviously the case than in free mining law.

The language of custom enabled miners to refute patrician definitions of them as lawless and barbaric. In answer to allegations of communism, the miners laid claim to an 'indubitable custom' which had by virtue of precedent, court ruling and continuous usage been 'strengthened by law as the warrant of their undertakings'. In protecting the 'custom of the myne', they defined themselves as the real defenders of law, contrasting their legitimacy to the 'lawless' and 'disorderly usage' of lords who employed 'hirelings'. Historians should not be deceived into seeing the free miners as

---

[1] J.G.A. Pocock, *The ancient constitution and the feudal law: a study in English historical thought in the seventeenth century. A reissue with retrospect* (Cambridge, 1987).

[2] See K.E. Wrightson, 'The politics of the parish in early modern England', in P. Griffiths, A. Fox and S. Hindle (eds.), *The experience of authority in early modern England* (London, 1996), 22–5; A. Wood, 'The place of custom in plebeian political culture: England, 1550–1800', *Social History*, 22, 1 (1997), 46–60. For an important earlier perspective on the politics of custom, see Tawney, *Agrarian problem*.

the opponents of private property. In the eyes of the common law, their mineshares were saleable and heritable as freehold. But neither did they welcome the increasing concentration of mining activity by the late seventeenth century into a smaller number of gentry-owned works. Instead, the miners saw custom as the potential basis for a bounded patriarchal democracy of individual small producers in which production would be regulated by strong institutional and cultural forces. In order to prevent over-production, barmote by-laws of the mid-sixteenth century limited the number of mineshares an individual could hold and tried to restrict output.[3] Like other early modern workers, the miners possessed a classically artisanal vision of an industrial moral economy.[4] Custom therefore found its legitimate defenders against both the 'rich & great' and 'psons of mean condicion' amongst the independent, artisanal free miners. Central to that defence was the barmote, conceived of as 'the constitution and frame of the miners', which was 'so beneficiall . . . that too break this custome is to break some part of the sinews of the nation'.[5] From confrontations over custom, the law emerged as a contested category. Experience of the expenses of litigation before central courts, and of the bias of the local common law courts against them, taught the miners that both the principle and the practice of the law in early modern society could be very political indeed. William Hooson understood this well enough, summing up generations of experience in 1747:

the fairest play is, when one Miner contends against another, as being Men of equal Size, but where great Men get footing amongst 'em, there is as great Knavery (and may be justly feared) Perjury and Injustice as in any Court, Law or Business whatsoever, for great Men and Money do great Things; and the Rule is not to starve the Cause; and no Money, no Mine.[6]

The miners approved of the cheapness, speed of action, use of English and easy accessibility of the barmote, and contrasted its advantages with the expense, delay and obscurantism of litigation at Westminster courts.[7] Their demand that mineral cases should be heard at the barmote 'and not elsewhere' therefore suggests a wider significance to the jurisdictional confrontation which developed between local and national legal systems.[8]

---

[3] PRO, DL3/61/V1.
[4] A. Randall, 'The industrial moral economy of the Gloucestershire weavers in the eighteenth century', in J. Rule (ed.), *British trade unionism, 1750–1850: the formative years* (London, 1988), 29–51.
[5] PRO, DL5/29, fols. 432–3; PRO, DL4/75/10; BL, Add. MSS 6677, fols. 49, 88–94, 6686, fol. 62.
[6] Hooson, *Miners' dictionary*, 15.
[7] PRO, DL4/66/6, /85/51; BL, Add. MS 6681, fols. 189–91; Hopkinson, *Laws and customs*, 13–14.
[8] PRO, STAC8/73/4, /226/27, /201/19; PRO, DL4/66/6, /120/1679/2.

While barmote custom excluded women and cavers, in its internal operation it was democratic and consensual. The barmotes relied upon no ultimate coercive sanction; rather their legitimacy rested upon tradition, common usage and the social standing of the jurors. Active participation in the formulation and execution of mining law gave miners a real authority as the governors of their own trade, reinforced by the recitation of the customs at each Great Barmote.[9] In their evidence to central courts, miners frequently referred to their experience as barmote jurors or as deputy barmasters to validate a particular point.[10] Experience of the enforcement of custom expanded miners' knowledge of the law itself, of precedent and legal forms, and could legitimate their recourse to strenuous resistance on occasion.

It was the custom of barmotes to 'borowe mynors out of An other manor' to make up juries, thereby creating important links between miners, and standardizing the practice of the local courts.[11] The barmote created an institutional space within which popular resistance could be planned. For that reason, barmote jurors and deputy barmasters were often to be found at the forefront of the miners' resistance.[12] A powerful legalism built up within the miners' political culture, evidenced in their fear of contradicting custom even where it stood to their disadvantage. Thus one miner recalled having refused payment of the lead tithe, 'but was satisfyed by the sight of the articles of the Liberties and Custumes of the Myne (which hee often Read) & saith that in the Raigne of Edward the Sixth the fowerth article & in Queene Maries tyme the Sixth article are to that purpose, and thereafter agreed to payment'.[13] The miners' knowledge of custom reinforced the tenacious pugnacity they showed in defence of their rights. Confronted by outraged lords of manors who sought to eject the free miners from their estates the miners would typically respond that 'they had good right to worke there', or 'good authority, it being the Kings Field'.[14] In this respect, as in others, the 'law was a part of popular culture'.[15]

The legitimacy of custom grew from its forceful appeal to the past. The requirement that claimants to custom demonstrate its origins in time out of mind engendered a developed sense of the past within many local plebeian cultures. In the Peak, the peculiarly intense and protracted disputes over free mining rights led to the emergence of an unusually detailed historical consciousness amongst the miners, as the past itself became a terrain of

[9] PRO, DL4/75/10.
[10] For examples, see Wood, 'Industrial development', 181–2.
[11] PRO, DL4/66/6.
[12] See Wood, 'Industrial development', 183–5.
[13] PRO, DL4/117/8.   [14] PRO, DL4/120/1678/1.
[15] Sharpe, 'The people and the law', 262.

conflict. Where customs were remembered and continuously asserted, they were more easily defended. The Earl of Rutland's attempt to reimpose a manorial monopoly over ore sales within Bakewell manor in the 1660s was only defeated because the mining community had remembered the customs it had extracted from the Earl's ancestor in 1608.[16] In contrast, the recodification of Wirksworth mining custom which occurred between 1549 and 1557 removed awareness of earlier customs. The miners' claim of 1525 to a right of election over the barmaster vanished for two generations after 1549. It was only in the mid-seventeenth century that the demand was renewed, upon the earlier discovery of a copy of the customary of the 1490s. Thereafter, the claim re-entered the miners' collective memory, remembered as a lost right.

It is easy for the modern historian to dismiss the validity and longevity of the plebeian memories recalled in the depositions transcribed by commissions of Westminster courts. It suits historians' self-perceptions as myth-breakers to present such accounts as fantasies, conflations or deliberate inventions. And, indeed, some were. But given a close contextual knowledge of the area and a long historical view, we can discern a real truth inhabiting many of the stories told by aged deponents. In 1610, deponents in their sixties and seventies could give wholly accurate accounts of the dispute of the 1530s in which cope duties had been raised in Wirksworth. Their sources were their youthful memories of the speech of 'ancient and aged men'.[17] In the 1680s, miners gave clear and accurate accounts of the legal cases of the 1610s and 1620s which had established a right of free mining across Wirksworth Wapentake. In 1692, aged miners were still gloating over their defeat of the minister of Wirksworth's claims on them for a tithe of lead in the 1620s.[18] In 1616, when the miners of Bakewell, Tideswell and Hope were involved in litigation and protest against the lead tithe, old miners justified their sons' resistance with reference to their own refusal to pay the tithe in the 1570s. Songs of the seventeenth century kept alive memories of how mining custom 'was made most firmly . . . in Edward's Days'.[19]

The miners had a strong sense of their own history. The overt and public political culture of the miners became apparent after the 1580s, and achieved its clearest expression in the mid-seventeenth century, at a time when the miners were still marked by their low levels of literacy. Despite historical claims to the contrary, literacy was not a precondition for the

---

[16] BL, Add. MS 6677, fol. 79.   [17] PRO, DL4/55/46.
[18] PRO, DL4/123/1684/4, /124/1686/7; PRO, E134/4&5Wm&Mary/Hil 15.
[19] PRO, E134/13JasI/Mich3; R. Kay, 'Songs of the Derbyshire lead-miners', *BPDMHS*, 6, 1 (1975), 7–8.

development of popular politics.[20] The spoken word continued to possess a considerable authority in the maintenance of local memory into the eighteenth century. Claims that the miners 'imbibed' their skills, language and laws 'in their infancy' were no great exaggeration.[21] Even in 1747, William Hooson based his varied account of mining law, methods and history upon oral tradition. The miners' sense of the past was, like all histories, based upon key fictions, exaggerations and silences. It did not present a chronological narrative, but rather focused upon key themes, the most important of which identified the existence of a broader realm of customary rights 'in past tyme' than operated in the present. That close sense of the past enabled the development of arguments for democracy.

Many miners of the seventeenth and eighteenth centuries felt aggrieved that the office of barmaster was held by gentlemen or nobles who were hostile to the miners' right. Feeling that 'the Barrmr ought to be an indifferent pson', and especially should 'doe right to them that be opprest', they reached back to an imagined point at which the miners had themselves elected the barmaster. The claim was recovered in 1644 from the structural amnesia which followed upon the recodification of mining custom in the mid-sixteenth century, when George Hopkinson noted the existence of an 'old Customary' which showed 'that the office of Barrmaster was Originally Elective', and observed that 'I have heard Many Ancient Miners of the 24ly affirm, that by the Custom they ought to chuse the Barmaster'. Over the 1640s and the 1650s, the miners pressed their claim 'by ancient custome' to elect the barmaster, but without effect; yet as late as 1774, they were still harping on the subject, using language lifted from the customary of the 1490s.[22] Similarly, the miners laid a claim to a right to take wood freely from across the King's Field, arguing that the testimony of 'antient miners' and the text of 'an auncient wrytinge' proved the existence of the right 'in tyme past'. That manorial dues had once been lower was apparent to the miners from the same evidence.[23]

Most commonly, the past was invoked to criticize the conduct of the church in the present. Between the 1590s and the 1740s, miners insisted that their ancestors had only paid lead tithes to the church as a gift and that in return 'they formerly used to have prayers att Sixe of the Clocke in the

---

[20] Tim Harris, for instance, has seen print culture and literacy as a precondition of an urban popular politics: *London crowds in the reign of Charles II: propaganda and politics from the Restoration until the Exclusion Crisis* (Cambridge, 1987), 27. In contrast, see A. Fox, 'Rumour, news and popular political opinion in Elizabethan and early Stuart England', *Historical Journal*, 40, 3 (1997), 597–620.

[21] BL, Add. MS 6681, fols. 189–91.

[22] PRO, DL4/127/1694/6; Manlove, 'Customs', 16; Hopkinson, *Laws and customs*, 11; PRO, SP23/151, fol. 99; DRO, 1495M/Z13.

[23] PRO, E134/2JasII/Mich21; PRO, DL4/55/46.

morninge'. Since the church had discontinued prayers for the miners' safety and good fortune, the miners argued, there was no longer any custom of lead tithes. In making the argument, the miners looked with rose-tinted spectacles upon their ancestors' religiosity. In a moment of clarity, one eighty-eight-year-old miner recalled in 1675 how as a lad he had been labouring at Anthony Younge's mine when one of the priest's tithe collectors approached and asked Younge for a contribution: 'For what [asked Younge], the other replyed for praying for you at Six of the clocke in the morninge And then the said Younge answered let other myners give what they please hee shall have noe oare of mine for prayinge for me, I hope I can pray for myselfe.' The belief that the tithe was a reciprocal gift embedded itself through repetition in the miners' historical consciousness. Thus in 1662 one Matlock miner explained to his vicar that the church had no right to a lead tithe, but that he would give the minister some of his ore as a gift, 'out of good will to him; and to pray for the myners, for they had formerly used to have prayers att sixe of the Clocke in the morninge for the Myners'.[24]

The miners drew important messages from their history. The key 'facts' which this historical consciousness planted in the miners' culture helped them to contextualize their collective identity, to rationalize the customs which identified that collectivity and to explain their own participation in conflicts over those customs. In particular, three messages stand out from the miners' construction of local history: that they were an 'ancient', and therefore a permanent, part of Peak society; that their customs and rights had once been more extensive than in the present; and that therefore present attacks upon their rights should be seen as a part of a historical continuum. This historical interpretation conceived of custom and plebeian rights as a contested category, produced out of earlier conflict. Victories in the past established bulwarks against future encroachment, while past defeats were to be remembered and brooded over. The past therefore strayed into the present, enforcing duties to defend ancient rights on the behalf of future generations. Thus, the lord of Litton's enclosures in 1650 threatened not only the present inhabitants of that village, 'but all those who shall succeed us here as inhabitants'. The miners of 1772 were warned that if they failed in the defence of their laws 'which have been sanctified . . . for a Thousand Years', then they would 'Become the Betrayers of . . . Custom, and rivet Slavery on their Descendants'.[25]

William Hooson felt the ideological force of the past most acutely. In 1747, he dedicated his account of mining history, laws and methods to

---

[24] PRO, E134/2JasII/Mich21, /13JasI/Mich3; BL, Add. MS, 6682, fol. 38; PRO, DL4/117/8.
[25] SA, Bag C 2094; BL, Add. MS 6681, fols. 335–58; DRO, 1495M/29.

'that Honest and well Experienced MINER John Staley of Youlgreave' who had been a member of the Harthill barmote of 1720 which had maintained free mining within that manor.[26] For Hooson, John Staley represented the best traditions of the free miner:

you have been the only Person that has of late Years stood up to Defend your Antient Mineral Customs and Privilidges acquired and settled many Ages ago, by the Care and Pains of your Worthy Ancestors that their Posterity might enjoy the Benefit thereof, and though they were just expireing at that Time, you happily stept in and was the Receiver, and supported your dieing Liberties and Customs.

In contrasting Staley's defence of custom to the conduct of those 'base and degenerate Miners' who failed to support custom, Hooson forthrightly stated the public politics which defined the honour of the free miner: a respect for the past, a concern for the future and a refusal to accept the illegitimate exercise of elite authority in the present. In a curious reference to Cromwellian republicanism, Hooson described the defence of custom as the miners' 'Good old Cause'.[27] But then, perhaps this terminology was not so odd. Perhaps to the Derbyshire miners, their defence of custom against successive threats seemed as dramatic and important as the struggle against arbitrary power within the national body politic.

GENDER, PLACE AND THE CONSTRUCTION OF SOCIAL IDENTITY

In tying production and the distribution of resources into cultural practice and social relations, custom always possessed a latent politics. Within the Peak Country, that latent politics was activated in the last years of the sixteenth century, generating a historical and legal consciousness which helped to define the miners as a collectivity. The emergence of the free mining community as a collective political actor depended upon a process of cultural integration around the inclusive functions of custom. Since the miners' customs were not closed, neither was their culture. The strong regional identity of the Peak did not generate the claustrophobic xeno-phobia to be found in, for example, the Forest of Dean. Unlike the laws of the Free Miners of the Forest of Dean, the right of free mining in the King's Field was not restricted to those born within that jurisdiction and appren-ticed into the trade.[28] Instead, Derbyshire custom guaranteed a universal right to any man with sufficient credit to dig within the King's Field, and

---

[26] Hooson, *Miners' dictionary*, 198–9, 63; BL, Add. MS 6682, fols. 80–5.
[27] Hooson, *Miners' dictionary*, 63.
[28] C.E. Hart, *The free miners of the Forest of Dean and the Hundred of St. Briavels* (Gloucester, 1953); C. Fisher, *Custom, work and market capitalism: the Forest of Dean colliers, 1788–1888* (London, 1981).

miners seem to have been happy to instruct newcomers in their customs. When Richard Browne first arrived in the Peak and 'beganne to be a myner . . . he enquyred of the Auncyent Myners wthin the kings feild what the orders & customes was', and they told him.[29] The miners did not, therefore, seek to regulate entry into their trade, but rather attempted to maintain and extend a relatively open and inclusive system. But all processes of cultural integration require the establishment of an external opponent. In the case of the miners identity after 1590, that 'other' was found amongst the opponents of custom: the 'rich and powerful oppressors' amongst the gentry and nobility. But the miners also built cultural buttresses against 'unskilful folke', whom they took to include the poor, semi-vagrant cavers, and the women of the mining villages.

The ordering of cultural practice in the Peak Country was intimately bound up with the organization and use of space. We have seen how in 1623 William Booth gave a totemic authority to the customary he could not read, seeing in the document a physical validation of the miners' rights. In 1661, the eighty-year-old Edmund Higton gave a similar meaning to another artefact. Describing the 'brazen dish' which had been given to the miners by Henry VIII in 1512 as a standard measure for their ore sales, Higton explained that 'there is some writinge about it, but what it is he knoweth not'. None the less the significance of the dish was apparent to him: it was an ancient guarantor of the miners' rights, 'free and open to every miner to bringe their oare to be measured accordinge to the Custome of the Myne'. The brazen dish was kept chained in the 'lower roome' of the moothall at Wirksworth, which had been built around the same time as the 'brazen dish' was granted to the miners, 'to keepe the kyngs courts therein'. As the moothall occupied an important site within Wirksworth town, placed just off from the market, so it did also within the miners' culture. Here were kept some of the most important artefacts on which the customs were founded, including the original articles of the mine. Here came aged miners to give their testimony as to the operation of the customs in ancient time. Here the customs were read aloud, twice yearly, to the Great Barmote and the assembled audience. In the 'upper roome' the deputy barmasters were publicly sworn to their duty, standing 'upon the chequer table'. The moothall functioned as the miners' memory palace, its fabric and contents acting as a permanent reminder of the ancient origins of their customs, and of the royal sanction given to them.[30]

---

[29] PRO, E134/13JasI/Mich3.
[30] PRO, DL4/105/1661/22, /75/10; PRO, DL1/18/V1. The original moothall was replaced in the nineteenth century. The brazen dish is still kept there, and the Great Barmote still meets in the building.

The moothall defined the public authority of custom within the physical landscape of Wirksworth town. As an outstanding feature of the town, much remarked upon by visitors to the place, it announced the miners as 'a commonwealth within our commonwealth, governed by laws peculiar to themselves'. Here were settled the 'subterranean quarrels and disputes' of the miners. The trials could be rowdy affairs, with litigants shouting denunciations at one another. Authority was both restated and contested within the moothall: it was here in 1661 that the miner George Thompson had told the controversial new steward of the court, George Hopkinson, that his deeds were 'but ballads', and then 'said unto the myners, look to yorselves that yew wronge not the customs for it is no matter what George Hopkinson saith'.[31] The moothall was also a centre of fraternity, the focus where miners gathered from across the King's Field of Wirksworth Wapentake to hear causes. In all these respects, the moothall was constituted as a male space.

Yet that space could be invaded by an assertive female presence. Alice Spenser of Matlock was present 'at the Hall in Wirkesworth', to hear a case concerning a mine in which her nephew had an interest. Her neighbour, Katherine Smedley stood up to denounce her nephew's evidence, thereby incurring Alice's wrath. 'Katherine, why doe you soe raile against the poore boy' she asked, at which the two women set to a public discussion of the matter.[32] Both before and after the barmote trial, Alice Spenser had briefed her nephew in the intricacies of mining custom, referring to him as 'child' throughout. Her deposition of 1667 betrays a developed understanding of mining law which stands at odds to the institutional exclusion of women from mining custom. Yet although it was very unusual for women to give evidence concerning mining disputes, where they did appear as deponents they typically displayed as developed an understanding of mining custom as that of their menfolk.[33] The lack of women deponents mirrored their wider structural exclusion from participation in the formal institutions of customary law rather than any lack of knowledge of custom itself.

In everyday practice, men and women learnt about custom in similar ways. The location of boundaries and the nature of rights upon commons were apparent from traffic and labour. Men and women alike were shown the bounds by their aged relatives or neighbours and told of their past use. Yet male knowledge of custom was more often produced in a formal context than was that of women. Peak women never referred in any of their depositions to having gone the bounds of a parish, manor or common upon

---

[31] T. Fuller, *The worthies of England* (1652; London, 1952 edn), 107; PRO, DL4/105/1661/22; Defoe, *Tour*, 460–1.

[32] PRO, DL4/110/1667/7.

[33] PRO, DL4/110/1667/7, /117/8, /64/11, /85/51.

Rogation week or on some other specific occasion. Rather, they learnt such knowledge in passing. For men, being shown the bounds, or instructed in the customs of the King's Field, was as much a rite of passage into a community of male householders or miners as it was a purely informative experience, and old men tended to date their 'remembrance' of their home village from the point in time at which they were instructed in its customs. Inherent to old men's understanding of custom was therefore the assumption that it was the property of the 'substanciall men of the . . . manor'.[34]

Women's near-absence from the institutional and ritual invocation of custom in the Peak did not imply their exclusion from knowledge of or interest in such matters. None the less, that absence had important implications for the way in which custom was perceived by men, and how its authority was rhetorically reconstructed for the benefit of Westminster courts. The evidence given by Anne Redfearne, a widow of Taddington, concerning the customs and boundaries of her village, to the Duchy Court on 23 September 1617 illustrates the point.[35] Of the thirty-five people who gave evidence that day, Anne was the only woman. Aside from a couple of young men, whose evidence was fairly brief, the male deponents gave long, complex descriptions of the area, its bounds, customs and local history. In contrast, Anne's deposition was short. The clerk of the commission wrote down her information that

about 30 yeares agoe she [Anne Redfearne] being then gathering wooll sawe one William Sheldon of Sheldon delving turves upon pte. of Greensall rake pcell of the waste grounds in question, [that is, the disputed area] and saieth that one old John Newton then one of the best freeholders in Taddington & now deceased came to the said Sheldon and in her . . . sight & hearing tooke the said Sheldons spade from him and told him the said Sheldon that neither he nor anie other of Sheldon had any right of turbarie there, whereupon the said Sheldon then dep[ar]ted wthout his spade, but howe afterwards they agreed she knoweth not.

Whereas male deponents typically placed interpretative burdens upon such stories, Anne did not. She stands outside the story she tells, as a passive witness to the words and actions of men. The confrontation between William Sheldon and old John Newton was about a number of things. It was about space: where the boundaries lay. It was about custom: who had the right to dig what. It was about the past: the right to dig devolved from the past. It was about age: old John Newton confronts William Sheldon, Newton's age giving authority to his opinion. It was about place: an insider confronts an outsider. And obviously it was about gender: Anne Redfearne stands by, apparently in silence, watching while the politics of the manor are enacted before her. Of course, she understood the significance of the

[34] PRO, DL4/41/51.   [35] PRO, DL4/67/59.

event. That was why she placed the discussion in her mind, and recalled it for the Duchy's Commissioners. Anne's memory of the events of that day helped to prove that the title to the turves of Greensall rake lay with the community of Taddington, and not with Sheldon. But Anne was only a partial member of that community.

Yet the rights and resources guaranteed by custom were essential to many women. Despite its heavy gender bias, this was especially the case with mining custom. Women could inherit mineshares upon the death of their husbands, and many did so. Eighty-seven of the 1,912 mining households listed in the 1641 petition were headed by widowed women. Moreover, as an example of how barmote custom could contradict common law, married women could hold mineshares in their own right. Female mine investors were therefore common, and one mine near Matlock gained the name Gentlewomen's Grove from its ownership by an all-female combination.[36] Women's ownership of mineshares seems to have encouraged an assertiveness which sat at odds to patriarchal conventions. In 1635 Elizabeth Ferne, a gentlewoman of Wirksworth, gave evidence to the Duchy Court in a case concerning the right of married women to hold mineshares in their own right. The aunt of John Ferne, she was a mine investor who in her widowhood diversified her interests into landholding and coal mining.[37] The clerk who took her deposition noted her statement that 'it is usuall for Gentlewomen & other women as well marryed as unmarryed to take & hould ptes of ground & maintayne the same wth workmanship & sayeth that she herself hath bought an hundred poundes worth of groves and sould an hundreth poundes worth'. That evidence was almost identical to that provided by male deponents. But scrawled in another hand was an addendum announcing Elizabeth's opinion 'that she thinketh tht by the custome of the mine [her mineshares] ought to stand as good as yf her husband had bought the stakes therein'.

In stating the formal exclusion of women from the institutions of mining custom, we should not therefore overstate their actual exclusion from knowledge of its provisions or involvement in its assertion. None the less, the miners' collective identity was bolstered by the attempt to lock women and the unskilled out of access to custom. Gloomy depositions given by miners in 1581 to a commission of the Court of Exchequer inquiring into the sustainability of the revival of the High Peak mining industry provide

[36] PRO, DL1/352, answer of Grace Columbell *et al.* Gentlewoman's Grove was not the only all-female mining enterprise. A major working in Wirksworth in 1689 contained 'the women's meare': Rieuwerts, 'Earliest lead mine soughs', 279. For a mining enterprise in which two of the four investors were women, see PRO, DL1/331, answer of John Ferne *et al.*

[37] PRO, DL4/85/51; PRO, E101/280/18; PRO, E317/9/28.

graphic evidence of how such closures operated.[38] Christopher Chapman told the commissioners that

there is no good order kepte for the gettinge of sive ewer for that the same is nowe used by men women and children that have little skill, and not by experte workemen that be miners . . . for the goodnes and purenes of the ewer he saithe the Bearmaster oughte to loke to it and to be judge thereof, and to refuse to measure suche as is not inchanttable ware.

In an unsolicited aside, Richard Milnes of Tideswell developed Chapman's critique. He felt that

If the Bearmr were emongste them everie weke . . . as by theire auncient orders he thinketh he oughte to be to see such orders kepte as are sett downe by the Jurie men would observe them the better. . . . if suche as be riche men and of abilitie otherwise to live whoe for a gaine sake doo sett women children and unskilfull folke to worke in the rakes mighte be forbidden the workes, and the order for the auncient and skilful miners to worke it as they were wonte it would continue the longer to the more b[e]nefitte of the comon wealthe.

A year later, other miners echoed these concerns, condemning the 'comon disorder' of the 'poore cuntrye people'. They claimed that if the mines were 'orderlie wrought uppe', they might provide employment for 100 years, but that the current disorder of the industry meant that they would be worked out within a decade. Their own honour as skilled men was distinguished from the dishonourable labours of 'unskilful' cavers by reference to a connection between custom and work. For the miners, their honour and authority came in 'synkinge wth stoes and Tymber and so to gett the ewer accordinge to the old Custome of the Mynes' rather than merely scraping for rubbish on the surface.[39]

We should observe the logic upon which the miners' critique proceeded. In identifying the 'comon disorder' which resulted from the employment of 'women children and unskilfull folke' in the mines, the miners defined themselves in masculine terms as skilled and orderly. The 'poore cuntrye people' digging in the old works were the mere tools of 'riche men' who were the enemies of custom, and who enjoyed the support of the corrupt barmaster. In contrast, the 'auncient and skilful miners' held custom as a plebeian possession, and saw in it the potential for a different ordering of the mining industry. If the industry were properly regulated and 'order' established, then 'Riche men' would 'be forbidden the workes', and production regulated so as to guarantee continuous and honourable employment. A closer statement of the male artisanal vision of an industrial moral economy is not to be found in early modern England.

The nobility and gentry were blind to the important internal divisions

[38] PRO, E178/611.   [39] PRO, E134/24Eliz/Hil4.

which existed within the mining workforce. Elite accounts of the plebeian inhabitants of the Peak tended to present the mining workforce as an undifferentiated, threatening mass. To Roger Kenyon, the miners were all of the 'poorer sort of people'. At times of dearth, the county bench worried over the concentration of masses of unruly industrial workers into the infertile north. The miners played knowingly upon their governors' anxieties. Petitioning the House of Commons for the repeal of the lead tithe in 1624, the miners warned of the results of their paying the tithe: 'being destitute of other Corses to maintain themselves both [the miners] as also their wives & children being almost Twenty Thousand psons will be enforced to begg & live upon the charity of others'.[40] Yet the mining workforce was by no means the homogeneous bloc imagined by contemporary elite observers. Rather, the growing self-identification apparent amongst the miners from the late sixteenth century turned upon the sharper specification of difference between themselves and the rest of the mining workforce.

Through most of the sixteenth century, it was very rare for extractive workers to identify themselves as miners when giving depositions to commissions of Westminster courts. Instead, occupational ascriptions more fitted to an agricultural economy such as 'labourer', 'husbandman' or 'yeoman' were preferred. But from the 1580s, it became much more common for men to announce their status as miners.[41] Such changing ascriptions were the most obvious aspect of the surprisingly rapid coalescence of the miners' collective identity traceable to the period *c.* 1590–1610. Mining courts stopped calling themselves 'the othe of the xxiiiitie of the myners or diggers', and instead became the barmote. The miners' workings became 'mynes' rather than mere 'hooles'. Some of the earliest documents for our period betray occasional references to women as miners. The last came in the 1560s. Thereafter, the only reference to a woman's extraction of ore refers to her as having 'broke the ground and gott oare', rather than as 'mining'.[42] These slips point to a distinctly gendered reclassification of work. The separation of labour from capital and the division of labour process evident in the mining industry after *c.* 1600 therefore bred changes in the meaning of work. The nature and implications of that reclassification are explored in the succeeding section.

---

[40] Sharpe France, *Thieveley*, 95; PRO, SP16/193/29; HLRO, MP 9 April 1624. For equivalent images of the mining workforce of the northern coalfield, see Levine and Wrightson, *Making of an industrial society*, 202–4.

[41] Blanchard, 'The miner and the agricultural community', 98. For an important exception concerning miners' rights, see PRO, STAC2/15/141–9.

[42] PRO, DL3/61/V1; PRO, DL4/120/1678/1; PRO, DL1/74/W1&2 and Chapter 2 above.

Our concern here is with shifts in the definition of skill and social place which fed into changing relations of production and exploitation.

The gentry and nobility regarded the miners as unruly, violent, stupid and unchristian. The miners did not agree. To them, mining was an 'eminent' trade. They had brought prosperity to a poor area, behaved in a 'Civil and Christian qualitty', 'Releeved the Poore' and performed many actions of charity.[43] Their public honour lay with their customs, and with their willingness to defend them. By the early seventeenth century, the free mining community was defined through a series of clear social, cultural and political exclusions. These gathered in the demarcation which the miners drew between themselves and the poor cavers. The 'gettors' and 'myners' of ore had since the early sixteenth century been distinguished from those who 'geyther oor . . . called . . . cavers or purcasers'.[44] By the early seventeenth century, the occupational category of the caver had been expanded into a criminal one. The existence of the caver category also helped to mark the miners' identity in space, as by-laws were introduced from the late sixteenth century which prevented the cavers from approaching the miners' works without permission, and thereby enabled the miners to engage in their own moments of theatrical patronage.[45] Hooson explained that out of goodwill, miners gave the cavers 'some part of the waste . . . which they are very thankful for'.[46] Manlove considered that one of the functions of mining law was 'to keep in awe Such as be Cavers, or do rob men's Coes'.[47] In 1681, cavers were identified as 'poor people that go about the mines to beg or steal from the miners'.[48] Cavers, therefore, were the other against whom the miners defined themselves. The pejorative category was used to describe the labour and social place of others, never of oneself. In 1622, recalling his work upon rubbish tips during the expansion of the High Peak mining industry in the 1570s and 1580s, the aged miner George Marple could not bring himself to admit to having 'caved' for ore. Instead, he insisted that he had been 'a washer of lead oare in the ould workes'.[49]

Inherent to the establishment of the miners' collective identity was the clearer specification of the difference between the miner and the caver. This formed an important part of the wider redefinition of custom which occurred during the late sixteenth and early seventeenth centuries. After the

---

[43] PRO, E112/75/165, /168/11; Hopkinson, 'Lead mining in the Eyam District', 80.
[44] PRO, DL1/10/F2.
[45] See for instance DRO, D1289B/L139; BL, Add. MS 6678, fols. 149–52.
[46] Hooson, *Miner's dictionary*, 128.
[47] Manlove, 'Liberties and customs', 14.
[48] T. Houghton, *Rara avis in terris, or the compleat miner* (London, 1681), 113.
[49] PRO, DL4/67/61.

High Peak industry was suddenly reborn after 1569, many lords initially came to informal, oral agreements with their tenants and newcomers concerning the exploitation of the lead deposits on their estates.[50] It was not until the first decade of the seventeenth century that the miners developed the political capacity to insist upon a full codification of their rights within individual manors. The intervening period is a shady one. But we are able to describe the changing relationship between economics, social relations and identities and customary law with some degree of detail for the manor of Calver in the late sixteenth century.[51] In 1569, the mining industry of Calver was as moribund as that of the rest of the High Peak. Nine years later, the lord of Calver found it necessary to take Chancery action against the local miners, who were insisting upon the introduction of the free mining customs of the King's Field into the manor. Following the lord's victory, the first mining customs were established for the manor in 1578. These announced that 'noe maner of pson' could dig within the manor without the lord's permission, and detailed a series of other restrictive clauses. Importantly, no mention was made in the 1578 customs of any distinction between miners and cavers. In 1593, the customs were recodified. By that date, the miners had developed more political punch. Their new authority was reflected in the fuller provisions of customary law, which allowed the miners a series of new rights, including an implicit right of free mining. At the same time, the 1593 customs laid down rules against the cavers. The closer specification of social and cultural divisions amongst the mining workforce of Calver touched upon broader changes within the local economy and social system. There had been no physical boundary between Calver and the neighbouring settlement of Ashford until the 1590s, when in the course of the enclosure of the manor's commons, boundary markers had been established. The spatial boundaries of community were reconceived at the same time as the reorientation of social and cultural boundaries. In 1583, the manorial customs of Calver had stated that every year two 'neighbors' should be appointed as 'sworn men' to oversee the administration of the common fields of the village. These sworn men were selected by 'going up one side of the towne of Calver & downe the other to household every yere, untill the same order have passed through all the sayd towne & then . . . to begyn agen in such order as is aforesaid'. That egalitarian method of selection was produced from the communal system of agriculture it was intended to maintain. As with changes to mining custom, the provisions of agrarian customary law were

---

[50] See for instance NAO, DD.P. 80/2. Revealing asides on the subject are to be found in PRO, DL4/64/11.

[51] The ensuing discussion is based on SA, Bag C 343 (1–4, 8–9); PRO, C21/D1/13; PRO, SP12/75/8; PRO, C2/Eliz/S12/18.

radically reworked in tune with economic change. In 1593, the Court Baron of Calver introduced new customs to govern the agricultural practice of the village. These recorded new concerns over encroachments upon the commons, and placed inhibitions upon the exercise of common right: 'noe cotager' could put cattle on the common fields 'without lycense of the inhabitants'. As with the new specification of the category of 'caver' by the barmote in that same year, growing economic differences between landed and landless were encoded in a new distinction between the 'inhabitant' and the 'cottager'.

The clearest statement of how the variegation of the mining workforce defined the miners' identity is to be found in the miners' petition of 1641.[52] Considered in Chapter 3 as a source of information about the social structure of the Peak in the mid-seventeenth century, and in Chapter 12 as representing a formative moment in the miners' politics, the petition of 1641 was both a declaration of the free miners' solidarity, and of the construction of that community of interest. The miners were listed by township group as individuals, followed by a statement of the number of 'dependants' upon the miner, and their place within the miners' household. At the end of each township list, the number of 'cavers and hirelings' and their dependants within each settlement were indicated by an anonymous statistic. The 'cavers and hirelings' were placed upon the textual margins of the 1641 petition, just as they stood on the social, economic and cultural margins of the Peak Country. Although women, children and servants made up a large proportion of the mining workforce, their place within the miners' petition again was marginal, appearing only as dependants within the household headed by the skilled free miner. In order to comprehend the political authority of the skilled adult man within the mining household, we must now turn to consider how work was culturally constructed in the early modern Peak Country.

[52] PRO, E101/280/18.

―✠ 8 ✠―

Community, identity and culture

GENDER, WORK AND IDENTITY

Both in free mining and in the large, deep mines which mushroomed across the lead field after the mid-seventeenth century, the household was central to the organization of labour in the mining industry. Qualitative and quantitative evidence suggests an average household size of five people in the late sixteenth and early seventeenth centuries.[1] The contents of the miners' petition of 1641 allows for a closer scrutiny of the structure of mining households.[2] In the case of 1,463 named miners, the structure of their households are described (see Table 8.1).

Unsurprisingly, given what is known of household formation in early modern England, the nuclear family predominated within the orefield in 1641. More unusually, few mining households of that year included servants, and none included any apprentices. Households which included servants tended to be headed by wealthier miners, and therefore were more likely to be found within the richer valley settlements. On the south-eastern margins of the lead field, where the mining industry may have remained in a state of flux in 1641, there was a higher proportion of shared households, perhaps suggesting a more fluid population than existed within the core of the lead field.

Whereas women's work underwent significant change in other areas of early industrialization, within the Peak after the mid-sixteenth century a basic continuity in the sexual division of labour within the mining household is apparent. In the late sixteenth century as in the late eighteenth century, adult men cut lead at the vein, adolescents and servants carried ore below ground, and children, women and aged men operated windlasses

---

[1] PRO, DL4/23/9, /69/56.
[2] PRO, E101/280/18. This suggests an average household size of 4.496. For a fuller discussion, see Wood, 'Industrial development', 88–91.

Table 8.1 *Structure of 1,463 Peak mining households in 1641*

Household formation	Number	Percentage
Nuclear	1,157	79%
Extended	51	4%
Headed by widow/widower	118	8%
Individual	47	3%
Shared with non-kin	90	6%
Total	1,463	
Total of households which included servants	131	9%

and dressed ore on the surface.[3] The household was the key unit of free mining production: John Pidcocke and his two sons all worked together in the same meer at Nesthouse mine. Similarly, John Bateman of Elton 'did gett the oare his son drewe and the said Ellen Peirson [Bateman's daughter-in-law] did picke or dresse the oare gotten'.[4] Broader kinship links were also important. The brothers Thomas, Richard and George Carrington had all been working as partners in the same free mining concern in Elton for twenty-five years by 1669, 'in lawfull possession according to the Custom of the Mine'.[5]

The coping system which had emerged by the mid-seventeenth century as the contractual basis of the relationship between labour and capital in large mineworkings was also founded upon the enduring importance of the household. The skilled miners who signed cope agreements also contracted their wives, children and servants to employment within the mine. The authority of the adult male within the household was therefore ensured, together with his continuing possession of skill and autonomy. By the mid-seventeenth century, to be a miner meant more than simply that a man worked underground. The term was applied only to those men who engaged at least some of the time in free mining activity, and who spent the rest working as skilled men 'upon a cope'. Unlike labour upon a flat rate, the skilled miner felt no shame in working upon a cope. George Frost explained that in his fifty years of working life as a miner he had worked 'sometymes for himself and sometymes for dyvers others', and remained a prominent member of Wirksworth's community of free miners. Those who worked for flat rates were mere 'labourers', 'servants' and 'hirelings', who worked 'only for wages'. This distinction between temporary and perma-

[3] Aikin, *A description*, 79.
[4] DRO, Q/SB/2/1297; PRO, DL4/118/4.   [5] PRO, DL4/112/13.

nent waged labour applied also to those lead miners who found work as paid labourers in the nearby coal pits at Duffield. In 1659 the free miner, landholder and alehousekeeper Richard Steere of Wirksworth found paid work as a coal miner in Duffield. He described himself at that time as a 'miner' in contrast to his fellow workers who were merely 'colliers'.[6]

Distinctions under the coping system between labour and capital could become unclear. In such circumstances, such distinctions between workers could matter as much as that between worker and employer. John White of Ashford was both a free miner and worked for wages, paid to him by two other free miners, whom he called his 'partners'.[7] The blurred divisions between labour and capital, and the large authority given to the skilled miner under the coping system complicate the history of waged labour in the mining industry. Rather than becoming alienated from the product of his labour, coping created an active interest on the part of the coper in the continuing success of the mining enterprise. The Derbyshire coping contract, like other systems of piece rates prevailing in early modern mining industries, therefore helped to reconcile the skilled worker to new divisions of economic power. The fact was recognized by the author of a 1699 pamphlet who recommended piece rates to mine-owners, since 'every miner will have an interest in the works . . . you may then . . . fear no Combination to destroy your works'.[8]

Most copers alternated labour in their own works with paid work in deep, capitalized mines. In 1772 it was noted that 'The labouring Miners, generally, work one Shift a Day at the Mines of Gentlemen, for Bread for their Families; and in an Evening, go a few Hours, to one of these poor Mines for themselves, for which they do not often get One Shilling per Week, but from Hope of some Discovery they toil on'.[9] Save for the rare lucky strike, little profit came to the miners from their continuing involvement in free mining. Yet if the free mining output contributed little to the output of the industry as a whole, it remained important to the domestic economy of the mining household. Moreover, the mirage of that lucky strike helped to maintain the spirit of free mining. In economic terms, that independence may have become illusory by the late seventeenth century. But in cultural terms, it was as solid as ever. The 'attachment and . . . chearfulness, that are increasing and invincible' with which free mining was prosecuted into the late eighteenth century might seem to fly in the face of economic reality, but none the less it maintained the authority of the skilled miner.[10] In the maintenance of custom and small-scale production, the

---

[6] PRO, E134/1659/East 27.
[7] PRO, E134/8ChasI/Mich26, /22JasI/East30.   [8] Waller, *An essay*, 52.
[9] DRO, D1495M/Z9.   [10] Whetstone, *Truths*, 9.

Derbyshire miner of the late eighteenth century continued to be touched by the dream of economic independence that had moved his ancestors.[11]

Unlike the Miners' Law Courts of the Forest of Dean, the barmotes did not maintain any formal apprenticeship system. Many Peak miners were born to the industry, and received their instruction in skill and custom over various stages of adolescence and early adulthood. Kenyon observed that most 'Derbishire men' were 'minerally disciplined, even from theire cradles'.[12] Certainly this was the case for John Elliott who told Duchy Court commissioners in 1675 that he was a miner '& hath beene all his lyfe tyme since able to worke'.[13] Most miners entered the industry in late childhood or early adolescence. One man recalled how he had graduated from underground carrying work as a boy, to paid work at the vein at the age of seventeen, and finally at the age of twenty-four to full partnership in free mining.[14] Children were sometimes contracted by their fathers to work as labourers in mining operations. While still a boy, Anthony Wood was employed as a jagger 'by leave of his father' for a number of gentry-owned smelting works. At the age of fourteen he began work as an underground carrier at Milne Close mine. By the time he was nineteen he was cutting ore at the forefield 'for wages'. The next eight years of his life were taken up with waged labour in a number of mines around Matlock. By the age of fifty-six, Wood had become a weaver, a trade he maintained for the next twelve years.[15] Wood's working life was typical of that of a poorer miner, shifting from one form of waged work to another throughout his life. For those former miners whose age or injuries prevented them from labouring underground, a poor living could be had as chandlers or shepherds; after the Restoration many more found themselves in the 'manufactures' established for the maintenance of the poor.[16] For those miners who came from a relatively wealthier free mining background, expectations could justifiably be higher. Beginning as Wood had done as underground servants, or as jaggers, upon the inheritance of mineshares and land, such slightly wealthier miners often remained within the village of their birth. They were more likely to have servants within their households, and themselves to send their adolescent children to serve within the households of close neighbours and kin.[17]

---

[11] For the enduring importance of notions of independence to Gloucestershire weavers, see Randall, *Before the Luddites*, 31. For an important general study, see J.G. Rule, 'The property of skill in the period of manufacture', in P. Joyce (ed.), *The historical meanings of work* (Cambridge, 1987), 99–118.

[12] Sharpe France, *Thieveley*, 163, 95.

[13] PRO, DL4/117/8.		[14] PRO, E134/3JasII/East15.

[15] PRO, E134/2JasII/Mich21; PRO, DL4/117/8.

[16] PRO, DL4/120/1678/1; PRO, RGO 33; DRO, QAB/1/6/3.

[17] For examples, see Wood, 'Industrial development', 120–1.

In spite of the neglect of the subject by historians, the relationship between age and work had important implications for plebeian senses of masculinity.[18] Skill, gender, age and custom connected to define the miners' identity. Thomas Bradwell was aged sixteen when he gave evidence to the Duchy Court in 1694. He was then described as 'a worker in the mynes', for he was too young to be thought of as a miner. In contrast, John Downes of Bonsall gave his trade as that of miner in 1689 when, aged sixty-six he gave a deposition. He explained that he had been a miner since the age of fourteen, and that his remembrance of the mining customs dated from when he was aged sixteen. Though it had been two years since he had 'turned up all his mynes to his sonne & his sonne is to mentaine him', he still thought of himself as a miner. William Ward laboured throughout his childhood 'as a boy' and into his early twenties 'as a workeman' pulling corves underground at Gentlewoman's Grove. It was not until he took up work at the vein that he became 'a miner'. Other deponents dated the point in their lives at which they truly took on the identity of a miner at when they first married and set up their own household.[19]

We have seen in Part I that mining was the main source of male employment within the early modern Peak Country. At some point or other, most lower-class men in the area became involved with the lead industry. William Fisher of Youlgreave was unusual in having 'never had no minerall occasions nor any groves but followed his owne pfession being a smyth'. William Bramwall of Litton, aged sixty-nine in 1694, was more typical: 'hee hath beene brought upp a myner'. His neighbour, Thomas Ragge, had been a miner 'always'. Some miners found other occasional employment: working 'with staffe and dogg' as shepherds; as jaggers 'following horses'; as quarrymen; as colliers; as weavers or chandlers. But most, like Robert Holmes of Wensley in 1689 had 'all his life tyme (since hee was able to worke at the lead mynes) beene a myner'.[20] In part, this strong attachment to the mining industry was born of the lack of any other significant form of employment in the area; and, in part, it came from the powerful pull exerted by the identity of the free miner.

---

[18] Very little has been written about the social and cultural meanings of men's work in early modern England. For a notable exception see J.G. Rule, *The experience of labour in eighteenth century industry* (London, 1981). For important contributions concerning women's work, see A. Clark, *Working life of women in the seventeenth century* (1919; 3rd edn, London, 1992); L. Charles and L. Duffin (eds.), *Women and work in pre-industrial England* (London, 1985). For a brief discussion of masculinity and early modern mining, see Wood, 'Custom, identity and resistance', 262–3. For a suggestive early modern German study, see M.E. Wiesner, 'Guilds, male bonding and women's work in early modern Germany', *Gender and History*, 1 (1989), 125–37.

[19] PRO, DL4/127/1694/6, /125/1689/2, /117/8, /124/1686/7.

[20] PRO, DL4/71/39, /127/1694/6, /123/1685/2, /125/1689/2; LJRO, B/C/5/1623, Bonsall.

Free mining partnerships often stuck together upon the extinction of one vein, to move on to another. The close associations which developed out of such partnerships formed the basis for collective action against tithe proprietors or lords. Shared experience of the underground danger drew miners together. The uniformity and consistency of miners' accounts of the hazards of their work remain striking. Not only might father and son work in the same pit: they might also die together, overcome by the 'damps' or crushed by rocks.[21] Danger and labour bonded the miners as a community. When four Wirksworth miners were 'damped' to death in their mines in 1628, their bodies were taken to be buried at the parish church. Since the miners would not pay the tithes demanded by the vicar, Richard Carrier, the curate refused to bury them. 'The friendes of the said deceased were ready to give their wages [than] leave the corpses aforesaid unburied being very much discontented and grieved thereof.' The matter became a local scandal, and was one of the causes of Carrier's eventual overthrow.[22]

Much of women's work did not, as patriarchal theorists desired, take place within the confines of the house. Instead, women made up a substantial part of the mining workforce. They worked in the fields at harvest time, looked to cows and sheep upon the commons and wastes, and led horses as jaggers. None the less, connected attempts were made to constrain women's work if not within the physical limits of the house, then within the household, and to denigrate its significance. Grace Oxley remembered in 1688 how she used to live in her uncle's house, and worked for wages for him as a surface labourer. In 1675, seventy-year-old Elizabeth Adams described how she had been employed as 'a labourer . . . in draweing & chipping of oare at sevrall lead mynes'. Aged eighty-seven in 1686, Jane Saunders gave the Duchy Court a detailed account of her deceased husband's activities as a free miner, and then added that 'Shee . . . hath often wrought att the said Mine & hath fetcht water to the same, and washt lead oare & done other things there as shee could.'[23] Women's accounts of their working lives reveal nothing of the pride, assertiveness and sense of control exhibited by male miners. The work which miners performed was arduous and dangerous. But as free miners and as copers, they also enjoyed considerable control over the circumstances of their labour, together with cultural prestige and political and social authority. As we will see in the succeeding section, underground labour could even have its rewards in moments of revelation and excitement. In contrast, women's work in the mining industry enjoyed none of these benefits. It was

---

[21] PRO, E134/13JasI/Mich3; PRO, DL4/75/10.
[22] LJRO, B/C/5/1628 and 1629, Wirksworth.
[23] PRO, E134/3JasII/East15; PRO, DL4/117/8, /124/1686/7.

repetitive. The meagre wages women produced passed into the hands of their father, master or husband. Women were excluded from underground work. Similarly, women could not sit on barmote juries or act as barmasters.

Many of the despised cavers were women. We know little about these people, other than the stereotypes offered of them by the miners. In evidence given to the Court of the Exchequer in 1581, miners had defined caving in feminine terms. They saw that 'there is a kinde of broken ower . . . that poore women doo finde', and knew that activity to be 'unskilful'. We have seen that where male deponents admitted to having caved for ore, they described such work in euphemistic terms. Women were less equivocal: Anne Wilson knew that she had once 'caved' for ore, and told the Duchy Court so in 1667.[24] To the free miner, dressing ore with caving hammers constituted a necessary if low-status part of the labour process which was best carried out by women and children. Where a caving workforce was not available within the household, but instead provided a poor but independent living to women cavers, it identified such women as dishonourable and dangerous. The stereotype persisted into the nineteenth century, but is best exemplified by the notorious fate of Dorothy Matley of Ashover. The parish clerk of Ashover noted against the entrance of her burial that on 23 March 1661 'Dorothy Matley, supposed wife to John Flint . . . forswore her selfe, Whe[re] upon the ground open & she sanke over hed.' Employed upon caving and dressing ore at an Ashover mine, Dorothy was alleged to have stolen tuppence from a local boy. Approached by her neighbours while she worked at her buckets, Dorothy denied the theft and said that the earth should swallow her whole were she to be lying. At that point, the ground gave way and she was consumed. The story was popularized by the London newsbooks, and given an obvious moral twist by Bunyan, who observed that Dorothy Matley 'was noted by the people of the town to be a great swearer, and curser, and liar, and thief'.[25] The intervention of providence was explained by Dorothy's neighbours with reference to her personal reputation, and that of her trade. Her ambiguous place within John Flint's household joined with her independent trade as a female caver to mark her as an outsider to the moral community of Ashover.

Women's independent involvement in the public world of work was always perilous in early modern England. We have seen in the preceding chapter how the formation of the miners' collective identity was built upon

---

[24] PRO, DL4/110/1667/7.

[25] DRO, D2537/Pl/1/1; *Two most strange wonders* (1661) BL, TT E.1874 (4); J. Bunyan, *The life and death of Mr. Badman* (1680; London, 1928 edn), 169–70.

an attendant categorization of caving as feminized, de-skilled, criminal and dishonourable. Similarly, women's engagement in the intense world of local politics could also be constructed by plebeian men as an opposite against which their own claims could be legitimized. Between 1619 and 1632, the miners of Wirksworth were drawn into bitter conflict with the minister of that parish, Richard Carrier, and his wife, Jennet. Through the agency of her uncle, brother and father, Jennet had secured Richard's place as vicar of the parish and as barmaster of the Wapentake of Wirksworth. Jennet was not only the source of Richard's parochial authority: her pugnacity also contributed to his downfall. She was heavily engaged in the collection of lot and cope duties and tithe payments from the miners, and like other gentry women in the town was an independent investor in the mining industry. The miners accused Jennet of having coerced and threatened them in her collection of the controversial tithes, claiming that on one occasion she had brandished a knife at some of their number. In action before Star Chamber the miners presented her actions as a part of the larger disorder which had followed from her husband's oppressions within the parish. Despite Jennet's denial of the charges, she was fined £100 and jailed in Fleet prison, and the Earl of Dorset was moved to comment that 'if Mris Jennet Carrier had been at home armed with her distaffe and spindle, and not with a knife and a tallye in the fielde, this might have been spared'.[26]

Women's public participation in the politics of the Peak could therefore be heavily circumscribed. Yet just as plebeians could override the official ideology of the age in refusing the deference expected of them by their social superiors, so the practice of gender relations in everyday life was not driven according to the strictures of patriarchal teaching alone. We have already observed the assertive, public presence of women in the male space of the miners' moothall. There were other sites within Wirksworth town in which women's voices were used to being heard in contest or collaboration with those of men. Surprisingly for such a rural area, women's words were more frequently remembered as spoken within the open places and streets of the Peak's small towns than in its fields or commons.[27] The marketplace of Wirksworth town was one such site. In a dispute over the tolls of that market in 1667, it emerged that the lease of the tolls was held by a woman. Uniquely, almost all the depositions in that action were given by women, who spoke of their knowledge of the market customs, acquired as traders

---

26 S.R. Gardiner (ed.), *Reports of cases in the Star Chamber and High Commission*, Camden Society, new ser., 39 (1886), 89–109; PRO, RGO 33 frontispiece; DRO, D258M/56/21; PRO, DL4/84/24.

27 For an outstanding study of gender and speech in an urban context, see Gowing, *Domestic dangers*.

and buyers.[28] Women's engagement within the public sphere could be fraught with danger. But it could also carry authority. It was in Wirksworth market that Jennet Carrier had 'demanded' of the miner Edward Worslowe information concerning his holdings in the Dovegang mine. Elizabeth Ferne had argued with John Austerby 'in Wirksworth town streete' over her right to hold mines in Steeple grounds. Here too Lydia Hale had 'scandalized' Elizabeth Milward 'in the breach of charity openly in the town street to her great defamation' in 1670.[29]

It was not only the plebeian men of the Peak for whom entry into a community was guaranteed by their gender. Women's depositions suggest that they regarded one another's opinions much more highly than did men. Yet men could not always afford to ignore the 'speech communities' generated by women. The rich yeoman George Wilson's adultery and violence towards his wife Mary was well known 'in the comon speache of the Cuntrye' around Crich in 1599. The male 'frendes' of Wilson intervened in the matter, having heard their wives and daughters speak about Mary's abuse. These women had in turn heard about the matter from the servants of the Wilson household, and from Mary herself. When the case came before the Lichfield Consistory Court, the gossip network which Mary and her female friends had been able to activate against George was powerful enough to silence his male 'frendes' within the village. Deprived of the support of his near neighbours, George Wilson was forced to turn to men from distant villages to give evidence as to his good character.[30] Some men recognized the authority of such female networks. In 1631, the gentleman Robert Eyre of Highlow at first declined to take Mary Barley as his servant and housekeeper, 'sayinge he feared she dwelled toe neare her freinds'. Yet he subsequently relented. Later, it was said by Eyre's neighbours that Mary came to exercise 'great power' over him.[31] Gender overlapped and conflicted with the other communities within which identities were formed in the Peak Country as elsewhere. But it did so in a local context which was made peculiar by the special claims that plebeian men made over custom, skill and community.

---

[28] PRO, DL4/112/21. On the role of women in markets, see W. Thwaites, 'Women in the market place: Oxfordshire, 1690–1800', *Midland History*, 9 (1984), 23–42; M. Prior, 'Women and the urban economy: Oxford, 1500–1800', in M. Prior (ed.), *Women in English society, 1500–1800* (London, 1985), 93–117.

[29] PRO, DL4/91/16, /85/51; DRO, QS/B/2/296.

[30] LJRO, B/C/5/1599: matrimony, Crich.

[31] PRO, C21/E1/E12. For women's gossip networks, see B. Capp, 'Separate domains? Women and authority in early modern England', in Griffiths, Fox and Hindle (eds.), *The experience of authority*, 125–40.

COMMUNITY AND LOCAL CULTURE

Upland, pastoral-industrial regions of early modern England such as the Peak Country have been supposed in one historical interpretation to produce more individualistic, less neighbourly local cultures than in downland, arable areas.[32] It is difficult to produce an index against which the extent of community can be gauged, but the evidence at least qualifies such a large generalization. Community is never a universal constant, regardless of the economic or ecological setting. But in given contexts, a broad, inclusive feeling of community was present within the plebeian culture of the early modern Peak Country. This sense of community crossed divisions of age, place and gender, but operated within prescribed social limits so as to exclude the gentry and nobility. In the latter half of our period, its grip was weakening upon the richest yeomen farmer. The reorientation of community was reflected in changing languages of social description as, after the Restoration, a variegated language of 'sorts' was more commonly deployed as a mode of social classification. Yet it is important that social distinctions were developed through a binary opposition between 'better' and 'poorer' sorts: the term 'middling sort' was not used in any surviving description of Peak society.[33]

The strong sense of local place which underpinned community was sustained by a surprisingly static population during the seventeenth and early eighteenth centuries. The employment afforded at most times by the mining industry, coupled with partible inheritance patterns and the resources of the commons created economic conditions which inhibited significant long-distance migration and thereby helped to tie down local identity.[34] In linking what he saw as the backwardness of his native culture to the structural characteristics of community in the late eighteenth-century Peak, Charles Whetstone saw the truth of this connection between culture and immobility:

Perhaps no part of England retained so much of ancient customs as were to be found amongst the inhabitants of the *Peak* in *Derbyshire*: their dialect, prejudices, and superstitions (all gross and of very long standing) were in great degree peculiar to themselves. Their blind and childish partiality in favour of nativity, and their

---

[32] Underdown, *Revel, riot and rebellion*, esp. chs. 1–4. See also his restatement in *idem*, 'Regional cultures?'.

[33] For important work on this subject, see K.E. Wrightson, 'Estates, degrees and sorts: changing perceptions of society in Tudor and Stuart England', in P. Corfield (ed.), *Language, history and class* (Oxford, 1991), 30–52; *idem*, 'Sorts of people in Tudor and Stuart England', in Barry (ed.), *Middling sort*, 28–51. For the 'language of sorts' in the Peak, see PRO, DL4/119/1, /121/1681/6; Slack, *Lands and lead-miners*, 78; BL, Add. MS 6681, fols. 360–71; HLRO, MP 9 April 1624.

[34] See Wood, 'Migration and local identity'.

total ignorance of the rest of the world, extinguished in their minds almost every spark of curiosity or enterprise after objects remote. If an individual made a journey of 80 or 100 miles . . . it was sure to be talked of by his neighbours as well as himself, as a great event, for a long time afterwards – '*He has never once been out of sight of the smoke of his own chimney?*' was a common *High-Peak* proverb; and all proverbs have their foundation in nature and truth.[35]

Localized migration fields created dense personal networks based upon kin, neighbourhood, credit and mutual interest. From those networks grew a community defined by mutual responsibilities. The Ashford free miner and freeholder William Platts recalled in 1618 how 'hee hath divers tymes found falt wth one Anthony Sheldon an ould man for gettinge turves upon windewalls [in Ashford] whoe would then often saie to this depont. and others yowe must beare wth mee I am yor neyghbor borne, or words to that effect'. Sheldon's words were calculated to pull on Platts' social conscience: here, community was defined within a moral economy which overrode local social distinctions to privilege a neighbourliness established by birth, place, custom and duty. In Platts' encounter with Sheldon, the older man retained his access to the turves of Windebanks by calling upon community, certain that Platts would privilege the moral community of the village above that of his own 'rational' self-interest. The same equation moved William Platts' neighbours in 1618. Edmund James, another long-established miner and tenant of Ashford, was enraged by the ejection of his poorer neighbours from the village's commons by the gentleman Rowland Eyre, seeing in Eyre's actions a threat to the larger body politic of the village. James was a relatively wealthy man within Ashford society, yet in his evidence to the Duchy Court he placed himself alongside his poorer neighbours, noting that many of his neighbours were very poor and that they got 'the best p[ar]t of theire meanes by keepinge of sheepe & other cattell upon the said comons'.[36] Social historians have grown used to regarding such protestations with a cold eye. Yet amongst both landed tenants and their landless neighbours there did exist a real mutual interest in the commons in the Jacobean Peak. Out of that mutuality grew one source of community: the 'comon welth' of the village. Constructions of community had implications for definitions of social conflict. In Ashford in 1618, that 'comon welth' was presented as a plebeian property threatened by 'rich men' such as Rowland Eyre.

The community of the village was regularly renewed in communal festivities. Commentators of the seventeenth and eighteenth centuries noted

---

[35] Whetstone, *Truths*, 14.
[36] PRO, DL4/67/59. For similar examples of richer villagers aiding the defence of communal interests, see PRO, C21/C11/10; SA, Bag C 2094; PRO, DL4/53/59, /77/3, /96/66.

the liking of the 'peakards' for 'foote races' which would take place 'in a winters day, ye earth crusted over wth ice'. Especially popular were those races which pitted the young men of the Peak against Moorlander lads from the neighbouring villages of Staffordshire, and great bets would be placed upon the outcome. Yet 'for generall inclination & disposition the Peakard & moorlander are of the same ayre, they are given much to dance after ye bagg-pipes, almost every towne hath a bagg-piper in it'. In extension of the random fortunes of their trade, miners were known for their 'love' of cards. Saints days and feasts were carefully recorded upon the clog almanacs by which innumerate Peakrills recorded the passage of the year. The Wakes were celebrated with great feasts and garlands in the market towns, and were occasions for the settling of scores and the promise of marriage. Over the two weeks of Christmas, the miners left off work to 'carry tenn or twentie pound about them, game freely & returne home againe all the yeere after very good husbands'. Some celebrations helped to define the longevity of community. In 1604, the Star Chamber Court learnt that it was the 'custom' of the 'yong people' of Ashford to 'go amaying' after evening prayer, 'as they doe many tymes in that Contrey'. On that occasion, the festivities ended in a drunken and humiliating assault upon the a wealthy freeholder as the youths made their way to Churchdale 'to make merry & to drynke of sillybowken there as hath byn a long tyme accustomed by younge people'. Churchdale had been the site of an earlier enclosure riot back in 1542, on which occasion the ancestors of the 'yonge people' of 1604 had also ended up before the Star Chamber. Such wild festivities continued in Ashford into the early nineteenth century. More formal occasions could also define plebeian communities. In the eighteenth century, miners decorated their coes with oak branches on 13 May before making their way to a festival at which a large, open-air dinner was provided with ale.[37]

The ideal of neighbourliness formed another source of community. Social historians have described the role played by wealthier yeomen and gentlemen in settling disputes between their humbler neighbours, finding in such events a neighbourliness which oiled the machinery of local social

[37] Anon., 'The journal of Mr. John Hobson, late of Dodworth Green', in *Yorkshire diaries and autobiographies in the seventeenth and eighteenth centuries*, Surtees Soc., 65 (London, 1875), 291–2; W.G.D. Fletcher, 'Philip Kinder's Ms. "Historie of Darbyshire"', *Reliquary*, 23 (1882–3), 10, 181–2; J. Smith Doxey, 'Notice of a clogg almanac, from Wirksworth, Derbyshire', *Reliquary*, 7 (1866–7), 173–4; LJRO, B/C/5/1628 and 1629, Wirksworth; PRO, STAC8/168/25; T. Brushfield, 'Customs and notions at Ashford-in-the water sixty years ago', *Reliquary*, 5 (1864–5), 13–14; *idem*, 'A second notice of customs, notions and practices at Ashford-in-the water sixty years ago', *Reliquary*, 5 (1864–5), 152–3; B. Bryan, *Matlock: manor and parish, historical and descriptive* (London, 1903), 305–6.

deference.[38] Yet in the Peak, at least before the middle of the seventeenth century, it was at least as common to find miners and poor husbandmen intervening to settle quarrels between their richer neighbours, and enjoining them to live together in a more Christian fashion. The small but distinct lesser gentry of early seventeenth-century Wirksworth often brawled drunkenly both with one another and with their poorer neighbours. Many ended up before the very Court Leet on which they and their relatives sat as jurors. On several occasions, the pride and violence of one particular offender, Anthony Hopkinson of Bonsall, drew sharp comment from his humbler neighbours. On one such occasion, Hopkinson and another local gentleman began a brawl in a Hopton alehouse, only to be quietened and turned out by a miner. Plebeian criticisms of their richer neighbours' conduct drew heavily upon a Christian rhetoric of neighbourly responsibility and mutual respect. On another occasion, Hopkinson tried to drive a poor miner from his cottage and 'Fearfullye and unchristianlye [did] sweare & vowe by the lorde that he would be dampned bothe bodye & soule yf he had not the lands in question, whereunto George madder [a free miner] then beinge psent replyde that he was like then never to be savede'.[39]

Despite this, the people of the early modern Peak were rarely the subject of praise by established Christian ministers. Like the good Methodist he was, Charles Whetstone noted the incompetence of the Peak's eighteenth-century Anglican ministers; but he also paid attention to the large size of the parishes, which resulted in the 'dilution' of parishioners' sense of loyalty to ecclesiastical authority, and the disinterest of their plebeian parishioners in religious matters.[40] The Presbyterian William Bagshawe, known after the Restoration as the Apostle of the Peak for his preaching activities in that area, spoke in his sermons of 'scarcity paucity & scarceness' of his co-religionists, and singled out the miners for condemnation:

As to miners: through the rich grace of God there are miners who not only dig into the bowels of the earth, but into the bowels of the scripture. They cry after knowledge and lift up their voice for understanding . . . There are miners who search the scriptures as knowing that therein they may have eternal life; but alas go to the generality of those who labour in the mines and you will find that they are not such labourers as I have commended.[41]

---

[38] J.A. Sharpe, ' "Such disagreement betwyx neighbours: litigation and human relations in early modern England', in J. Bossy (ed.), *Disputes and settlements: law and human relations in the West* (Cambridge, 1983), 167–87. For an example, see PRO, DL4/8/4.

[39] PRO, DL4/43/24, /68/55, /67/64, /64/14. For the Wirksworth court leet's prosecutions of the local gentry, see DRO, D258M/58/18b.

[40] Whetstone, *Truths*, 17–21; R. Clark, 'Anglicanism, recusancy and dissent in Derbyshire, 1603–1730', DPhil thesis, University of Oxford, 1979, 2–7.

[41] JRL, Bagshawe Muniments B23/1/2; W.H.G. Bagshawe, *A memoir of William Bagshawe . . . styled the apostle of the Peak* (London, 1887); for a fuller account of Bagshawe's ministry, see J.M. Brentnall, *William Bagshawe: the apostle of the Peak* (London, 1970).

The vicar of Ashover Immanuel Bourne saw popery and superstition all around himself in the mid-seventeenth century, lamenting the 'gross & *popish* ignorance of his congregation'. Bourne's comments echoed long-standing fears of the Catholic sympathies of the Peak's plebeian inhabitants. In 1590, the Peak was described as 'where the papists have their harbours and are relieved by shepherds', and as 'more dangerously infected than the worst of England' with Catholicism. Yet in spite of the presence of powerful gentry recusant families such as the Fitzherberts and the Eyres, and the attentions of Jesuit priests, late sixteenth-century popular appeals to Catholicism amounted to little more than nostalgic references back to the days of church ales and chantry priests. The absence of any under-current of recusancy within the mining villages is made all the more surprising by the close proximity of a substantial recusant community to the northern edge of the lead field, at Hathersage. It is an overstatement to suggest that 'Catholicism remained entirely alien to the mining commu-nities' of the Peak, for by the Restoration most villages contained one or two recusant households; but only a slight one.[42] Accounts of the 'popish' tendencies of the Peak's inhabitants had more to do with contemporary elite prejudices against inhabitants of mountainous 'dark corners of the land' than with popular religious culture, and speak of the cultural distance which existed between ministers like Immanuel Bourne and their flock.

Immanuel Bourne was also given to exaggerated fears concerning the growth of religious dissidence within his parish. In 1659 he saw in the miners' refusal to pay tithes the seed of organized antinomianism, believing that if his tithes were not paid then preaching would become the preserve of 'Taylors, and Tinkers, Mercers, Bakers Boyes and Carpenters' and that his parishioners, 'instead of being fed with Heavenly Manna, the truth of the Gospel, [would] be choaked with error and heresie'.[43] Yet religious radicals thought as little of the Peak's inhabitants as more conservative clergy. The Quaker John Gratton dreamed of walking into Wirksworth market to 'declare against the wickedness of the people . . . for I knew the People many of them to be a rude, wicked, drunken, swearing people', but

---

[42] J. Bossy, *The English Catholic community 1570–1850* (London, 1975), 84, 87. On fears of Peak Country recusants, see LPL, Talbot MS CA/H, fol. 215, /I, fol. 29, /N, fols. 128, 136; PRO, SP12/241/23, 241/25, 245/131, 251/13. On popular memories of the pre-Reforma-tion church, see PRO, E134/38&39Eliz/Mich 29; PRO, DL4/18/38, /57/57, /20/9. On the extent of recusancy, see J.C. Cox, *Three centuries of Derbyshire annals*, 2 vols. (London, 1890), I, 260–3, 287–8; G. Lyon Turner, *Original records of early nonconformity under persecution and indulgence* (London, 1911), 52–3; LJRO, B/V/1/26, 59, 41; Clark, 'Anglicanism, recusancy and dissent', 38–43.

[43] I. Bourne, *A defence and justification of ministers maintenance by tythes* (1659); BL, Add. MS 6675, fols. 379–80. On Bourne, see also R. O'Day, 'Immanuel Bourne: A defence of the ministerial order', *Journal of Ecclesiastical History*, 27, 2 (1976), 101–14, and Chapter 12 below.

found that he was unable to muster the courage to do so. Instead, he spent most of his time engaged in sectarian disputes with the scattering of Baptists, Muggletonians and Presbyterians who huddled in the local market towns.[44]

In spite of the enthusiasm of individual puritan vicars and the establishment of preaching ministries by godly gentry, pre-civil war puritanism seems to have had little impact upon plebeian inhabitants of the Peak.[45] Despite late seventeenth-century claims that Protestant dissenters in the Peak were drawn from 'the meaner sort of common people', most of its local adherents were of the lesser mercantile gentry and richer yeomanry, supplemented by the occasional wealthy free miner. Support for post-Restoration dissent was strongest in the wealthier and more literate valley settlements.[46] By the early eighteenth century, old Dissent had closed itself off from the burlesque popular culture of the Peak. John Gratton's Quaker autobiography of 1726 reveals the same contemptuous disassociation from the rough, plebeian culture into which he had been born as the Methodist Charles Whetstone was to exhibit a full century later. Early Methodism had little effect within the area, and it was only after 1770 that it developed any force within popular culture. Religious censuses of 1676 and 1751 therefore reveal very similar official religious popular cultures. At both dates, the typical Peak parish contained a scatter of Catholics and dissenters, including perhaps some isolated member of one of the more exotic sects, notable in a sea of apparent religious conformity.[47]

That appearance of conformity should not blind us to the alternative spiritual beliefs of the Peak's plebeian population. Those ministers of the established church who drew the warmest welcome from their humbler parishioners were those who were most willing to join actively in the festive, alehouse-frequenting culture which dominated the mining villages. At the end of the sixteenth century, it was well known in the 'comon report' of Castleton that its vicar Thomas Furnace 'Lovethe good drinke verie well'. That he had conducted marriages while drunk, had nearly married one village lad to another (the would-be bride was in drag), and had himself changed his surplice for a woman's petticoat, seemed to merely improve his standing amongst the adherents to festive village culture.

---

44 J. Gratton, *Journal of the life of that ancient servant of Christ* (London, 1720), 23–6, 31, 47–8, 87–8.

45 LPL, Talbot MS CA/K, fol. 173; BL, Add. MSS 6694, fol. 178, 6672, fol. 167; Clark, 'Anglicanism, recusancy and dissent', 124.

46 Lyon Turner, *Original records*, 52–3; Wood, 'Industrial development', 148–9.

47 Robson, 'Aspects of education', 116; J.C. Cox, 'A religious census of Derbyshire, 1676', *DAJ*, 1st ser., 7 (1885), 31–6; A. Whiteman and M. Clapinson (eds.), *The Compton census of 1676: a critical edition*, British Academy records of social and economic history: new ser., 10 (London, 1986).

Furnace kept the goodwill of his humbler parishioners, together with most of the 'best sort' of the parish who gave evidence on his behalf when he was excommunicated after running foul of a clique of rich farmers who had bought the lease of the parochial tithes.[48] Local culture disparaged religious innovation, and the collection of tithes was actively and even violently opposed. Thus Richard Carrier, the unpopular vicar of Wirksworth was unfavourably compared by his parishioners to his predecessor, Mr Billing, who was 'Carefull to preserve the rit[e]s of the Church and one that had the love of his neighboures'. In contrast, Carrier was condemned for his disputatious claims to tithes, his 'oppressions' as barmaster, and his wheedling demands that the parish pay for the cost of communion wine. Carrier was the object of further condemnation for his employment of a drunken and libidinous curate and his refusal to lead the parish on their yearly perambulation of the bounds on Rogation Sunday.[49] Carrier's great sin lay in his breach of the values of neighbourliness, and his failure to appreciate the limits of his authority.

By the eighteenth century, the lack of affection between the inhabitants of the mining villages and their ministers was notorious. The miners were warned in 1701 by one pamphleteer that if they allowed the passage of a parliamentary bill which would standardize the payment of the lead tithe across every parish within the lead field, they would be thrown onto the mercy of 'the country parsons whose charity God knowes to the myners will bee as cold as the season is here'.[50] The longevity of the miners' resistance to the demands made upon them by vicars and tithe proprietors for a tenth of their production is suggestive of the frequently antagonistic relationship which existed between clergy and plebeian laity within the Peak. One of the sanctions deployed by the ecclesiastical authorities in the pursuit of this claim was that of excommunication. Yet miners were compensated for their loss of the sacrament by their continuing membership of the community of pugnacious, independent free miners which their public resistance guaranteed.[51] The place given by some historians to the church in the 'political socialization' of the lower orders into the acceptance of authority is, in this instance, obviously misplaced. Rather, the miners had been politically socialized into a different community: one whose rules, traditions and customs they had themselves created.[52]

[48] LJRO, B/C/5/1600, Castleton; PRO, STAC5/B15/1; PRO, STAC7/9/1; PRO, STAC8/209/5, /283/25.
[49] PRO, C21/C11/10; LJRO, B/C/5, 1628, 1629, Wirksworth.
[50] BL, Add. MS 6682, fol. 134.
[51] HLRO, MP 9 April 1624.
[52] G.J. Schochet, 'Patriarchalism, politics and mass attitudes in Stuart England', *Historical Journal*, 12, 3 (1969), 413–41.

THE SUPERNATURAL AND THE UNDERWORLD

Running alongside the outward conformity of the Peak's plebeian population to the teachings of the established church was a less obvious but perhaps more deeply felt belief in the operation of magical and supernatural forces within the everyday world. The people of the Peak were tempted to find extraordinary explanations to everyday events: we have already seen how the fate of the unfortunate Dorothy Matley of Ashover was ascribed to the force of providence. Stories concerning the intervention of the supernatural were set firmly within a context which shaped popular culture within a distinct body of local knowledge.[53] The Peak's landscapes sometimes became magical, their enchantment deriving from marks left upon them by their forgotten use in past time. 'Monster beings, called Hobthursts' inhabited the exposed side of the Iron Age hill fort at Finn Copp, near Ashford. They could turn milk sour, send cows barren, and stole from the nearby villagers. Fairy Ring mushrooms which were to be found around Finn Copp owed 'their peculiar form and greeness to the nightly moonlight revels' of fairies.[54] The inhabitants of Castleton rose early on Easter Sunday to watch the sun dance up and down over the hills which girdled their valley. One of those hills, Mam Tor, was topped by the remains of another Iron Age fort. Below Mam Tor was Odin mine, thought to have first been worked when the mining customs were established by the Vikings. Two other hills, named Win Hill and Losehill, were said to take their names from their occupation by opposing armies who had fought a battle there in times past.[55]

Above Castleton village loomed the Peak Cavern, known as the Devil's Arse, associated from medieval times with a diabolic presence. Long ago a shepherd of Castleton was said to have become lost within the Devil's Arse, and after a long underground journey had 'found a Passage into a delightful, plentiful Country, wherein were vast Pools and large Rivers, with verdant Meadows and Pastures'. The enchanted environment within which the inhabitants of early modern Castleton lived and worked sometimes intruded upon them. In 1758, five Castleton miners were at work in Winnats Pass near the village when one of their number, James Ashton, persuaded the rest to murder a passing gentleman and 'his lady'. They took £200 from the murdered couple, and left their bodies in a barn. That night, the miners returned to bury them, but, according to Ashton, 'they were so

---

[53] On legends and local culture, see D. Hey, 'The Dragon of Wantley: rural popular culture and local legend', *Rural History*, 4, 1 (1993), 23–40.

[54] Brushfield, 'Customs and notions', 11–12, 14.

[55] Glover, *History*, I, 312–13; Bray, *Sketch*, 103.

terrified with a frightful noise tht they durst not move them; and so it was the second night. But the third night, Ashton said, it was only the Devil, who would not hurt them, so they took the Bodies away, & buried them.' The supernatural proved less benign than Ashton had imagined: as he remembered events, providence intervened. One of the miners fell from a precipice near Winnats Pass and died. Another hanged himself. A third was walking near the Pass when he was killed in a rockfall. The fourth went mad and died miserably. Ashton survived until 1778 when, eager for death and in great pain, he was unable to pass away until he had unburdened himself of the tale to a local gentleman.[56]

Past, present and future blurred at moments and places within this charmed landscape. Joseph Bradbury 'heard it reported' that if he sat within Castleton church on the Eve of St Mark's Day, he 'shod see between the hours of 11 & 12 the spirits or resemblances of all such of that parish as shod die the ensuing year'. He decided to test the local legend, and placed himself

on the East side close to the door where he had not sat above a quarter of an hour but there came as out of faintish air (as he express'd it) which made him sick & tremble which made his Hair stand on end – immediately after which came the likenes of one widow Barton (a pour woman then alive tho' sick) of Castleton & as she came in at the entrance of the Church Porch the Church Dore flew open he look'd her in her face & she had a Death's Visage & a red Coat on all patched such as she used to wear she went by him into the Church as fast as a Man can go.

There followed other ghostly figures, most of whom Bradbury could not recognize, for 'he durst not look any more of them in the face . . . he wod rather chuse Death than watch it again'.[57]

The educated classes of eighteenth- and nineteenth-century England held such beliefs in contempt. Their basis in speech and tradition was seen as a further invalidation of oral tradition and local culture, presented as backward, irrational and thereby as feminine. For Farey in 1815, local legends were maintained only by 'childish nurses and Grand-Mothers'.[58] The connection was an ideologically important one, establishing orality and local culture as antique and static, and enabling a bourgeois and urban

---

[56] BL, Add. MSS 6668, fol. 470, 6670, fol. 342.

[57] SA Bag C 3470. The magical properties possessed by Castleton parish church on St Mark's Eve were shared by other churches within north Derbyshire and south Yorkshire. See BL, Add. MS 24544, fols. 99–101; BL, Lansdowne Ms 207c, fols. 193–5. For John Aubrey's account of a similar belief in the West Country, see BL, Lansdowne MS 231, fol. 161. Samuel Bamford recalled that such beliefs still existed in the Lancashire villages of his boyhood in the late eighteenth century: *Early days* (London, 1849), 160–1.

[58] J. Farey, *A general view of the agriculture and minerals of Derbyshire*, 3 vols. (London, 1815), II, 627.

culture to pose as modern, improving and rational. Some nineteenth-century radicals were drawn into the association: William Bamford remembered local legend as the property of his female relatives, and was thereby able to contrast the irrational, rural, feminine world he had left behind with the ordered, urban world of the radical male artisan. Historians have been gulled by such accounts into assuming that the nineteenth century saw the decline of oral tradition and local culture in the face of the rise of a national, literate modernity.[59]

Miners were especially reviled for their 'silly' beliefs, which were presented as the product of their degeneracy and illiteracy. Since miners worked in 'dismal obscure cells', they were cut off from enlightenment. Therefore 'the product of their six days work is generally on the seventh expended in Drunkeness and Lewdness'. The miners' 'ignorance' led them to 'superstition' and 'wickedness . . . their morals being inconsistent with any religion'.[60] Eighteenth- and early nineteenth-century elite observers of the miners' beliefs and culture were able to list the miners' supernatural beliefs, but were unable to see them for anything other than evidence of the miners' backwardness. Influenced by structuralist anthropology, modern social historians of the period have been more willing to see sense in plebeian beliefs in magic.[61] Certainly, the powerful sense of the supernatural which pervaded the miners' experience of underground work fulfilled a need within their culture. Miners believed that whistling underground frightened away the ore. Supernatural creatures known as 'knockers' were thought to inhabit the mines, whose hammering noises, which warned of danger or of the presence of ore, could sometimes be heard by the miners. Ore was believed to grow in the veins from a substance called 'Ghurr'. Miners claimed to be able to identify the location of a vein through observation of surface foliage, or 'by the use of an Hazel stick'. Elaborate ritual was attached to the construction and use of such divining rods; they had to be cut at certain phases of the moon and the planets; improvements to the technique of 'wagging' for ore were made over time, and the possession of the requisite skills brought a man great prestige. The flowering of pease was thought to contribute to underground

---

[59] Bamford, *Early days*, 159–69; D. Vincent, 'The decline of oral tradition in popular culture', in R. Storch (ed.), *Popular culture and custom in nineteenth century England* (London, 1982), 20–47. But see P. Joyce's recent rehabilitation of the place of speech in late nineteenth-century working-class culture: *Visions of the people*, chs. 8, 11–12.

[60] Leigh, *Natural history*, 79; SA, Bag C 3438; Cotton, *Wonders of the Peak*, 33–4; Farey, *General view*, III, 620.

[61] See especially Thomas, *Religion and the decline of magic*; B. Bushaway, '"Tacit, unsuspected, but still implicit faith": alternative belief in nineteenth century rural England', in Harris (ed.), *Popular culture*, 189–215.

methane concentrations, while 'choke damps' were believed to accumulate during periods of damp or cloudy weather.[62]

It is not necessary to replicate the elite outsider's contempt for these beliefs. Some of the miners' ideas were not unique to them. The belief that a connection existed between the movement and position of the planets and the geology of the earth was shared by a number of prominent early scientific thinkers. Other ideas were the miners' gifts to the learned culture of their betters. Hooson observed that 'some Men who were never perhaps down in a Mine in all their Days are the best acquainted' with the existence of Ghurr. Webster found that mine-owners as well as the 'vulgar' believed in its existence, and had himself obtained several pounds of the substance (upon payment) from a miner's son.[63] Many of the miners' beliefs reconciled them to the dangers and surprises which they encountered underground. The 'solemn expression' spoken by all miners before starting work on a new vein – 'By the grace of god and what I can find here' – called on providence to back up the miners' own luck.[64] Similarly, the miners' belief in the benign presence of the 'knockers' helped to sustain them in facing the daily dangers of their trade. Derbyshire miners were not alone in holding such beliefs. Cornish tin miners were guided underground by imps known as 'noggies', while Austrian miners received the aid of the 'Berg-mann'.[65]

Seventeenth-century miners were, in a sense, subterranean pioneers. They dug deeper than had been attempted since the Romans, and further still. As they descended, they encountered the unknown: sometimes unusual, sometimes marvellous. One miner recalled having met

with large hollow caves, the roof, and sides, and bottom full of congealed stone like ice; and in one there was a spring of water which fell from the roof, and had made a hollow place at the bottom, in which were 12 stones of the shape and bigness of a moor hen's egg, and speckled like them, which he supposes were formed by the motion of the water turning them round in the hollow where they lay.[66]

Other miners encountered the skeletons of prehistoric mammoths, holes which seemed to have no bottom, cathedral-like caverns which still have the power to amaze late twentieth-century tourists. As they broke through into the ancient abandoned workings which they knew as the work of 'T'Owd man', miners found themselves face to face with the past. T'Owd

[62] Bryan, *Matlock*, 297; Hooson, *Miner's dictionary*, 85–8, 78–9, 177–86; K.H. Johnson, 'Folklore and superstition in mines', *BPDMHS*, 5, 3 (1973), 156–7; BL, Add. MS 6682, fols. 254–303; Rieuwerts, 'Early geological concepts', 56–7; J. Pettus, *Fodinae regales* (London, 1670), 3; Glover, *History*, I, 312.

[63] Hooson, *Miners' dictionary*, 78; Rieuwerts, 'Early geological concepts', 56–7.

[64] BL, Add. MS 6682, fols. 254–303.

[65] L.B. Williams, 'Derbyshire mining', *Mining Magazine*, 47, 2 (1932), 89.

[66] Anon., 'Journal of Mr. John Hobson', 296.

man was the collective spirit of earlier miners, and where his presence was mentioned, it meant that the miners had encountered the underground works or remains of their predecessors. The first reference to the presence of T'Owd man occurred in 1625, and as the miners delved deeper, so they encountered him with greater frequency.[67] T'Owd man's remains could be grisly, and his proportions suggested that he had sometimes taken gigantic form. In 1663 miners at Ball Lee mine discovered 'an open place as large as a church and found the skeleton of a man standing by the side, rather declining . . . his braine-pan would have held two strike of corn, and . . . it was so big they could not get it up the mine they had sunk without breaking it'. New discoveries implied that perhaps T'Owd man had not been entirely human. In 1730 a miner working in Hazelbadge found a skull, 'and in it several large teeth, which were made into candle sticks'. Forty years later Bradwell miners found a tooth 'of a wonderful proportion' which measured some thirteen and a half inches long. On this occasion, the miners had the best of the 'learned', who believed the tooth to be that of a giant man. The miners disagreed, arguing that it was that of an elephant, 'and for this opinion, they produce some Elephants Bones found near Castleton'. One antiquary concluded airily that 'The most possible conjectures about these Phaenomena are, that they are the Exuvine of those Creatures brought hither by the general deluge.'[68]

The discovery of such remains could lodge in a man's mind. In 1686, the aged Matthew Berisford still had vivid memories of the strange underground discoveries he had made as a youth while working in some 'old works'. He explained that he

beleeves that the same might have bin wrought above a hundred yeares before & saith that by the surface of the earth they could not tell that it had beene an old worke for that the earth was even & grasse grew there but saith that in their workinge they found the same were old works . . . when they had sunke about Five Fathoms they found three mens skulls one whereof was of an extraordinary bignesse & some of the bones were very great ones but the rest were but of an ordinary bignesse.[69]

There is no way of knowing what Berisford had chanced upon; but it should hardly be surprising that such discoveries sparked off tales of supernatural beings inhabiting the miners' underworld. For many miners, the forces of the past moved about them as they worked. Bradwell miners

---

[67] The first reference is at PRO, E134/5ChasI/Mich6. For subsequent seventeenth-century mentions of T'Owd man, see BL, Add. MS 6686, fols. 57–8; PRO, DL4/112/12, /120/ 1678/1.

[68] J. Pendleton, *A history of Derbyshire* (London, 1886), 50; Anon., 'Journal of Mr John Hobson', 296; BL, Add. MS 6670, fol. 343r.

[69] PRO, DL4/124/1686/7.

left candles burning underground on Christmas Eve, as a mark of respect to 'T'Owd man', for it was thought best to placate such spirits.[70] For T'Owd man, the spirit of those miners who had gone before, looked over the subterranean people in their underground labour. T'Owd man forms an appropriate symbol of the miners' culture: a distant, powerful, masculine figure formed out of collective memory and a brave leap of imagination. That the miners were able to articulate a collective identity, define a political project and, albeit for a few fleeting moments in the mid-seventeenth century, imagine a different ordering of industry and local society, had much to do with the force which the past held over them. Without a history, there can be no culture. And the miners knew their history. The past suffused their world: in the emblematic figure of T'Owd man; in the landscapes of the Peak; in the artefacts and ordered memories upon which they built their knowledge of custom; in their recollections of battles lost and won. It is to the history of those battles that we now turn.

[70] Johnson, 'Folklore and superstition', 157.

Part III

THE POLITICS OF SOCIAL CONFLICT

9

'Pyllage uppon the poore mynorz': sources of social conflict, 1500–1600

LATE MEDIEVAL QUIESCENCE

In 1497, the Court of the Duchy of Lancaster heard complaint from Henry Foljamb esquire, a prominent member of Derbyshire's gentry, and the lessee of its right of lot and cope within the Wapentake of Wirksworth.[1] Foljamb objected to an alliance formed against him by two other powerful gentry families: the Leakes and the Babingtons. At some time in the 1470s, the Leakes had prevented the free miners of Wirksworth from entering the fields of neighbouring Cromford to dig for ore. The miners were still barred in 1497, and Foljamb thereby lost valuable revenue from his tolls upon their production. Moreover, he was hindered in his collection of lot and cope by the intransigence of the barmaster, Roger Vernon. As for the miners, they lacked sufficient assertion to challenge the Leakes, and told Foljamb that they 'durst not' enter Cromford, for George Leake had 'discharged all the myners that they shuld geytt no hoore [ore] bott if it were doin be his Comandment'. Furthermore, the inhabitants of Cromford were ready to 'damme theyr owin sawles [souls]' to give evidence in favour of Leake and the Babingtons. Yet Foljamb insisted none the less 'that theyr was no man lyffyng that cowyde prefe [prove] bott as the kinge hathe had Allway the Lott and Cowpe here of all the town & felds of Cromforthe', and hence that a right of free mining existed there.

Thus the custom of free mining had found its champion. Yet that champion was not drawn from the ranks of the free miners of Wirksworth, but rather from amongst the county's gentry. The miners themselves appear in the proceedings of 1497 as impotent pawns in a game of power politics played amongst the county elite. The miners had no voice within the proceedings, and no role in their initiation. Knowledge of mining custom was presented as an elite possession, and as a subject of dispute between rival gentry families rather than as a source of plebeian rights and

---

[1] PRO, DL3/2/F3.

203

independence. Within a century, all that was to change. By 1600, Wirksworth miners scarcely needed a gentlemen to tell them of their 'ancient custom' of free mining in Cromford; for they were laying claim to such rights far and wide. In 1497, the only reference to the Quo Warranto proceedings of 1288 which formed the source of mining custom came from the gentleman who occupied the office of barmaster. By 1600, miners were circulating transcriptions of the documentation which proved their rights, and committing their contents to memory. The miners were to use the barmote court as a forum for self-organization, rather than to see their participation within it as a sign of their subservience to their lord. In the century which followed 1497, the miners' lack of collective self-confidence suggested in the legal proceedings of that year was to be replaced by their emergence as an organized interest group in local politics. The transformation which occurred in plebeian political culture over the course of the sixteenth century will form the subject of this chapter.

After 1600, the dominant conflict within the Peak centred upon the control of the mining industry. Prior to 1570, however, most social conflicts concerned agrarian custom. Such disputes were much less intense than those of the early seventeenth century, and the relative social demarcation of conflicting interest groups less clear. In some cases, a straightforward conflict between organized groups of tenants and their lord is obvious. Such confrontations typically concerned the enclosure of common land or the suppression of common rights. In 1542, sixty-eight 'evell disposed' villagers of Ashford broke down the fences with which the Earl of Westmorland had enclosed some 300 acres of Churchdale meadow. In symbolic assertion of their right of common, they then drove their cattle into Churchdale.[2] The Ashford tenants' collective action drew upon their common interest in the maintenance of rights which were threatened by a powerful noble. On other occasions, lords rallied their tenants to demonstrate against neighbouring villagers over boundaries or manorial rights. Here, a mutuality of interest can be detected between individual lord and tenant in the protection of local custom. In such instances, conflict was not drawn around social place, but was instead defined around an antagonism between highly localized interests.[3] Prior to the rapid increase of population after 1569, therefore, conflict over agricultural resources simmered on a very slow heat. This muted conflict resulted from the absence of any

---

[2] PRO, STAC2/19/270; see PRO, DL3/49/C1, /22/J2; PRO, DL5/8, fol. 119; PRO, DL41/2/11, for a similar long-running dispute in Ashbourne. For contemporaneous disputes over commons in Hartingdon, see PRO, DL3/36/R8, /79/H1; PRO, DL4/1/8. For riotous conflict over pre-Dissolution Granges, see PRO, DL3/79/H1, /36/R8.

[3] See PRO, STAC2/3/19–20, for an example. For accounts of the leadership of such struggles by local gentry, see Manning, *Village revolts*, 38.

significant pressure upon the land, and the relatively light hand of manorialism. This was especially true of the Duchy of Lancaster's large estates. The Elizabethan Duchy's fairly relaxed attitude to its Peak tenants enabled them to develop and extend their freedoms and privileges, the continuous exercise of which built up a hard shell over innovations in common right, and transformed them into 'ancient' custom.[4]

In contrast to the relative freedoms of agrarian custom, and in spite of the remarkable liberties allowed to them by the 1288 Quo Warranto proceedings, the miners of early sixteenth-century Wirksworth were bonded into a subordinate relationship with the powerful brenner families of that neighbourhood. Miners appear in the records of disputes between rival cliques of gentry families in the role of clients of one side or another, or as neutral onlookers.[5] Unlike their successors of a century later, miners rarely represented their own grievances to the Duchy Court, but rather relied upon a wealthy interlocutor. Thus in 1553, Edward Lowe made complaint to the Duchy Court in his capacity as barmaster of Wirksworth along with three prominent free miners of that town against Edward Bland, a gentry opponent of the right of free mining. Lowe and the miners recited the basis to their case: that a custom had existed time out of mind, founded upon the provisions of the 1288 Quo Warranto, whereby miners could search wherever ore was to be found within the Wapentake. The case itself is assertive. But the terminology of their case is still more enlightening. Lowe and the miners argued that in obtaining an injunction from another central court, Bland threatened to undo the mining laws and thereby to impoverish 2,000 or 3,000 poor people, 'as they be the most porest creatures that can be and not of habilitie to sue nor yet to answeare in any Courte for the Triall of their right . . . other then in the small courte of Beremote onely'.[6] In the future, the miners would not retreat from the basic case which Lowe made on their behalf in 1553, and would cling tenaciously to the claim that their barmote court should be the main, or the only, forum for hearing 'mineral cases'. Yet they would do so in their own voices, and without referring to themselves in such demeaning terms.

Yet even by the mid-sixteenth century there were signs that the quiescence of the miners was evaporating. As we saw in Chapter 6, four years before Lowe's complaint to the Duchy, the Great Barmote of Wirksworth Wapentake had begun to redefine mining custom, rendering it more certain and taking upon itself greater regulatory powers. Lowe's action at the Duchy resulted in a further recodification of the laws in 1557, in which the right of free mining received its clearest and most assertive specification.

---

[4] See for instance PRO, DL4/19/7, /38/17.
[5] PRO, DL1/29/G2, /28/B10a.   [6] PRO, DL1/34/L6.

We must turn again to a wealthy interlocutor of the miners to hear something of their discontents in the mid-sixteenth century. At some time in the 1530s, James Else, an orebuyer of Matlock, gave a very revealing answer to the complaint of Sir Godfrey Foljamb, the lessee of the lot and cope of Wirksworth Wapentake. Foljamb was suing Else for his refusal to recognize the increase in cope duties from four pence to six pence upon the sale of each load of lead. Claiming to speak for the miners who were his neighbours, Else defined a basic social antagonism between the free mining interest and the gentry. In his account, this antagonism was presented as rooted in the experience of oppression and informed by a memory of lost freedoms. He told the Court that he had heard from 'old Auncient mynrs and Brenners of lead And Also the Chartr of the myne will Testifie the same tht the mesure tht shuld be made by bothe their Assents And tht mesure to be delyved unto suyche pson as the mynerz and Brennerz shuld chose for the Beremaistr'. Thus, as Else saw the matter, not only had Foljamb taken upon himself to raise the level of manorial dues, but at some point in the past Foljamb's predecessors had expropriated the office of barmaster, which had at one time been filled by election from amongst the miners and orebuyers. To Else, it was the duty of the barmaster to deal equally with all comers 'wtoute Any Reward'. The barmaster should be properly rewarded for his neutrality by taking a dish of ore from every newly opened mine, and by his receipt of the costs and fines of litigants at the barmote court. Yet not only had Foljamb increased the cope duties, he had also altered the customary dues such that the poorest miners and cavers were required to pay duties. This was 'Contrarie to the old Custome And to the utter undoyng of the said poore mynorz'. All of this contradicted custom as it had prevailed in 'old tyme'. Most importantly, Else perceived a clear connection between the loss of the elective office of barmaster and the increased exploitation of the buyers and miners:

> nowe of late tyme . . . his ma. the kynge And his noble pgenytors have taken From the mynerz and Brenerz the namyng of the Beremaistr and have gevyn thoffyce of Beremaistr unto ther s[er]vauntz which the said s[er]vauntes have made deputiez doe Gyffe great somez of money unto evy Beremaistr And doe Raise the same by pyllage uppon the poore mynorz in Somych tht at this dey the said deputie beremaistr wyll meyt noe oore of any pson but he wyll Take a pte of the same oore for meytynce.[7]

The recodified barmote customs of 1557 entitled the miners to dig for ore in any land, regardless of its ownership, within the Wapentake of Wirksworth. By the 1580s, a solid core of territory centred around the towns of Matlock and Wirksworth, and including the villages of Cromford,

---

[7] PRO, DL1/10/F2.

Middleton and Bonsall, had been established as the heart of free mining territory. Yet within the Wapentake, large tracts of land remained in which the right of free mining was either allowed only by licence of a resident lord, or had been banned altogether. At various points between 1561 and 1591, the Wirksworth miners were driven from the manors of Ballidon, Bradborne, Elton, Cowley, Alsop, Wensley and Snitterton and from Steeple, Griffe, Aldwark and Willersley Granges (see Map 14). Typically, lords or major freeholders led their tenants and servants in armed attacks on the miners. Following the expulsion of the miners, the lead deposits were worked by waged labourers, or lead was compulsorily purchased from miners at low prices under the manorial right of pre-emption of sales. Moreover, many freeholders within the Duchy's large manor of Wirksworth also barred miners from working on their land, and denied them their customary right to wood.[8] Thus, while in theory the customs of 1557 confirmed free mining, in practice the miners' lack of assertion and organization prevented them from exercising that right.

The matter came to a head in litigation before the Courts of Exchequer and the Duchy of Lancaster between 1591 and 1593. For the first time, the free mining interest in Wirksworth received the powerful support of the Talbot Earls of Shrewsbury. Like his father, the sixth Earl of Shrewsbury, Earl Gilbert held the lease of the Duchy's rights of lot and cope in the Queen's Fields of Wirksworth Wapentake and the Hundred of High Peak. Unlike his father, he was prepared to back up his interest in the collection of the Duchy's lot and cope (thereby confirming the right of free mining, as supported by the Duchy) with the force of law. In 1591, he initiated legal proceedings against the lord of Wensley and Snitterton, Henry Sacheverell, who had barred the miners from his land and taken the lot and cope to himself.[9] The case is important in the development of the legal and social conflicts over mining rights in three respects. This was the first case in which a Westminster equity court issued a clear judgement concerning the character of mining rights within the lead field and the extent of the Queen's Field. In this case, Shrewsbury and the miners were victorious, as the Duchy Court announced that the provisions of the 1557 Great Barmote concerning free mining applied to Wensley and Snitterton. Secondly, the case had been won due to a coincidence of interest between the Duchy's lessee of the rights of lot and cope, who sought to exact tolls upon the industry in Wensley and Snitterton, and the miners, whose right of free

[8] PRO, E134/32&33Eliz/Mich28; PRO, DL4/34/22.

[9] On this litigation, see PRO, E134/32&33Eliz/Mich28; PRO, DL4/34/22, /34/47; PRO, DL1/91/D2, /144/B16, /159/S15, /187/E22. On earlier action at the Duchy concerning Wensley and Snitterton, see PRO, DL1/44/B24. On the mutual hostility of the Talbots and Sacheverells, see LPL, Talbot MS CA/F, fol. 225.

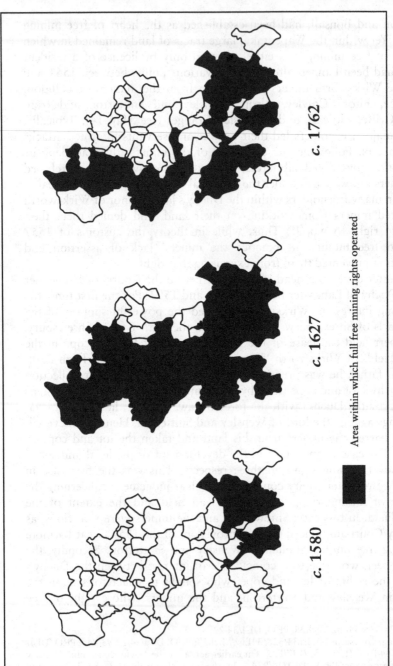

Map 14 The assertion and defence of custom: the extent of free mining rights, c. 1580–1762.

These maps are necessarily sketchy. It is of the essence of custom that it defies the kind of simplistic representation attempted here. Moreover, the surviving written information about customary law on which the maps are based is itself of varied quality. Full free mining rights are here taken to include all of the following: a clearly stated, free and open right to all the Crown's subjects to dig for lead on all ground within the jurisdiction in question, regardless of tenure (save for roads, graveyards, gardens, etc.); the absence of manorial

c. 1580 *c. 1627* *c. 1762*

■ Area within which full free mining rights operated

mining confirmed him in his entitlement to this duty. Thirdly, legal action had for the first time coincided with an organized invasion of Wensley and Snitterton by the miners of Wirksworth, Cromford, Matlock and Bonsall. The miners would combine crowd action with collective litigation on many more occasions in the years ahead.

None the less, important differences existed between the miners' defence of their customs in the Wensley and Snitterton case, and the form they would assume after *c.* 1600. In their depositions to the Courts of the Duchy of Lancaster and Exchequer of 1591, only one miner cited the key provisions of the 1557 Great Barmote. The miners mentioned some part of their customs, but did not provide a full and detailed recitation. Neither did they refer to the provisions of the 1288 Quo Warranto, nor to any other customary. Their only source for the assertion of the 'Auncient' origins of their customs was the physical evidence of earlier workings upon the ground. A fighting fund, or 'common purse' to pay for the action had been levied upon the miners by Earl Gilbert, rather than collected upon their own initiative. Neither was there any evidence that any barmote meeting had been utilized to plan legal action or resistance. In all these respects, the miners' defence of custom in the 1590s seems muted.

THE 'TROUBLESOME PEOPLE' OF THE TUDOR HIGH PEAK

Within the Hundred of High Peak, where population had expanded so rapidly after 1570, the Earls of Shrewsbury were cast in opposition to the miners. Unlike in the mining disputes of 1561–93 in the Wapentake of Wirksworth, the assertion of free mining rights in the High Peak was closely connected to disputes over enclosure and agrarian custom. In the decade which followed the introduction of Humphrey's ore hearth mill and sieve in 1569, a complex and poorly documented battle was fought over the control of the High Peak industry between George Talbot the sixth Earl of Shrewsbury, William Humphrey, other leading gentry families who held manors within the High Peak lead field, and the miners and tenants of the area. The sixth Earl, anxious to raise revenue upon his Derbyshire estates, aspired to a monopoly over all sectors of the lead industry. As lessee of the rights of lot and cope within both the Queen's Field of Wirksworth Wapentake and the Queen's Field of the High Peak, as lord of the various manors which made up Ashford lordship, and as the major smelter and lead merchant in the Peak, he was well placed to establish such a monopoly. Through his control of the institutions of the mining industry, the Earl hoped to impose a pre-emption of all the miners' ore sales within the Queen's Field of the High Peak and Ashford lordship. He would thereby be able to ensure a cheap and permanent supply of ore to his smelting works.

William Humphrey entertained still more grandiose pretensions. Claiming that his Crown patent granted him a pre-emption over the sale of all ore produced using his innovations, and that this pre-emption applied across the whole lead field regardless of manorial distinctions, he too attempted to extract ore from the miners at deflated prices. Similarly, by the mid-1570s, leading gentry families in the High Peak such as the Manners and Foljambs had recognized the potential of the new industry and set about imposing a pre-emption of ore sales, or banning free mining altogether. Finally, the hugely expanded but increasingly harassed group of High Peak miners stood in opposition to all of these powerful interests.

Of all the miners' opponents of the 1570s, William Humphrey was the easiest to frustrate. Opposed by all the major gentry and noble families in the Peak, and without any effective means of imposing his claim to pre-emption on to the miners and cavers, by 1578 he had been defeated by 'the disobedience of the country people'.[10] Secure in their victory over Humphrey, the miners became increasingly troubled by the activities of the lords of a number of manors in the High Peak. As the miners explained in 1581, these 'riche men' banned them from the lead deposits, and gave them over to the cavers, or to servants who would work them for wages. Yet for all that the miners fulminated against such 'disorderly' practices, their main confrontation with these authorities still lay three decades in the future. Instead, the miners turned to opposing the Earl of Shrewsbury's claims.

Like many noble men and women, by the late 1570s the Earl of Shrewsbury was becoming increasingly desperate for money as the inflationary pressures of the period undercut his rents. He was further harassed by the financial demands of his pugnacious wife Bess of Hardwick, and by the need to maintain the imprisoned Mary Stuart, Queen of Scots, in secure but commodious accommodation at Chatsworth. Further to his demands upon the miners of the High Peak, he therefore set about a second money-making scheme. In the decade after 1575, complaints reached the Courts of the Duchy of Lancaster and Chancery and the Privy Council from Shrewsbury's tenants in Ashford and Peak Forest within the High Peak lead field, and from Glossop in that part of the High Peak which lay amongst the gritstone levels beyond the lead field. In all three manors, Shrewsbury had attempted to raise rents and entry fines, to redefine agrarian custom in his interest, and in the case of Peak Forest and Ashford, to enclose parts of the commons and wastes. And in all three manors, these efforts were opposed by the tenants.

For all that Shrewsbury dismissed his opponents as 'simple fellows', these lowly men and women were organized, articulate and assertive. Led

---

[10] Kiernan, *Lead industry*, 169.

by men such as 'Black' Harry Botham, a 'notorious trouble-maker', the Glossop tenants played upon the Privy Council's fears concerning Shrewsbury's ability to maintain order so close to the site of Mary Stuart's incarceration. The leaders of Ashford and Peak Forest's resistance were more shadowy, but were equally well placed to embarrass Shrewsbury before his peers. The Peak Forest tenants initiated legal action against Shrewsbury at the Court of the Duchy of Lancaster in 1576, claiming that he had denied them their 'aunciente customs & liberties'. That same year, Shrewsbury gave voice to his irritation that the Peak Forest inhabitants had come to London and criticized him before the Queen as though he were 'a great wronge doer'. In 1579, the 'unreasonable people' of Ashford also attempted to place a complaint before Elizabeth concerning Shrewbury's behaviour. They were prevented from doing so; but if their timing was not co-ordinated with the Glossop tenants' complaints, it was at least fortuitous. In that year, the tenants of Glossop had also been pestering the Queen and Privy Council with complaints. This combined lobbying exercise resulted in the intensification of royal anxieties concerning the security of Mary Stuart at Chatsworth. The pressure pushed Shrewsbury towards a change in his estate policies. Between 1581 and 1585, Shrewsbury and his officers engineered compromises with the three groups of tenants. A settlement was agreed with the Glossop tenants in 1581–2. The Peak Forest inhabitants had their customs confirmed by the Duchy Court. And in 1585, the tenants and miners of Ashford lordship came to a settlement with their lord. Under a Chancery agreement, Shrewsbury's authority as lord was recognized by the tenants, together with his ability to impose a manorial pre-emption over lead ore sales. The price at which ore was to be sold was set at the nine shillings then pertaining on the open market. In return, Shrewsbury confirmed a right of free mining within the lordship, and allowed the tenants wide tenurial and common rights.[11] His change of policy not only brought Shrewsbury a measure of peace upon his estates. His officers now advised him that he was able in turn to rely upon his tenants' support against Bess of Hardwick and her equally troublesome Cavendish offspring, who by the mid-1580s were challenging Shrewsbury's entitlement to a number of his High Peak manors.[12]

For all that the sixth Earl of Shrewsbury was remembered in King James'

---

[11] S.E. Kershaw, 'Power and duty in the Elizabethan aristocracy: George, earl of Shrewsbury, the Glossopdale dispute, and the Council', in G.W. Bernard (ed.), *The Tudor nobility* (Manchester, 1992), 266–95; PRO, DL4/18/20; PRO, DL1/93/M7; LPL, Talbot MS CA/P, fol. 733, /F, fol. 331; BL, Add. MS 6685, fols. 66–70; SA, JC 384.

[12] LPL, Talbot MS CA/G, fol. 280; on the disputes between Shrewsbury's disputes with Bess of Hardwick and her Cavendish sons see PRO, SP12/207, *passim*.

reign as having been the 'cheefe barmr of the high peake . . . and had the firste refusall of the lead oare through the queenes field', the story of his attempt to impose a pre-emption on ore sales within the High Peak between 1569 and 1590 is as chequered as his troubles with the tenants of Ashford, Peak Forest and Glossop. His status as a broker in the world of late Tudor court politics was not sufficient to intimidate the truculent miners of the High Peak. Rather, they simply ignored his barmasters' instructions to sell their ore to Shrewsbury at compulsory low prices. Similarly, his claim to a tithe of one tenth of their lead production met with consistent frustration. By 1585, John Booth and Arthur Barker, the Earl's head barmasters, wrote bleakly to him of their inability to impose a pre-emption of ore sales, concluding from their sorry experiences that 'the lord of the Feld shall not have [the miners'] oorre but by force'. As we shall see, leading gentry families such as the Foljambs and the Manners successfully established a monopoly over ore sales within their own estates. But by 1585, the enforcement of Shrewsbury's claim to a pre-emption over the large tracts of the Queen's Fields and Ashford lordship had been exposed as a practical impossibility. Shrewsbury's officers advised him to learn the same lesson that they had been taught by the struggles over pre-emption: that the miners were 'wilfull and must be used quietly'.[13]

The preceding discussion of the disputes which Shrewsbury and his officers faced between 1569 and 1585 in the High Peak has artificially separated contests over mining custom and agricultural custom. Many of the inhabitants of Ashford and Peak Forest who complained to the Queen in their capacity as tenants were themselves miners or orebuyers, and hence were caught up in the conflicts over mining rights. Just as the revitalization of the High Peak mining industry led to new conflicts over mining custom, so the accompanying growth in population placed pressure upon agricultural resources. While the central conflict in the period c. 1570–1600 was that over mining rights, these thirty years also saw intensified conflict over enclosures and common rights. As with earlier in the century, the settled inhabitants of one Peak village sometimes found themselves drawn into conflict with a nearby settlement. Most of these disputes were small scale and relatively insignificant. But some, such as that between the inhabitants of Elton, Winster, Bonsall and Brassington, were to stretch over several generations. In this case, the villages had initially intercommoned. Growing population pressure forced a closer demarcation of boundaries, and a clearer specification of exclusive rights to settled inhabitants. Disputes over

---

[13] PRO, DL4/67/59, /64/11; PRO, E134/13JasI/Mich3; PRO, E178/611; SA, BFM2/78; Kiernan, *Lead industry*, 214.

rights of common and turbary, the exact whereabouts of parochial, manorial and township bounds and, after the 1620s, lords' rights over sheepwalks defined the interests and identity of villages in opposition to one another. Community and social space were thereby reimagined at the same time as communal resources were redefined, articulating a more separate and distinct set of village identities which remain historically observable into the 1680s.[14]

But just as in disputes over mining rights, conflict over land and common right in the late sixteenth century Peak was most apparent between plebeian and elite. Many of the former monastic Granges of the Peak which came on to the land market following the Dissolution of the monasteries were purchased by local gentry families. Also a source of contention over mining rights, these Granges became the cause of riot, dispute and litigation between their new owners and the inhabitants of nearby villages. In some cases, such as the dispute between the inhabitants of Youlgreave and Overhaddon and the owners of Medowplecke Grange, post-Dissolution disputes represented a continuation of a long-running conflict which stretched back to before the Reformation. More typically, gentry owners of Granges used their acquisition of former monastic estates to press long-forgotten rights over commons. Just as some disputes over the rights and boundaries of Granges stretched back into the fifteenth century, so many others therefore extended forwards in time into the seventeenth and eighteenth centuries.[15]

The key subject of contention between lord and tenant became that of enclosures of common land. Anxious to raise revenue, the Duchy leased out bundles of its rights in feefarms to gentlemen, who used them to extort new fines and rents upon existent land, and to impose enclosures upon the commons. On the large tracts of land which were not held by the Duchy within the High Peak, lords also tried to raise revenue by increasing rents, suppressing common rights on demesne land, and carving enclosures out of the commons. In some instances, wealthier freeholders can also be found making enclosures upon the commons. A united communal response was typically solicited by such attacks on common lands and rights. Manifest in the breaking of enclosures, in armed demonstrations, in threatening speeches against gentlemen and freeholders, and after the 1570s in a growing tendency on the part of tenants to engage in litigation, such

---

[14] On these disputes, see for instance PRO, DL4/32/26, /59/42, /123/1685/2. For other inter-community disputes of the late sixteenth century, see DRO, D258M/61/9; PRO, DL4/26/33, /10/23, /19/7, /38/17, /27/83.

[15] PRO, DL4/56/22, /59/22, /67/61, /40/18, /37/14, /32/26; PRO, E134/9Jasl/Mich5, /10Jasl/East32, /11Jasl/Trin5; PRO, STAC5/B52/9.

conflict became increasingly confrontational during the late 1580s and 1590s.[16]

The increasing aggression displayed in enclosure disputes at the end of the sixteenth century was a part of a general shift in local plebeian politics. Whether dealing with mining rights or enclosures, lower-class inhabitants became much more assertive than in earlier years. In response, the gentry and nobility of the area intensified their attacks upon common rights and free mining customs. Alignments of interest in this gathering social conflict were redrawn by the death of the sixth Earl of Shrewsbury in 1590, which opened a power vacuum in the politics of the Peak. The local authority of Earl George had a number of sources: the large number of manors he held either as a Duchy lessee or as their lord; his considerable wealth in an unusually impoverished part of the country; his domination of the lead industry; and his close connections to Elizabeth's court. Upon his death, lesser figures took up the fragments of his empire. The lease of the lot and cope rights in the Queen's Field of Wirksworth Wapentake passed to his son, Earl Gilbert, who continued to foster the Duchy's rights there. The lot and cope of the Queen's Field in the Hundred of High Peak was transferred to Rowland Eyre of Hassop.

While the sixth Earl lived, his policies in his own manors and those he leased from the Duchy had developed along similar lines. By the 1590s, the Shrewsburys had run the affairs of the High Peak for so long that the boundaries between the different manors over which the sixth Earl had held authority had become indistinct. This vagueness was further complicated by the descent of the Earl's territories and leases, and by the impact of late sixteenth-century population expansion upon local memory. On the death of Earl George, Ashford lordship was temporarily broken up. Part of the lordship passed to Earl Gilbert, and the rest to Bess of Hardwick and her Cavendish sons. Furthermore, much of the population of the High Peak villages were first or second generation migrants, having arrived in the wave of population increase which followed the revival of lead mining in the High Peak. Therefore, there were relatively few aged local inhabitants able to make clear distinctions between Shrewsbury's private manors within Ashford lordship and the territories he had leased from the Duchy of Lancaster. For all of these reasons, Rowland Eyre, as the new lessee of the Duchy's lot and cope rights in the Queen's Field of the High Peak, was impelled to define the spatial limits of the High Peak Queen's Field through legal actions. As the new lessee he had an obvious interest in the establish-

[16] PRO, C21/D1/13; PRO, DL4/11/45, /10/23, /19/7, /38/17, /21/31, /26/4, /26/28, /27/67, / 27/87, /27/49, /28/6, /37/4, /41/51, /67/59; PRO, E134/38&39Eliz/Mich29, /39&40Eliz/ Mich1; PRO, STAC5/V1/25; *APC, 1597–8*, 442–3; BL, Add. MS 6668, fol. 289.

ment of as wide a Queen's Field as was possible, so as to be able to levy tolls upon the miners and orebuyers there. In 1593, therefore, Eyre initiated the first case at the Court of the Duchy of Lancaster concerning the boundaries of the Queen's Field within the Hundred of High Peak, laying claim to Ashford as a part of the Duchy's estates. That same year he displaced Shrewsbury's deputy barmasters, and appointed his own men. Although the Duchy threw out Eyre's claim upon Ashford lordship, in the last years of the sixteenth century he initiated several cases against lords of manors within the High Peak who would not accept his claims to lot and cope upon their territory.[17] Again, an important watershed had been reached in the history of mining rights in the Peak Country. Hitherto, Peak mining cases heard before the Court of the Duchy of Lancaster had concerned the customs within the Wapentake of Wirksworth. Now the Court was to become the main focus for litigation over mining rights in the Hundred of High Peak as well.

In order to prove his entitlement to the lot and cope duties of the territories which he claimed as part of the King's Field, Rowland Eyre had to amass a body of both written and oral evidence. The latter category of evidence took the form of depositions, taken upon a specified day by a commission of local gentry empowered by the Duchy Court to hear evidence as to the past history of a manor from local aged inhabitants. Eyre therefore required a certain degree of local support in order to win his case at law. It is significant that in only a single case did Eyre's litigation of 1593–1602 reach the stage at which depositions were taken and judgement issued; and in that case, the deponents were uniformly hostile to Eyre. In no small measure, this was due to his attempt to claim further duties upon the miners and orebuyers. Not only was Eyre trying to extend the territory over which he could collect the Duchy's lot and cope duties. In laying claim to a right to cope payments upon the 'purcassed' ore produced by the poor cavers, who were traditionally exempted from payment of duties on grounds of their poverty, he was also attempting to increase the depth of such duties.[18]

Rowland Eyre was hampered in his attempts to extend the Duchy's lot and cope rights by a lack of support from any significant interest group within Peak society. By the time at which he was pressing his claims, the miners had started to emerge as one such interest group. Rowland Eyre's sons Adam and Thomas succeeded him as lessees of the Duchy's lot and cope. They did not make the same mistake as their father. For all that the

---

[17] PRO, DL1/148/T2, /160/E1, /163/F4, /165/M8, /168/E3, /171/A6, /175/W1, /177/E2–5, /178/S8, /179/A28, /179/A57, /181/E1, /181/E7, /185/S14, /187/E8–9, /188/E40–3, /199/S7; Meredith, 'Eyres of Hassop: I', 34–7.

[18] PRO, DL1/177/E5; PRO, DL4/40/34.

miners remained hostile and suspicious towards them, on both sides a common willingness to compromise in pursuit of their mutual interests allowed for the prosecution of successful actions at the Duchy Court in the Jacobean period. These actions both increased the area over which the Eyres could claim lot and cope duties, while at the same time confirming the miners in their right of free mining within those territories. The story will be told more fully in the succeeding chapter, but it should be noted that it begins at the close of the sixteenth century, in 1597. In that year, John Burton, a 'poore mynor' of Tideswell, defended the right of free mining in Little Hucklow against its powerful lords, and also insisted upon the right of the barmote to hear the case. Burton lost the action, but his actions presaged future developments. A year earlier, he and other miners had been prosecuted at the Court of Exchequer for refusing payment of a one tenth lead tithe claimed upon them.[19] These legal actions formed the opening shots in the High Peak miners' battles to extend the limits of the Queen's Field and to defeat the claim to a tithe upon their labours. In the years ahead, both matters were to preoccupy a series of Westminster courts, and to determine the miners' political culture. For the miners just as for the Eyres, the successes of the early seventeenth century were founded upon their willingness and ability to build alliances: in this case, with those individuals within Derbyshire's ruling elite who possessed an interest in the success of their cause. And like the Eyres, they learnt this lesson in the years between 1570 and 1600.

As we have seen, the sixth Earl of Shrewsbury was advised in 1585 to take care in his dealings with the miners. That advice needs to be placed into context. Like his peers, Shrewsbury had been brought up with the idea that the social order was built upon hierarchy, paternalism and deference. Yet we have seen how one of the most powerful noblemen in Elizabethan England was advised to approach 'quietly' a group of poor but 'wilful' workers. Out of his conflicts with the miners and his tenants, Shrewsbury had learnt the hard lesson that the hierarchical ideal was a fiction. While not yet possessed of the organization and traditions which were to define them as a local political body, the miners were established as an interest group. Like the tenants of Glossop, the High Peak miners had acquired a sense of tactics. As tenants and as miners, they had played upon the Privy Council's concerns as to Shrewsbury's ability to maintain order in what was perceived to be an unruly and lawless area. Shrewsbury and his officers ultimately recognized the importance of placating the interests of the tenants and miners. By 1585, the sixth Earl was forced to back down from

[19] PRO, DL1/185/S14, /199/S7a; PRO, E112/9/75.

his demands for a pre-emption upon the miners and orebuyers, and to come to a compromise settlement with his tenants.

The sixth Earl lived in two interconnected political worlds: that of the court, and that of the Peak. In the former, the tenants and miners of the Peak were outsiders. Yet none the less they were able to embarrass Earl George before his peers. In the latter, by the end of the sixteenth century, they were becoming players in a game of local power politics. The rules of that game were biased against them, yet increasingly the miners could not be ignored. Relations within and between these political worlds did not move according to some well-oiled function. Instead, the place which the free mining interest occupied within the power politics of the Peak was to be bought through conflict, threat and negotiation. After the 1580s, in order to pursue their own material interests – to enclose land, deny rights, impose and exact duties and tithes – noble magnates, gentlemen and ministers were required to face down or to come into conflict with increasingly organized plebeian resistance. Alternatively, as Shrewsbury had recognized, they could negotiate. In such moments of compromise, the outward form of deference was respectfully maintained by tenants and miners, just as their social betters took on for a moment the Emperor's new clothes of silken paternalism. But by the last years of the sixteenth century, both sides were aware of the hard reality which underlay those fleeting moments.

10

'All is hurly burly here': local histories of social conflict, 1600–1640

The potential for conflict over customary law in general, and mining custom in particular, was realized in the Peak Country during the period between the end of Elizabeth's reign and the outbreak of the civil war. Miners and tenants struggled with the greater gentry, nobility and clergy of the region over a series of connected issues: free mining custom; the enclosure of common land; the denial of common rights; and parochial tithes. The subject matter of such disputes was far from exceptional. Across early Stuart England, but especially in the pastoral-industrial uplands, in forests and in the East Anglian fens, custom and common right were hotly contested between lord and tenant, minister and parish, landed and landless. What made local disputes in the Peak unusual was their connected character, their longevity and seriousness, and the relatively clear social division which separated opposing sides. This chapter will chart the twists and turns in the development of that conflict. It will focus first of all upon developments within the Wapentake of Wirksworth, describing in turn the renewed struggle over mining rights; the conflict between the parishioners and minister of Wirksworth; and the intervention of the central state to crush the right of free mining in the Dovegang circuit just north of Wirksworth town. Attention will then turn north to consider developments within the High Peak, charting the struggles over the lead tithe, enclosure and free mining rights. In the succeeding chapter, the pattern of social conflict in the Peak Country will be placed in the wider context of historical debate over riot and popular politics in early Stuart England. Both chapters will concern themselves with the differing motives, interests and shifting alliances of key players in local politics. We will see in Chapter 11 how the evidence presented in this chapter bears upon social historians' reconsideration of politics in early modern England.

THE CONFRONTATION OVER FREE MINING IN THE WAPENTAKE OF WIRKSWORTH

The free mining community of the Wapentake of Wirksworth first revealed its collective capacity for organized political engagement in the middle years of the reign of King James I. In the late sixteenth century, the miners of Wirksworth had been reluctant publicly to oppose the manorial interest without the support of a powerful patron such as the Earl of Shrewsbury. By 1613, that was no longer the case. In that year, a group of miners led by Anthony Cadman of Wirksworth entered Steeple Grange near Wirksworth and started to dig for ore. They were violently ejected, but returned thereafter to exercise their rights. Around the same time, organized invasions of Tissington and Newton Grange by Wirksworth miners also occurred. Cadman is an interesting figure. Four years prior to his involvement in Steeple Grange, he had given evidence against the owner of Wigwell Grange near Wirksworth, who was impinging upon the town's commons. In 1623, he gave evidence in favour of the common rights of Bonsall, together with Robert Shawe, a notable defender of free mining rights in Stanton. In his seventies, Cadman was again to be active in defence of free mining, giving evidence against Sir Robert Heath's claims to the Dovegang mine.[1] Possessed of a close understanding of local custom, prepared to defend his rights through direct action and at law, enmeshed in a network of similarly minded individuals, Cadman typified the leadership of the miners' struggles in the early and mid-seventeenth century. His invasion of Steeple Grange marked the first shot in a larger confrontation over mining rights within the Wapentake.

At the time of Cadman's invasion of Steeple Grange, the lease of the Duchy of Lancaster's lot and cope duties in the Wapentake of Wirksworth was held by the parvenu gentleman Thomas Parker and his son Robert. The Parkers were using their family links and control of local office to build up a power base within the Wirksworth area. Thomas's daughter, Jennet, had married Richard Carrier, whom the Dean of Lincoln Cathedral (Thomas Parker's brother) had appointed as minister to the parish of Wirksworth and as rector of the adjacent parish of Carsington in 1619.[2] Immediately upon his appointment to the parish, Richard Carrier renewed an old claim to a tithe upon the miners' ore. The barmaster, William Bamford, helped to organize the miners' resistance to his demands. As lessees of the Duchy's lot and cope, Thomas and Robert Parker were

---

[1] PRO, DL4/72/31, /54/36, /73/26, /85/58.
[2] The parish of Wirksworth was in the gift of the Dean and Chapter of Lincoln, who had once owned a decayed manor in the town.

entitled to appoint the barmaster for the Wapentake. The Parkers therefore displaced Bamford as barmaster, and appointed Carrier to the important local office in his place.[3] As we shall see, Jennet and Richard Carrier became loathed within the parish for their exactions as tithe proprietors, and for Richard's actions as barmaster. None the less, the Carriers and Parkers had a common interest with the miners in the extension of the King's Field within the Wapentake of Wirksworth.

The miners sought the Duchy of Lancaster's support in their claim to free mining rights on those manors and Granges where the custom was denied. Hence, the affirmation of free mining entailed the recognition of the Duchy's authority, which in turn meant that the miners had to pay lot and cope duties to the Parkers and Carriers. As in the High Peak, the Wirksworth miners were therefore drawn into an alliance with the gentry family which they found the most obnoxious. Both sides were cynical about that alliance. While making common cause with him and his family against the greater gentry of the Wapentake, the miners continued to oppose Carrier's tithe claims. Yet from 1621 to 1632, Carrier and the Parkers initiated actions in the Duchy Court against those lords of manors and owners of Granges in Wirksworth Wapentake who denied the miners the right of free mining. Ironically, the miners and their hated minister therefore became joint upholders of the laws of the King's Field.

In legal action commencing in 1622, the mining rights of some sixteen manors or granges in the Wapentake of Wirksworth were called into question.[4] Miners had been barred by the lords of these territories in the late sixteenth century. Initiated in the names of Richard Carrier and the Parkers, the actions were enthusiastically supported by the Wirksworth miners. The lords of the manors and Granges in question responded with counter-actions, and with organized violence against the miners. In Tissington, Sir John Fitzherbert ejected the miners from his land, as did Sir Francis Foljamb in Elton. In Smerrill Grange, Lady Grace Manners of Haddon made 'threatening speeches' at the miners while leading armed attacks upon them by her tenants. In at least seven other manors or Granges the miners were threatened with action at common law for trespass if they did not leave their works.[5]

[3] PRO, SP14/80/129.   [4] PRO, DL4/72/31, /85/58.
[5] PRO, DL4/123/1684/4; PRO, STAC9/1/13; PRO, DL1/293, Att.-Gen. v. Sir Fras. Foljamb, *et al*, /296, replication of Att.-Gen. v. Sir William Withypool, /298, Att.-Gen. v. Lady Grace Manners, /300, replication of Att.-Gen. v. Sir Fras. Foljamb; BL, Add. MS 6677, fols. 40–3; PRO, DL5/29, fols. 321–2. Following the ejection of the free miners, waged labourers or servants were typically employed to dig and carry away ore to smelting mills which were frequently also owned by the lord. See PRO, DL1/293, Att.-Gen. v. Sir Fras. Foljamb *et al.*; PRO, DL4/72/31, /75/10; PRO, DL5/29, fol. 289. For memories of these disputes in the 1680s, see PRO, DL4/123/1684/4.

The miners' collective assertion of free mining rights was planned and organized in advance. So too was their opponents' defence of their estates. As the miners and their supporters saw the issue, some of the most important gentry families in the county were involved in a concerted attempt to deny the 'free liberty' of mining. The Wirksworth miners received the support of two lesser gentlemen, Anthony Ferne and his son, John.[6] John Ferne's role in the downfall of Richard Carrier will be described later in this chapter. In 1623, in the course of legal proceedings concerning the mining rights of Steeple Grange, Ferne gave a lengthy deposition to the Duchy Court. His reading of the history and character of mining custom has been already discussed in Chapter 6. In a series of asides to that deposition, Ferne described what he saw as the social basis to the developing confrontation over mining rights in the Peak. For John Ferne, the miners were threatened by 'powerful men' who

by violence [have] holden the myners down by their own combynacion [and] do now bandy themselves [to claim] . . . that the myners . . . have never wrought in their lands wch this deponent taketh to bee untried for that itt appeareth in many townes and places in the said Wapentake where the mynors for His Matie have been inhibited or else kept out by strong hand . . . that there are mynes of ancient tyme wrought wch now in pte are for lett which argueth that the myners ought to worke ther.

These 'powerful men' used 'Terrer & Feare' to prevent the miners from exercising their rights. In this, the 'powerful men' were aided by their social position and political authority: 'Some of them had a great Comande in Wirkesworth parishe by themselves their kindred and alleyances'. Thus 'poore men for want of supportacon are driven from their right and thereby the King looseth his privilidge of lot and cope'. John Ferne's father, Anthony, agreed with this interpretation and went further, presenting a vision of a direct conflict between rich and poor over mining custom:

hee did not ever hear of any yeom[an], husbandma[n] or other Ordinary psones keepe oute the Kinges Minors or stop the[m] from searching or digging for lead Oare . . . manie of them are great men that doe stopp and keepe the mynors for digginge & gettinge lead oare in their grounds . . . most of the sd great men doe keep the said myners forth of their grounds rather for fear of their greatness & displeasure then by any just Tytle.

The words of Anthony and John Ferne were echoed by the miner Francis

---

[6] John Ferne succeeded Anthony as Bailiff of the Duchy manors of Wirksworth and Ashbourne. See R. Somerville, *Office-holders in the Duchy and county Palatine of Lancaster from 1603* (Chichester, 1972), 177. As such, the Fernes had their own interest in the extension of the Duchy's rights in Wirksworth Wapentake. See PRO, DL4/64/14. For continuing memories from 1666 of John and Anthony Ferne as defenders of common rights, see PRO, DL4/109/8.

Toft in his answer to the complaint of Sir Francis Foljamb at Star Chamber in 1625. To Toft, Foljamb and his ancestors had kept the miners out of Elton 'by reason of their greate power & commaunde in those p[ar]ts and not by anie just tytle or p[ro]perty they had thereunto'. For Toft, the 'miners . . . wrought and ought there to have to have libertie of digging & gettinge lead oare'.[7]

Initially, the litigation which Carrier and the Parkers commenced in 1622 was mounted in separate complaints against each lord of each manor or Grange where free mining was denied. But by 1625, the matter had devolved upon two test cases which would establish the validity of a general custom of free mining across the whole of the Wapentake of Wirksworth. That test case concerned two purported manors: Elton and Tissington. The miners, backed by Carrier and the Parkers, claimed that their 'free liberty' to search within the whole Wapentake was proved by their continuous usage of a custom of free mining, and by the provisions of the 1557 Great Barmote. It will be remembered that the 13th injunction of the 1557 Great Barmote of Wirksworth manor had laid down a right of free mining across the whole Wapentake, and that by King James' reign miners were committing this injunction to memory and repeating its provisions verbatim when giving verbal evidence in mining disputes. Despite the production of documents suggesting that some of the Granges and manors in question had never been held by the Dukes of Lancaster, in a judgement of 1627 the Duchy Court ruled in favour of the operation of free mining law within Elton and Tissington.[8] At that point, the lords of the remaining manors and Granges dropped their opposition to free mining. Further litigation ensued in 1634 after Carrier's removal as barmaster, but citing its judgements of 1627, the Duchy Court again declared in favour of free mining (see Map 14).[9]

Although the gentry coalition lost their case, this was by no means a foregone conclusion. Carrier and the Parkers lost confidence at various points between 1622 and 1625, but were forced to maintain their actions due to the independent action of the miners. In spite of prosecution for trespass by the Manners of Haddon, the Wirksworth miners persisted in digging in Smerrill Grange, while the tenacity of the local miners and deputy barmaster in the face of Star Chamber action, where Sir Francis Foljamb accused them of riot, kept the Elton case before the Duchy Court.

---

[7] The Fernes' remarks are at PRO, DL4/72/31; Toft's are at PRO, STAC9/1/13.
[8] PRO, DL5/29, fols. 33, 39–40, 74, 84–5, 115, 142–3, 159, 166, 168, 169, 181, 215, 228, 272, 278, 289, 303, 306, 314, 321–2, 432–3, 467, 523. The crucial judgements are at fols. 159, 432–3r See also BL, Add. MS 6678, fols. 58–61.
[9] PRO, DL5/31, fols. 496, 503, 641.

The victory of the miners and their unlikely allies strengthened the legal basis of free mining within the Wapentake of Wirksworth, and set an important precedent.[10] Yet the victory of the free mining interest was by no means complete. Since the opponents of free mining had withdrawn from legal action in 1627, no specific verdict concerning manors other than Elton and Tissington was established. While the right of free mining had been advanced through a combination of litigation and crowd action, the legal judgements obtained in the miners' favour only contributed to a strengthening of the 'generall custome' across the whole Wapentake, rather than securing free mining within specific jurisdiction. Once law courts turned against such general, vague customs in favour of a closer specification of the claimants to and geographical operation of customary law, this lack of specificity was to imperil the right of free mining. This represented more than a mere legal technicality, and had repercussions which were to be felt after the Restoration when free miners were once again excluded from some manors and Granges in the Wapentake of Wirksworth.

THE POLITICS OF A PARISH AND THE KING'S ATTORNEY-GENERAL

From his appointment to the parish of Wirksworth in 1619 to his removal in 1632, neither Richard Carrier nor his wife Jennet seem to have understood the politics of that parish. Vigorously prosecuting his claims to tithes on wool, corn, lambs and most importantly on lead production, Carrier sued a growing number of husbandmen, yeomen and miners at the central courts of Chancery and Exchequer and at the Consistory Court of the diocese of Lichfield and Coventry.[11] The replacement of William Bamford with Richard Carrier as barmaster in 1619 seems to have merely hardened opposition to his claim to a tithe of lead. Nor did Carrier's appointment to the county bench improve his local standing. The more that Richard accrued institutional power to himself – as minister, as a Justice of the Peace, as barmaster – the more he seemed to lose informal, local authority. As the Carriers set about inventing tithe rights, they met with mounting hostility. In Carsington, Richard used his new authority as a Justice to gaol his opponents, and threatened them with ruin at the Westminster courts. His deputy barmasters made similar threats against miners who refused to pay an invented tithe called 'Gifter ore'. Richard was accused of assaulting his parishioners in Carsington in pursuit of his tithes, while Jennet was

[10] BL, Add. MS 6677, fol. 49.
[11] PRO, C2/Jas I/C20/15; Cox, *Derbyshire annals*, II, 241; PRO, DL4/84/24; SA Bag C 549 (9); LJRO, B/C/5 1613, 1621, 1624, 1622 Wirksworth; PRO, E112/168/5, 34.

alleged to have brandished a knife at miners while taking Gifter ore from them.

As barmaster, Richard packed and intimidated barmote juries. He refused to allow the miners use of the 'brazen dish' to measure their ore before sale, thereby rendering their sales illegal under mining law. Richard's drunken and libidinous curate refused burial to the bodies of those miners who had opposed the Carriers' demands. As vicar, Justice and barmaster, Richard Carrier's monopoly of local authority brought bitter comment. On one occasion, Carrier was alleged to have told the miners that 'hee was barmaster, Judge, Justice & lord of the myne & whosoever resisted hee would set them in the stocks by the neck, middle or legg'. Richard Carrier would later be given cause to rue his 'thretes' to use 'his own greatnes and the greatnes of his freinds' against the inhabitants of Wirksworth and Carsington. Throughout the 1620s, the parishioners responded to the Carriers' behaviour with organized tithe strikes, threats of murder, maiming the Carriers' cattle, and with their own legal suits. In Wirksworth parish, a common purse was maintained by the parishioners in the 1620s to pay for legal action against the Carriers' tithe demands. A second common purse was gathered by 300 miners of Wirksworth and Carsington to oppose the demand for Gifter ore. In alliance with the miners of the parishes of Bakewell, Tideswell and Hope, the Wirksworth miners presented a petition against the lead tithe to the Privy Council.[12] Over the 1610s and 1620s, the Wirksworth miners' opposition to the lead tithes developed in tune with their hostility to those lords who opposed free mining. Jennet and Richard Carrier therefore ran into the hardening face of the miners' growing assertiveness. The development of a dense network amongst leading resisters to lords and ministers can be traced from around this time.

Thomas Godberhere, a Cromford miner, is one example of a miner who distinguished himself both against Carrier and the manorial interest. He led opposition to Carrier's claim to Gifter ore in the 1620s, and was prosecuted by Parker at the Duchy Court in 1628 for his refusal of the duty. This was no new experience for Godberhere, for five years earlier he had been sued by Richard Carrier at Chancery. In 1632, Godberhere was to be prosecuted yet again, this time for organizing the non-payment of lot and cope duties to Carrier. Godberhere's organizational activities did not end there. He was to challenge Sir Robert Heath's seizure of the Dovegang works in 1638, and to petition for the right to elect the barmaster in 1651. Variously

---

[12] PRO, C21/C11/10; Gardiner, *Reports*, 90; PRO, RGO 33, frontispiece; LJRO, B/C/5, 1628, 1629, Wirksworth; BL, Add. MSS 6704, fols. 4–5, 6677, fols. 1–8, 6681, fols. 360–71; PRO, SP14/163/81, /123/12.

described as a 'yeoman' and 'husbandman' before the civil wars, by the 1650s Godberhere had become an important investor in the highly profitable works on Cromford moor. He was a prominent figure within his village, serving as a Headborough and frequently deposing in court actions. His fame as an opponent of 'oppressors' spread to the High Peak, and he was called upon to give evidence against the lead tithe in Bakewell, Tideswell and Hope parishes in 1628.[13] Godberhere was typical of the miners who formed the hard core of opposition to the Carriers and to later opponents of the free mining interest. Such men were joined by a small but important clique of local lesser gentry, irritated by Carrier's and later by Sir Robert Heath's disruption of communal harmony. John Ferne typified the Wirksworth miners' allies amongst the town's lesser gentry. He was on personal terms with Godberhere, and they co-operated together against Carrier, whom Ferne described as the 'arch enemy of o[u]r parish'. Ferne had reason to dislike the vicar, having been the object of court action by Carrier for his opposition to the collection of Gifter ore; the purpose of this action was, as Ferne put it, to 'molest' him and 'terrify' others. He was well known within the town as 'Mr. Carrier's enemy', and as a defender of free mining and common rights, representing cases in both barmote and Westminster courts. Like Godberhere, he became a leading protagonist against Sir Robert Heath in the 1630s.[14]

By 1629, Richard and Jennet Carrier had managed to alienate all the key interest groups within local society. Despite the money which they had spent on legal action, the lead tithe remained difficult to collect. Furthermore, in pressing their claims to Gifter ore and lead tithes with such extremity, the Carriers had alienated themselves from the miners. Their allegedly violent and oppressive conduct was perceived by their social peers as straining local social relations.[15] Finally, in their strange alliance with the miners against the manorial interest within the Wapentake, the Carriers had earned the hostility of the greater gentry. Only their links to the Parkers and Richard's command of local office sustained them in power by the late 1620s. In 1629, however, Carrier was suddenly removed as barmaster through the intervention of the King's Attorney-General, Sir

[13] PRO, DL5/29, fol. 556, /31, fol. 218; BL, Add. MS 6681, fols. 360–71; PRO, DL4/90/24, / 109/8, /91/16; PRO, SP23/151, fol. 99; PRO, DL30/54/664, 54/671; DRO, D258M/28/ 20c.

[14] On Ferne, see Chapter 6 above, and DRO, D258M/60/11, /X/77c, /50/52h, /42/29e. For his depositions, see PRO, DL4/85/51, /72/31; PRO, E134/11ChasI/Mich 20. On his activities as a mine-owner and lead merchant, see DRO, D258M/58/24c, 20c; PRO, E317/9/28. Despite his sympathy for popular interests in Wirksworth, his tenure as bailiff of Wirksworth manor led to him taking action against miners and smallholders: see PRO, DL1/352, answer of Anthony Harding et al. and attached depositions; PRO, REQ2/404/101.

[15] See for instance Ferne's letters to Thomas Gell: DRO, D258M/56/52i, /54/19p.

Robert Heath. Carrier had opposed Heath's decision to take possession of a large mine near Wirksworth town called the Dovegang. In this, Heath was also opposed by the miners of Wirksworth Wapentake, to whom the seizure of the Dovegang represented a direct assault upon free mining law. The barmastership of Wirksworth at first passed into the hands of John Ferne.[16] As the conflict of interest between Heath and the miners became more apparent, Heath himself acquired the right of appointment of barmaster.[17] But just as the miners had been able to put aside their growing hatred of the Carriers and Parkers in pursuit of free mining rights within the Wapentake between 1622 and 1627, so they now made common cause with the King's Attorney-General against the minister of Wirksworth and his wife. Heath ensured that Robert Parker and Richard Carrier were removed from their respective positions as lessee of the lot and cope rights and barmaster of the Wapentake. The miners were only too ready to testify against their barmaster, just as they were two years later when Heath placed Richard and Jennet Carrier before the Court of Star Chamber, accused of the riotous extraction of Gifter ore and alleged criticisms of church policy.[18] In this action, leading miners enthusiastically gave evidence against the Carriers, giving full voice to the resentments which had built up against the Carriers since 1619. The Star Chamber found against the Carriers, imposed a heavy fine upon them, and removed Richard as minister of Wirksworth. He was replaced by Martin Topham, who discovered that he was as unable to collect tithes of lead upon the miners as his predecessor had been.[19]

Thus far, we have focused almost exclusively upon struggles within the small world of the Peak Country. Indeed, the Carriers' conflicts with their parishioners literally defines the politics of a parish. But like so many other small worlds, the early Caroline Peak became the sudden focus of attention of one of the 'great men' of King Charles' court. As in the fenlands and the forests of the West Country, existent social conflicts were intensified and given new definitions by the incursion of a powerful courtier into the locality. Reference to similar disputes in the fens and the West Country

---

[16] BL Add. MSS 6681, fols. 132–3; DRO, D258M/54/19p; although the office of barmaster was removed from Carrier, he continued to press his claim to lot and cope payments throughout the 1630s: see PRO, DL1/352, complaint of Richard Carrier, /349 Att.-Gen. v. Henry Travis.

[17] PRO, DL5/30, fols. 34–5; Dias, 'Lead society and politics', 49.

[18] The precise nature of these criticisms remains unclear. Carrier is reported to have made contradictory comments, apparently sympathetic to both puritanism and Catholicism. See Gardiner, *Reports*, 91–2, and DRO, D258M/56/21. Both Richard and Jennet Carrier sided with the King on the outbreak of war: *Theeves, theeves, or a relation of Sir John Gell's proceedings in Derbyshire* BL, TT E.100 (13).

[19] PRO, DL5/34, fol. 436.

forests is more than merely comparative. At the same time as his involvement in the Dovegang affair, Heath was also drawn into conflict with the Free Miners of the Forest of Dean, where other courtiers were attempting to redefine forest law and ban free mining. The same connections exist with fenland disputes. Heath's partner in his dealings in the Dovegang was Sir Cornelius Vermuyden, made famous by his attempts to drain the Bedford Level in the face of bitter opposition from the local inhabitants.[20] As in the Forest of Dean and the fens, the combined forces of the Privy Council, Star Chamber, the common law and the Courts of the Duchy of Lancaster and Exchequer were mobilized to crush local custom. The Dovegang dispute of 1629–32 represented the only attempt at the outright abolition of the laws of the King's Field. Elsewhere, mining law was either marginalized, or its basis in common usage disproven within specific jurisdictions. In contrast, both sides in the Dovegang dispute accepted that a right of free mining had existed prior to Heath's interest in the mine. Instead of developing an argument from law, the King's Attorney-General therefore relied upon his authority and connections as a 'great man' to break local custom.

The story told here has its own relevance. But it is also part of a bigger picture, providing a further example of how a Caroline courtier was able to shove his own interests down the gullet of a plebeian community at a time of wider disenchantment with a national government which was coming to be perceived as hostile to the national custom of the ancient constitution. Heath was aided in this project and others by the Crown's need for revenue. Up to the 1640s the Duchy Court was generally sympathetic to mining law and local custom on its Peak estates. But where the Crown wished to raise revenue, the Duchy Court became a means of securing exactions upon local inhabitants. One method pursued across the Duchy's territories, and in particular in the pastoral and industrial 'Northern Parts' of its estates where the value of land had risen while rents and fines remained set, was to force tenants to compound with the Duchy upon cash payments for the confirmation of their customs and rents. Hence the Duchy's tenants in the manor of Wirksworth were forced to pay a fine of £1,193 for the confirmation of their customs in 1621. In the same fashion, feefarms of Duchy offices and rights were granted to gentry entrepreneurs, who used these titles to exact new tolls upon tenants, and

---

[20] The interconnections of such courtiers involved in these disputes would repay closer attention. On the Forest of Dean, see Sharp, *In contempt*; Hart, *Free miners*. On the fens, see Lindley, *Fenland riots*; L.E. Harris, *Vermuyden and the fens: a study of Sir Cornelius Vermuyden* (London, 1953). On the Dovegang, see Kirkham, 'Tumultuous course'; F.N. Fisher, 'Sir Cornelius Vermuyden and the Dovegang lead mine', *DAJ*, 2nd ser., 72 (1952), 74–118; Dias, 'Lead, society and politics', 48–51.

to enclose land.[21] Sir Robert Heath was a key adviser on means of raising Crown revenue, and was therefore ideally placed to benefit from developments in its estate policies.[22]

Sir Robert Heath's attentions had been attracted to Wirksworth by the possibilities afforded by the large Dovegang works. As well as holding office as the King's Attorney-General, Heath was also something of an entrepreneur.[23] Relying upon the technical expertise of Sir Cornelius Vermuyden, a Dutch drainage engineer, he proposed to drain the inundated Dovegang deposits. Consisting of about a square mile just north of Wirksworth town, the Dovegang was said to contain the richest ore in the lead field. By 1629, the deposits had been exploited down to the winter waterline. Yet good ore was known to lie beneath the waters. All previous attempts at drainage had failed, but limited work was still possible in the summer. Under early seventeenth-century barmote law, any mine which was not worked for a period of more than six weeks passed to the barmaster, who reassigned the meers of the mine to other owners. But a clause of mining custom specifically exempted mines which were hindered by drainage or ventilation difficulties from this law. Small free mining operations, funded by the mercantile lesser gentry of Wirksworth, therefore continued in the summer months.[24] The defence of free mining rights in the Dovegang therefore united both free miner and lesser gentleman in common cause.

In 1629 Heath secured an order from the Duchy Court which placed the barmastership of Wirksworth and the Dovegang mine in his hands.[25] Yet by custom his seizure of the Dovegang was illegal, since the mines were still in occupation. Heath and Vermuyden proposed to drain the inundated deposits by means of an underground channel or sough. They acknowledged that the project promised to be highly expensive, but Heath argued that if successful it would provide employment for many hundreds of labourers. The owners of the mines on the Dovegang were unimpressed by this argument, and even less pleased when, utilizing his new powers over the barmaster, Heath removed the Dovegang altogether from the King's Field and appointed a special barmaster for those works.

---

[21] PRO DL5/28, fols. 368–80; PRO DL43/1/36A; Manning, *Village revolts*, 132–3. On the broader context of these developments, see R.W. Hoyle ' "Shearing the hog": the reform of the estates, *c.* 1598–1640', and 'Disafforestation and drainage: the Crown as entrepreneur?', in *idem* (ed.), *The estates of the English Crown, 1558–1640* (Cambridge, 1992), 204–62, 353–88.

[22] Harris, *Vermuyden*, 43.

[23] P.E. Kopperman, *Sir Robert Heath 1575–1649: window on an age* (London, 1989), 247–77.

[24] PRO, E317/9/29b; BL, Add. MS 6686, fols. 61–3.

[25] PRO, DL5/30, fol. 234. This was backed up by a further order of 1632: PRO, DL5/31, fol. 218.

In 1631 the new barmaster empanelled a barmote jury to survey the Dovegang. Having been told that the survey did not in any way prejudice the ownership of the works already in operation within the circuit, and threatened by Vermuyden's lieutenant Johannus Molanus, the jurors put their marks to the document placed before them, only to discover that it authorized Heath to take control of the workings. A subsequent jury introduced a new injunction that those Dovegang mines which had not been worked for two weeks were forfeit to Heath. Once again, the jurors later claimed to have been intimidated into this breach of custom by the 'terrifying' behaviour of Heath and Molanus.[26] The Dovegang therefore passed into the hands of Sir Robert Heath, 'to his great p[ro]fit and advantage'. Although the free miners and lesser gentry lost their mines, the poorer inhabitants gained from employment in the construction of Vermuyden's sough. By 1641, the workforce employed on the construction of Vermuyden's sough was estimated at around 200. The internal divisions within the extractive workforce therefore operated against the free mining interest; for the poorer miners and 'hirelings' had little interest in resisting the possibility of long-term employment.[27] None the less, resistance to Heath's seizure of the Dovegang continued after 1632. A number of miners were indicted for 'inactinge an assault' against Heath's men, and the newly appointed barmaster of the Dovegang was instructed by the Duchy Court to inform against any disturbers of the works. In spite of further injunctions from the Duchy Court, 'interruptions' of the soughing operations continued. Heath and Vermuyden pursued cases at common law against miners who took ore from the Dovegang rather than in the barmote, presumably fearful that barmote jurors would be sympathetic to the accused.

A different sense of economic priorities from that of their rulers informed the free miners' continuing opposition to Heath and Vermuyden. Lawrence Stokes was amongst those who had lost works on the Dovegang. He argued that he was able to make a good living from his work there, and that 'if the miners had been suffered to work in the [Dovegang] . . . according to the . . . custome they might have gott four or five hundred loade of oare there in a year'. Stokes complained that Molanus had threatened him and had cut down and burnt the 'stowes' which marked possession of the small workings in the Dovegang. Miners argued that by undercutting custom, the Attorney-General was both setting a precedent for other wealthy men and

[26] PRO, DL44/1121; PRO, DL4/91/16. It is interesting to note that the tenants of Gillingham Forest in Dorset, also subject to the rapacious activities of a Stuart courtier who had acquired a lease of office within the Forest, complained that they had been tricked into signing a document which effectively gave away their customary rights. See PRO, E134/3ChasI/East17. For similar actions in the fens, see Lindley, *Fenland riots*, 31.

[27] PRO, DL4/85/58, /92/55; PRO, E101/280/18.

striking at the liberties of the common people.[28] John Ferne again gave voice to the miners' frustrations. Writing to the attorney Thomas Gell, he remarked that

people have been so terrified and oppressed with [Heath] . . . that they dare not draw breath agt. him for the vulgar sorte doe beleeve that nothing wilbe done against him but all wilbe with him as it hath beene and then he would torment them that either say or doe agt. him that they dare not openly be seen to doe any thing for I protest I think that many poore stand more afraid of him then they doe either of God or the Kinge.

Gell agreed with Ferne's assessment of the situation, concluding that Heath threatened to 'destroy the miners utterly'.[29] Ultimately, King Charles himself intervened, ordering the ringleaders to 'suffer' Heath's employees to work the Dovegang upon the pain of a £500 fine.

Although Heath secured possession of the Dovegang, he ultimately gained little by it. Vermuyden's drainage works took many years to complete, and by the time the mine was turning a profit Heath was dead. That the methods by which Heath seized the Dovegang works were never again to be repeated is of considerable significance. At the same time as Heath had been manipulating his position as Attorney-General to secure the Dovegang, he had also set the Duchy Court into motion upon a matter which posed a much greater threat to the free mining interest than the seizure of a square mile of lead deposits. In 1627, the Duchy started to inquire into the legality of re-establishing a pre-emption of all ore sales within both the King's Field of Wirksworth Wapentake and the High Peak. We have already seen how, during the late sixteenth century, the lords of non-Duchy manors had used their manorial right of pre-emption to force miners to sell their ore at rates below the market price. Another part of the Crown's estates, the Duchy of Cornwall, occasionally followed the same policy in the Cornish tin mines. But in the King's Fields of High Peak and Wirksworth Wapentake, the Duchy mysteriously lost interest in the matter after 1634. The Duchy may have been dissuaded from this course of action by the intensity of local hostility generated by the seizure of the Dovegang.[30]

In part, Heath's methods were a product of the particular circumstances of the 1620s and 30s. The story of an enterprising and autocratic courtier, reinforced by the power of the central law courts and the patronage of the

---

[28] DRO, QSC/62. For particularly strenuous assertions of the miners' case, see BL, Add. MS 6686, fols. 61–3; PRO, DL4/90/24, /91/16; DRO, D258/28/20r. See BL Add. MS 6678, fol. 39, for the complaints of the barmote against Heath.

[29] PRO, DL4/92/55, PRO, DL5/31, fols. 201, 242–3, 301–2, 540; BL, Add. MS 6686, fols. 158–60; PRO, PC2/44, fols. 614–20; DRO, D258M/56/52i, /58/49.

[30] PRO, PC2/44, fols. 614–20; PRO, SP16/78/20; BL, Add. MS 6686, fols. 57–8. For the Duchy's declining interest in the matter, see PRO, SP16/310/11, /341/129, /377/5; PRO, DL4/91/16. For the Duchy of Cornwall's right of pre-emption, see PRO, SP12/255/58.

King, imposing his interests over those lower down the social scale in spite of local custom was not an uncommon one at this time. The unique nature of Heath's arbitrary actions speaks volumes both for the antipathy raised against the Attorney-General and, paradoxically, of the strength of the free mining interest within Wirksworth Wapentake before the civil wars. The free miners of Wirksworth were no passive, disorganized victims of economic change. They successfully defended their rights against a coalition of some of the most important gentry families of the county, and engaged in continuous resistance to the lead tithe. In forcing through his demand to remove the Dovegang works from the King's Field, Heath alienated local opinion and enraged the miners. The role of the Wirksworth miners in the fall of Richard Carrier suggests how the alienation of an important plebeian interest group could destroy the authority, and ultimately the position, of a 'powerful man'. The Dovegang disputes tell a different but related story. In that matter, the miners were defeated. In the tenacity of their struggle over the Dovegang, the Wirksworth miners revealed themselves as a key collective interest group within local politics. The revelation to the Duchy and the Privy Council of the potential for organized, collective plebeian opposition to their decisions was not lost upon them.

THE 'ILLEGAL COMBINATIONS' OF THE HIGH PEAK

Over the early seventeenth century, the miners of the High Peak were learning the same lessons as their brethren further south, and teaching them to their social betters. The subject matter of disputes within the High Peak in these years was similar to that in Wirksworth Wapentake. Ministers and tithe proprietors demanded a lead tithe from the miners. Lords of manors and Granges attempted to prevent free mining upon their estates, leading to legal and physical contests over mining rights. But the context in which these disputes were fought out was rather different. While the High Peak miners were also able to exploit differences of interest amongst their betters, and while they also combined litigation and petition with obstruction, demonstration and crowd action, they were rather less successful than the Wirksworth miners in their opposition to lead tithes, or in advancing the right of free mining.

We shall concentrate first of upon the conflict over the tithe of lead. This story centres upon the three large mining parishes of Bakewell, Hope and Tideswell (see Map 2). Prior to the Reformation, the Priory of Lenton had held the lease of these tithes. Upon its dissolution in 1539, the lease passed to the Gells of Hopton and Talbot Earls of Shrewsbury. Initial attempts at the collection of the lead tithe by Earl George met with frustration, as the miners refused to pay the duty. The subsequent history of the lead tithe within these three parishes is vague until 1613, when the Shrewsburys' part of the lease passed to the Leakes of Sutton.[31] Upon his acquisition of two-thirds of the lease, Sir Francis Leake combined with John Gell of Hopton to raise the lead tithe upon the miners of the three parishes. The miners' opposition to the lead tithe after 1613 was more coherent than that of the late sixteenth century. More than any other single issue in the years before 1641, the matter of the lead tithe united the High Peak miners. Organized resistance to the tithe spread swiftly from Ashford after 1613. In consequence, Gell and Leake decided upon court action to restore their title. Their first action at law sought the recovery of the documentation which proved their right to the lease, which had been stolen by some of the miners. Thereafter, they sued in Chancery and Exchequer against leading opponents of the tithe for the recovery of the tithe itself.[32]

At first, the miners responded to Gell and Leake's demands by simply hiding their ore, or by assaulting the tithe gatherers. But after 1615, the miners gathered in barmote meetings to collect common purses as fighting funds, and to appoint attorneys as legal advisers. Gell and Leake's complaints to central courts provide lurid accounts of the miners' organization, describing them as 'illegal combinations of the myners . . . being a multitude, and making a general purse'. This 'multitude' was led by 'unquiet and turbulent spirits' who drew 'great sums of money from their common purse' to frustrate the will of their betters.[33] Such rhetoric was characteristic of many gentlemen's complaints to central courts, and both echoed and played upon wider elite anxieties concerning autonomous plebeian organization. It was also to appear in complaints against, for example, the raising of collective purses by defenders of common rights in the East Anglian fens and in the tenant right disturbances of the northern border counties. Accounts of crowd gatherings and the collection of common purses were presented as the prelude to possible wider disturbances, as gentry complainants hinted at possible parallels with the peasant rebellions of early Tudor England, or worked on more sharply felt memories of the 1607 Midland Rising.[34]

[31] Kiernan, *Lead industry*, 78; PRO, E126/2, fol. 85; PRO, E134/13JasI/Mich 3.
[32] PRO, E112/75/151; DRO, D258/28/20m, /59/13L.
[33] BL Add. MSS 6681, fols. 360–71, 6686, fol. 147, 6704, fols. 4–5; DRO, D258M/59/13L, / 42/15 unlisted interrogatory; PRO, E112/168/12, /75/128.
[34] For the levying of common purses outside the Peak, see for instance PRO, STAC8/7/3, 27/8, 34/4, 161/16; Manning, *Village revolts*, 152; C. Holmes, 'Drainers and fenmen: the problem of popular political consciousness in the seventeenth century', in A. Fletcher and J. Stevenson (eds.), *Order and disorder in early modern England* (Cambridge, 1985), 185. For comparisons of smaller-scale riots with the Midland Rising of 1607, see PRO, STAC8/ 18/19, 129/13, 219/20, 15/13.

We need not rely solely upon the overblown rhetoric of the tithe proprietors to find evidence of the miners' growing organizational assertiveness. The first major crowd actions within the High Peak in support of free mining rights occurred in 1606, in Ashford. As we have seen, the Wirksworth miners first asserted free mining rights on territory from which they had been hitherto excluded in 1613. The first statement of the miners' capacity for organized collective action can therefore be dated within the whole of the Peak Country to the period between 1606 and 1613. Legal cases concerning the lead tithes of Bakewell, Tideswell and Hope continued until 1642. From the records of these proceedings, and from attendant documentation in the papers of John Gell, it is possible to draw a detailed picture of the methods by which the miners organized their opposition to the tithe, and of the complex and extensive social networks on which that opposition was founded.[35] Just as within the Wapentake of Wirksworth, the larger miners' network depended upon a substantial core of men who were consistently prosecuted for their opposition to lead tithes and to the manorial interest. Often connected by kin, neighbourhood and the experience of labour within the same mineworkings, such men were sometimes selected to represent the miners' grievances to the authorities. Such elections occurred at meetings in private houses or at barmote sessions, at which the collection of common purses to fund legal actions were also planned. The opinions of attorneys hired with that money were communicated by their presence at these meetings, or by the 'publicacion' of their letters, which advised the miners of their legal rights. In other cases, miners stood up in parish churches 'in a publique manner in or after the tyme of divine service upon the Saboth day' to read declarations made by barmotes against the tithe. The collection of common purses and the non-payment of the tithe were communal actions which sometimes required a degree of intimidation on the part of the 'neighbours' against those individuals who gave in to the tithe gatherers. So canny was the High Peak miners' use of the law, that their gentry opponents resorted to the more traditionally plebeian complaint that legal proceedings were being dragged out by the other side in order to exhaust and impoverish their opponents.[36] By 1615, the geographical basis of resistance had broadened from Ashford to include men drawn from all the mining townships of the

---

[35] Lists of tithe resisters are to be found in PRO, E134/17ChasI/Mich4, /18ChasI/East12, / 13JasI/Mich3, /4ChasI/Mich33, /8ChasI/Mich26; PRO, E126/2, fol. 122; PRO, E126/4, fols. 18–19; PRO, E112/75/128, /129, /151, /165, /9/75, /168/11, /12, /24; DRO, D258M/ 28/20n, /42/15 .

[36] DRO, D258M/28/20n, /42/15; BL, Add. MS 64908, fol. 134; PRO, E112/168/24, /75/151; PRO, E134/8ChasI/Mich26, /18ChasI/East12; APC, 1616–17, 361–2; PRO, SP14/123/12, /94/47.

parishes in question, which covered some two-thirds of the High Peak lead
field. Despite the distances involved, many of these men were well known
to one another and were drawn closer together as deponents in court
action, barmote jurors, petitioners, rioters, and tithe resisters. Some seem
to have made the defence of the miners' interests one of their prime
concerns in life. Raphe Oldfield, a free miner and minor landholder in
Litton, was one such man. He led the extension of free mining rights into
the neighbouring manors of Great and Little Hucklow in 1613. In
Tideswell and Litton, his involvement in crowd protests against enclosures
and infringements of free mining law led to his regular appearance before
the Court of Star Chamber. Oldfield's extensive knowledge of mining law
made him a frequent deponent, and his hostility to the lead tithe brought
him before the Exchequer Court in 1615, 1625 and 1632. In his seventies
he was one of a number of prominent miners arrested for his role in the
mass demonstrations against the tithe in 1634, in which his son-in-law
William Bagshawe also played an important part.[37] Like Oldfield, Bagshawe was a relatively wealthy, independent-minded man. He too was
named as a tithe resister and a defender of free mining rights. He served as
a constable for his township in the same year as he was jailed for his part in
the major demonstrations of 1634. Four years later, he was barmaster of
Tideswell. On the death of his first wife, he married the daughter of
another miner who was prominent as a tithe resister.[38] The miners'
resistance also drew upon networks based upon kinship and the household.
The brothers John and George Brewell jointly operated mineworkings in
Ashford. Both were prominent men in the township, helped to organize the
collection of common purses and were named as leaders of the non-
payment of the lead tithe. A number of Raphe Oldfield's sons were involved
in resistance to the tithe and in the defence of free mining and common
rights within the Tideswell area.[39] Similarly, the Heawards of Ashford, the
James of Wardlow and the Sellars of Taddington, all smallholding or
landless families with strong free mining connections, featured prominently
in tithe and manorial disputes throughout the first half of the seventeenth
century. The tithe issue drew such men together in a common cause which
cut across the boundaries of the township, parish and manor, creating
lasting personal associations.

---

[37] PRO, STAC8/226/27, /64/4, /271/3; PRO, DL4/66/6; PRO, E134/4ChasI/Mich33, /13JasI/
Mich3; PRO, DL5/27, fol. 183; BL, Add. MSS 6680, fols. 24–5, 64908, fols. 128, 130–1.
[38] Newton, 'Gentry', 11; PRO, E101/280/18; SA, Bag C 549 (1); Cox, *Derbyshire annals*, I,
288, 319; Dias, 'Lead, society and politics', 48.
[39] PRO, PC2/41, fol. 291; DRO, D258M/28/20n; PRO, E126/4, fols. 18–19; SA, Bag C 549
(1), 2094; PRO, STAC8/64/4, /271/3; PRO, DL1/323, complaint of Att.-Gen. v. John
Manners.

Within the townships of Tideswell and Litton in the early seventeenth century one such close personal network centred upon Raphe Oldfield. His sons, son-in-law and close neighbours were all pulled into the same court cases and disturbances as himself. Oldfield rented land from Thomas Simpson, with whom he was prosecuted at Star Chamber on two occasions for riot. He shared a prison cell in 1634 with John Mitchell, another Litton miner who had been involved in the miners' mass gatherings of that year and who was an almost constant associate of Oldfield in the tithe struggles of the 1620s. The three men were not only united in their hostility to tithe proprietors, but also held a particular animosity for the Bagshawes of the Ridge, a Recusant gentry family who laid claim to the mineral rights and common fields of Litton.[40] Personal associations created in the course of mutual engagement against tithe proprietors or manorial authorities can be glimpsed in the surviving wills of such individuals. The will of George Frost of Sheldon, an opponent of the lead tithe, was witnessed by men with whom he had been involved in the defence of free mining rights. The occasion of Frost's demise revealed another form of association between the defenders of mining custom. We saw in Chapter 3 that early seventeenth-century miners relied upon orebuyers to advance money to them. Like other miners, Frost owed money to such orebuyers, many of whom doubled as miners themselves, and whose interests were also threatened in disputes over lords' claims to monopolize the lead trade on their estates. Miners involved in struggles with lords and tithe proprietors tended to borrow money from the same orebuyer, who was also sometimes caught up in those conflicts.[41]

The common purses raised by the miners were well spent. The progress of Gell and Leake's initial case of 1613 through the Court of Exchequer was frustrated by the miners' attorneys. In spite of injunctions and rulings in favour of the tithe proprietors thereafter, the miners were still organizing against the tithe in the late 1620s. The early 1620s saw the intervention of the Privy Council on the side of John Gell and Sir Francis Leake (by then the Baron Deincourt), which resulted in the miners' referral of the matter to parliament. In 1624, they were able to secure the placement of a bill in the Commons against the tithe which, although it got nowhere, resulted in further delays. Upon the bill's failure, the miners continued to refuse payment of the tithe despite injunctions against their leaders. Deincourt and Gell were forced into the expense of the exhibition of further complaints to Exchequer. For a brief period between 1628 and 1629, some

---

[40] PRO, STAC8/51/15 , /271/3, /81/20; PRO, DL4/64/11; PRO, E112/168/3.
[41] Wood, 'Industrial development', 213–14.

miners paid the tithe, but only under duress. Meanwhile, moves were underfoot to organize the miners' next action.

Following an unsuccessful attempt to disprove Gell and Deincourt's claim to the tithe at Exchequer, the miners once again refused payment, resulting in the proprietors taking action at common law, and the imprisonment of some of the refusers. By 1632, Deincourt was so wearied by the 'litigious' miners that he tried to find a buyer of his part of the tithe lease. Hearing that the Countess of Devonshire was interested in the purchase of Deincourt's rights, the miners sent Raphe Oldfield, John Mitchell and some Ashford men to persuade her to lease the rights to them.[42] For once, their social betters had the best of the miners. The Countess told them she was uninterested in the purchase of the tithes; Sir Robert Heath led them to understand that the tithe was a 'thing not lawfull to be sould'; the miners stopped pestering the noble lady; and she promptly bought Deincourt's interest in the lease. The bitterness caused by the Countess's dealings sparked off further non-payment of the tithe in 1632. Once again, miners who had been prominent in the affair since 1613 therefore appeared to answer contempt charges at the Court of Exchequer.[43]

By 1634, the miners of the parishes of Bakewell, Hope and Tideswell had been frustrated in every attempt they had made to be rid of the hated tithe: litigation, petition, negotiation and even outright physical opposition had all failed. The presence in the county of King Charles on a royal progress offered them the opportunity of direct appeal to the monarch. They therefore set about the organization of a mass appeal to the monarch. Gathering in smaller numbers in their own villages, they converged on Baslow, from where they intended to cross over the hills to Chesterfield to make their case to Charles. A series of breathless and increasingly frightened letters from local gentlemen to Sir John Coke, and from Coke to the Lord Lieutenant, the Earl of Newcastle, describe the unfolding events.

On 30 of July 1634, Sir John Coke warned Newcastle that 'a great multitude of miners assemble themselves at Baslow with purpose to come tomorrow morning to your house to present a mutinous petition, which is not sufferable in a well-ordered state'. The King ordered Newcastle to raise the trained bands, suppress the miners' march, 'and imprison the chief authors thereof'. In this, Newcastle was unsuccessful, for by 3 August

---

[42] The minister of Eyam, wearied by the miners of that parish's refusal of the tithe, had come to such an arrangement in 1611. See PRO, E134/13ChasII/East23.

[43] *APC, 1616–17*, 361–2; *APC, 1619–20*, 78; PRO, SP14/123/12; PRO, SP14/163/81, /123/ 12; HLRO, MP 9 April 1624; *Journal of the House of Commons 1547–1629*, 758, 787; BL, Add. MS 6681, fols. 360–71; DRO, D258M/44/2r, /42/15 unlisted order to constables of Eyam and unlisted orders of Chancellor of the Duchy of Lancaster, 1629; PRO, E112/ 168/12, /32; PRO, E126/3, fols. 40–1, /4, fols. 18–19; PRO, C21/N9/10; PRO, C2/JasI/ G2/48.

Christopher Fulwood, the lord of Middleton by Youlgreave and an opponent of free mining, had been ordered to arrest Raphe Oldfield at Chesterfield. Oldfield had led the miners there with the intention of presenting a petition to the King. In spite of hearing a royal proclamation commanding them to depart, the miners remained in the town. Despite Fulwood's best efforts, they were still on the road the following day, where William Wright, who was subsequently to oppose the right of free mining in the Earl of Rutland's manor of Netherhaddon, encountered about 400 of them. The miners were following the King to Nottingham, where they intended to present a second mass petition. In this, as Wright had heard, they had been motivated by William Bagshawe, who wrote to them from Derby Gaol, his letter having been 'openly read upon Sunday last after evening prayer at the Cross at Tideswell, and thereupon the miners came forward upon Monday towards Nottingham'.

Having captured Raphe Oldfield and his son-in-law William Bagshawe, the authorities were now concerned to lay their hands on Oldfield's long-time associate John Mitchell. William Wright was able to report that Mitchell was amongst the miners marching to Nottingham, who were now demanding the release of their leaders as well as the removal of the tithe. Two days later, Wright informed Coke that 'all is hurly burly here, and few or none of the miners work, but come up or down about these matters'. Despite their exertions, the miners were refused a royal audience. Their leaders were left in Derby Gaol until October, where they were forced at last to humiliate themselves by asking the Countess of Devonshire to intercede with the King for their release.[44] Not until 1641 was organized opposition to the lead tithe to resume within the three parishes; and then within a very different context.

The intensity of the conflict over the tithes of lead within Bakewell, Hope and Tideswell dissuaded lessees and ministers in the other High Peak parishes from pressing their tithe claims too strongly. Occasional lead tithe disputes developed in the parish of Castleton during the first half of the seventeenth century. In Youlgreave parish, the lead tithe was not collected until the 1650s, when the Earl of Rutland acquired the lease. In Darley, tithe collectors were driven off by the miners in the early seventeenth century. Miners in Stoney Middleton and Eyam leased the tithe from the ministers upon a yearly composition, both sides thereby avoiding conflict. It was really only after the Restoration that ministers and tithe lessees elsewhere within the High Peak started to press the miners for payment.[45]

[44] BL, Add. MS 64908, fols. 112, 128, 134, 130–1; PRO, SP16/275/73.
[45] PRO, E134/26 Chas II/East 34, 3 Jas II/East 15, 13ChasII/East23; DRO, D258M/54/19ha.

RIOT, LITIGATION AND FREE MINING RIGHTS IN THE HIGH
PEAK

The historical record of the lead tithe struggle has allowed us to illuminate
some of the central features of the High Peak miners' political culture and
organization. The pugnacity and commitment exhibited in the tithe
dispute, coupled with the miners' capacity for self-organization, stand at
odds to historical accounts which emphasize the deference and pre-political
character of early modern plebeian cultures. Just as within the Wapentake
of Wirksworth, tithe disputes within the High Peak occupied the miners at
the same time as they were contending with the manorial interest over
mining rights. But the legal and jurisdictional context of the struggle over
mining custom in the High Peak differed in important respects from that of
the Wapentake of Wirksworth. This context fundamentally affected the
character and outcome of disputes over mining rights. An appreciation of
the complexity of the manorial structure of the High Peak is therefore
essential to understanding the history of free mining disputes (see Maps 5
and 14).

We have seen that the assertion of free mining rights in the Wapentake of
Wirksworth met with surprising success between 1613 and 1627. The free
mining interest within the Wapentake had been aided by the continuous,
uninterrupted exercise of free mining within some parts of the Wapentake,
and by the specificity of the provisions of the Great Barmote of 1557.
Under those provisions, which were given the force of law by the Duchy's
judgements of 1622–7, that right extended beyond the Duchy's manor into
the whole of the Wapentake. Under the aegis of the Duchy, free mining
custom within the Wapentake therefore possessed a firmer legal basis than
that within the High Peak. The manorial structure of the High Peak was
considerably more complex than in Wirksworth Wapentake. The Duchy's
possessions within the lead field of the Wapentake of Wirksworth comprised a single, large, unified manor: the manor of Wirksworth. In contrast,
there were no less than five manors within the High Peak lead field which
had at some point come under the jurisdiction of the Crown or the Duchy.
Two of these, Youlgreave and Tideswell, had been leased to gentry families
for so long that they were claimed as private mining liberties.[46] Peak Forest
township, although still the core of an extensive royal forest up until 1640,
was administered by the Duchy of Lancaster down to 1630. Hence, a right
of free mining was embedded there.

The manors of Castleton and High Peak comprised the most important

[46] PRO, DL5/25, fols. 816, 924; J. M. Fletcher, 'Notes on the history of Tideswell and its
manor', *DAJ*, 1st ser., 41 (1919), 1–37.

Duchy territories within the High Peak lead field. Yet they were by no means clear in their limits, and far from composite as administrative and geographical units, being divided into a number of scattered and sometimes separated townships. The manors of Castleton and High Peak collectively comprised the lordship of High Peak; hence the parts of this lordship which fell within the lead field comprised the King's Field of the High Peak. Sections of the Duchy's two manors had for many years been leased to noble or gentry families, creating further confusion as to the boundaries and title of manors within the High Peak.[47] As we have seen, the most important of these lessees had been George, Earl of Shrewsbury. Over the long tenure of the Shrewsburys' lease of the Duchy's manors and rights within the Hundred, the distinctions between one manor or lordship and another had become blurred. This situation was further complicated by the death of Gilbert Talbot, the seventh Earl of Shrewsbury, in 1616, and the consequent breaking up of the remaining Shrewsbury estates in the High Peak. Much of Earl George's estates had passed to Bess of Hardwick's Cavendish sons, together with his house at Chatsworth. Created Lord Cavendish in 1605 and Earl of Devonshire in 1618, Sir William Cavendish was keen to establish the former Shrewsbury possessions as manors independent of any Duchy claim upon them. A second powerful gentry family, the Manners of Haddon, likewise to be ennobled before the civil war, also held a large and composite estate within the High Peak. Following the death of Sir George Vernon in 1565, John Manners inherited the Vernon estate centred upon Haddon Hall. Thereafter, he and his successors bought leases of tithes upon their manors, and exchanged or bought manors adjacent to Haddon in order to create Haddon lordship. A smaller number of manors within the High Peak were also held by individual members of Derbyshire's greater gentry, such as the Meverells and Foljambs. Finally, as in Wirksworth Wapentake, the High Peak lead field was also punctuated by a series of small former monastic Granges which, by 1618, were mostly held by the Cavendish Earls of Devonshire.

Two salient points should stand out from the baroque complexities of the Jacobean High Peak's manorial structure.[48] First, the Duchy's estates were confused and scattered. Secondly, two very powerful families held composite estates within the lead field. As we shall see, the policies pursued by the Cavendishes of Chatsworth and Manners of Haddon

---

[47] PRO, E317/9/12, /20, /24; PRO, DL1/340, Att.-Gen. v. Earl of Arundel *et al.*

[48] The Elizabethan and Jacobean Duchy was rather confused as to the boundaries and titles of its jurisdictions within the High Peak, and could be encouraged to imagine that the manor, lordship and Hundred of the High Peak constituted a single entity under its jurisdiction. This confusion can also be found in the work of some historians of the subject. See for instance, Dias, 'Lead, society and politics', 39–41.

towards free mining custom initially converged in their mutual hostility, and then very swiftly diverged. Again, differences in the subsequent estate policies of the two families make the story of free mining disputes within the Hundred of High Peak very much more complicated than that of the Wapentake of Wirksworth.

Yet despite fundamental differences in manorial structure and the legal basis of mining custom, miners within the High Peak saw the firm and extensive customs of their brethren in the Wapentake of Wirksworth as the ideal at which they should aim. In legal actions between 1616 and 1657, High Peak miners argued that the Duchy King's Field, together with its attendant free mining laws, constituted a single entity which covered the whole of the Derbyshire lead field without reference to hundredal or manorial boundaries.[49] In making this argument, the miners ignored important differences in the histories of customary law in the High Peak and the Wapentake of Wirksworth. First, the King's Field had never been the homogeneous unit claimed by the miners. Even prior to the incorporation of the Duchy into the Crown's estates, the Dukes of Lancaster had held separate barmote courts for their estates in the two Hundreds, which administered subtly different mining codes. Secondly, an important break had occurred in High Peak lead mining which prejudiced legal arguments for the application of free mining across the High Peak. Whereas the origins of free mining in Wirksworth Wapentake did indeed lie in time 'beyond the memory of man', and had been subject thereafter to continual usage, mining in the High Peak had virtually died out by the end of the fifteenth century, only to recommence 100 years later. In consequence, a number of early seventeenth-century legal cases turned on the continuous usage of mining rights. Thirdly, Duchy territory in the High Peak had never been as extensive as in the Wapentake. The effect of these distinctions was to militate against the miners' claim to a general custom of free mining which transcended manorial and hundredal boundaries.

The organized assertion of free mining rights within the High Peak can first be traced to 1606–7. Between the 1580s and the early seventeenth century, lords had tightened the manorial regulation of mining activity. Since Earl George had tried to impose a pre-emption of ore sales within the High Peak King's Field and within his private Ashford lordship, and since many other lords followed a similar policy in the late sixteenth century, differences between mining jurisdictions had meant little to the miners.[50] Depositions taken in or referring to the 1590s suggest that miners possessed

[49] BL, Add. MSS 6682, fols. 65–75, 6677, fol. 49; PRO, DL4/64/12/4, /64/11; PRO, DL1/ 340, Att.-Gen. v. Earl of Arundel *et. al.*
[50] PRO, DL4/38/17, /64/11.

little sense of demarcation between one manor and another. But with Earl George's death, and with the steady rise in lead prices after 1600 which lifted the market price of ore well above the prices set by lords under their right of pre-emption, differences between the King's Field and other manors became more meaningful. This had an important effect upon the High Peak miners' political culture in the early seventeenth century, which was made evident in their complaints and depositions to Westminster courts, in which many miners identified their customs with those of the Duchy's King's Field of High Peak.

The perceived link between customary rights and the jurisdiction of the Duchy of Lancaster meant that, as in the Wapentake of Wirksworth, High Peak miners looked to the lessee of the Duchy's lot and cope in the High Peak King's Field for support. Unfortunately for the miners, that lease had passed to the recusant Eyre family of Hassop. Like Richard Carrier, the Eyres were hated by their tenants in Hassop, Rowland and Calver, and by the miners of the whole Hundred. Rowland Eyre, who first acquired the lease, had depopulated Hassop with violence in the 1590s. Local gentlemen spoke of him as a 'Rich & potent . . . Ad[ver]sarye', while his tenants referred to his 'accustomed maner of malice & vexacone'. His son Thomas, who inherited the lease, was seen in similar terms. If the miners' complaints are to be believed, Thomas administered mining law in a corrupt manner. In his activities as a lead merchant and creditor, he was known to drive 'verie hard bargaines'. The miners recognized that he held the office of barmaster due to its 'great pfitt and commoditie', and out of the hope that it would give him 'rule and commande over the . . . minors', rather than out of any desire to support their customs. When one barmote attempted to raise a levy for a common purse against the lead tithe, Thomas Eyre prevented its collection. So unpopular was he that some miners went so far as to accuse him of cheating them at cards. Thomas's son, another Rowland, was the subject of similar criticism. This Rowland Eyre, who raised a regiment for the King in 1644, can be found amongst a crowd of armed and mounted gentlemen and their retainers, riding down miners who were digging in the Earl of Rutland's manor of Netherhaddon in 1657.[51]

Whereas Richard Carrier was universally loathed by the miners and gentry of Wirksworth Wapentake, the Eyres retained important links with the Manners of Haddon. Long antagonistic to the Cavendishes of Chatsworth, the Eyres were quite happy to support miners of the King's Field in their attempts to extend their laws into the Cavendish's lordship of Ashford. Similarly, Eyre backed the miners' cause against other lords, most

---

[51] PRO, C21/E6/2; PRO, STAC5/E12/14; PRO, DL4/69/51; PRO, E112/168/24, /294/31.

notably the Foljambs of Walton. But when the High Peak miners found themselves in conflict with the Manners of Haddon, they were opposed by Thomas and Rowland Eyre. This coincidence of gentry alliances was unfortunate for the miners, since the Manners were the most steadfast opponents of free mining within the whole Peak Country. In the same fashion, Thomas Eyre bridled when the miners attempted to claim free mining rights in his own manors of Hassop, Rowland and Calver.[52] In their joint pursuit of free mining rights within certain parts of the High Peak lead field, the miners and the Eyres' alliance was therefore based upon temporary mutual interest, rather than any kind of patron–client relationship. The miners of the early seventeenth century had become players in the local game of power politics. The prize, so far as the miners were concerned, was the control of customary rights and thereby of material resources. To that end, the miners were prepared to make temporary alliances with individual gentry and noble houses.

In 1612, a crowd of Litton and Tideswell miners, led by Raphe Oldfield, began digging in the manor of Little Hucklow. They were opposed by Lady Isabel Bowes, the former wife of Sir William Foljamb of Walton, whose family had run the manor's lead industry under a pre-emption of ore sales since the mid-1570s. The dispute developed apace over the succeeding three years, resulting in action against the miners in the Courts of King's Bench, Common Pleas and Star Chamber. At the same time, Oldfield was involved with other leading miners and tenants in enclosure disputes with the recusant Lord of Litton, Thomas Bagshawe of the Ridge. In 1613, a local attorney was accused of organizing and leading a crowd of fifty miners into Little Hucklow to assert the right of free mining.[53] By 1614, they had managed to secure the support of Thomas Eyre against Bowes. Over the next three years, Eyre went on to claim the lot and cope upon almost every High Peak manor which was not held by the Manners, or which was not already accepted to lie within the Duchy's estates. Save for such disputes as concerned manors within the Cavendishes' Ashford lordship, Eyre received the enthusiastic support of the High Peak miners. Rulings at the Duchy Court between 1619 and 1622 guaranteed the right of free mining within the manors of Great Hucklow, Little Hucklow, Winster and Youlgreave, and extended the Duchy's King's Field into the

[52] Meredith, 'Eyres of Hassop: I', 16–18, 41; *idem*, 'Eyres of Hassop: II', 73–5; PRO, DL1/323, complaint of Att. Gen. v. John Manners, /344, answer of Thomas Eyre. As Earl of Rutland, John Manners protected Eyre's sequestered estates during the Commonwealth period. See R. Meredith, 'A Derbyshire family in the seventeenth century: the Eyres of Hassop and their forfeited estates', *Recusant History*, 8, 1, (1965), 23.

[53] PRO, STAC8/64/4, /81/20, /209/7. An earlier, less organized, attempt to extend the King's Field into Little Hucklow occurred around 1610. See PRO, STAC8/211/10.

first three manors. But Eyre's actions against the Cavendishes at the Duchy Court were almost entirely unsuccessful.[54]

In his actions against other lords, Eyre had been able to rely upon miners from across the High Peak to give evidence in support of his case. Taken between 1616 and 1620, their depositions provide detailed evidence of the rapid development and growing sophistication of mining custom within the High Peak. Eyre was able to produce High Peak miners as witnesses in support of his claims against the Cavendishes as well. But the Cavendishes countered by turning out the miners of Ashford lordship to give evidence on their behalf. The ability of the Cavendishes to secure the support of the free miners of their own estates was central to their victory at law, for these men were able to present detailed accounts of the local history of Ashford lordship which demonstrated the descent of the territory to the Cavendishes. Many of these miners were also tenants of the Cavendishes. On the surface, therefore, it may seem that new evidence has been found of the thick-headed tenant deference sometimes assumed to operate within early modern society. But the reality was rather more complex.

In 1585, in order to allow for changing agricultural practices and for the emergence of a mining industry, the customs of Ashford lordship were redefined by agreement at Chancery, thereby ending a period of conflict between the Earl of Shrewsbury and his tenants. One aspect of this settlement concerned the manorial pre-emption of ore sales. Shrewsbury secured the monopoly of all ore sales within the lordship, provided that he paid nine shillings for every load purchased from the miners. Since this was the then market price, this was acceptable to the miners. But by 1602, the market price of ore had risen, and the Cavendishes' attempts to maintain the price set in 1585 was causing difficulties. An early hint of that trouble came when Henry Hurst and his partners were instructed by the barmaster of Ashford, Thomas Hadfield, to sell their ore for nine shillings. Feeling that he and his partners 'should be att libtie to sell their ore where they would', Hurst and his partners sold their shares in Ashford, and moved to the freer environment of the neighbouring King's Field. Real trouble broke out over the matter four years later.

According to the subsequent complaint of William Cavendish to the Star Chamber, on 4 June 1606, seventy miners from both Ashford lordship and

---

[54] Depositions in these cases are at PRO, DL4/60/16, /64/11, /68/52, /64/12/4, /67/63, /67/61, /68/50, /67/70, /71/36, /69/51, /69/72, /67/62. The progress of the ensuing legal cases are set out in PRO, DL5/27, pp. 150, 152, 198, 223, 235, 527, 610, for Stoney Middleton; PRO, DL5/27, pp. 183, 196, 255, 485–6, 674, for Little Hucklow; PRO, DL5/27, pp. 768, 773, / 28, fols. 35, 38, 58–61, 47, 441, 468, for Ashford lordship; PRO, DL5/25, pp. 816, 905, 924 /27, pp. 183, 196, 255, 485–6, 630, 671, 674, 724, 727, 742, 831, 839, 1019–20, 1027, 1249, /28, fols. 47, 130, 284, 591, for other manors.

the King's Field assembled with an attorney in the village of Ashford upon the 'measuring day' when the barmaster was meant to take their ore at the set price. They refused to allow the barmaster to measure their ore, and a violent riot ensued. The miners claimed that no riot had occurred, but agreed that they had refused to sell the barmaster their ore, saying that the price was unfair and that in any case the matter should be heard by the manor's barmote, and not by the Star Chamber.[55] The outcome of the case is not known, but it clearly resulted in victory for the miners, for in 1626 the barmote laws of Ashford recorded a curious custom in which the lord held a theoretical right to take ore at nine shillings per load, but noted that 'it hath pleased the lord' not to maintain this right. The barmote customs went on to specify a full right of free mining within the manor, and observed that the barmote was to levy tolls upon the miners for a common purse against the lead tithe. The customs of 1626 therefore validate Gell and Deincourt's periodic complaints that the Devonshires' barmasters were involved in the organization of the miners' resistance to the tithe.

Around the same time, Sir Charles Cavendish responded to a complaint at Chancery from his tenants in a dispute over copyhold fines, in which he discussed the earlier history of disputes over the customs of Ashford. Remarkably, he accepted that his family had in the past 'dealt hardlye wth the copiehoulders in this behalf', and explained that he felt they had been 'well recompenced' with the granting of free mining rights.[56] A compromise had been struck, whereby the miners gained full rights of free mining, the removal of pre-emption and the effective control of the barmote, while the Cavendishes received their lot and cope and were guaranteed social peace upon their estates. Moreover, they were also assured of the support of their miners and tenants against Eyre in the legal actions of 1616–20 at the Duchy Court. Thus, Henry Frost of Sheldon, a consistent opponent of the lead tithe, saw no difficulty in deposing against the extension of the Duchy's King's Field into Ashford lordship. In 1619, he explained that the mining industry of Ashford lordship was regulated 'according to the use & custome of the myne'. The miners of Ashford lordship had therefore been able to extend their rights without appeal to the repulsive Eyres. Local hostility towards the Eyres was complemented by that of their lord. Thereafter, the Cavendishes and their tenants continued to co-operate amicably against Eyre's attempts to take Longstone common as his own. Here, local plebeian memories of Rowland Eyre's oppressions and depopulations on Hassop in the 1590s were a motivating factor, for as the Ashford inhabi-

---

[55] PRO, DL4/67/59; PRO, STAC8/201/19.
[56] CHT, Hardwick MS Mineral Court Roll ii, reproduced and misdated in G. Steer, *Compleat mineral laws of Derbyshire* (London, 1734), 27–30; PRO, C2/ChasI/A51/87.

tants noted, many had 'the best pt of their meanes by keepinge of sheepe & other cattell upon the said comons' which were now threatened by Thomas Eyre.[57] What at first sight appears as tenant deference to the great lords of Chatsworth therefore emerges as a careful, and very political, social alliance of lord and tenant, forged out of prior conflict and the subsequent presence of a mutual enemy.

Relations between the neighbouring Manners of Haddon and the local miners followed a very different path. There is no easy explanation for the consistent hostility displayed by the Manners of Haddon to the right of free mining. Quite possibly, the Manners simply pursued an estate policy inherited from their predecessors as Masters of Haddon, the Vernons. Since the fourteenth century, the Vernons were notable for the close control they exercised over their estates. The Vernons held extensive demesne upon their estates, and continued to enforce labour dues from their tenants at a time when such practices were being commuted into cash payments elsewhere. That direct control was maintained through the early fifteenth century, as the Vernons raised rents on their estates, forcing out the tenantry of the manor of Netherhaddon, such that by 1431 Richard Vernon was listed as the sole tenant of that manor. The land was emparked and turned over to deer and sheep, and the church of Netherhaddon incorporated as a chapel into the fabric of Haddon Hall.[58] It was not only the village that was lost with the death of Netherhaddon; popular access to the agricultural and mineral resources of the manor were lost as well.

The Dissolution of the monasteries offered further opportunities to the Vernons to close their grip upon their estates. Like other lords, they bought up former monastic granges and tithe rights; unlike those of other lords, the rights and territories lay on or very close to their existent properties. John Manners acquired the Haddon estate upon the death of Sir George Vernon in 1565.[59] Both in his acquisition of rights and manors, and in his policy towards his tenants, Manners maintained the policy established by 'tht moste Drad sovaign lorde . . . George Vernon'. To this, Sir John Manners added a hostility to the custom of free mining. Taking to himself the right of free mining, unlike other lords he did not permit the formation of any barmotes which might subsequently become an institutional basis to custom. Instead, barmasters were 'placed & displaced' at his will, and 'good orders' imposed upon the miners in his manor of Bakewell 'for the

---

[57] PRO, DL4/69/51; PRO, C21/D1/13. The disputes over Ashford lordship had their parallel in events in Tideswell: see Wood, 'Industrial development', 220.
[58] Blanchard, 'Economic change', 22, 39, 42; on the desertion of Netherhaddon, see *idem*, 'Industrial employment', where a demographic interpretation is offered.
[59] John Manners was knighted in 1603.

Reformacion of abuses'.[60] But in 1607, he faced a challenge to his authority.

As a Justice of the Peace, on 4 June of that year, Sir John Manners received news of the rising of the labourers and artisans in Warwickshire, Leicestershire and Northamptonshire which became known as the Midland Rising. Warned to keep a close watch upon potential disorder within the Peak, the news may have affected Manners' response to local developments. On 28 September, a group of miners gathered from nearby villages at Youlgreave and, carrying weapons, marched to Stanton moor, within Haddon lordship. Here they declared themselves to be a lawful barmote in session, announced that a custom of free mining henceforth applied within the manor of Stanton, and allegedly 'did . . . agree to stick together and to keep the said [barmote] court by force if any resistance should be made'. Having asserted their rights, they returned to Youlgreave. Manners responded with prosecutions at the Quarter Sessions and Star Chamber for riot. Many other members of the gentry and nobility in the months immediately following the Midland Rising were wont to read local riots in the light of this larger and more threatening insurrection, and Manners may have been no exception.[61] In the aftermath of the Midland Rising, England's gentry were enjoined by the Crown to punish riotous offenders swiftly, but also to inquire into the causes of popular discontent. Manners' punishment of the miners before the Star Chamber may be read in this light, as might his calling of a barmote court for his neighbouring manor of Bakewell in 1608.

The Stanton disturbance had no direct connection with the Midland Rising, save perhaps in the mind of Sir John Manners.[62] It should rather be related to the growing local assertiveness of the miners. The introduction of a barmote system in Bakewell manor represented an important, if limited, gain for them. The customs laid out by that barmote guaranteed the miners the right to dig for ore upon payment of lot to the lord, and on recognition of his right to a pre-emption of ore sales. Trouble continued within Bakewell manor over pre-emption at a further barmote in 1621, in which orebuyers from Ashford lordship and the King's Field were prosecuted for infringing the lord's right, and in which punitive penalties were set out for further offences. The local miners were clearly also implicated in attempts to overturn the Manners' right of pre-emption, as injunctions were made

[60] BL, Add. MS, 6668, fol. 472; PRO, STAC2/17/138; PRO, DL4/98/34; Kiernan, *Lead industry*, 204; SA, PhC 328; DRO, D1289B/L139; LPL, Talbot MS CA/L, fol. 87.
[61] For the Stanton 'riot', see PRO, STAC8/219/4. It is important that the defendants admitted that they had brought weapons to Stanton moor.
[62] For an attempt to connect isolated enclosure riots elsewhere in Derbyshire to the Midland Rising, see Martin, *Feudalism to capitalism*, 164, 167, 174.

against their hiding ore from the barmaster of Bakewell. Unlike the Cavendishes, therefore, the Manners did not step back from conflict with the free mining interest following an initial clash. Moreover, for all that a truncated version of free mining custom was allowed after 1608 within the manor of Bakewell, within the other manors which made up Haddon lordship it was still banned.[63]

Over the rest of the pre-civil war period, there was no peace on the Haddon estates. On 20 January 1617, following upon violent enclosure riots in the Manners' manor of Rowsley, rioters allegedly came with weapons to Haddon Hall and warned Sir George Manners, who had become Master of Haddon upon his father's death, that any of his servants sent to dispossess them 'should bee shot to death'. They added ominously that 'they would pull downe Haddon House' if Manners resisted them. Sir George revealed something of his equally antagonistic attitude to his plebeian neighbours when he prayed for 'better tymes and fortunes then always to live a poore base Justice, recreatinge myselfe in sendinge roges to the gallows'. He was still enmeshed in litigation over the mining and manorial rights of Stanton in 1622. In January 1624, Sir George's widow, Lady Grace, led attacks by her tenants upon miners digging in the Granges of Aldwark and Cole Eaton within Wirksworth Wapentake.[64] By the time that John Manners became Master of Haddon in 1628, his family were therefore well established as the leading opponents of free mining within the Peak. John Manners continued the family tradition. In 1630, he organized attacks on free miners from the Tideswell area who, led by John Mitchell of Litton, had entered into his manor of Hazelbadge. Further trouble developed in 1634 over the Haddon estates, as the miners prosecuted Manners at the Duchy Court, claiming free mining rights there.

In 1641, upon the death of his cousin the seventh Earl of Rutland, John Manners inherited the Earldom of Rutland. To his peers, the eighth Earl seemed a 'harmless soft man'. The miners' perception of the Earl of Rutland was rather different. Looking upon his 'countenance and power', they concluded that he was their 'implacable enemy'.[65] By the time that he entered the House of Lords, Manners had identified himself as the chief opponent of the right of free mining within the High Peak, uncompromising in his hostility to the 'free liberty' claimed by the miners, and fully

[63] SA, PhC 328; DRO, D1289B/L139.
[64] L. Stone, *The crisis of the aristocracy, 1558–1641* (Oxford, 1965), 391; PRO, C142/401, fol. 128; PRO, WARD7/68/70; PRO, DL1/298, complaint of Robert Parker v. Dame Grace Manners; for the Rowsley case, see PRO, STAC8/212/28, continued at /212/29, /216/25.
[65] PRO, DL1/323, complaint of Att.-Gen. v. John Manners, /378 complaint of Rowland Furniss; BL, Add. MSS 6682, fols. 87–9, 6677, fol. 49; Davies, 'The Dukes of Devonshire, Newcastle and Rutland', 127.

prepared to back his legal power with physical force. It is within this context, and that of the relative freedom of the miners elsewhere in the Peak, that the violent dispute between the Earl of Rutland and the miners during the years of the civil war and Interregnum must be set. This dispute had its immediate origins in the conflict between the miners and the Manners over the preceding decades. Its long-term causes can be found in the dispossession of Netherhaddon's inhabitants in the early fifteenth century. But the uniquely politicized flavour of that dispute can only be understood in the context of the English Revolution. That story forms the core of Chapter 12. But in order to appreciate the significance of the events which unfolded within the Peak between 1641 and 1657, we must first survey the key characteristics of local plebeian political culture, and its implications for our understanding of social conflict in England before the civil wars.

The Peak in context: riot and popular politics in early Stuart England

REDEFINING POPULAR POLITICS

The historiography of so-called 'protest movements' has often been informed by a mechanistic economism. Like the histories of Luddism, the rise and decline of Chartism, and support for the organized socialist and labour movements of the early twentieth century, 'upsurges' of early modern popular protest have sometimes been interpreted as the product of 'crisis' years in, for instance, the late 1540s, the mid-1590s and the late 1620s.[1] It is certainly true that dearth, population pressure and inflation often formed the backdrop to enclosure and food riots, planned and actual insurrections, and to the seditious mutterings transcribed in countless court papers. But social conflict in early modern England cannot be explained by economic pressure alone. Otherwise, national periods of economic crisis should have provoked a uniform pattern of popular protest across the country. Instead, historians of riot and protest in early modern England have repeatedly made the point that disorder was typically local or, at best, regional in character. That point is usually made in order to emphasize the allegedly conservative, limited nature of protest.[2] Such a reading of local social conflicts is, at best, only two-dimensional.

Early modern plebeian politics were typically produced out of local cultures and local contexts. That relationship was a circular one, driven by the dynamic of social conflict. Political engagement in turn altered local identities and refashioned social collectivities, thereby both reproducing and refashioning local cultures. We have seen how the emergence of the Peak miners' identity in the c. 1590–1610 period coincided with their entry into local politics. By 1610, to be a Peak miner was to claim an identity

---

[1] Manning, *Village revolts*, 55; B.L. Beer, *Rebellion and riot: popular disorder during the reign of Edward VI* (Kent, Ohio, 1982), chs. 1–2.

[2] P. Clark, 'Popular protest and disturbance in Kent, 1558–1640', *EcHR*, 2nd ser., 29, 3 (1976), 365–82; C.S.L. Davies, 'Peasant revolt in France and England: a comparison', *AgHR*, 21 (1973), 122–34; Lindley, *Fenland riots*; Manning, *Village revolts*.

which was simultaneously occupational, local and political. The establishment of that identity had larger implications for local culture. It forced a fundamental reworking of social relations, as the newly assertive miners publicly rejected deference to the gentry and nobility. And it reworked gender relations, providing a new way of fashioning plebeian masculinity and of claiming community and custom as a male preserve.

Shifts and changes in local identities shaped outbursts of 'social protest'. Thus the so-called Western Rising of 1628–31 had as much to do with the longer development of local, plebeian collectivities out of conflict with their social betters over matters of custom and common right as it did with enclosures and the high price of corn in those years.[3] Local cultures could therefore engender popular politics. But such cultures were not homogeneous or stable. The collapse of common interest between richer and poorer villagers within downland, agrarian England, for instance, undermined the broad definition of community and mutual responsibility which had formed the moral ideology of Kett's Revolt of 1549. The Fakenham man who was called to answer for his proposition of 1597 that 'There should be a camp at Whissonsett, meaning such as Kett's camp was, and there men should fight for corn' was one victim of the withdrawal of Robert Kett's descendants from the leadership of protest in late sixteenth-century Norfolk.[4] The plebeian collectivities from which grew consistent, long-term resistance were therefore no more predetermined than the timing and spread of riots can be plotted according to a 'distress index' alone.

By the early seventeenth century the bulk of the inhabitants within many villages in the Derbyshire Peak had become dependent upon lead mining. If we are to plot a 'distress index' which enables us to make sense of the changing pattern of social conflict within the Peak, it might therefore be

---

[3] My gloss upon B. Sharp, *In contempt*. On the West Country disturbances, see also D.G.C. Allan, 'The rising of the West Country, 1628–1631', *EcHR*, 2nd ser., 5, 1 (1952), 76–85; E. Kerridge, 'The revolts in Wiltshire against Charles I', *Wiltshire Archaeological and Natural History Magazine*, 57 (1958), 64–75; J.H. Bettey, 'The revolts over the enclosure of the Royal Forest at Gillingham, 1626–1630', *Dorset Natural History and Archaeology Society*, 97 (1975), 21–4. There was something distinct about the popular cultures of the larger West Country area, and of the cultural provinces it contained, which allowed for the maintenance of a complex tradition of riotous behaviour over a long period of time. This may have had something to do with the relationship between the pastoral economy, migration patterns and forest law. The full story requires further investigation, but for the moment see the suggestive comments in Underdown, 'Regional cultures'.

[4] Quoted in Amussen, *An ordered society*, 145. On the long-term implications of the withdrawal of the involvement of 'middling sorts' from the leadership of plebeian politics in parts of arable England, see Walter, 'A "Rising of the people"?', 120–2; J.S. Morrill and J.D. Walter, 'Order and disorder in the English Revolution', in Fletcher and Stevenson (eds.), *Order and disorder*, 151–2.

with reference to movements in the price of lead ore (see Fig. 3.3). Using lead prices as an indicator of the level of 'distress', we might assume that where the price of lead fell, so 'social protest' increased. In fact, the reverse was the case. Over the period between *c.* 1600 and the early 1630s, the price of lead rose in tune with the miners' growing assertiveness. The rising lead prices of the early seventeenth century coincided with the full flourishing of free mining law across much of the lead field. Perhaps, freed of the manorial price-setting under lords' right of pre-emption, and emboldened by the new strength of their customs, the miners felt sufficiently confident to demand higher prices for their ore. When lead prices fell back in the late 1630s so did the miners' resistance to the tithe and to the opponents of free mining. We will see in Chapter 12 that high lead prices in the late 1640s and 1650s coincided with the violent, protracted, and highly politicized dispute over the mining rights of Haddon lordship. And as we shall see in Chapter 13, the long fall in lead prices between the late 1660s and the mid-1690s coincided with the collapse of the miners' overt resistance. Explanations of the growing assertiveness of the miners must therefore be sought outside a blunt economism.

The origins of the miners' tradition of self-organization originated in the 1580s and 1590s. Elsewhere within pastoral-industrial England, plebeians felt emboldened at around the same time. In his study of the changing patterns of prosecutions of enclosure rioters at the Court of Star Chamber, Roger Manning found that the period after the 1590s saw an increase in the number of such cases and that 'social conflict . . . becomes more explicit'. The period also saw a locational shift in enclosure disputes towards pastoral-industrial regions of the country. Manning finds an economic explanation for this change in the increased demographic pressure which occurred within the less rigidly controlled pastoral zone of England, caused by in-migration and natural increase due to the availability of work opportunities and open common rights. For Manning, this led to conflict between newcomers and established tenants and, more typically, between lord and tenant. The importance which Manning gives to such structural factors as an explanation of the conflicts he describes is necessary, but scarcely sufficient. He goes on to note that in their resistance to manorial authorities, 'Early Stuart enclosure protesters were probably more sophisticated than their Elizabethan predecessors.' Central to this growing sophistication was their use of the law. Whereas only 7 per cent of complaints to the Elizabethan Star Chamber referred to the collection of common purses by their opponents, about one fifth of Jacobean complainants did so. Moreover, many groups of lower-class litigants were alleged to have bound themselves into covenants to maintain their case until the defeat of their opponent. Finally, Manning detects a dramatic decrease in lower class dependence upon gentry support in such cases.[5] In the developing assertiveness of the miners after 1590, the fuller and more articulate statement of mining custom, the gathering of common purses and the organization of crowd action, as in the growing polarization of social groups into opposed blocs around the matter of mining custom, the experience of the Peak in the period between the accession of James I and the outbreak of the civil war therefore appears as an extreme example of a wider pattern.

The inherently political character of these developments should be apparent. Yet for Manning, early modern rioters 'may be regarded as displaying primitive or pre-political behaviour because they failed to develop into some modern form of protest or participation in the political nation'. Manning's interpretation finds support elsewhere. Keith Lindley remarks that fenland rioters were not 'politically educated', thereby explaining the 'defensiveness, conservatism and restraint' of their protests. To Alan Everitt, 'for most of the people, most of the time, political matters scarcely existed'.[6] In such accounts, politics seems to be conceived of as comprising the governmental activities of the ruling elite vested in the central state, and any state-centred disputes generated thereby. As such, the lack of any organized, national plebeian political movement defines the absence of politics from early modern 'social protest'. As in characterizations of early modern social relations, a nineteenth-century definition of politics is removed from its historically specific context, to be reified as an overarching category, in which politics is conceived of as an organized activity focused upon the central state.

Such views have not gone unchallenged. In 1989, Patrick Collinson spoke of the need to 'explore the social depth of politics, to find signs of political life at levels where it was not previously thought to have existed'. In search of the antecedents of the radicalism of the 1640s and 50s, Christopher Hill made periodic forays into the world of plebeian politics. In his essay on the political consciousness of the fenland inhabitants, Clive Holmes found exactly what Hill had sought, and was able to connect the politics of fenland custom to the politics of the Agreement of the People.[7]

---

[5] Manning, *Village revolts*, 55, 58–9, 84.

[6] *Ibid.*, 2; Lindley, *Fenland riots*, 253, 257; Everitt quoted in A. Hughes, 'Local history and the origins of the civil war', in R. Cust and A. Hughes (eds.), *Conflict in early Stuart England: studies in religion and politics* (London, 1989), 225. For the concept of 'pre-politics', see E. Hobsbawm, *Primitive rebels: studies in archaic forms of social movement in the 19th and 20th centuries* (New York, 1965), 2–3. For a more nuanced vision of the ideology of 'pre-industrial' protest, see G. Rude, *Ideology and popular protest* (London, 1980), chs. 1–2.

[7] P. Collinson, *De republica anglorum, or, history with the politics put back in* (Cambridge, 1990), 15; Hill, *World turned upside down*, esp. chs. 1–3, 5; Holmes, 'Drainers and fenmen'.

More recently, Keith Wrightson has broadened the definition of popular politics, hitherto focused upon plebeian interventions in and acquisitions from the world of the central state and the political theorist. Identifying the key components of any politics as constituted from 'the social distribution and use of power', he has anticipated a social history of 'the manner in which relationships of power and authority, dominance and subordination are established and maintained, refused and modified'. The possession of social power, however, was intimately interwoven with the ownership and control of resources. The development theorist Adrian Leftwich has provided a materialist definition of politics which, while giving a large autonomy to process and agency, recognizes the importance of economics and resources. To Leftwich, politics is drawn from 'all the activities of co-operation and conflict, within and between societies, whereby the human species goes about organizing the use, production and distribution of . . . resources'.[8] Leftwich's formulation is useful in assessing the development of a broadly plebeian politics within the Peak. Much of this section of the book has been concerned with a chronology of the recreation, assertion and defence of customary law. In Chapter 6, custom was presented as occupying a key site at the junction of ideology, economics, and social and cultural practice. In Chapter 7 we saw how the acquisition of a local hegemony by settled, male plebeians over the language and institutions of custom helped to constitute plebeian social identities as gendered and discriminate. As such, following both Leftwich and Wrightson, custom constituted both a field of conflict and a building block of the plebeian politics of the Peak. The localism of custom did not deny it political potential. Rather, the authority of custom within plebeian politics derived from its role in the articulation of local identity.

Throughout the preceding discussion, plebeian politics have been given specific geographical locations. Struggles over resources, rights and power have been presented as developing within, and thereby actively shaping, a series of boundaries: the parish, the manor, the lordship, the King's Field and ultimately the Peak Country. Wrightson has eloquently described one location within which popular politics was to be found: that of the small world of the parish. We have seen in Richard and Jennet Carrier's downfall how relations within the parish could become very political. The parish was indeed a 'political forum', and an 'authentic unit of everyday life . . . replete with "power laden situations"'. But as Wrightson acknowledges, the

---

[8] Wrightson, 'Politics of the parish'; A. Leftwich, *Redefining politics: people, resources and power* (London, 1983), 1–27. Anthropologists have long been wise to the slippery character of the political. For important recent examples of political anthropology, see R. Maddox, *El Castillo: the politics of tradition in an Andalusian town* (Urbana, 1993); F. McGlynn and A. Tuden (eds.), *Anthropological approaches to political behaviour* (Pittsburgh, 1991).

parish was not hermetically sealed. Like customary law, the importance of the parish in plebeian politics was not predetermined. Rather, the parish gave a legal and cultural focus to struggles between interest groups and to contests over local identities. Wrightson's focus upon the parish does not, therefore, preclude the possibility that other administrative units may have provided plebeian political cultures with a spatial definition.[9] Most of Chapter 10 has not focused upon the politics of a parish. Rather, the plebeian politics of the Peak was formed within a confused web of jurisdictions, customs, alliances and interest groups. We have seen how, on occasion, plebeians were able to manipulate fissures within the gentry and nobility of the Peak to their own end. On other occasions, the lower-class inhabitants of one village found themselves set in opposition to those of a neighbouring settlement. None the less, after the late sixteenth century inter-community disputes were relatively rare and lacked the intensity of social conflicts. By the 1590s, confrontations over rights and resources were more likely to be drawn according to social divisions than parochial or manorial boundaries. While particular disputes were obviously specific to localities, they were given a similar political flavour and form. Public plebeian politics was defined upon the mining customs of the King's Field, and was built upon the limiting structures of community, gender and local identity.

GENDER AND THE SOCIAL BASIS OF PLEBEIAN POLITICS

There was a special quality to disputes over customary law in English free mining areas. In the Forest of Dean, the Somerset Mendips and in the Derbyshire Peak, miners can be found alongside their neighbours rioting, litigating or protesting against enclosure or attacks on common or forest rights.[10] This contrasted to the pattern of conflict in those mining areas where free mining custom did not prevail. Here, disputes more typically saw the existent tenants of a place attacking miners who had been employed by a lord to dig deposits of coal, iron or lead.[11] Within free mining areas, many miners were also tenants and saw no obvious distinction in the defence of different aspects of custom. Similarly, the members of a landless mining household had as important an interest in the defence of the commons as they did in free mining law. The defence of agricultural custom in the mining area of the Peak therefore often took a very similar

---

[9] Wrightson, 'Politics of the parish', 11–12.
[10] Wood, 'Custom, identity and resistance'; Sharp, *In contempt*, 100. For a Forest of Dean example, see PRO, STAC8/303/7.
[11] See for instance PRO, STAC5/D23/29, /33; PRO, STAC8/292/1, /224/19, /50/23, /24/21, / 106/7, /227/3, /154/12, /228/13, /174/16, /227/17.

form to the defence of free mining rights. Riotous demonstrations against the lord's claims upon the commons of Stoney Middleton between June and September 1617 saw up to 100 people, many of them miners, assemble from 'divers cuntries & places' symbolically to assert common rights. The Duchy of Lancaster's lessees were attempting to enclose commons and raise rents within the manor of Wirksworth only a few years before Sir Robert Heath's seizure of the Dovegang. Both events inspired opposition from the same people: that broad stratum of householders which encompassed both the near-landless and relatively wealthy farmers. The inhabitants of Taddington and Chelmorton, within the Duchy's lordship of the High Peak, were drawn into escalating conflict with the Cavendishes of Chatsworth over James I's reign. Again, many were miners. Their opposition to the Cavendishes followed the same tactics as those they employed in disputes over mining rights and the lead tithe: the Taddington and Chelmorton inhabitants gathered common purses to fund legal actions, marched in groups on to land from which they were banned in assertion of their rights, and contended at law with their opponent. As with mining disputes, that which the tenants of Chelmorton and Taddington fought with the Cavendishes was protracted, and helped to generate a closer and more specific definition of local custom and identity.[12]

The outstanding difference between Peak Country disputes over agricultural and mining custom lay in the differing roles assumed by men and women. During the Elizabethan period, women were prominent in the defence of agricultural custom against lords and enclosers.[13] There is nothing surprising in this. In other parts of early modern England, women assumed a large responsibility for the assertion of common rights, and an equally large part in their defence. As women gathered wood or looked to their cows, their presence upon the commons informed them of boundaries and rights, and made them sensitive to infringements. In parts of agrarian England, the right of gleaning was typically exercised by women. Elsewhere within the country, women can be found throughout the seventeenth century organizing and leading crowd protests against enclosure or the denial of common rights.[14] But in the Jacobean and Caroline Peak Country,

---

[12] PRO, STAC8/298/8, /103/6; PRO, E308/43/426; PRO, DL4/58/5, /7; PRO, DL5/27, p. 768; PRO, DL4/58/27, /56/17, /60/16.

[13] PRO, DL4/27/87; PRO, STAC5/E12/14, /B25/37; BL, Add. MS 6685, fols. 66–70r; SA, JC 384.

[14] On women's defence of gleaning, see King, 'Gleaners', 120–4, 131–6; J.A. Sharpe, *Crime in seventeenth-century England: a county study* (Cambridge, 1983), 169–70; R. Houlbrooke, 'Women's social life and common action in England from the fifteenth century to the eve of the civil war', *Continuity and change*, 1 (1986), 175. The historiography of women's involvement in pre-civil war riot is surprisingly slight. See *ibid.*, 176–86; Walter, 'Grain riots'. For examples from beyond the Peak Country of women's involvement in, and

the defence of both agricultural and mining custom became an increasingly masculine activity. After *c.* 1600, women were only very rarely prosecuted for their involvement in enclosure riots.[15] Their involvement in public disputes over mining custom was still more marginal.[16] There are two possible explanations for this.

First, while many plebeian women possessed detailed knowledge of mining custom, both the institutions of barmote law and the control of free mining were defined in masculine terms. After *c.* 1600, the central matter of dispute within the Peak shifted from the communal defence of common right to the male defence of free mining. In at least one dispute over free mining rights, the matter of gender loomed as large as did that of social conflict. In 1630, a crowd of Tideswell miners marched into John Manners' manor of Hazelbadge to dig for ore. They were stopped by Manners, who sent his tenants to attack them. A few weeks later, the Tideswell miners returned, only to be ejected once again; but not by John Manners. A crowd of Hazelbadge women, led by Anne Daniell and Mary Bradwell confronted the miners, and prevented them from digging the fields. We can only beg the question; but it may well be that Daniell, Bradwell and the other women of Hazelbadge felt that they had little to gain from the establishment of free mining upon their commons.[17]

Secondly, as mining disputes were fought increasingly out before Westminster law courts, the process of equity law acquired an important role in that larger conflict. According to patriarchal theory, married women were the subordinates of the male head of the household. Westminster law courts embodied this assumption within their practice. Even in the Yorkshire valley of Nidderdale, where local women had established a strong tradition of autonomous collective action by 1600, women rioters were expected to refer questions as to their activities and motivations to their husbands.[18] Peak Country miners resented the interference of Westminster law courts in their customs. None the less, by *c.* 1600 they were not only becoming more litigious, but also more legalistic. The barmote code was assuming a larger importance within their culture, and the miners were adapting the practices they were witness and subject to in Westminster and common law courts to their own purposes in the formulation of mining custom. Here, too, women were being squeezed out of involvement in the

---

leadership of, riots over enclosure and common rights, see PRO, STAC5/S57/23, S76/16, L2/39; PRO, STAC8/17/11, 5/21, 42/11, 129/13, 205/23, 203/30, 308/13, 193/10, 219/23.

[15] For an exception, see PRO, STAC8/212/28.

[16] Exceptions are at PRO, DL4/103/18; SA, PhC 329.

[17] PRO, DL1/323, complaint of Att.-Gen. v. John Manners.

[18] For women's tradition of riot, see PRO, STAC5/D23/29. For their interrogation, see PRO, STAC8/227/3. I hope to write about rebellion and popular culture in Nidderdale, *c.* 1590–1620, elsewhere.

institutions of plebeian political life. Women's place in the defence of mining custom was therefore an ambiguous one, and is perhaps best summed up by an incident which occurred in the course of the miners' demonstrations against the lead tithe in 1634. Following the imprisonment of the miners' leaders for their defiance of King Charles, their wives presented a petition for their release to the Queen. The act implies a sense of tactics about it. In order to secure their object, the women acted collectively. In approaching Henrietta Maria rather than Charles, they were effectively making the point that they were not repeating the husbands' presumed impudence. Moreover, in petitioning another woman, they played upon the fact of their gender, and the patriarchal assumption of their weakness.[19] As we have seen in Chapter 7, the women of the mining villages were not always so willing to play upon such sensibilities. But on this occasion, their politic deference paid off: their husbands were subsequently released.

Just as the proscription or limitation of women's involvement in public politics has come to be seen as an integral part of the establishment of a working-class politics in the early Industrial Revolution, so the creation of the Peak miners' identity in the early modern period entailed the restriction of women's political engagement.[20] But just how 'plebeian' was that political culture? We have seen that legal complaints against miners and tenants for riot sometimes refer to attorneys as leading popular resistance. Moreover, from the late sixteenth century the miners were drawn into a series of tangled alliances with elements of the gentry. To what extent did the miners and tenants of the Peak merely follow where lesser gentry and rich farmers led?

Debates over the social character of the leadership of popular politics in early modern England have adapted an earlier dispute between Boris Porschnev and Roland Mousnier over the leadership of French peasant uprisings in the seventeenth century.[21] Mousnier confirmed his view of early modern France as a hierarchical 'status' society by claiming that 'the

---

[19] BL., Add. MS 64908, fol. 134. For a similar example, see Kershaw, 'Power and duty', 281. For the rhetorical construction of female weakness, belied by the reported facts of the case, see PRO, DL1/323, answer of Anthony Harding *et al*, incl. attached depositions.

[20] For the early industrial period, see most obviously Clark, *Struggle for the breeches*; B. Taylor, *Eve and the new Jerusalem: socialism and feminism in the nineteenth century* (London, 1983). Early modern social historians have not been overly interested in the gendered constitution of social identities in their period.

[21] P.J. Coveney (ed.), *France in crisis, 1620–1675* (Totawa, 1977); R. Mousnier, *Peasant uprisings in seventeenth century France, Russia and China* (1967; Eng. trans. London, 1971); R. Mousnier, *Social hierarchies: 1450 to the present* (1969; Eng. trans. London, 1973). For a perceptive critique of Mousnier's description of early modern society, see Arriaza, 'Mousnier and Barber'.

peasants were the agents of the nobility' in their revolts against the central state. Following the rigid Marxism required of Soviet academics, in contrast, Porschnev interpreted French peasant uprisings as class conflicts produced out of the contradictions of early absolutism. In the work of Keith Lindley and Buchanan Sharp we find similarly opposed interpretations, adapted to the context of early modern English social structure. Lindley finds that fenland rioters were led by wealthy farmers, backed by discontented members of the greater gentry. In contrast, Sharp has discerned from his study of enclosure and food riots in the West Country the existence of an organic leadership amongst a discontented class of landless rural labourers and industrial workers.[22] Other studies have tended to confirm Lindley's findings, pointing to the importance of local 'middling sorts' in the organization and leadership of protest. The experience and status which such men had acquired from holding local office, it is suggested, equipped them to lead their poorer neighbours. Finally, it has been argued that the local gentry provided the legal brains behind the defence of custom.[23] The leadership of popular protest has therefore become something of a litmus test of the character of social relations in early modern England.

At least one example can be found from the early Stuart Peak of a lord leading his tenants in action against the inhabitants of a nearby settlement. In the course of a drawn out boundary dispute, Lord Cavendish led tenants of Ashford lordship against their Monyash neighbours in 1616.[24] Yet the Ashford inhabitants make a poor example of tenant deference. They had defied Cavendish ten years earlier in his attempt to fix ore prices, after which lord and tenant had arrived at a compromise settlement. That Cavendish's tenants stood with him in 1616 says more about the accident of their mutual interest in the maintenance of the boundaries of Ashford lordship than it does of any inherent lower-class deference. Yet evidence can be found of the leadership of Peak tenants and miners by wealthier, more educated individuals. In his account of the miners' demonstrations at Chesterfield in 1634, Christopher Fulwood remarked that 'almost xxtie of the psons that weare so assembled & ptended themselves myners are

[22] Lindley, *Fenland riots*, 255–6; Sharp, *In contempt*, 97–104, 126–34, 240–2. Sharp overstates his case. See for instance JRL, Nicholas MS 72/8, 'A noat of further passages', which suggests the importance of local lesser gentlemen in encouraging lower-class men and women to take action in Gillingham Forest. See also Underdown, *Revel, riot and rebellion*, 108–9.

[23] Holmes, 'Drainers and fenmen', 183–5; Underdown, *Revel, riot and rebellion*, 123; for examples of crowds led by local officers, see PRO, STAC8/146/29, 129/13, 253/17, 15/13, 34/4.

[24] PRO, DL4/67/59.

wealthy & sufficient freeholders, and able to pay good fines'. An attorney employed by the miners on that occasion was certainly active in carrying messages and offering advice. Nine years earlier, the Exchequer Court heard allegations of how another of the miners' attorneys, named Henry Lightfoot, had 'gone about from towne to towne [and] from libtie to libtie to animate & encourage the said Minors' against the lead tithe. Superficially, such evidence tends to support the view that the miners' grievances were organized and articulated by their attorneys in coalition with a local middling sort. Yet Henry Lightfoot answered the allegations against him by stating that he had no hand in the miners' resistance, and that it was the miners themselves who had collected common purses and refused the tithe. In the wake of the 1634 disturbances, the county's gentry did not bother themselves with tracking down any of the miners' attorneys: it was Raphe Oldfield, John Mitchell and their comrades they were interested in. Within Wirksworth, John Ferne played an important role in defining the legal and historical basis of the miners' claims to custom; yet he did so on the basis of documents lent and advice offered by the miners themselves.[25] We should not write off the importance of those few lesser gentlemen who offered their legal services to miners' and tenants' defence of custom. But nor should we exaggerate it. Men like Ferne were sympathizers; men like Lightfoot were hired attorneys. Neither were leaders.

In their disputes with their social superiors, the miners and tenants of the Peak produced their own leaders, and developed their own organizations and ideas. Yet in their complaints to Westminster courts, lords and tithe lessees often spoke of how the lower orders had been led to oppose them through the malign involvement of other 'great men'. Such complainants both spoke of their own fears, and played upon the prejudices of their class. Even in resistance, plebeians were assumed to need the leadership of their social betters. Definitions of the miners as violent, lazy and lawless therefore dovetailed with paranoid accounts of the movement of threatening, shadowy, wealthier men amongst them.[26] Other sources provide a closer sense of how the Peak's gentry understood the social background of their opponents. In the 1630s, Sir William Armyn had two poor men whipped through the streets of Cromford for taking timber from his woods. In response, the inhabitants of Cromford and Wirksworth took legal action against him. Feeling that the two poor men were the stooges of the settled inhabitants, Armyn told his opponents that 'hee would desire them if they

[25] BL, Add. MS 64908, fols. 128, 134; PRO, E134/22JasI/East30; PRO, DL4/72/31.
[26] PRO, E112/168/12, 19; BL, Add. MS 6681, fols. 360–71; DRO, D258M/47/17h, 28/20n, 42/15 unlisted interrogatory; Kershaw, 'Power and duty', 279. Some historians have been tempted into accepting such assumptions as fact: see for instance Lindley, *Fenland riots*, 255.

pceeded further in their suite to pduce their Accion upon such men that had woolle of their backes'.[27]

The men with 'woolle of their backes' were the same men whose names featured in lists of tithe resisters, or in Star Chamber prosecutions for alleged riot in the advance of free mining rights. Sometimes, the men with 'woolle of their backes' held land; sometimes, they did not. Typically, they were free miners with experience of barmote service who had served as deputy barmasters or in other local offices. They brought that experience to bear in the depositions which they gave to commissions of central courts, in which they articulated their strong sense of rights and custom. They had their equivalents elsewhere: with the relatively poor but independent artisans who comprised both the body and head of popular resistance in the forests of the West Country, or amongst the small master craftsmen of urban centres, concerned to defend the customs of their trade against those both above and below their social position.[28] That they were not a part of a local social elite was fundamental to their identity. Yet they were emphatically not of the poor, either. From the perspective of the gentry and nobility, such people were undoubtedly plebeian. But that overarching term, while it identifies the hard, blunt social polarities within which early modern social relations were conducted, none the less obscures the subtler distinctions which operated amongst the lower classes of early modern England. The men with 'woolle of their backes' were not especially wealthy, but neither were they of the 'hirelings and cavers'. Their most visible leaders, men like Raphe Oldfield of Litton or Thomas Godbehere of Cromford, were generally of slightly wealthier estate, but not so much as to lead them to feel part of a 'middling sort'. Indeed, as we have seen in Chapters 3 and 4, that important 'middling sort' group of agrarian England scarcely existed in the mid-seventeenth-century Peak, and no contemporary reference to the term can be found within the area. If the men with 'woolle of their backes' marked themselves out, it was as 'miners', thereby identifying themselves as adult, male, settled, skilled and independent.

The identity of the miner was simultaneously inclusive and exclusive. Unlike amongst the Free Miners of the Forest of Dean, Peak mining custom did not require either apprenticeship or birth into the trade. Instead, any man with sufficient access to capital (typically loaned) was able to set himself up as a miner, and to dig wherever he pleased within the King's Field or other free mining territories. The potential social basis of resistance

---

[27] PRO, DL4/109/8.

[28] Sharp, *In contempt*, 5–6, 126–55, 261–3. On the politics of urban labour identities, see the still durable G. Unwin, *Industrial organization in the sixteenth and seventeenth centuries* (Oxford, 1904). For a local study, see D.M. Palliser, 'The trade gilds of Tudor York', in Clark and Slack (eds.), *Crisis and order*, esp. 104–9.

was therefore very wide. None the less, it is important that the very poorest members of the mining workforce were not drawn into the developing struggle over the industry. The dispute over the lead tithes of the parishes of Bakewell, Hope and Tideswell provides the clearest illustration of this. Those miners listed as tithe resisters between 1615 and 1641 came almost exclusively from the wealthier parishes of Bakewell and Tideswell. As we saw in Chapters 3 and 4, the social structures of the parish of Hope were built upon deep poverty, heavy wage dependency and extreme landlessness. The miners of Hope were doubtless amongst the 'poorer sort' who were forced to compound with the tithe lessees. The implications of these contrasting social structures for the local character of social conflict find their expression in the dispute over the mining rights of Hazelbadge in 1630. Here, John Mitchell of Litton had led free miners from the Tideswell area into the manor to assert the right of free mining against that of its lord, John Manners of Haddon. But in recruiting his workforce, John Manners had drawn upon the deeper poverty of the neighbouring miners of Bradwell, within Hope parish. To the Tideswell miners, the fact that the Bradwell men were prepared to accept the price of nine shillings for their ore meant that they were 'noe miners', but merely Manners' 'servants'.[29] Similarly, in Wirksworth the very poorest miners benefited from the increased employment which resulted from Sir Robert Heath's seizure of the Dovegang works. Just as gender both defined the miners' political culture while undercutting a plebeian unity of interest, so social divisions amongst the mining workforce undermined the efficacy of popular resistance to tithes and manorial authorities.

TRADITIONS OF RESISTANCE

Although wage dependency was growing within the early Stuart Peak, the development of large mines and the collapse of lead prices had not yet forced free miners into waged work. Women, hirelings and cavers could be excluded from the free miners' political culture, and yet its social basis remain firm enough. Indeed, the maintenance of their exclusion became essential to the miners' collective identity. The miners' control of the language and institutions of custom legitimated the boundaries of their identity. But within that identity, custom operated in an inclusive fashion, naming skilled, settled adult male miners as a part of a definable collectivity. On the practical level, the institutions of mining custom provided both legitimacy and organizational focus to the miners' resistance.

---

[29] PRO, E112/168/24; HLRO, MP 9 April 1624; PRO, DL1/323, complaint of Att.-Gen. v. John Manners.

Instances of miners who had sat as barmote jurors or held office as deputy barmasters using their positions and legal experience to articulate, organize and lead tithe strikes, demonstrations, petitions, litigation and riot are not hard to find.[30] Still more importantly, the ideal of free mining custom defined the lead field of the Peak as the geographical unit within which this plebeian politics operated.

Miners in the High Peak saw the freedoms of the King's Field within Wirksworth Wapentake as the model of order and good government for the mining industry, and attempted to introduce it within their own manors. While proponents of free mining custom in manors within which the custom was banned tended to come from free mining manors immediately adjacent to the disputed territory, the struggles over the lead tithe and the Dovegang drew in large numbers of miners from a relatively wide area. Similarly, key leaders of the miners' cause travelled across much of the orefield. Thus Raphe Oldfield of Litton can be found disputing the free mining rights of Meadowplecke Grange, and Thomas Godbehere of Cromford questioning the lead tithe of Bakewell, Tideswell and Hope.[31] None the less, the miners and tenants of the Peak Country made no concerted attempt to link their own struggles with those going on elsewhere. The Peak produces no equivalent of the despatch by the defenders of Gillingham Forest in Dorset of their 'Colonel' to the inhabitants of Braydon Forest in Wiltshire to ask for support against enclosers.[32] Although some Peak miners tried (and in one case succeeded) in introducing their laws into other lead fields, those who stayed within the region made no attempt to link their struggles to those occurring in other free mining areas.[33] The only occasion on which the Peak miners joined with another group of free miners came in 1621 when the Peak and Mendip miners jointly petitioned the Privy Council against Captain Henry Bell's attempt to impose quality restrictions upon the sale of smelted lead.[34] Closer to home, the Wirksworth miners had no hand in the enclosure disturbances which gripped Duffield Forest four miles south of their town between the 1620s and 1650s.[35] Where miners were interested in disputes

---

[30] For examples, see Wood, 'Industrial development', 181–5.

[31] BL, Add. MS 6680, fols. 24–5; PRO, E134/4ChasI/Mich33.

[32] Underdown, *Revel, riot and rebellion*, 112.

[33] For Derbyshire miners in North Wales, see Williams, 'Mining laws in Flintshire and Denbighshire', 66. For Peak Country law as a model for Lancashire and Yorkshire lead miners, see Wood, 'Custom, identity and resistance', 274–5; Raistrick and Jennings, *Lead mining*, 110–14.

[34] *APC, 1619–21*, 140–1; on Bell's patent, see PRO, SP14/111/13, 109/164, 109/165.

[35] For a brief discussion of the Duffield disturbances, see Sharp, *In contempt*, 223; *VCH*, I, 420–1. This well-documented conflict would repay closer attention.

outside their village, they only concerned those occurring elsewhere within the lead field.

The lead field therefore contained and defined the miners' political culture before the civil war. Finer geographical limits can also be discerned. Proponents of free mining tended to come from territories immediately adjacent to those under contention. It was the miners of Wirksworth, Cromford, Middleton, Bonsall and Matlock who won the physical and legal battle over the mining rights of the rest of the Wapentake in James I's reign. Within the Haddon estates, the proponents of free mining came largely from Youlgreave, Bonsall, Overhaddon, Winster, Tideswell, Litton and Ashford lordship. Initially at least, the indigenous inhabitants of disputed manors were not actively drawn into the conflict on the miners' side. But as free mining rights were confirmed or allowed in one form or another across larger parts of the lead field after the 1590s, the numbers of manors from which new proponents of the right were drawn snowballed. It was out of this gathering confrontation that was drawn the network of free miners who were prepared to defend their rights across a wide swathe of the Peak.

In identifying the spatial limits of many local plebeian political cultures, social historians need to avoid the trap of demarcating lower-class politics within an arbitrary, closed unit.[36] We have seen that the Peak miners' attentions seem to have been closed by the boundaries of the lead field. It is therefore ironic that their politics have become historically observable through the study of the records of central equity courts based in Westminster. Although the central place held by custom gave the Peak's plebeian politics an inherently local quality, in the circumstances of the pre-civil war period the defence of custom required a growing involvement with the legal and political institutions of the central state. We have seen how Sir Robert Heath used his office and political weight in his intrusion into the affairs of the Peak miners. In response, much as they had been doing for a generation by the time of the Dovegang conflict, the Peak miners themselves intruded into the political centre. In 1632, hearing word that a new parliament was to be called, the Great Barmote of Wirksworth Wapentake drew up a petition denouncing the Attorney-General. It may have been with this in mind that Heath told his subordinates that he did not wish to know of their assaults upon the Wirksworth miners, warning 'I do not love to heare

---

[36] For a long time, historians of gentry politics tended to assume that 'county communities' constituted the essential basis of governance and identity, thereby downplaying ideology and conflict in pre-civil war England. For the classic statement of that view, see A. Everitt, *The local community and the Great Rebellion* (London, 1969). For important critiques of that interpretation, see C. Holmes, 'The county community in Stuart historiography', *Journal of British Studies*, 19 (1980), 54–75; Hughes, 'Local history'.

language in Parliament . . . sayinge . . . act your parte below and I will act my parte above.'[37] That such appeals might matter within the world of the political centre is evidenced by Heath's eventual fall from office as a result of growing disenchantment with his and Vermuyden's corrupt dealings in enclosures in Somerset and elsewhere.[38] The miners' ability to place the matter of the lead tithe before parliament in 1624, for all that their attempt to secure legislation failed, provides further evidence of their willingness to appeal to the political centre. But such appeals found their clearest articulation in legal proceedings.

For many historians, riot presents the primary, or even the sole, form of popular politics in rural England before the civil wars.[39] Other historians, assuming that riots occurred only after the exhaustion of more orderly forms of representation, find confirmation in riot of the orderly nature of early modern society. Riot, and therefore pre-civil war popular politics, has come to be seen as 'essentially defensive, conservative and restrained'.[40] Neither interpretation finds much support in the evidence of social conflict in the early Stuart Peak. It is now well known that early modern English rioters did not involve themselves in bloody jacqueries. Indeed, the term 'riot' itself denoted an offence in law, rather than any necessary violence against person or property. Heavily influenced by Edward Thompson's work on eighteenth-century food rioting, historians of riot in the sixteenth and seventeenth centuries have emphasized the orderly, non-violent, limited nature of crowd actions.[41] Indeed, riot and crowd actions within the early Stuart Peak correspond exactly with this picture. But this should not be taken as evidence of the deferential nature of plebeian society in the Peak. Riot, or more properly, crowd action, did not occur as a spasm of frustration following upon the denial of plebeian appeals to authority, or the failure of their legal action. Rather, as we have seen in the case of the invasion of private manors within Wirksworth Wapentake in the course of free mining disputes there between 1613 and 1627, crowd action was combined with litigation. Riot and demonstration was only a part of the armoury of plebeian politics, and was deployed with a large sense of tactics: to apply pressure; as a threatening display of potential force; collectively to demonstrate a claimed right. Within the Peak's plebeian politics, the collective use of the law was of equal importance as riot. The tithe lessees were exhausted by the High Peak miners' combination of tithe

[37] BL, Add. MS 6678, fol. 39; PRO, DL4/90/24.
[38] Kopperman, *Heath*, 231–44.
[39] See for instance Underdown, *Revel, riot and rebellion*, 106.
[40] Lindley, *Fenland riots*, 57.
[41] Thompson, *Customs in common*, ch. 4, and Walter and Wrightson, 'Dearth and the social order'.

strikes, physical violence, and the clever use of the courts. Similarly, in disputes over enclosure and mining rights, petition, negotiation and demonstration were all used in conjunction with riot.

We misread early modern popular politics if we define it on the basis of riot and 'disorder' alone. Similarly, we misread riot if we see it solely as a product of a 'traditional' plebeian culture threatened by the insidious creep of modernization. It is notable that crowd actions and riot in the Peak possessed few identifiable ritual elements. Unlike in the fens and the West Country forests, the rising in the Midlands in 1607, or the rather more closed local culture of the Yorkshire valley of Nidderdale, there are no elements of symbolic inversion to be found in the ordering of crowd protest in the Jacobean and Caroline Peak. We find no references to men dressed as women; no use of maypoles or football; no militia-style organization, or mysterious 'Captain Pouches' leading and organizing resistance. There are no mocking rhymes, burnings in effigy or exaggerated threatening letters.[42] There is a pattern to crowd action in the Peak, but no obvious ritual. At the same time as advancing their cause at Westminster courts, tenants and miners might organize a crowd to march on to and sometimes around the boundaries of a disputed manor or common. Cattle might be led onto commons, or lead ore dug, in symbolic assertion of customary rights. Similarly, opposition to such rights had by James' reign acquired a particular, and very obvious, form. Cattle would be driven off commons, and boundary markers removed. The stowes which marked a free miners' possession of a mineworking would be removed, and sometimes publicly burnt. If a miner was found working underground, earth would be cast in upon him.[43] None of this is very striking. The miners and tenants of the Peak did have traditions, and as we have seen in Chapters 7 and 8, these were central to their collective and individual senses of identity. These traditions were vested in notions of law and good order which connected in custom. Theirs was a rather less colourful tradition than that in the fens or forests; but it was perhaps a rather more public, organized and assertive one.

[42] For the Midland Rising, see E.F. Gay, 'The Midland Revolt and the inquisitions of depopulation of 1607', *Transactions of the Royal Historical Society*, 2nd ser., 18 (1904), 195–244; Martin, *Feudalism to capitalism*, chs. 9–10. On the long persistence of ritual forms in some areas, see A. Howkins and L. Merrick, ' "Wee be black as hell": ritual, disguise and rebellion', *Rural History*, 4, 1 (1993), 41–53. On the symbolism of 'skimmington' riots, see Underdown, *Revel, riot and rebellion*, 110–12. Historians of crowd action in early modern England have been heavily influenced by N.Z. Davis' readings of contemporary French disorders: see her *Society and culture in early modern France* (Stanford, 1975), esp. chs. 4–6.

[43] See for instance PRO, DL1/378, complaint of Richard Furniss, /366, complaint of William Goodwin; PRO DL4/120/1678/1; PRO, STAC8/219/4.

Plebeian politics in the Peak did not stem from a 'traditional' lower-class culture. Miners made the claim that their customs were 'ancient' while simultaneously introducing innovations into them. Their politics was neither conservative nor defensive. Instead, it was consciously and deliberately pro-active, their tactics well capable of responding to changed circumstances, of exploiting divisions amongst their opponents, and manipulating legal process. They did not aim merely at the defence of existent custom. Rather, by 1640 the political project envisioned by the miners entailed the perfection of free mining law in those territories where it already existed, and its advance across those manors where the right was denied. This project was to find its clearest articulation, and to experience its greatest defeat, in the years of the English Revolution.

'Prerogative hath many proctors': The English Revolution and the plebeian politics of the Peak, 1640–1660

WAR AND ALLEGIANCE

Modern historians have found the Peak miners as difficult to understand as did their early modern rulers. In an economy which is conventionally described as pre-industrial, the lives of the mining workforce were dominated by the experience of industrial labour. In a society whose norms were supposedly built upon the reciprocal ideals of plebeian deference and elite patronage, the miners stand out as unusually assertive. It should therefore come as no surprise to find that popular allegiances in the Peak at the outbreak of the first civil war run against the grain of the contending historical explanations of that subject. The political loyalties of the miners and tenants of the area did not follow those of the local gentry and nobility. Popular deference to the political decisions of their social betters can therefore be ruled out.[1] Neither did the miners enlist as a composite social bloc for one side or another, thereby frustrating a simple class interpretation of allegiance.[2] The same goes for suggestions that religion constituted the key factor in individuals' and groups' choice of sides.[3] While religion proved a motivating factor for some people within the Peak, religious divisions were not as deep as elsewhere within England. Instead, the plebeian inhabitants of the Peak followed their own circuitous and divergent paths into civil war.[4]

In his study of popular politics within the West Country, David Under-

---

[1] For the view that the lower orders followed where their social betters led, see most importantly A. Everitt, *The community of Kent and the Great Rebellion, 1640–60* (Leicester, 1960). For a useful survey of the different models of allegiance, see D.E. Underdown, 'Community and class: theories of local politics in the English Revolution', in B.C. Malament (ed.), *After the Reformation: essays in honor of J.H. Hexter* (Manchester, 1980), 147–65.

[2] Manning, *English people*.

[3] Morrill, *Nature of the English Revolution*, ch. 3.

[4] For a fuller account of popular allegiances in the Peak during the first civil war, see A. Wood, 'Beyond post-revisionism? The civil war allegiances of the miners of the Derbyshire Peak Country', *Historical Journal*, 40, 1 (1997), 23–40.

down observed a similar lack of correspondence between the pattern of allegiance in 1642, and the conventional tools of explanation deployed by historians of the subject. His innovative solution to that problem grew from his claim that 'the patterns of civil war allegiance in the western counties have an unmistakably regional character'. He had already noted a basic difference in the character of popular culture, social conflict and social structure between downland, arable areas and the pastoral-industrial uplands of the West Country. Within the former, he found hierarchical communities in which the traditional norms of deference and hierarchy were widely accepted. Within the latter, he detected a greater popular independence, deeper social conflict, and a broader distribution of wealth. He also found that popular puritanism was more likely to develop in upland, pastoral-industrial regions than in downland, arable areas. Finally, he claimed that in 1642 a close correspondence emerged between ecology and allegiance. Whereas 'the royalism of the downland villages was an appropriate expression of the local culture', the individualism and puritanism of pastoral-industrial localities manifested itself in support for the parliament.[5] Long extrapolation from a basic truism concerning the differing structural and ecological characteristics of agrarian and pastoral England therefore provided the interpretative base of the model. In spite of corrosive criticism, Underdown's interpretation has been adopted by other historians.[6] Based as it was upon a contextual, long-term understanding of regional and cultural difference, Underdown's interpretation seemed to offer a clear and persuasive explanation of the formation of opposing sides in England in 1642. Moreover, it appeared to grant an autonomy to plebeian politics which many earlier explanations, founded upon the assumption of a broad deference on the part of the lower orders to their rulers, had lacked. Unfortunately, in spite of its apparent logic and clarity, the ecological interpretation of allegiance flew in the face of the historical pattern of allegiance.

Flat, agrarian Norfolk and Suffolk remained securely parliamentarian throughout the first civil war. Mountainous Cornwall and North Wales, like many parts of Lancashire and Yorkshire, sided with the King. The parliament's grip upon much of the agrarian Home Counties never loosened until the second war. And within the Peak Country, in spite of claims that it provided strong support for the parliament, King Charles was able to recruit a 'Life guard' from amongst the miners at his 'first entrance

---

[5] Underdown, Revel, riot and rebellion, 165, 180.
[6] For a powerful critique of Underdown, see Morrill, Nature of the English Revolution, ch. 11. For adaptations of Underdown's interpretation, see A. Hughes, Politics, society and civil war in Warwickshire, 1620–1660 (Cambridge, 1987); idem, The causes of the English civil war (London, 1991); idem, 'Local history'.

to this Warr'.[7] Underdown's predictive model cannot therefore bear the weight of the historical evidence. Yet his achievement lay in the contextual attention he gave to the political and cultural worlds which existed below that of the gentry. In particular, Underdown's recognition that popular responses to civil war had much to do with the pre-existence of local plebeian political cultures stood in opposition to the short-term high-political accounts of the causes of civil war then prevailing. It is this aspect of Underdown's interpretation which endures. Civil war allegiances in the Peak had a lot to do with the alliances and divisions of interest created by earlier conflicts over the lead industry, and should be read against the pre-war development of an assertive politics amongst the free miners.[8] For it was not ecology which determined allegiance in the Peak in the August of 1642, but rather the contingent interests of a large section of the mining workforce.

As we have seen, the pre-war politics of the Peak was far from isolated from the central state. Prior to the calling of the Long Parliament, the miners had already drawn the Westminster courts, the Privy Council and the parliament into their struggles. Like elsewhere, the Peak's inhabitants were formally pulled into the constitutional and religious politics of the centre in 1641. On 14 March of that year, a petition of some 7,077 people was presented to the Long Parliament from the inhabitants of Derbyshire. Like other county petitions, it praised the Commons for its 'blessed work of reformation' of religion and government. Two months later, the parliament reciprocated by requiring all loyal subjects to sign its Protestation in favour of the established Protestant religion. In April 1642, the Peak's inhabitants were again enjoined to put their names to a petition from the county's inhabitants, this time directed to the King, and calling upon him to maintain Protestantism, the liberties of his subjects, and the parliament.[9] The two Derbyshire petitions had been written by leading members of the county's gentry, and the collection of signatures was organized through ministers and constables by Sir John Gell. One reading of the petitioning movement of 1641–2 has drawn the conclusion that such petitions represented the grievances of the county community of the gentry,

---

[7] BL, Harl MS 6833, fol. 61.

[8] Jill Dias has recognized the importance of earlier conflicts over the lead industry in conditioning allegiance in 1642, but has inaccurately characterized the nature of that allegiance. See Dias, 'Lead, society and politics', 51–2; Wood, 'Beyond post-revisionism', 28–32, 35.

[9] On the petitioning movement of 1641–2, see A.J. Fletcher, 'Petitioning and the outbreak of the civil war in Derbyshire', *DAJ*, 2nd ser., 93 (1973), 34–7. The only surviving Protestation returns from the Peak Country are at DRO, D258M/60/6, and DRO, D2537/Pl/1/1. Names collected from fifteen lead mining townships for the 1642 petition are at HLRO, MP 26 February 1642.

organized through their traditional control of local government.[10] Other historians have seen the collection of petitions as evidence of the growing politicization of ordinary people.[11]

Grievances given formal expression in the petitioning movement did not only concern constitutional and religious matters. Some linked economic difficulties to the growing political crisis.[12] The miners of the Peak were not isolated from these developments. In 1635, King Charles had doubled the duties taken by the Exchequer upon the export of smelted lead to forty-eight shillings per fother. Hit by falling lead prices, the miners recognized that the increase of duties was likely to hurt their industry still further. The calling of parliament provided the miners with an opportunity to influence events. Early in 1641, signatures were collected from amongst the miners to a petition which was to be placed before parliament calling for the reduction in duties to twenty-eight shillings. The petition is important in three respects.[13] First, the miners' petition was a clearer statement of popular hostility to the Crown's actions than were the county petitions of 1641 and 1642. Whereas the county gentry had given the lead in the collection of the county petitions, no such hierarchy can be drawn from the text of the miners' petition. It listed by name the 1,912 individuals who had given their support to it, headed by Lionel Tynley, a minor lead merchant who can subsequently be identified as a Presbyterian. A few orebuyers and lesser merchants were mixed with the other signatories, all of whom were miners. Secondly, the petition spoke volumes as to the presence of the miners as a coherent interest group within the politics of the Peak. While it included as signatories those women who held mineshares (most of them widows), it excluded the names of 'cavers and hirelings' and ancillary workers, who appeared only as crude statistical totals. It therefore constituted the clearest statement of the limits within which the miners' collectivity was defined. Finally, while the tone of the petition was less explicitly political than those concerning (for example) the decay of trade in textile areas, it pointedly referred the increase in tolls as 'theise late illegal ymposicions'. The miners' petition should therefore be seen as part of the growing national critique of the arbitrary and oppressive nature of Caroline economic policy. The petition was placed before a Commons committee in July 1641, who recognized that it was 'a matter of great moment to the miners of the Peak', and promptly agreed to a reduction in duties.[14]

---

[10] A.J. Fletcher, *The outbreak of the civil war* (London, 1981), 196.
[11] Hughes, *Causes*, 166–75.   [12] Fletcher, *Outbreak*, ch. 6.
[13] For its use in the study of social structure, see Chapter 3. For its significance in defining the miners' collective identity, see Chapter 8.
[14] PRO, E101/280/18; PRO, SP16/341/130, /14/35, /431/32, /432/16; BL, Add. MS 64922, fol. 47.

By August 1642, the miners of the Peak had become used to setting their names to petitions concerning events in the national political centre. In that month, Derbyshire began its collapse into civil war.[15] On 3 August, a committee was appointed by parliament to take control of the county. On the 15th, King Charles published an appeal to the miners in which he offered to exempt them from duties of lot and cope if they joined his army at Nottingham. He was answered by a new petition from the High Peak miners on 31 August, signed by twenty-eight of their number, in which they agreed to form a regiment if, instead of exempting them from lot and cope, he lifted the 'oppression' of lead tithes. 'Being graciously inclined to ease them by Our Princely indulgence', and also desperate for infantrymen, Charles agreed to their request.[16] Importantly, the negotiations were communicated through the medium of printed handbills.[17] The King instructed barmasters and ministers to collect miners for his army, and by early September some 400 miners had mustered for his army at Nottingham.

In spite of the formation of a county committee and the independent mustering of other High Peak miners for the parliament, gentry supporters of the parliamentary cause were slower off the mark than their opponents. Marching from Hull to Derby, Sir John Gell, the leading parliamentarian of the county paused at the puritanically inclined town of Chesterfield, and again at Wirksworth in mid-September, where he recruited 140 men to serve as foot and dragoons. Within a month, therefore, the outbreak of war had divided the mining community. The breach in popular allegiances within the Peak remained obvious throughout the first war. In spite of the miners' historic hostility to his family, Rowland Eyre was able to raise a second royalist regiment from amongst them in 1644, while the muster rolls of the parliamentarian regiments of Gell and Thomas Sanders included the names of many miners, mostly drawn from the Wirksworth and Youlgreave areas.

Within the Peak, popular allegiances were influenced by a series of contradictory factors. The twenty-eight signatories of the miners' petition which answered Charles' appeal were all drawn from the parishes of Bakewell, Hope and Tideswell. Sir John Gell had been their prime antagonist over the matter of the lead tithe, and they saw in the King's need for soldiers an opportunity to press their case upon him with greater force than they had managed in 1634. Moreover, most of the signatories had

---

[15] The ensuing discussion is based on Fletcher, 'Petitioning', 38–40; Wood, 'Beyond post-revisionism?', 32–5.

[16] On Charles' need for infantry, see J.L. Malcolm, *Caesar's due: loyalty and King Charles, 1642–1646* (London, 1983), ch. 4.

[17] Copies survive in BL, Add. MS 6677, fol. 48; BL Harl MS 6833, fols. 58–9, 61.

distinguished themselves as leaders of resistance to lords and tithe lessees. Their royalism was more the product of long-standing conflict and a sense of tactics than the result of the deference sometimes ascribed to popular support for the King. But it is important that initial support for the King came only from the High Peak. The plunder of Wirksworth and adjacent settlements by Colonel Wortley's cavalry shortly before Gell's arrival in the town cannot have done much to engender support amongst its inhabitants for the King. Yet the tenants of that town were, in his right as Duke of Lancaster, the King's tenants. Within the Wirksworth area, the central authorities had appeared as the greatest opponents of popular rights. The backing given to Heath's seizure of the Dovegang, the large fine levied upon Wirksworth's inhabitants in 1622, the attempted enclosure of the manor's commons and the interference in the ordering of the industry by the Privy Council over the course of James I's and Charles I's reigns must all have acted to create a perception of the Crown as 'an oppressive, alien force'.[18] High Peak miners arrived at their royalism through their antagonism to Gell. Wirksworth miners and tenants may have given their support to Gell at least in part out of their hostility to the Crown. We might therefore be tempted to propose a model of popular allegiance which operated according to inverse deference, whereby the lower orders of certain areas perversely supported the opposite side to that of their local social superior.

Yet no single issue can be privileged in explanation of the multiplicity of popular reactions to the outbreak of the war. While the religious issue was not as much to the fore as that of local social antagonisms within the Peak in August and September 1642, it is notable that shortly before the outbreak of fighting, on hearing rumours that papists were coming to burn Wirksworth, the town's population had panicked. Moreover, the Wirksworth area was the only locality within the post-Restoration Peak to harbour a clique of relatively wealthy Presbyterians. Contrarily, some of the men whom Eyre recruited to his regiment in 1644 were, like him, Catholic recusants. William Bagshawe and John Mitchell of Litton, long united against tithes and oppressive lords, split in their reaction to the civil war. Mitchell signed the petition of 31 August which offered support to the King, while Bagshawe was a supporter of the parliament, a noted Commonwealth Presbyterian, and the father of a man who became known after the Restoration as the 'Apostle of the Peak' for his preaching activities. Although lead merchants tended to support the parliament, the greater gentry were as divided by the war as were the miners. In spite of decades of social conflict within the Peak Country before the civil war,

---

[18] Here quoting Underdown, *Revel, riot and rebellion*, 112.

patterns of allegiance were therefore not demarcated by clear social solidarities.[19]

Within the Peak, initial patterns of popular allegiance were instead drawn around three factors, in order of descending priorities: the specific configuration of local social conflicts before the civil war; the experience of plunder; and, in the case of a minority, religious belief. Given the powerful importance of religion as a motivating factor in political allegiance elsewhere within England, readers may find these priorities rather odd. Indeed, Mark Stoyle's impressive study of popular allegiances in Devon has recently given qualified support to Underdown's connection between regional variation and allegiance, and has found in differing popular religious cultures the key to the manifestation of popular support for the King or the parliament.[20] Yet the religious divide opened by the Reformation and deepened in the early seventeenth century had little significant effect upon popular culture within the Peak.

In spite of the presence of important recusant gentry families, the attentions of Jesuits in the late sixteenth century, and the existence of a large community of plebeian Catholics in nearby Hathersage, popular Catholicism within the mining area of the Peak appears as insignificant. Equally, despite the attentions of godly ministers and preachers, the hotter sort of Protestantism was given a decidedly cool reception by the miners and tenants of the Peak. The signature of many miners to the county petitions of 1641 and 1642 in support of the work of reformation of the Long Parliament should be set against the appearance of the names of the same men on the petition of 31 August 1642 to the King. After the Restoration, a small but coherent group of dissenters can be found in towns lying along trade networks and possessed of relatively high rates of literacy. Quite conceivably, post-Restoration Presbyterianism in the Wirksworth area had some roots in the locality before the civil war. But if so, the historical evidence suggests that such roots were weak. Moreover, post-Restoration dissenters were mostly minor lead merchants and wealthier freeholders.[21] The hotter sort of Protestantism was largely restricted to the literate, numerically insignificant 'middling sort' of the largish, socially complex valley market towns.

The absence of any strong popular religious conviction within the Peak, coupled with the historic autonomy of local plebeian politics, formed the background to popular support for the King. The miners' response of 31 August to their monarch's appeal should therefore be set in the longer

[19] Newton, 'Gentry', 2, 8.
[20] M. Stoyle, *Loyalty and locality: popular allegiance in Devon during the English civil war* (Exeter, 1994).
[21] Newton, 'Gentry', 8; Wood, 'Industrial development', 148–50.

context of their political culture. By that time, the miners had developed a sensitivity to local and national divisions amongst their rulers. Their ancestors' ability to embarrass the sixth Earl of Shrewsbury at court, their tactical alliances with Carrier and the Eyres, and later with Heath against Carrier, form the context within which their answer of 31 August should be set, rather than the ecological typology of the Peak Country. In 1642, the miners of Bakewell, Hope and Tideswell who mustered for Charles were playing the same game as they had for generations. But on this occasion, the stakes were higher than the lead tithes of their parishes, or their mining customs; and this time their alliance set them in opposition to their neighbours and brothers in their trade.

The war in the Peak Country was dominated by semi-permanent garrisons in strongpoints such as Chatsworth and Hassop Hall, and by the movement of small mounted raiding forces. Continual skirmishing between parliamentary and royalist cavalry and dragoons continued between 1642 and 1645, interrupted on occasion by the arrival of larger field armies, but no major engagements were fought. None the less, the endemic fighting dislocated trade and forced the division of communities down partisan lines. In particular, the lead industry was badly affected by the war. In 1643 the royalist Earl of Newcastle ignored miners' complaints and began a blockade of the movement of lead ore to Hull, arguing that the trade benefited the parliament. The following year, the parliamentarian Earl of Manchester stopped the lead trade on the grounds that sequestered ore from delinquents' estates was included amongst that being sold. That year saw the almost total collapse of lead mining within Wirksworth, with all the consequent unemployment amongst the town's industrial workforce. Throughout the war, the military vacuum in the High Peak resulted in the dislocation of trade networks, disrupting the movement of food into this barren, overpopulated area.[22] Finally, while parliamentarian troops tended to restrict themselves to plundering the houses of royalist gentry, their opponents became notorious for their widespread pillage. But if the war brought with it economic disruption, it also created new possibilities.

Between 1640 and 1643, in tune with the growing crisis at the political centre, enclosures were cast down within large parts of England. Such riots became a matter of political comment, reported in the growing number of

---

[22] *Certain Informations*, 13–20 February 1643, BL, TT F. 90 (3); DRO, 803M/Z9, fols. 88–9; DRO, D258M/60/11. It is significant that the Wirksworth mining industry swiftly recovered in 1645, and that record amounts of lead were shipped from Hull during the war years to feed the parliament's demand for lead shot: Kiernan, 'Lawrence Oxley's accounts', 123. On wartime disruptions in the larger North Midlands area, see M. Bennett, '"My plundered townes, my houses devastation": the civil war and North Midlands life', *Midland History*, 22 (1997), 35–50.

London newsbooks and prosecuted before both houses of parliament. Commons enclosed with the backing of the central law courts by entrepreneurial courtiers such as Heath and Vermuyden were once again laid open, and lost common rights restored. As Derbyshire's member in the Commons wrote to his father in May 1641, 'This is no time to try titles of common . . . [or] to prosecute the enclosures of commons whilst the common people are at so much liberty.'[23] The Peak's inhabitants took the opportunity to effect a reformation of some of their own grievances. Enclosure markers on the moors of the Duchy's manor of High Peak were removed. In riots just south of the Peak in Duffield Frith, the tenants cast down enclosures made by the Duchy in the 1630s. In the same year as the miners collected their petition to parliament, barmote courts met to renew organized opposition to the lead tithe in the parishes of Bakewell, Tideswell and Hope, and the miners of the Youlgreave, Bakewell and Ashford areas combined in a mass invasion of the Earl of Rutland's manor of Harthill.[24] On the outbreak of hostilities, manor courts in many parts of the Peak stopped functioning. The collection of lot and cope and of tithes in the High Peak ceased. In the first few months of the war, more attacks on enclosures in the High Peak and Duffield Frith occurred, and the documentation proving enclosure was destroyed. At both Newton Grange in Wirksworth Wapentake and in the Earl of Rutland's manors of Harthill and Netherhaddon the miners took the opportunity of the collapse of manorial authority to resume free mining. Hearing of the invasion of his lands, Rutland called upon parliament to despatch soldiers to guard his lands and his steward from attack.[25]

The parliamentary soldiery were also enjoying the benefits of new-found freedoms of action and thought. The men of the Peak Country who had joined Sir John Gell's and Thomas Sanders' regiments found that military experience brought with it a perceptible broadening of intellectual and political horizons. In particular amongst the cavalry and dragoon units, there developed an antipathy amongst the soldiery to the authoritarian conduct of Sir John Gell and a willingness to question, criticize and, on a number of occasions, to rebel. Differences between Gell and his men occurred not only over matters of pay and conditions, but also over the direction of the war and religious policy. Major Thomas Sanders, whom Sir

---

[23] Manning, *English people*, 190–211; Morrill and Walter, 'Order and disorder in the English Revolution', 139–42; Underdown, *Revel, riot and rebellion*, 159–62.

[24] Somerville, 'Commons and wastes', 20; PRO, DL4/120/1680/13, /126/1691/3; PRO, E134/17ChasI/Mich4, /18ChasI/East12, /1659/East 27; PRO, DL1/366, complaint of William Goodwin *et al.*

[25] PRO, E317/9/10; Somerville, 'Commons and wastes', 19–20; PRO, DL4/124/1686/7; HLRO, MP 20 February 1643 and 16 March 1643; *Journal of the House of Lords 1642–3*, 624, 651; PRO, DL5/34, fols. 228, 249.

John Gell accused of being a Brownist, became the leading critic of Gell. Threatened by Sanders' power base amongst the cavalry, Gell restricted payments to the horse soldiers in order, as another of his critics Captain Nathaniel Barton put it, 'to destroy the regt. of horse'. Sanders, enraged at Gell's attempts to destroy what he considered 'the best regiment of horse in the north of England', took strength from the fact that 'both officers and soldiers refuse to go under [Gell's] command'. Both Barton and Sanders subsequently took their men to fight under different commands.[26]

Wirksworth miners who had joined Gell's regiment may have taken special pleasure in plundering the houses of those gentlemen, such as John Lowe, George Hopkinson and the Fitzherberts of Tissington, who had earlier opposed their right of free mining and who now supported the King.[27] When not disputing with their colonel, or settling old scores, some of the soldiers of the Derbyshire regiments found time to expose themselves to the radical religious ideas then gaining influence in the parliament's forces. Immanuel Bourne, the puritan minister of Ashover, had before the civil wars despaired of what he regarded as the 'popish' habits of his flock. In 1646, as he recalled in a letter of the following year, he had occasion to despair again: but this time of the penetration of religious radicalism into the Derbyshire parliamentary forces. Having observed a troop of horse led by 'a scout master named Smedley' destroy Wingfield Hall he watched them mount and set off, singing psalms, in the direction of his parish church. He recalled that

For feare they should prophane or injure the house of God I did soon follow after and to my great surprise did find scout master Smedley in the pulpit, where he did preache a sermon two hours long about popery, priestcraft and Kyngcraft; but Lord what stuff and nonsense hee did talke and if he could have murdered the Kyng as easily as hee did the Kyngs english the war would long since been over then singing a psalm they prepared to go but some of the pyoneers seeing the stayned window once belonging to the Reresbys on which was paynted the crucifiction they said it was rank popery and must be destroyed; soe they brought their mattocks and bars and not only destroyed the glass but the stone work also they then found out the prayer booke and surplice and the old parishe registere being old and partly in latine they could not reade it so they said it was full of popery and treason and tooke the whole to the market place and making a fyre did burn them to ashes. They then mounted their horses and sung another psalm and rode awaye.[28]

---

26 DRO, D258M/34/10; DRO 1232M/011. The dispute between Gell and Sanders is more fully explored in L.N. Beats, 'Politics and government in Derbyshire 1640–60', PhD thesis, University of Sheffield, 1979, 142–54, 196–203.

27 Newton, 'Gentry', 24; Hopkinson, *Laws and customs*, 3.

28 DRO, D267/229c. This is a nineteenth-century copy of the original, which has been lost. On the provenance of the copy, see BL, Add. MS 6675, fols. 379–80. On its validity, see C.E.L., *The 'saints and sinners' of Ashover* (Leicester, 1924), 54–5.

THE LEVELLERS, THE MINERS AND THE EIGHTH EARL OF
RUTLAND

The radicalization and polarization of the late 1640s electrified the miners' final attempt to extend the right of free mining within the Peak Country. By the time of his ascent to the peerage as the eighth Earl of Rutland, John Manners of Haddon had identified himself as the chief opponent of the right of free mining. The miners' invasion of his manor of Harthill in 1641 must be seen in two contexts: that of the new popular liberty extending across much of England at that time; and that of the long-standing conflict between the miners and the Manners of Haddon. Between 1641 and 1658, Rutland and the miners dug themselves into opposing trenches over the matter of the mining rights of two manors within Haddon lordship: Harthill and Netherhaddon. The dispute had many of the qualities of the pre-civil war conflicts, but in exaggerated forms. Events in Netherhaddon and Harthill involved the greatest violence of any free mining dispute of the early modern period. Moreover, the confrontation in the Peak between plebeian and elite collectivities acquired its sharpest focus in these years. Whereas popular allegiances in 1642 had cut across social divisions, open class conflict was explicit in the Haddon dispute. The coalescence of opposing class forces in Netherhaddon and Harthill was stark. The miners who confronted the Earl of Rutland were all men of small estate, shorn of almost all support from amongst the lesser gentry.[29] Rutland's local supporters, on the other hand, were almost all drawn from the county's greater gentry. On both sides, leadership came from people with long experience of struggles over mining custom. And on both sides, the conflict was described in extreme terms.

In their published and reported remarks, miners drew upon a language of class to define their opponents as oppressors and tyrants, and were given to expropriatory fantasies in which they imagined taking not only the lead ore of Haddon lordship, but the estate and the Hall itself.[30] In response, the Earl and his supporters described the miners as violent, disorderly men driven by a communist impulse that led to the levelling of all property and order.[31] Most dramatically, the Haddon dispute developed important national connotations, as it came to express on a micro scale the political and social divisions of 1649. The Leveller movement was drawn into the conflict on the side of the miners, while Rutland received the support of the

---

[29] For the humble backgrounds of the miners' leaders in 1648, see PRO, DL5/34, fol. 302, and below.
[30] On the context of this language, see Wood, 'Social conflict', 43–7, 50. For an exception, see BL, Add. MS 6682, fol. 46.
[31] See Chapter 6 above.

parliament, the common law and Westminster courts, the county gentry, the Council of State and the Army. The remainder of this chapter will focus upon the course, implications and outcome of the Haddon dispute. First, a narrative of events will be developed. Secondly, the support for the Leveller movement shown by some Peak miners will be placed in the context of developments in the miners' political culture in the mid-seventeenth century. Finally, the eventual resolution of the Haddon dispute in the interests of the nobility and gentry will be shown to mark a decisive turning point in popular politics in the area, in the history of disputes over mining custom and thereby in the history of the lead mining industry itself.

The mass invasion of Harthill by the miners in 1641 was greeted by their violent ejection by the Earl of Rutland and his armed and mounted retainers. Using his authority as Justice of the Peace, he bound their leaders against entering his estates. In response, William Goodwin of Ashford, a known tithe opponent and soon to be a signatory to the petition of 31 August 1642 to the King, placed the matter before the Duchy Court, which ruled in favour of Rutland. Two years later, following the outbreak of war and Rutland's removal from the warzone to London, the miners again entered Haddon lordship, allegedly declaring that there was 'no law'. They were driven out on separate occasions by both parliamentary and royalist forces, but by the time of the Earl's return to his Derbyshire estates in 1647 were still to be found digging within the lordship.[32] In the intervening period, two connected events had pointed to important changes in the miners' political culture. The first event concerned the office of barmaster. The delinquency of Rowland Eyre led to his removal as barmaster of the High Peak. Consequently, the Duchy appointed a new barmaster who found his authority undermined by the election, for the first time since the late fifteenth century, of a rival barmaster from amongst the miners' ranks. The miners' candidate for the office was David Frost of Sheldon, who styled himself as a gentleman, but was the son of a miner and barmote juror who had taken part in resistance to the tithe in the 1620s.[33] Secondly, in 1645 an important pamphlet was published by a former miner and parliamentary soldier. Its author, William Debankes of Cromford, had been a tithe resister before the civil war and by 1644 was enlisted as a parliamentary trooper in Sanders' regiment. Entitled *The liberties and customs of the miners*, the pamphlet presented the legal and historical basis of the miners' claim to dig for ore anywhere within the lead field. The

[32] PRO, DL1/366, complaint of William Goodwin *et al.*; HLRO, MP 20 February 1643; BL, Add. MS 6677, fol. 49.
[33] PRO, SP19/159, fol. 125; PRO, DL5/34, fols. 228, 249, /35, fol. 74; PRO, E317/9/24; LJRO, B/C/11, will of George Frost, 20 Dec 1636; PRO, E101/280/18; PRO, E134/8ChasI/ Mich26, /13JasI/Mich3.

pamphlet went into a second edition in 1649, in time for the climax of the Haddon dispute.[34] The election of a barmaster and the publication of their customs suggested that the miners' ambitions were expanding beyond the already wide bounds established before the wars.

On his return to Haddon, Rutland therefore faced the occupation of his estates by a still more militant band of miners than that which he had confronted in 1641. Initially, and quite uncharacteristically, he attempted to compromise. Calling the miners to a meeting, he formed a Great Barmote for Harthill manor and allowed free mining there in return for stringent controls upon the miners, recognition of his authority as lord and the exaction of severe manorial tolls upon them. The compromise broke down as, unhappy with these limited gains, the miners pressed their claims into the manor of Netherhaddon in which Manners' mansion house of Haddon Hall was located. On 11 May 1648, Rutland procured an order from the House of Lords which prevented the miners from entering Netherhaddon. Upon the miners' refusal to leave the manor, Rutland led another armed attack upon them. His servants filled in the mine-shafts, while in his capacity as a Justice, Rutland bound the miners over to keep the peace and threatened that he 'would lay them in Gaole and ruine them'. The miners, despite their claims to having been overcome by 'the countenance and power of the . . . Earl of Rutland their maister', responded with their own prosecutions at the Court of the Duchy of Lancaster and, the following week, launched a mass invasion of Netherhaddon. In all of this, their candidate as barmaster was to the fore, organizing the legal action at the Duchy, and leading riots.[35]

Over three days in late May 1648, crowds of up to 200 miners entered Haddonfields in Netherhaddon manor to dig for ore. The Earl's stewards, his retainers and freehold tenants sallied forth from Haddon Hall to confront them. One of the stewards, William Savile, himself a Justice of the Peace, read out the House of Lords' proclamation of 11 May and ordered the miners to depart. At this, one miner was reported to have responded

that there was lead oare to be gotten there [in Haddonfields] and that they would worke there whosoever said nay, and that they would bring thousands to assist them, and many of the minors then said that they had nothing to loose, and that they cared not for their carcasses, and some . . . said that if they were interrupted and those they looked for came to them it was not working there [in Haddonfields]

---

[34] BL, Add. MS 6682, fols. 65–75. For Debankes, see Wood, 'Beyond post-revisionism', 36.
[35] BL, Add. MSS 6682, fols. 80–5, *Journal of the House of Lords 1647–8*, 252–3; *Journal of the House of Lords 1648–51*, 303. For the case at the Duchy, which was eventually thrown out, see PRO, DL1/378, complaint of Rowland Furniss, /379, answer of Latham Woodruffe *et al.*; PRO, DL6/95/26, /54, /69; PRO, DL5/34, fols. 296, 300, 302, 305, 310, 314, 317, 324, 336.

should serve their turne, for they hoped to have the house meaning thereby the Mannour House of Nether Haddon.

A fracas between the miners and the Earl's men ensued, in which the miners gave as good as they got. Thereafter, the Earl initiated new prosecutions for riot at the Quarter Sessions, Assizes and the House of Lords. Eleven miners, many of them prominent in earlier tithe disputes, were brought to London and imprisoned at the order of the House of Lords in Fleet Gaol. Two of the miners incurred the House's wrath for 'refusinge to submitt to this house or to acknowledge their offence'.

Despite the imprisonment of their comrades, the miners continued to disturb the peace of the Haddon estate. Further prosecutions at Assizes, Quarter Sessions and the Court of King's Bench resulted in the punishment of more miners, but by March 1649 the Earl could still find cause to complain to the House of Commons that his estates were subject to invasion. In that month, the Earl and other leading members of the gentry of the High Peak petitioned the House of Commons for the restitution of order.[36] Rutland was supported in his public campaign against the miners by both the royalist and parliamentarian press. The almost total uniformity of the response of the London newsbooks to the affair was not coincidental. As the Leveller journal *The Moderate* was careful to report, one of the Earl's stewards was feeding lurid stories of the miners' communistic tendencies to the newsbooks.[37] The propaganda war was not, however, a wholly one-sided affair. Both the miners and the Earl of Rutland and his supporters published a series of declarations and petitions which were distributed over the spring, summer and autumn of 1649.

The miners answered the Earl's petition to the Commons with one of their own.[38] The House refused to hear the petition, and so the miners had it printed and distributed both in London and in Derbyshire, where their declarations and handbills were posted up in the county's market towns.[39] This petition was signed by three men: William Heaward, Nathaniel Middleton and Captain Thomas Robinson. Their backgrounds and political sympathies are important. William Heaward was an Ashford free miner and a significant man in his community. He occupied a prominent place within the seating arrangement of the parish church, and sat on the manor's Court Leet. Possessed of a growing estate in the manor in the

[36] HLRO, MP 19 June 1648, 16 August 1648; *Journal of the House of Lords 1647–8*, 335; *Journal of the House of Commons 1648–51*, 175; PRO, SP18/26/93; BL, Add. MS 6682, fols. 30, 33.
[37] *The Moderate*, 4–11 September 1649, BL, TT E. 573(7).
[38] BL, Add. MS 6677, fol. 49, published in *The Moderate*, 4–11 September 1649, BL, TT E. 573(7); *Perfect Occurrences*, 17–23 August 1649, BL, TT E. 532 (24); *A Perfect Diurnall*, 20–7 August 1649, BL, TT E. 532 (28).
[39] BL, Add. MS 6677, fol. 51.

1630s, in 1641 his household included two servants. By 1643, Heaward had left Ashford to serve in Sir John Gell's infantry regiment. Five years later, he was to be found with his fellow petitioner Thomas Robinson and another opponent of the Earl of Rutland, William Wombwell, operating as sequestrators of the estates of royalist delinquents. That same year the Earl of Rutland singled him out for prosecution at the Court of King's Bench for trespass and riot in Netherhaddon.[40] Heaward's social background was more typical of the bulk of Rutland's opponents than was that of his co-petitioners.

Little can be discovered of Nathaniel Middleton. He was described as a gentleman, and held freehold land in Eyam township where he lived in 1638. Possibly he was a lead merchant.[41] Thomas Robinson, like Heaward, had served in the parliamentary forces in the first civil war. His name appears on muster rolls for both Sanders' horse regiment and Gell's regiment. He may have been one of those dragoon officers who transferred his troop to Sanders' command. By 1649, like many other ex-parliamentary soldiers, Robinson was in a state of penury. Petitioning the Committee for the Advance of Money, he explained that he had spent £225 in raising a troop of dragoons at his own expense for the parliament's service, and lost a further £268 when his property was plundered by the royalists. The committee agreed that in return for his service he would receive one half of all Papists' and delinquents' estates he discovered in the county. Accordingly he set about hunting down such individuals, together, as we have seen, with Heaward and Wombwell.[42]

The petition which bore Heaward's, Middleton's and Robinson's names was laced with a bitterness at the parliament's betrayal of the popular cause which is reminiscent of the Leveller critique of the new regime. It complained of the partial treatment of the miners' case at the hands of both houses of parliament before describing how the right of free mining was being 'persecuted and destroyed . . . by some few persons the greatest whereof is the Earl of Rutland'. From this, it spoke of the petitioners' disappointments with the parliament:

[We] did not doubt but by our appeall unto your honours (who ought to be the conservators of all the peoples customes and immunities) to obtain not only speedy

---

40 PRO, E101/280/18; CHT, Book of Rentals 1634–8; SA, Bar D 44; PRO, SP28/128/15; PRO, SP18/26/93; PRO, SP19/139, fol. 36; DRO, D307/Box H, 1632 Ashford Church plan; there were at least four Ashford men named William Heaward in 1638. This reconstruction of Heaward's background may therefore be flawed. See PRO, SP16/405, Pt 2.
41 PRO, SP16/405, Pt 2; CHT, L/20/5/xxvi, /8/vi, /20/25/xxvi; Anon., 'Vills and freeholders of Derbyshire, 1633', *DAJ*, 1st ser., 6 (1884), 71.
42 PRO, SP19/134, fols. 391, 393; PRO SP19/7, fol. 321; PRO, SP28/226, muster roll 1645; DRO, 1232M/0110b; *Calendar of the Committee for the Advance of Money*, 78.

protection, but also such relief against [our] adversaries . . . but so it is . . . to our great grief and amazement we finde that prerogative hath many proctors, by whose power and policy justice is either denied or delayed, the oppressors because rich and powerful cherished; and the oppressed though many thousands, ready to perish for bread; because poor altogether neglected, and not only so, but more oppressed and absolutely exposed to the power of an implacable enemy who leaves no way unattempted to destroy them.

Thomas Robinson and William Heaward obviously felt that they had gained little from their armed support of the parliament's cause: 'When Kingly prerogative was at its height [the right of free mining] was a sufficient bulwark to protect [the miners] against the malignity of their most potent enemies; being now in these times of Reformation and redress of grievances [that right is now] persecuted and destroyed.' Not all High Peak miners possessed such impeccably parliamentarian credentials as did Heaward and Robinson. Indeed, their partner in the post-war pursuit of local royalists, William Wombwell, had himself signed the petition to King Charles of 31 August 1642, as had other miners who were prominent against Rutland.

Despite its bitter tone, Heaward's, Middleton's and Robinson's petition emphasized their continuing adherence to the parliament, on whose side they were at pains to show they had fought. This relatively ambiguous position is, again, typical of many Leveller writings in the aftermath of the King's execution. By the summer of 1649 there is some evidence that the Leveller leadership was attempting to broaden the geographical range of the movement's interests, and to expand beyond its support amongst the civilian population of London and the Home Counties.[43] It should not be surprising, then, that The Moderate should be the only newsbook to write with overt sympathy for the miners' cause.[44] The first evidence that some of the miners had placed their political loyalties with the Levellers came in July 1649, when Mercurius Elencticus announced that 'The miners of Derbyshire, encouraged by the Saints of the Levelling Tribe, are at deadly feud with the Earle of Rutland.' Mercurius Pragmaticus parroted the same line, accusing the miners of taking advantage of 'this loose time' to 'work their levelling end'. By August, hysterical claims were being voiced that 'most of the towns and villages [in the Peak] . . . have great plenty of Levellers, who stir up the Minors and others to a rising'.[45] The existence of

[43] Brailsford, The Levellers, 400–52.
[44] The Moderate, 19–26 June 1649, BL, TT E. 561 (19); The Moderate, 4–11 September 1649, BL, TT E. 573 (7).
[45] Mercurius Elencticus, 25 June–2 July 1649, BL, TT E. 562 (18); Mercurius Pragmaticus, 26 June–3 July 3 1649, BL, TT E. 562(21); The Kingdomes Faithfull Scout, 24–31 August 1649, BL, TT E. 532 (30); see also The Moderate Messenger, 27 August–3 September 1649, BL, TT E. 532 (33).

Leveller ideas in the Peak was confirmed, if somewhat downplayed, by a letter printed in *A Modest Narrative* in August. The writer described the circulation of a Leveller tract called *The serious representation*. This publication, allegedly written by *The Moderate*'s Derby correspondent, gave support to the miners' case, and connected their grievances to wider issues: it was said to be 'full of menaces and saucy language against the Parliament, Committee, Judges and Nation as I must confess I never heard greater insolence'. The correspondent to *A Modest Narrative* noted the activities of 'a few factious, Malignant and Levelling persons, seven or eight at the most' amongst the miners. Still more mysterious, the author of a broadsheet hostile to the miners noted the presence of 'some strangers to that country that gain by these controversies [who] set [the miners] on foot for their own particular profit'.[46] By late August such stories had acquired a firmer foundation with the information from the Derby correspondent of *The Moderate* that 'our country is in great expectation of the response of the Parliament upon the petition of the miners who are conceived by all to be much wronged by the Earl of Rutland, and if they have it not according to their ancient interest its much feared the Parliament may gain many stubborn and resolute opposites . . . the Levelling party in the towns adjacent promise them assistance in the prosecution of their just desires'.[47]

In September, the House of Commons finally declared against the miners' claim upon Netherhaddon manor, and imposed Colonel Thomas Sanders as barmaster.[48] This decision solicited a quick response from some of the miners, as reported in *The Moderate*:

The Miners of this county seem much discontented at some of the proceedings at Parliament, and especially at their owne business depending before them; there hath been severall meetings this week of many of the chief of them, and we are informed it is about the Draught of a Declaration against the present Authority, upon publication whereof they intend to be ready to maintain the same with their lives and fortunes and likewise the Agreement of the People and the [Leveller] petition of the 11 of Septemb. and likewise a declaration either of the city, or some members thereof, which I cannot yet inform myself of.[49]

The suppression of the radical press shortly after the publication of this

[46] BL, Add. MS 6677, fol. 50; no copy of the *Serious representation* has survived. For the letter to *A Modest Narrative*, see Anon., 'Letter from Derbyshire concerning lead-mining, 1649', *DAJ*, 2nd ser., 10 (1936), 130–2.
[47] *The Moderate*, 21– 8 August 1649, BL, TT E. 572 (1).
[48] *Journal of the House of Commons 1648–51*, 298. The heated issue of entitlement to the office of barmaster within the King's Field in the High Peak had been given added fuel in early 1649 with the Earl of Rutland's attempt to secure the Duchy's lease of the lot and cope there. See PRO, SP19/159, fol. 125. Veiled hints in two documents suggest that Sanders and Nathaniel Barton were themselves treating with the miners at this time and after. See PRO, SP18/26/93; BL, Add. MS 6682, fol. 34.
[49] *The Moderate*, 4–11 September 1649, BL, TT E 572 (7).

report hampers our detection of further Leveller activities amongst the miners. After the suppression of the mutiny of Leveller soldiers amongst the Oxford garrison in mid-September, the interrogation of mutineers revealed their expectation of support from Leveller risings in Northamptonshire, Leicestershire and Derbyshire.[50] Following reports to the Council of State in October of gatherings of 5,000 or 6,000 armed and mounted men on the border with Staffordshire, the potential threat of Leveller risings in the Peak may have influenced its decision to maintain troops of Sanders' regiment there.[51] The authorities remained concerned about the possibility of risings amongst the miners into the 1650s. Troops were despatched to the Peak when trouble flared following renewed dispute over the Dovegang, and inquiries were made into rumours of a planned rising of miners against the Commonwealth led by both ex-royalist and ex-parliamentary officers in the Youlgreave area in 1651.[52]

The despatch of troops into the Peak, the imposition of Colonel Sanders as barmaster and the declaration of the House of Commons in favour of the Earl of Rutland all formed part of the reimposition of elite control across the Peak. The early 1650s saw the minister of Wirksworth again collecting his tithe of lead upon the miners. As in Netherhaddon, miners who had reclaimed Newton Grange for free mining after July 1642 were ejected following the end of the wars. By the later 1650s, officers of the Commonwealth had come to see the inhabitants of Duffield as seditious rioters rather than (as in 1649) the defenders of their legitimate common rights.[53] In this changed atmosphere, it is therefore indicative of the strength of feeling against Rutland that resistance to him was renewed in the late 1650s.

In its proceedings of 1641 and 1648, the Duchy had refused support to the miners. The King's Bench rulings of 1648 and 1649, and that of the Commons of 1649, secured Rutland's hold over his estates. These categorical verdicts closed the miners off from their traditional avenue of legal action. Undeterred, in their last confrontation with Rutland, the miners found a novel legal sanction for their demands. In 1656 Francis Staley, Thomas Lock and Benjamin Bradborne purchased a patent which granted them licence to search for Mines Royal within Derbyshire. Staley was a Youlgreave free miner, and had sat upon the barmote jury for Harthill

[50] *Mercurius Pragmaticus*, 17–24 September 1649, BL, TT E. 574 (20).
[51] *CSPD, 1649–60*, I, 335, 337.
[52] *CSPD, 1649–60*, XLI, 222, 255–6; J.T. Brighton, *Royalists and Roundheads in Derbyshire* (Bakewell, no date), 45–6; Historical Manuscripts Commission, *Report on the Manuscripts of . . . the Duke of Portland*, 10 vols. (London, 1886–1931), I, 578.
[53] PRO, DL5/35, fols. 87, 359–60, /40, fols. 269–70; on Duffield, compare the tone of PRO, E317/9/10, with PRO, E134/1659/East 27, and PRO, DL5/35, fol. 54.

when Rutland had attempted a compromise with the miners in 1647. Nothing is known of the other two men.[54] Under the patent secured by Staley, Lock and Bradborne, the patentees and their agents (which effectively meant the rest of the miners) were entitled to dig any land within the county regardless of its ownership, ostensibly in search for silver bearing lodes. All lead carries some small deposits of silver; the patent therefore seemed to provide a back-door means of claiming free mining rights. In compensation to the lords of manors in which they exercised their patent, the patentees were to pay a composition of one tenth of lead ore produced, provided that they were unsuccessful in their supposed search for precious metals. Furthermore, as the patent had been secured through the Commonwealth Exchequer, the patentees were entitled to receive the support of the Court of Exchequer in any dispute which resulted from their exercise of the patent. The practical effect of the patent was to provide a novel form of legal support to the miners' claim to a right of free mining within the whole of the lead field. Unsurprisingly, they decided to test their new rights first of all against their greatest opponent: the Earl of Rutland.

This last phase of the Haddon dispute combined many of the earlier features of the conflict.[55] At some time prior to August 1657, miners once again entered Netherhaddon manor and began to dig for ore. The Earl was swift in his response. Bradborne complained that 'severall tymes' he, the miners and his 'workmen' had been attacked by the Earl, his son Lord Roos, their servants and retainers, and the local gentry 'on horsebacke & on foote', and were 'driven from theire workes'. Rutland took action against the patentees at the Courts of King's Bench and Common Pleas, and against forty-two miners at the Quarter Sessions. Arguing that the conditions of his patent were being frustrated by Rutland's actions, Thomas Lock complained directly to the Council of State and initiated legal action at the Court of Exchequer. Staying legal proceedings, the Council of State ordered the matter to be placed in the hands of the Assay Master, who was to determine the silver content of the lead deposits in Netherhaddon.[56] Typically, the miners had therefore combined litigation and petition with crowd action.

Late in 1657, Bradborne was arrested by warrant of the county bench for trespass into Netherhaddon. The miners responded with a mass demonstra-

---

[54] A Thomas Lock was listed as resident in Bakewell in 1638: PRO, SP16/405, Pt 2. Bradborne was a Youlgreave surname.

[55] An account of the 1656–8 dispute is available in N. Kirkham, 'A royal mine in Netherhaddon?', *DAJ*, 2nd ser., 75 (1955), 20–35. What follows is based upon Kirkham, and PRO, E112/294/31.

[56] The proceedings at the Council of State are at PRO, SP25/78, fols. 91–2, 365, 511, 642, 759–60, 799–801. See also *CSPD, 1649–60*, XI, 100 (I have been unable to trace this calendar reference in the original).

tion. On 3 December they gathered at Youlgreave and marched across Haddonfields in assertion of their rights. Some miners reopened the workings from which they had been driven on various occasions over the intervening sixteen years. In display of their potential power, the miners also accompanied Bradborne to his interrogation by the Justices. On 20 January of the following year, Bradborne led another crowd into Haddonfields. By that point Lock, Bradborne and Staley had been joined as patentees by Colonel Edward Ashenhurst of the Staffordshire militia, who brought some of his troops to join in another invasion of the Haddon estates.[57] In all, a crowd of one hundred miners, ten horsemen and thirty militia soldiers were present in Youlgreave churchyard where Bradborne made a 'sollempne speech'. The crowd then moved off into Haddonfields, where an officer of the bailiff, having been warned that a gathering was imminent, was present. He attempted to arrest Bradborne, but the crowd prevented him. One of the freeholders of Netherhaddon, Henry Buxton, tried to prevent the miners from digging in his field, but was threatened by the soldiers with mutilation. In a theatrical display, swords were drawn, and pistols discharged by the soldiery, and the local gentry put to some fright.

The crowd actions of 1657–8 only biased the Council of State against the miners. Despite the miners' temporary seizure of Haddonfields, they lost their case both at law and before the Council of State. Lock and Bradborne maintained their claim to a Mine Royal in Haddonfields into the 1660s, but with no success.[58] The riot of 20 January 1658 marked the closing act in the collective assertion by riot and demonstration of the right of free mining. In itself, this gives the disputes over the Haddon estate of 1641–58 some importance. But the events here charted have a greater significance.

THE TRANSFORMATION AND DEFEAT OF THE MINERS' POLITICAL PROJECT

The men who made up the crowds of miners which invaded the Haddon estates represented the archetypal free miner of the mid-seventeenth century. Neither of the poorest nor the wealthiest of their villages, these free miners were joined by ties of blood, friendship, partnership and common interest. Their names are known to us from the list of miners attached to the Harthill agreement of 1647 and the legal proceedings and

---

[57] I am grateful to John Sutton for his help in identifying Ashenhurst.
[58] BL, Add. MS 6677, fol. 79; BL, Loan MS 16 (2), fols. 132–8.

petitions concerning the 1641–58 dispute.[59] Taking these sources together, we learn the names of some 121 of Rutland's opponents. These men can be found labouring together in the same mineworkings or fields, living in the same village, sitting on the same barmote jury or jointly refusing payment of the lead tithe. As in pre-war conflicts, this network of miners depended upon a hard core of men who appeared repeatedly amongst rioting crowds between 1641 and 1658, initiated legal actions and were named as key defendants in Rutland's prosecutions. Unsurprisingly, such men had often been involved in pre-civil war mining disputes. The ubiquitous Anthony Sellars was one such man. A signatory to the miners' petition to King Charles of 31 August 1642, in 1648 he had been imprisoned by the House of Lords for his part in the riots in Haddonfields. He returned to that place again in 1658, leading to his prosecution at Quarter Sessions. In 1641, together with many other later opponents of the Earl, he held shares in High Stoole rake mine, had taken a leading part in renewing opposition to the tithe and had moved a resolution in a barmote court against the tithe. One of his partners in High Stoole rake was David Frost, the miners' preferred candidate as barmaster who had led the miners on to Haddonfields in 1648; another was Thomas Mosley, a free miner and cottager of Youlgreave who sat as a barmote juror for that manor, and who was also prosecuted by Rutland at the Quarter Sessions in 1658. Whereas the large majority of Rutland's antagonists were drawn from the free mining manors immediately adjoining Haddon lordship, their leaders tended to come from further afield. Furthermore, such leading figures were far more likely to have been in trouble with the authorities on previous occasions, and to have served on barmote juries.[60] The miners' organization against Rutland was therefore built upon the networks established in the years before the civil war.[61] None the less, the Haddon dispute was marked by important discontinuities.

Most obviously, opposition or support for the miners' case crystallized around class polarities. Unlike before the civil war, the miners were unable to exploit internal divisions amongst their opponents, or to establish tactical alliances with elements of the elite. Their failure to secure the

---

[59] BL, Add. MS 6677, fol. 49; BL, Add. MS 6682, fols. 80–5; HLRO, MP 19 June 1648, 16 August 1648; PRO, SP18/26/93; PRO, E112/294/31; PRO, DL1/378, complaint of Rowland Furniss, /366, complaint of William Goodwin *et al.*; DRO, QS/B/2/103. Locations have been primarily determined from PRO, SP16/405, Pt 2, and PRO, E101/280/18.

[60] Wood, 'Industrial development', 252–3. On the wider social networks of the leaders of the abortive 1596 Oxfordshire rising, see Walter, 'A "Rising of the people"?', 102, 118.

[61] Oddest of all continuities was the importance of 20 January as a date on which hostility to the Manners of Haddon was expressed: the first intrusions into Harthill were made on that date in 1641; the riot of 1658 occurred on the same date, which was also the anniversary of the threats by rioters in 1617 to 'pull downe Haddon House'.

support of the Duchy Court exposed the weaknesses of a political culture which had in part been drawn around legalism and a strong sense of immediate tactics. From this failure resulted a more immediate resort to riot, and the greater violence of those riots. It also led to the attempt to construct a broader alliance with constituencies outside the Peak Country. Print played a vital role in that attempt.

We saw in Chapter 6 that the Peak miners of the mid-seventeenth century were notably illiterate. Yet in 1642 this had not prevented them from conducting their negotiations with King Charles through published declarations. Nor did it preclude William Debankes' *Liberties and customs of the miners* from providing a popular definition of the legal and historical basis of mining custom, or from expressing the political project which envisaged the extension of free mining across the whole lead field. The climax of the Haddon dispute in 1649 therefore clarified the new importance which print assumed in local struggles.[62] Hitherto, appeals by miners to the political centre had focused upon institutions: parliament, the Privy Council, or the Westminster law courts. But while the law courts and parliament remained important to the miners' activities in 1649, the existence of a more nebulous yet none the less significant force within London was intruding upon the miners' awareness: a politicized reading public. Both the miners and the Earl of Rutland attempted to secure support from the London press, and published declarations and petitions which were distributed in London and in the Peak. While the object of Debankes' *Liberties and customs* of 1645 was to reinforce the miners' own knowledge of custom, and hence had been written upon the assumption of the readers' prior knowledge of mining law, the miners' declarations and petitions of 1649 made no such presumption. Instead, as the miners tried to reach to a wider national audience, they extended, if only for a few dramatic months, the spatial limits of their politics. It is no accident that Debankes had been a parliamentary trooper. Combined with their experience of war and revolution, and their perceived sense of betrayal, the readership of printed political appeals radicalized many parliamentary soldiers in the mid- and late 1640s. The embittered tone of Heaward's, Middleton's and Robinson's petition of 1649 found its immediate antecedents in the enraged outbursts of the soldiers' representatives at the debates in Putney church in the October of 1647.[63] We here find further evidence of the intimate connection which existed between print culture and radical politics in mid-seventeenth-century England. Yet print and literacy did not create popular

---

[62] By the end of the seventeenth century, commoners in the fens were using printed papers to organize riots: Lindley, *Fenland riots*, 59.
[63] For the comparison, see Wood, 'Social conflict', 46.

politics, either in the Peak or elsewhere. The support given to the Leveller movement by some Peak miners finds its immediate cause in the parliament's refusal to consider their petitions, and the hostility of the parliamentary newsbooks to their cause. But the appeal of the Levellers' politics touched on deeper forces within the miners' political culture.

Historical interest in the Leveller movement has tended to focus upon its leadership to the detriment of the social basis of its support. The political philosophy of men like John Lilburne, William Walwyn and Richard Overton has been exhaustively analysed and debated. Their relations with the Army officers, the Agitators, the Gathered Churches and the leadership of factions within parliament have all been carefully scrutinized.[64] Most recently, historical accounts of the Leveller movement have tended to be rather dismissive. Some historians of high politics have come to see the movement as born solely out of the crisis of the late 1640s.[65] The acceptance of the claim that 'the Levellers have been cut down to size' by the sharp pen of revisionist historiography has led one leading social historian to conclude that the movement has been over-studied.[66] Social historians' lack of interest in civil war radicalism is all the more regrettable, in that the few contextual studies of popular support for the Leveller movement have pointed to a correspondence between key aspects of the Levellers' programme and pre-existent local political cultures.[67] To the opponents of enclosure in the fens, as to London artisans and some Derbyshire miners, Leveller ideas made sense.

Amongst the contradictory ideas which for three years defined the Levellers as a political movement, certain basic, defining principles stand out. The Levellers were hostile to oppressive manorialism, tithes, arbitrary government, the complexities and expenses of litigation at central courts, the prerogative courts, the House of Lords and the priorities and social

---

[64] For the Leveller leadership, see P. Gregg, *Free-born John: a biography of John Lilburne* (London, 1961); J.R. McMichael and B. Taft (eds.), *The writings of William Walwyn* (Athens, Ga., 1989). For relations with the Army, see A. Woolrych, *Soldiers and statesmen: the General Council of the Army and its debates, 1647–1648* (Oxford, 1987). On the Gathered Churches, see M. Tolmie, *The triumph of the saints: the separate churches of London, 1616–1649* (Cambridge, 1977). The best study of the Levellers (in spite of its odd sub-title) remains J. Frank, *The Levellers: a history of the writings of three seventeenth-century social democrats: John Lilburne, Richard Overton, William Walwyn* (Cambridge, Mass., 1955).

[65] C. Russell, *The causes of the English civil war* (Oxford, 1990), 8–9.

[66] F.D. Dow, *Radicalism in the English Revolution* (Oxford, 1985), 30; Sharpe, *Early modern England*, 24–5.

[67] Holmes, 'Drainers and fenmen'; N. Carlin, 'Liberty and fraternities in the English Revolution: the politics of the London artisans' protests, 1635–1659', *International Review of Social History*, 39 (1994), 223–54. For an outstanding study of the differing patterns of local support for the Diggers, see J. Gurney, 'Gerrard Winstanley and the Digger movement in Walton and Cobham', *Historical Journal*, 37 (1994), 775–802.

consequences of early agrarian capitalism. They envisaged a limited, patriarchal household democracy of small producers as the bedrock of a more equal society and polity. The law sat at the heart of their ideology. In their proposals for legal reform, proceedings at law would be swift and just, and conducted in English. Officers and representatives at all levels of government would be elected on a household suffrage. Tithes would be abolished, as would the manorial system. The relevance of such an agenda to the Peak miners should be obvious. Like the involvement of the Levellers in the fens, their intervention into the politics of the Peak was short-lived. But that should not blind us to their importance. A section of the mining workforce had chosen to stand beside the Levellers in their moment of crisis, in August and September 1649. Outrage at the parliament's hostility to them played a part in the miners' motivations, and would thereafter find expression in insurrectionary talk in favour of the King. Moreover, the presence of Leveller ideas in the Peak allows us to hold up a mirror to the miners' political culture at this moment of their own, more local, crisis.

By 1640, the free miners' conflicts with their social superiors were organized by a political project. In space, that political project was settled upon the lead field, and defined by a series of oppositions: its plebeian quality was guaranteed by its antagonism to the interests of the gentry and nobility; its focus on skilled, male, settled workers excluded women, the transient and the unskilled. The miners emphasized their support for free mining law and for the authority of the barmote. Like the Levellers, the Peak miners regarded the election of officers as a subject of keen concern. At some point after 1644, the High Peak miners elected their own bar-master. In their publications of 1649, the miners justified the act by reference to suppressed ancient custom, arguing that before they reintro-duced election of the office 'many of the Bar-maisters [were] judges in their own cases, or malignants, and some unfit, taking no care to uphold the laws and customs of the Mynes, but aym[ed] at their private ends'. In 1651, the Wirksworth miners elected a barmaster by 'the general consent and approbriation of the Miners accordinge to theire ancient custome . . . it being against law and reason that any man should be his own judge'. Old grievances were renewed. In May 1652, the miners again petitioned parliament for the abolition of tithes. In 1649, they remembered Heath's oppressions upon them, and denounced the manorial right of pre-emption as 'too great an oppression to a free-born People'. The long struggle against pre-emption dovetailed with Leveller demands for free trade and opposi-tion to monopolies. Attempting to secure support from the Cornish tin miners, Levellers in that county petitioned in November 1648 against 'the unconscionable oppression' of pre-emption.

Growing frustration with the parliament's historic indifference to the miners' complaints was realized at some point in the mid-seventeenth century when the householders of Wirksworth drew up an undated petition for a borough franchise. The petitioners drew attention to their town's status as 'very ancient', and its importance in the 'well ordering' of the customs of the mining industry. As they noted, in spite of the 'great importance' of the industry, 'The said Mynors have noe voyces' in elections, and they therefore demanded a household suffrage.[68] Again, we should remind ourselves of the similarity of such ideas with Leveller proposals for political reform. Hostile to tithes and manorialism, like the Levellers, the miners saw their object as the establishment of a culturally bounded democracy of small producers. This democracy already existed in embryonic form, given institutional body in the barmote and the elective officer of barmaster, and provided with ideological force in the plebeian possession of customary law. That some of the miners should have declared their support for the Leveller movement should not therefore be seen as an anomaly. Rather, it represented one possible destination for the miners' political project in the conditions of the late 1640s.

Local demonstrations of support for the Levellers frequently coincided with growing popular royalism. As in Cornwall, Kent and the fens, the two political trajectories coincided in the Derbyshire Peak. That coincidence was less contradictory than it might seem. Leveller leaders themselves flirted with the exiled Stuart court in the 1650s, and had been enmeshed in serious negotiations in 1647. Although deriving from very different ideological sources, after the regicide royalist and Leveller ideas tried to organize similar popular experiences. The popular royalism of the 1650s focused hostility to a centralizing state which was perceived as alien, brutal, arbitrary and interventionist. Within the Peak, post-regicide outbursts of popular royalism seem more committed than the miners' tactical manoeuvrings with the King in the August of 1642.

William and Mary Greaves of Ashford were not alone in their opinion that 'the Parliament and Army was murthering men tht they murthered men and threw them in ditches & tht they had murthered the King & they hoped that the tyme would come when they should be murthered'. Hatred of the Commonwealth regime endured into the Restoration: one High Peak man was alleged to have remarked in an alehouse in 1661 that Charles II was 'a knave and a fool if he made [the Act of Oblivion] not voyde & hanged not upp all the Roundeheads'. Other drunken words in High Peak

---

[68] *The case of a publique business*; PRO, SP23/151, fol. 99; BL, Add. MS 6682, fol. 38; *The Moderate*, 18, 7–14 November 1648, BL, TT E. 472(4); *The Moderate*, 21, 28 November–5 December, 1648, BL, TT E. 475(8); DRO, D258M/31/10da.

alehouses suggest something of the contradictory political alignments involved in the Haddon disturbances. In September 1651, two Youlgreave miners who had been earlier involved in the disputes over Harthill manor were to be found in an alehouse 'drinking the King's health'. One was heard to say 'God blesse king Charles & put of his hatt & said he wold raigne ere long'. This may have been more than wishful thinking. Rumours reached the Council of State in that year that John Shalcross, a former royalist colonel with interests in the Youlgreave mines, was organizing a rising amongst the miners.[69] The meetings of armed men on the moorland border with Staffordshire in October 1649 were claimed by one royalist newsbook as the work of its party. Rutland's supporters argued in print in the same year that the miners' allegiance to the King was a source of 'dangerous consequence in those parts'. In another broadsheet published against the miners' cause, it was argued that they had shown 'the same zeale and fervency' to the royalists in the second civil war as they had in 1642–4. Thomas Bushell, the mining expert who had helped to recruit miners to the King in 1642, was present amongst them again in 1649, ostensibly to offer advice in their legal case against Rutland.[70]

In 1642, the free mining community had been divided by the civil war. But in the resurrection of the Haddon dispute after 1648, that community recoalesced around opposition to the Earl of Rutland. Rowland Furniss, who had served as a corporal in Eyre's regiment, led miners on to Haddonfields in 1648.[71] He apparently saw no contradiction in standing alongside William Heaward who, as we have seen, served in Gell's regiment. Meanwhile, both their erstwhile Colonels gave their support to Rutland: Gell signed a petition of leading gentry in support of Rutland, while Eyre was included amongst the mounted gentry who rode down the miners in 1657 and 1658. Class did not determine civil war allegiances; but it did continue to divide miner against gentleman in Haddonfields. Heaward, Robinson and Wombwell turned a blind eye to Rowland Furniss' wartime loyalties. Instead, their attention focused on their real enemies: Robinson fingered William Wright, a lead merchant and an agent of the Countess of Devonshire as a civil war royalist supporter. Wright had helped to track down the leaders of the miners' demonstrations in 1634, and in 1649 signed the gentry petition in support of the Earl of Rutland.[72]

[69] DRO, Q/SB/2/132, /630, /650; Newton, 'Gentry', 26–7.
[70] *Mercurius Elencticus*, 15–22 October 1649, BL, TT E. 575(27); BL, Add. MS 6677, fols. 50–1; 'Letter from Derbyshire', 131.
[71] Brighton, *Royalists and Roundheads*, 71; DRO, Q/SO/1/fol. 59; PRO, DL1/378, complaint of Rowland Furniss; PRO, DL5/34, fols. 305, 317; BL, Add. MS 6681, fols. 178–81; *Journal of the House of Lords 1647–8*, 335, 442, 595; HLRO, MP 16 August 1648.
[72] BL, Add. MSS 64908, fols. 130–1, 6682, fol. 33; Newton, 'Gentry', 30; PRO, SP19/134, fols. 391, 393, /7, fol. 253, /139, fol. 36.

Robinson's attentions were also drawn to John Briddon of Youlgreave, a minor gentleman who had been a steward of the Manners estates in Wirksworth and had ejected miners from those lands in 1624. He was prosecuted in October 1649 for having raised arms and troops for the King. In 1651, Briddon's continuing hostility to the miners' cause showed itself again when he tried to displace the miners' candidate as barmaster. The miners called a meeting at which 150 of their number declared their refusal to accept him as barmaster and denounced him as having 'been in armes against the parliament'.[73] The only men who accepted Briddon's authority were almost all lesser gentry with a history of opposition to free mining, including John Greaves, another steward of the Rutland estates who had led attacks on the miners on the manors of Hazelbadge in 1630 and Harthill in 1641.[74]

On both sides of the conflict over Haddon lordship, class interests therefore transcended civil war divisions. The Earl of Rutland, who had been at best a lukewarm supporter of the parliamentary cause, received the backing of John Gell, the leading figure in the Derbyshire parliamentary forces, together with George Hopkinson and Rowland Eyre, who had both supported the King. These men were united by their long-standing hostility to free mining. George Hopkinson and his son William were, between the 1620s and 1680s, leading opponents of free mining in Wirksworth Wapentake. George supported Sir Robert Heath's dissolution of free mining law at the Dovegang in the early 1630s, and was rewarded with the stewardship of those deposits. William was present amongst the gentlemen who attacked miners at Netherhaddon in 1657, and was a key deponent against the right of free mining in Newton Grange in 1686. The Hopkinsons owned the manor of Ible within the Wapentake of Wirksworth, the mineral deposits of which they jealously guarded against free miners, whom they ejected on various occasions in the 1640s and 1650s, and again in 1678. Following this, William Hopkinson set up a mine in Ible 'wherein his servants were at worke as mynors'.[75] Also to be found amongst the mounted gentry who attacked the miners in 1657 was William Savile. One of Rutland's stewards, he had led violent attacks upon the miners in 1641 and 1648. He was sufficiently unpopular in the area for Rutland to request a garrison to secure his safety in 1643.[76] Henry Buxton, the lord of

---

[73] PRO, SP19/21, fol. 144; PRO, DL1/298, complaint of Robert Parker v. Dame Grace Manners.
[74] PRO, DL5/35, fol. 74.
[75] Fisher, 'Vermuyden', 105, 110, 116; DRO, D258M/56/52i, /X/77; PRO, DL4/124/1686/7, / 120/1678/1.
[76] PRO, DL1/366, complaint of William Goodwin; HLRO, MP 16 March 1643, 19 June 1648.

Youlgreave, also took part in the gentry's attacks upon the miners in 1657. He had been responsible in 1630 for driving Tideswell miners out of Hazelbadge, in the course of which he had been attacked by the miners. In a striking demonstration of their sense of tenant deference, the miners (many of whom held land in Youlgreave) threatened to hack off Buxton's foot in the course of their riot of 20 January 1658.[77] Both the miners and the Earl's supporters in the Haddonfields confrontations included men who had come from a considerable distance, suggesting that both sides planned the confrontations in advance. From far afield, then, plebeian and gentleman came to batter one another in Haddonfields.

There is a sense of finality about the dispute over Haddon lordship. It constituted the most naked confrontation of class interest of any dispute concerning Peak mining custom. As such, it represented the culmination of that larger conflict. The Haddon dispute therefore has a symbolic quality about it. It also possessed a contemporary legal significance, as the withdrawal of the Duchy Court from the matter, and the judgements secured in Rutland's favour at King's Bench, became important precedents.[78] Related to this was the longer-term significance of the miners' defeat in Haddonfields for their broader political project. The dispute involved real issues of political and social power, and of access to resources which were crucial to both the great House of Haddon and to the miners who had set their faces against the interests of their 'rich and powerful . . . oppressor'. The Haddon dispute therefore provides a neat illustration of just how political a dispute over some fields of pasture could be in early modern England. The historian can detect this with hindsight. But in 1660, all that the miners could see was that their workings in Haddonfields had been replaced by large, complex mining operations, worked day and night by wage labourers, from which the House of Haddon reaped great profits, and which were shortly to displace their precarious economic independence.

---

[77] PRO, DL1/323, complaint of Att.-Gen. v. John Manners; BL, Add. MS 6682, fols. 33, 87–9.

[78] BL, Add. MS 6682, fols. 90–1; PRO, E317/9/24. The miners recognized the significance of the dispute as a test case: see PRO, DL1/378, complaint of Rowland Furniss.

The experience of defeat? The defence of custom, 1660–1770

The miners' defeat in Haddonfields concluded the last attempt to extend the free mining laws of the King's Field. Over the forty years that followed, free mining rights were subject to continuous, piecemeal erosion. Miners were unable to mount effective resistance to attacks upon their rights due to the coincidence of important economic and social changes with the declining sympathy of law courts for their cause. After 1660, the small but important group of mercantile lesser gentry who had often hitherto supported the miners sided instead with the manorial interest. The gentry's and nobility's hand was greatly strengthened by the close grip which leading families developed upon local office within the Peak, which prevented the miners from exploiting any internal elite divisions. The dramatic fall in the price of lead which occurred between the late 1660s and the 1690s hit the free miners hard, coming as it did at the same time as large-scale enclosure. Both the industrial and agrarian sources of the free miners' economic independence were therefore undercut, and the close network upon which their collective opposition had been mounted was broken down. Finally, the Court of the Duchy of Lancaster, hitherto a generally consistent supporter of the free mining interest, reversed a number of its pre-war rulings to side with the manorial interest. It should therefore be unsurprising to find that the free miners' resistance to these developments was generally disorganized and ineffective. It is argued here that the post-Restoration period saw the partial depoliticization of the miners' culture.

After 1700, the miners recovered some collective agency. The eighteenth century saw the miners establish a forthright tradition of riot in defence of mining rights, and in opposition to high food prices and government interference. None the less, crowd actions were typically defensive in nature. Whereas our preceding discussion of the formation of plebeian politics after c. 1580 emphasized the dynamism and assertiveness of the miners' political culture, discussion of the plebeian contestation of authority after 1700 will instead highlight a more negative agenda. This was produced out of a conservative popular culture more given to protest and resistance than to the ambitious formulation of new political methods, alliances and ideas.

CHANGING INTERESTS, CHANGING ALLIANCES

The religious politics of post-Restoration England failed to connect with the plebeian politics of the Peak. Although some Tory commentators imagined that the isolated nonconformists of the Peak's market towns were hatching conspiracies against the Crown, low levels of literacy and the lack of a substantial 'middling sort' within the region deprived organized dissent of a favourable environment.[1] More importantly, post-Restoration dissent in the Peak did not flow out of any established tradition of religious radicalism. John Harrison of Ashford, turning the 'fine sword', given him by his former parliamentary commander, the regicide Colonel Francis Hacker, decided to retain his weapon in order to 'put them to death [those] which had putt his good Coll[onel] to death'.[2] Yet few amongst Harrison's neighbours shared his brooding hostility to the later Stuarts. Beyond the market towns, Presbyterianism, Quakerism and other forms of dissent made little headway. Indeed, far from becoming seen as leaders of popular causes, the few prominent Presbyterians within the mining villages tended to be regarded as un-neighbourly and avaricious.[3]

Opportunities for the plebeian contestation of authority were limited by the local recoalesence of elite power after the Restoration. After 1660, the nobility and greater gentry returned to their traditional domination of county government, incorporating into the Commission of the Peace some of those humbler gentlemen who had held authority during the revolutionary decades.[4] The reconsolidation of the gentry's and nobility's hold on county administration was paralleled within the Peak by the extension of their economic power and their exertion of a new hold on the administration of the mining industry. We have seen how, before the civil wars, the division of local offices and leases of rights between opposing gentry interests provided the miners with the opportunity to exploit such divisions in the pursuit of their own interests. After 1660, that was no longer the case.

Following the Restoration, the Earl of Rutland expanded and consoli-

---

[1] For such fears, see PRO, SP29/275/172; PRO, SP31/1/69.
[2] DRO, QS/B/2/295.
[3] See the case of Robert Heaward of Carsington: PRO, E134/6Wm&Mar/Mich10, / 6&7WmIII/Hil15, /7WmIII/East5, /8WmIII/East11. For Heaward's religious politics, see G. Darnborough, 'A Wirksworth mine agent's letter', *BPDMHS*, 7, 6 (1980), 326.
[4] Beats, 'Politics and government', 335ff; Newton, 'Gentry', 7–8.

dated his estates and titles within the Peak, purchasing the manors of Darley and Youlgreave and the lease of lead tithes within Youlgreave parish, while the Earl of Devonshire bought the lease of the Duchy's lot and cope in the King's Field of High Peak. The lease of the lot and cope in the King's Field of Wirksworth Wapentake passed first to the Earl of Northampton and subsequently into the Devonshires' hands. The Devonshires retained the lot and cope rights in both King's Fields until the late nineteenth century. With their control over the whole of the Duchy's King's Fields and their ownership of Ashford lordship, the Earls (later the Dukes) of Devonshire established a firm grip on the administration of much of the mining industry. Coupled with their acquisition of the lead tithes of Bakewell, Hope and Tideswell, this remarkable consolidation of interests gave the Devonshires a tighter hold over the miners than any noble or gentry house had been able to exert since the days of the Talbot Earls of Shrewsbury.

The extension of post-Restoration noble power had significant implications for the miners' collective ability to influence the course of events. Before the civil war, the miners had been able to play off the contending interests of one gentleman or noble against another. After 1660, the concentration of lot and cope leases, tithes and manorial authority into the hands of the two leading families of the region effectively closed down that avenue of local politics. The many-headed monster of social disorder which the nobility and gentry had seen in the corner of their minds' eye during the English Revolution returned to its obscure lair. Hostility to the Rutlands still simmered, but took the form of covert, small-scale acts of social crime rather than public opposition. John Harrison, the former trooper of Colonel Hacker, stole Rutland's tithe hay. Francis Smith of Youlgreave, caught poaching game in Haddonfields in 1674, said of the Earl's son that 'hee cared neither for My Lord Rosse not his Lady'. Fisher had taken no recorded part in the earlier riots in Haddonfields, but as a barmote juror he sat with many who had.[5] But for most, to give voice to such resentments in the worsening conditions of the late seventeenth century was a luxury they could ill afford.

Many accommodated themselves to the changed circumstances, finding work in Rutland's new deep mines in Haddonfields, or gathering outside Haddon Hall amongst the rest of the poor to receive the traditional dole of tuppence from the Earl's gracious hand.[6] Never inherent to early modern social relations, for many plebeians deference could become a fact of public

---

[5] DRO, QS/B/2/295, /303; SA, Bag C 702(1), Youlgreave barmote lists, 1672–4.
[6] DRO, QS/B/2/303; SA, PhC 342; SA, Bag C 702(1a); Davies, 'Dukes of Devonshire, Newcastle, and Rutland', 219.

life. In some cases, no doubt, respect was genuinely felt for a decent lord or a good master, who reciprocated in kind. But in many others, public deference was the product of cruel necessity. Before the Restoration, many free miners had been able to escape the humiliations of those 'labouring poor Men, which in Times of Scarcity pine and murmur for Want of Bread, cursing the Rich behind his Back; and before his Face, Cap and Knee and a whining countenance'.[7] But after the Restoration, the social structures within which the miners' political culture had hitherto developed were broken by rapid economic change.

In the forty years which followed the conclusion of the Netherhaddon dispute, some miners maintained a faltering defence of free mining custom against the backdrop of falling lead prices, growing landlessness, the large-scale enclosure of commons, and the ever-increasing productive capacity of large works. The solid network on which the miners' politics had been based broke down as growing differences of material interest underwrote the separation of wealthier villagers, orebuyers and lesser merchants from the defence of custom. With the emergence of large capitalized mineworkings, merchants and smelters could maintain supplies of ore without recourse to the traditional free mining group. As we have seen in Chapter 4, many merchants therefore became investors in large mines. Such men and women were better able than the miners to stave off the effects of the dramatic fall in prices which lasted from the late 1660s to the 1690s. Since merchants and orebuyers required the mortgage of free miners' mineshares in return for the advance of capital, the fall in lead prices and the resultant foreclosure of loans led to the miners' losing their mineshares and land to their creditors amongst the mercantile lesser gentry.

Structural change therefore led to a separation of economic interest, as wealthier yeomanry and lead merchants distanced themselves from the struggles of poorer miners, tenants and cottagers. This development must be seen within the larger context of the changing role of men and women of 'middling' status within local body politics in early modern England. The growing identification of the rural 'middling sort' with the central state, in particular effected through their increasing involvement in local government, constituted one of the most important but least remarked upon aspects in state formation in early modern England.[8] Moving in close relation to local processes of social differentiation and polarization, this shift occurred earlier in downland, agrarian England than in regions like the Peak Country. None the less, the wealthy yeoman farmer of the

---

[7] Quoted in Morrill and Walter, 'Order and disorder', 154.
[8] See especially S. Hindle, 'The political culture of the middling sort in English rural communities, *c.* 1550–1700', in Harris (ed.), *Politics of the excluded.*

agrarian south-east found his equivalent in the post-Restoration lead merchant of the Peak who combined large-scale sheep farming with some beef fattening and the ownership of mineshares.

The post-Restoration fortunes of William Bagshawe of Litton, whom we last encountered leading the miners' demonstrations of 1634, provides the most telling example of the disassociation of the upper yeomanry from their poorer neighbours. A son-in-law of Raphe Oldfield, Bagshawe had been a central figure in agitation against the tithe and a consistent advocate of free mining. His interests shifted in the years of the Interregnum, after he bought the sequestered lands and titles of delinquent royalists. By the 1650s he no longer described himself as a yeoman, and had instead taken the title of gentleman. Bagshawe bought the manor of Great Hucklow in 1654 and the lead tithe of Tideswell and Litton three years later. By the 1660s, he had earned the acrimony of his erstwhile comrades amongst the free miners for his collection of the very lead tithe he had himself opposed in the 1630s, and for his enclosure of Great Hucklow's common fields.[9] As the wealthiest inhabitant of Great Hucklow in 1664, Bagshawe was not only economically differentiated from his neighbours, but was also set apart by his Presbyterianism. Bagshawe communicated the faith to his son, also named William and known as the 'Apostle of the Peak' for his preaching, who was to lament the lack of religion amongst the 'generality' of the miners. As within the Essex village of Terling two generations earlier, a 'cultural wedge' was being driven between the material, religious and political world of William Bagshawe and that of his neighbours.[10]

Whereas the latter half of the seventeenth century was a dark time for the landless free miner, the period presented new opportunities for investment and profit to the landed lead merchant typified by Bagshawe. Such men and women had frequently identified with the miners' cause in earlier years out of a mutual antipathy to tithes and manorialism. But now their interests lay elsewhere: in the profits to be made as partners in the new deep mines, and in the enclosure of commons and wastes. It is therefore significant that the last recorded attempt by a lord to impose a manorial pre-emption of ore sales within his territories should occur in 1662. As we have seen, lords who tried to impose a monopoly over the purchase of lead on their estates under their right of pre-emption were faced with the united hostility of miners, orebuyers and lead merchants. The declining enthusiasm of lords

---

[9] Newton, 'Gentry', 11; PRO, E112/382/35; J. Thirsk, *The agrarian history of England and Wales. V.I: 1640–1750. Regional farming systems* (Cambridge, 1984), 136; on Bagshawe's speculations in land in the 1650s see SA, Bag C 2098–105. For another example, see the subsequent career of Robert Ashton, who in his youth had led Tideswell and Litton miners against John Manners in Hazelbadge: Newton, 'Gentry', 10–11.

[10] Quoting Wrightson and Levine, *Poverty and piety*, 162.

for such conflicts enabled orebuyers and merchants to withdraw from conflict with the manorial interest. In some cases, local social alliances were thereby reconfigured, as lead merchants and mine investors moved to support lords against the miners. While the closure of manors like Nether-haddon to free mining hit the interests of the miners, it could actually benefit entrepreneurs. The capital which financed the deep works at Haddonfields after 1658 came both from Rutland's coffers and from the pockets of the lesser gentry of the area. Bluntly stated, the marginalization of free mining could result in the reshaping of class interests.

The reworking of local social alliances was also apparent in disputes over enclosure. After the Restoration, the officers of the Duchy of Lancaster ably exploited divisions amongst those who had hitherto opposed their attempts to enclose the large commons of High Peak lordship. In their renewed enclosure of the commons, Duchy officials ensured that opposition from richer freeholders of the adjacent townships was reduced through the grant to those freeholders of land out of the division of the wastes.[11] Whereas the Duchy's first attempt to enclose the High Peak commons had met with the combined opposition of the inhabitants, the drawn-out enclosure of the commons after 1675 encountered only fractured opposition from amongst the poorer landed inhabitants, resulting in only one known deliberate breach of enclosures.[12]

After the Restoration, a series of factors combined to break down the networks through which the miners had hitherto advanced their political project. Falling lead prices and the enclosure of commons undercut the free miners' precarious economic independence. The changed interests of wealthier villagers and lead merchants marginalized miners within their own villages. The consolidation of authority in the hands of the Rutlands and Devonshires prevented the manipulation of divisions of interest amongst the elite. And changes in the sympathy and authority of the Duchy Court in mineral cases, more fully charted in Chapter 6, removed the powerful legal support provided by that body. Most importantly, the miners' declining capacity to defend their earlier gains was indicative of the larger decomposition of their politics.

The miners' political weakness in the late seventeenth century was most apparent in their defence of free mining. Yet it is a tribute to the miners' enduring control of custom that even through the dark years of the late seventeenth century, knowledge of their rights and laws remained em-bedded deep within their collective identity. As Edward Thompson has

---

[11] Somerville, 'Commons and wastes'; PRO, DL4/121/1681/6. For similar developments elsewhere, see Manning, *Village revolts*, 141, 147; Underdown, *Revel, riot and rebellion*, 113.

[12] PRO, DL4/123/1684/12.

remarked in relation to the defence of the commons, 'it is sentimental to suppose that . . . the poor were always losers'.[13] Between the 1590s and the 1640s, the miners had won a series of remarkable victories. Within Elton, where the right of free mining had been won in 1627, the free miners were still 'in lawfull possession' of their mines 'according to the Custom of the Mine' forty-two years later. They retained sharp memories of that victory, and harped upon it. We should not, therefore, overstate the experience of defeat in Haddonfields. Many of the Elton miners of 1669 had been involved in the riots against the Earl of Rutland. But in recalling the days when Elton did not lie within the King's Field, 'nor any barghmaster there, neither was any myner pmitted to work there, but by lycense of the lord of the manor', they recalled their distant victory, rather than their more recent defeat.[14]

Memory became increasingly important after the Restoration to the defence of free mining rights. Riding on a crest after his extinction of free mining in Netherhaddon, in 1662 the Earl of Rutland tried to reintroduce a fixed price for lead sales within Bakewell manor under his right of preemption. He was unsuccessful, for the miners, orebuyers and merchants retained copies of his ancestor's agreement at the Bakewell barmote of 1608 that the lord should pay the market price for ore.[15] That the barmote remained an important guarantor of the miners' freedoms was evidenced by the development of disputes between lords and entrepreneurs on the one side, and the miners on the other, over the authority and autonomy of the barmote.[16]

Before the civil war, the miners had held the initiative in their attempt to extend free mining across the whole lead field. After the Restoration, it was the greater gentry of the area who took the offensive, and the miners who sat in static defence of their rights. This was most obvious in the renewal of legal attack upon the right of free mining within the Wapentake of Wirksworth. After the conclusion of the Haddon dispute, lords of manors within Wirksworth Wapentake again pressed for the removal of their manors from the King's Field. Since the Duchy Court's judgement of 1627, the right of free mining in all territories within the Wapentake had been protected by the Duchy of Lancaster. The extension of the right into the manor of Ible was called into question once again in 1641, but the outbreak of civil war had prevented a verdict.[17] Over the 1650s, attempts by lords within the Wapentake to drive the miners from their estates had

---

13 Thompson, *Customs in common*, 103.
14 PRO, DL4/112/13.
15 BL, Add. MS 6677, fol. 79.
16 BL, Add. MS 6677, fols. 88–94; PRO, DL4/120/1679/2.
17 BL, Add. MS 6678, fols. 14–18.

resulted in violence.[18] Following the Restoration, the attack on free mining rights within Wirksworth Wapentake took a legal form. In judgements between 1661 and 1663, the Duchy recognized Sir John Gell as sole owner of the mineral rights of Griffe Grange. Legal action commenced over the mining rights of Ible and Newton Grange between 1678 and 1686, in which once again the Duchy overturned its previous rulings to give verdicts in favour of the manorial interest.[19]

Even within those manors where free mining was not challenged, limitations were placed upon mining custom. The Tideswell barmote's jurisdiction was further restricted by the commandment of the lord in 1675. Miners' property rights over inundated deposits within Wirksworth Wapentake, already restricted in 1655, were further constrained in 1680. George Hopkinson gave influential opinion in 1684 that although miners were entitled by custom to seek for lead ore within the Duchy's possessions, 'if they finde noe vein they are trespasser from the beginning of their worke', and could be prosecuted before the common law. In 1689, Sir John Harpur, the lord of Wensley, defied custom by granting consolidated leases of lead deposits to entrepreneurs over the miners' heads.[20] Unlike before the civil wars, there is no evidence that the miners rioted or took collective legal action in defence of their rights. Although the miners of the Restoration period resented the growing encroachment upon their customs, they seem to have experienced a loss of collective agency.

In 1686, the miner John Derbyshire, who had been the lone defender of free mining within Newton Grange in the early 1680s, met the barmaster of the neighbouring Duchy sub-manor of Brassington at Ashbourne fair. The barmaster offered Derbyshire his moral support in the dispute. In response, Derbyshire explained how, following his imprisonment and the harassment of his family by the owners of Newton Grange, he had been forced to sign an undertaking that he would never again work there. The forced extraction of such agreements may have been more common at this time than the historical record suggests. Our history of disputes over mining custom is heavily reliant upon the record of legal proceedings before Westminster courts. Without the backing of the lessee of the Duchy's lot and cope, it was difficult for the miners successfully to sue their opponents at law. It could well be the case that the three disputes over mining rights heard by the

18 PRO, DL4/123/1684/1, /124/1686/7.
19 BL, Add. MSS 6682, fols. 49–50, 90–1, 6686, fols. 129–32, 136–42; DRO, D258M/59/ 3e; PRO, DL4/106/1, /105/1661/33, /105/1661/2, /105/1661/22, /108/31, /120/1678/1, / 123/1684/4, /124/1686/7; PRO, DL5/40, fols. 178, 181, 187, 189, 191, 201, 210, 269, 369, 384, 385, 387, 393, 397, 399, 408, 410, 418, 425, 427, 428.
20 CHT, 1675 Tideswell barmote articles; DRO, D258M/61/47t; PRO, DL4/123/1684/4, / 125/1689/2.

Duchy Court after the Restoration represent only a small proportion of those occasions on which miners found themselves banned from manors where they had hitherto exercised free mining rights. It is therefore significant that an agreement of 1680 survives in the Gell family papers in which seven Wirksworth miners were bound by Sir John Gell never again to dig on Hopton moor, and to recognize that such an act 'is not according to custom'. In fact, the right of free mining had been exercised within Hopton since the late sixteenth century.[21] As with John Derbyshire's experience in Newton Grange, the Wirksworth miners were being forced to cede control of custom to their social superiors.

RESISTANCE, PROTEST AND SURVIVAL

Renewed dispute at the beginning of the eighteenth century over the lead tithe suggests something of the miners' place within local politics at that point, and of how changing circumstances conspired to breed a stouter defence of custom. Whereas the miners had seen their free mining rights diminish after the Restoration, they had been more successful in preventing ministers and tithe lessees from establishing new lead tithes over them. This was in spite of the Crown's refusal to support the miners over this matter. In expectation that the Restoration government would honour Charles I's promise to exempt such miners as had joined his colours from payment of the lead tithe, older miners made a point of mentioning their wartime service for Charles I in their depositions to courts adjudicating in tithe cases. Some miners went so far as to petition the King to honour his father's promise. Yet Charles II took no action.[22] Betrayed by the Crown, the miners were still able to claim support from the merchants and mine-owners, whose profits were hit by the tithe proprietors' claims. Moreover, by the Restoration earlier parochial settlements between ministers and miners over the lead tithe had acquired the force of custom, and proved difficult to defeat at law. In most cases, tithe proprietors' claims were therefore rejected by the Exchequer and Duchy Courts.[23]

By the turn of the century, the collection of lead tithes was subject to considerable parochial variation. In some parishes, such as Bakewell, Tideswell and Hope, tithes were paid with little interruption after the

---

[21] PRO, DL4/123/1686/7; DRO, D258M/28/20v.

[22] PRO, DL4/123/1685/2, /124/1686/7; *CSPD, 1680–1*, 126. Upon petition to the Privy Council from the miners in 1681, the matter was passed to the Duchy. There is no record in the Duchy Court's books of any action taken, and the disputes continued.

[23] PRO, E112/383/68, /69, /83, /91, /96, /112, /382/35, /41; PRO, E134/23ChasII/East5, /26ChasII/East34, /3JasII/East15, /2JasII/Mich21, /6Wm&Mar/Trin1, /4&5Wm&Mar/Hil15; PRO, DL4/106/1, /117/8; DRO, D258M/54/19ha; BL, Add. MSS 6685, fol. 54, 6688, fols. 398–403.

Restoration. In others, such as in Eyam and the chapelry of Stoney Middleton, compromises agreed by ministers in the early seventeenth century endured. In a third group of parishes, most notably in Darley, Matlock, Bonsall, Ashover and Carsington, central courts accepted that no customary lead tithe existed. But in 1701, the ministers and tithe lessees ensured the placement of a bill before the House of Commons which proposed to override parochial difference and standardize a tithe payment across the whole of the lead field. The miners and mine-owners within those parishes where a compromise had been struck or where the tithe had been disproved mobilized against what became known as the Parsons' Bill. Defining themselves as the 'freeholders' of the parishes in question, the lead merchants, mine-owners and the wealthiest free miners combined to publish appeals against the Parsons' Bill. These publications cited earlier court judgements, arguing that the passage of the bill would diminish profits and impoverish the miners.

Pressure was applied through representation within the political system as well as through publication. On 22 April 1701, Lord Roos met with 'the best of the yeomanry in the high and low peake the lead merchants there and in Scarsdale with a number of the most substantiall myners' concerning 'the Parsons Bill as they call it'. This broad front threatened to withdraw their votes for Sir Philip Gell 'who they take to be the setter up of it', if the bill secured passage through the Commons. Through such selective pressure, the bill was defeated.[24] Like other electors in early eighteenth-century Britain, the public opponents of the Parsons' Bill were able to influence the course of events due to their possession of a freehold franchise. In that respect, the confrontation over the Parsons' Bill points to the continued presence of at least the 'most substantiall myners' within the local political system. As with the organization which underlay the miners' 1641 petition, the dispute over the Parson's Bill points to the overlapping interest between miners, orebuyers and lead merchants. But whereas the 1641 petition had included all miners, whether possessed of freehold or not, the negotiations of sixty years later were restricted only to a small segment of the mining community, acting in combination with their betters.

The defeat of the 'Parsons' Bill' at first gave confidence to poorer men. After 1701, the miners of Stoney Middleton refused payment of the tithe composition upon which their ancestors had agreed to the minister of their chapelry. Yet this spirit of resistance did not endure for long. Whereas the Stoney Middleton miners of King James I's reign had been economically independent, their eighteenth-century inheritors were not. In 1733, Ben-

24 DRO, 1289B/L158, /160–2; BL, Add. MSS 6682, fols. 125–33 , 155, 6681, fols. 359, 377–9.

jamin Ashton, a powerful employer in the area, supported the minister's renewed demands for a tithe of lead. The miners were 'afraid of disobliging him and being turned out of his business', for 'Mr Ashton . . . had a very great influence over the Myners at Stoney Middleton & most of them were servants or workmen under him.' Calling the miners to a meeting, Ashton 'grew angry' with them, and instructed them to pay the tithe.[25] Opposition to the Duke of Rutland's claim to tithe ore in Youlgreave parish in 1733 came from amongst the free miners of Birchover. But this took the form of the concealment of ore, rather than the more public politics of crowd action and litigation characteristic of their forefathers' resistance to tithes. In 1730, Sir Philip Gell directly echoed his ancestor's complaints against a 'combination' of miners in Bakewell, Hope and Tideswell who refused to pay the lead tithe. But on closer inspection, the defendants listed in the Gell's action prove to be lead merchants and mine-owners.[26] We should not therefore assume too readily that the miners of the eighteenth-century Peak had forgotten the hard times of the post-Restoration period.

The eighteenth century saw new attacks upon the right of free mining, the history of which is difficult to reconstruct with any precision. In most cases, eighteenth-century battles over free mining rights are heard only distantly in the documentation. Again, we are reminded of how dependent we are upon the records of legal proceedings, and how dependent in turn such legal action was upon the miners' collective ability to maintain their customs at law. In an undated petition to Lord Edgecombe, the miners complained of infringements of their 'immemorial . . . Laws and Customs' without which the industry would be destroyed 'to the utter impoverishing of many 1000. families'.[27] Upholding the jurisdiction of the barmote, they argued that the Duchy's authority as the final arbiter in mineral disputes was being undermined by other Westminster courts, such that cases were tried 'before Incompetent Judges ignorant of their Laws and Customs to their utter ruine'. Other complaints listed included the farming of the office of barmaster, the decline in the authority of barmote courts, the loss of their customary right to wood and the imposition of new taxes. The miner William Hooson wrote in similarly vague terms of an attempt of 1743 by the Duke of Devonshire, as lessee of the rights of lot and cope, 'to destroy the Priviledges and Customes of the Miners throughout the High Peak' by attempting the abolition of the barmote.[28] We can therefore detect a high

---

[25] PRO, E134/6GeoII/Mich4.
[26] BL, Add. MSS 6685, fols. 32–49, 168–70, 6682, fols. 111–14; Willies, 'Lead mining customs', 17. See also DRO, 504B/L221.
[27] BL, Add. MS 6682, fol. 212. Lord Edgecombe was Chancellor of the Duchy of Lancaster between 1743 and 1758.
[28] Hooson, *Miners' dictionary*, 63.

level of anxiety amongst the miners, and a continuing sense that their customs were threatened by 'great men'.

For a fleeting moment, the geographical extent of eighteenth-century free mining rights becomes clear. The survival of some manuscript notes concerning the state of mining law in 1762 provides us with the opportunity to survey manorial difference in customary provision in that year (see Map 14).[29] The 1762 notes show that despite Hooson's obscure reference to the events of 1743, free mining had been most successfully defended within the Duchy's King's Field. Still covering about half of the total lead field at that time, the King's Fields of High Peak and Wirksworth remained the heartland of free mining territory. Outside the King's Field, the miners' rights were less secure. The manors of Grindlow, Peak Forest, Rowland, Netherhaddon, Harthill, Bakewell and Stanton had by 1762 all been closed to free mining and the mineral rights taken to the lord as his or her 'exclusive property'. In the case of some of these manors, we have no evidence of how they had been redefined as 'closed liberties'. But we do know that the Rutlands' historic opposition to free mining continued into the eighteenth century. The free miners of Harthill manor, for instance, were ejected by 'force majeure' after 1748. And as we have seen in Chapter 5, the banning of free mining often preceded the lease of large mineral deposits as consolidated leases to mine investors. After 1660, the manorial interest therefore continued to set itself against the free mining interest in time-honoured fashion. In other manors, however, free mining rights faced erosion from a new source: that of wealthy freehold tenants.

Disputes between miners and freeholders over mining rights on enclosed land gave legal expression to the separation of material interest between richer and poorer inhabitants observed in the preceding section. Such disputes were a peculiarity of the post-1660 period. Following the defeat of free mining claims, mineral deposits on freehold land could be let on consolidated leases. Some freeholders were themselves investors in the deep mines established under consolidated leases. By 1762, manors where free-hold tenants held the mineral rights of their land included Great Longstone, Little Longstone, Hassop, Calver, Ashover, Eyam and Stoney Middleton. Within these manors, free miners were required to 'compound' with land-owners before digging for lead. Free mining still continued on the commons and copyhold land of such manors. But as large-scale enclosure proceeded in the later eighteenth century, the practical possession of mineral rights often passed into the hands of the freeholders. The 1762 notes therefore freeze a very fluid situation. None the less, while the eighteenth century saw the retreat of free mining rights within many individual manors, large parts

---

[29] BL, Add. MS 6677, fols. 78–80, supplemented by BL, Add. MS 6685, fols. 177–8.

of the lead field remained open to the miners. Furthermore, although the miners of the eighteenth century were operating within a less favourable economic and legal context than had their early seventeenth-century predecessors, they stuck to a dogged defence of mining custom. That defence is best studied with reference to the local case-study.

Surviving documentation allows us to investigate in some detail the history of two mining disputes which developed between 1713 and 1749. These concerned the manors of Eyam and Stoney Middleton, and the manor of Grindlow. Both disputes provide evidence of eighteenth-century miners' renewed willingness to take collective legal and crowd action in defence of custom. A custom of free mining had operated within Eyam and Stoney Middleton from the late 1580s to 1662, when the manor passed to Sir George Savile, the first Marquis of Halifax. After 1662, manorial custom was redefined, and the free miners excluded from freehold land. Conceivably, the plague which afflicted the village of Eyam in 1665–6 may have impaired the continuity of local memory on which custom depended. For the next forty years, the freeholders were untroubled by the dispossessed miners, whose activities were restricted to the manor's commons.

But at some time before 1702, the Eyam miners discovered a mid-seventeenth-century document which provided evidence of the past existence of a free mining custom. Their search into the history of the manor may have been motivated by the impending enclosure of the commons of Eyam, which the freeholders carried out in 1702, thereby limiting still further the area open to free mining. There is no evidence of organized crowd action by the miners over the matter, but in 1713 they started proceedings against the freeholders at the Court of Exchequer. At the same time, they were also mounting a defence of free mining custom in the adjoining manor of Foolow. Noting the 'generall dislike the freeholdrs have there to [the mining] customes', the miners cited the provisions of the 1288 Quo Warranto and subsequent proceedings as evidence of their right. Without the backing which their ancestors had received from the lessee of the Duchy's lot and cope, and without the organizational capacity to collect common purses, the miners proved unable to bear the costs of litigation. Moreover, the miners received no aid from the lead merchants of the area, whose interests lay in securing the freeholders' right over the minerals so that rationalized consolidated leases of the deposits could be granted to them. The agreement with the freeholders of 1715 which ended the dispute was therefore made on 'very hard terms' for the miners.[30]

---

[30] Hopkinson, 'Lead mining in the Eyam district', 82–3; SA, Bag C 703, 3355; CHT, 1713 declaration of the freeholders of Hathersage parish; BL, Add. MSS 6682, fols. 126–33, 6685, fols. 83–4, 89, 94–110, 6677, fols. 75–82, 84–6.

The dispute over the mining rights of the manor of Grindlow was drawn around a rather different series of social alliances from that in Eyam. Like Eyam, Grindlow had been open to free mining since the late sixteenth century.[31] And like Eyam, the removal of that right appears to have been very sudden, following in this case upon the purchase of the manor by Lord Cullen in the early 1730s. The discovery of the rich vein at Eyam Edge in the early 1730s, which passed through Grindlow, had led to the establishment of large-scale workings at Bank and Little Pasture mine. These workings were owned by a coalition of lead merchants, who employed the miners on a coping system. As was typical elsewhere, the large, gentry-owned mines operated alongside small free mining operations, worked by the miners when they were not at labour in the deep mines. Cullen's claim upon the mining rights therefore prejudiced both the title of the investors and the miners' livelihood as copers and free miners. Unlike in Eyam, the alignment of opposing interests in Grindlow pushed the miners into alliance with the mine-owners. The mine-owners started legal action against Cullen at the Derby Assizes in 1737, who passed the matter on to the Court of Common Pleas in 1738. In July 1738, the Common Pleas ruled in favour of Lord Cullen's possession of the mineral rights of Grindlow. This judgement was both preceded and followed by a series of increasingly violent confrontations which formed the basis of further action by Lord Cullen at the Court of King's Bench in 1739. The narrative of events which emerges from the legal papers of the King's Bench case deserves recounting, pointing as it does to the potential willingness of the eighteenth-century miners to resort to strenuous action in defence of their rights.[32]

In March 1738, Lord Cullen's agent, Warren, raised the freeholders of Grindlow in an attack upon the miners, after which he took forcible possession of the mines. In an act of deliberate provocation, Warren burnt the stowes which marked possession of the mine. A threatening crowd of miners gathered, and Warren's men left off. Early in June, Warren again attempted to take the mines, but was driven off by crowds of miners. On 10 July 1738, in defiance of the Common Pleas' verdict, the deep mines were formally reopened by the mine-owners. Two days later, officers of the county's sheriff arrived to enforce the law. The deputy sheriff gave an account of the events of that day. When he and forty of his men came to the mine, 'there was a very great number of people . . . two hundred or more about the said mine called Bank . . . many of them swore that they valued no writts or power And that if the Sheriff or any man took poss'ion of the

31 NAO, DD.P. 80/2.
32 The subsequent discussion is based on: SA, Bag C 704 (1–16); SA, SpSt 60498–50; SA, WHC 34; BL, Add. MSS 6682, fols. 204–7, 6678, fols. 155–200; Hopkinson, 'Lead mining in the Eyam district', 83–91.

sd mines they would have his blood'. The crowd, made up of both men and women, threw stones at the sheriff's officers. Despite the reading of the Riot Act, the deputy sheriff was 'advised . . . . to get off the ground and told . . . that as they believed he wo'd [be] kill'd or spoil'd or to that effect if he did not . . . as soon as he could he got through the Crowd not daring to stay for fear of injury'. One of the sheriff's men was attacked by members of the crowd, at which point 'a bloody battle ensued', as others turned on the deputy sheriff crying 'Damm him kill that Blue Coat Dog . . . he's Warren's man.' The officers of the law were driven off by this little insurrection, following which the entrances to the mines were blockaded and the drainage engines buried. An armed guard of thirty or forty men was mounted upon the mines, who maintained their watch in eight-hour shifts, and word given out that 'the partners wo'd raise all the miners in the High Peak and take possion of the sd mines back again'.

Rumours circulated that Warren would attempt to retrieve possession by force, that he would bring soldiers for that purpose 'and that in case any resistance was made he would murther or destroy them all'. Finally, on 22 July the sheriff's men approached the mine again. 'They heard . . . people on the sd mines give several great shouts . . . and also beat a drum upon the mines', which the sheriff's men 'took to be a signal to call in people to their assistance'. A crowd of allegedly armed and drunken miners, 'picked and chosen from other mines and other places in the County as a set of daring and desperate fellows fittest to undertake any wild enterprise', rallied support. A crowd of 200 people assembled from the neighbouring villages, many also armed. 'Several of the rioters [swore] . . . that no possion should be taken & that they would lose their lives before.' The Riot Act was read by the sheriff, but to no effect. Two of the miners 'shook their sticks and swore that these were their acts of Parliament & that they would use them as such'. One announced that 'he valued neither sheriff or any body else for that no body should take possion'. According to the miners, the Sheriff's men attacked them, but they held back, crying to one another 'good lads, hold your hands, pray don't strike'. By the evening, the crowd had grown to 500 people, again comprising both men and women. The sheriff sensibly recoiled from confronting such a large crowd and retired.

In the two riots of July 1738, Cullen's opponents had succeeded in driving off the sheriff and his officers. But advice from the mine-owners' solicitor that the sheriff had 'the power of the Countrey to assist in the execution of the writ' led to the dissolution of crowd protest. The inhabitants of the mining villages around Grindlow were prepared to defend their right to employment with demonstration and threat, but not with the use of armed force against the state. When the sheriff's officers returned on 2 August 1738, they encountered no resistance and took the mine 'by force'. The mine-owners came to a settlement with Lord Cullen in 1749, upon his agreement to more reasonable terms for the continuation of deep mining in Grindlow. The miners, of course, gained nothing from that compromise. They and their families had been persuaded into action on the mine-owners' behalf out of a mutual interest in the protection of the right of free mining. Yet for all the unconscious, distant echoes of the mid-seventeenth-century confrontations in Haddonfields to be heard in the words and actions of the rioters at Grindlow in 1738, the key actors in this confrontation were not the miners, but rather their employers.

The Eyam and Grindlow disputes suggest that while the Peak miners of the eighteenth century remained committed to the defence of free mining, they were rather less able to assert their collective, independent agency in the matter than their ancestors had been. We have already seen how dependent the miners were on the support of the mine-owners and merchants in their defeat of the 1701 'Parson's Bill'. Opposition to the Duke of Devonshire's attempt to extend the payment of lot and cope duties to the 'smitham' ore dug by cavers and the poorest miners presents a similar picture. As we saw in Chapter 6, the introduction of new smelting technology in the mid-eighteenth century rendered the processing of such smitham ore cost effective, and therefore its production from deep, gentry-owned works increased. In subsequent litigation stretched between 1750 and 1776, the Duke of Devonshire succeeded in claiming duties on smitham in the face of combined opposition from miner and mine-owner.[33] Once again, local circumstances produced an alliance between the miners and the mine-owners, in which the latter formed the leadership of opposition to the manorial interest.

Not for the first time, the language of custom formed the discursive terrain of local conflict. But on this occasion, that language was commandeered by a local elite operating in the name of the popular interest. In 1766, 'many hundred miners' from Wirksworth Wapentake put their names to an agreement that a committee of five mine-owners and lead merchants be formed 'to defend the customs'. Amongst the five men nominated to the committee was Anthony Tissington of Swanwick, who published a number of broadsides and a pamphlet in defence of mining custom. He explained in his publications that he spoke for the 'thousands of the industrious poor', within which category he included the miners. Explaining later events in 1772, Tissington described how the Duke of Devonshire's demands 'alarmed the country in general; publick meetings

---

[33] For this litigation, and public debate, see DRO, D504B/L420; BL, Add. MSS 6676, fols. 1–41, 44–49, 96–131, 6677, fols. 65–7, 6686, fols. 1–37, 82–104. For a similar dispute in the Yorkshire lead industry, see PRO, E134/6GeoII/Mich2.

were had; many Gentlemen Maintainers attended, who were petitioned by many Hundreds of the miners to defend them against the said Demand; offering to contribute all in their Power towards such Defence'.[34] Swanwick saw the smitham case in whiggish terms, as a confrontation between 'the people' and a 'tyrannical' aristocratic interest. His definition of the people was sufficiently broad to include both mine-owner and miner, but in its practical operation the opposition to Devonshire was both initiated and led by the employing class.

While the miners may have lost agency with the closure of elite unity against free mining and the growing hostility of the law courts to barmote custom, the public world of eighteenth-century plebeian politics in the region may have become more inclusive. The large crowds which gathered so rapidly in Grindlow in 1738, and the inclusion of women in those crowds, suggests that unlike the miners' crowd actions of the early seventeenth century, the Grindlow riots represented a more authentically communal protest against the loss of employment. With the growth of wage dependency amongst skilled miners, who alternated coping with small-scale production from free mining, distinctions between 'hireling' and free miner had become blurred. The watch kept by the armed miners upon the Grindlow workings operated on eight-hour shifts, in imitation of the shift system by which waged labour was ordered. The blocking of the mine entrances, and the burying of machinery, are paralleled in other mining areas of the country where colliers combined strikes, demonstrations and riots with organized sabotage.[35] These were the actions of wage labourers connected by mutual interest in the maintenance of their employment rather than those of free miners protecting their works. And like other industrial regions in eighteenth-century England, the Peak had become an important focus for food rioting.

Still noted for their 'riotous disposition' in 1800, the miners were singled out for their involvement in food riots in that year, as in 1757 and 1796. Miners were also identified as the main culprits in resistance to forced service in the county militia which in 1757, 1760, 1796 and 1797 developed into demonstration and riot.[36] As we have seen in Chapter 4, mining formed the primary form of male employment in the lead field villages of the mid-eighteenth century. Yet the area involved in such protest included Peak villages which lay outside the lead field. Moreover, other

[34] SA, Bag C 670; BL, Add. MSS 6681, fols. 335–58, 6677, fol. 65.
[35] See for instance Levine and Wrightson, *Making of an industrial society*, 399–403.
[36] M. Thomas, 'The rioting crowd in eighteenth century Derbyshire', *DAJ*, 2nd ser., 95 (1975), 40–1, 44; M. Thomas, 'Friends of democracy: a study of working-class radicalism in Derbyshire, 1790–1850', MPhil thesis, University of Sheffield, 1984, 88; Hopkinson, 'Lead mining in eighteenth century Ashover', 5–6.

accounts described public hostility to the Militia Acts as coming from 'tenants' and 'neighbours'. The same connection is apparent in earlier accounts of the threat of 'insurrections' of Peak miners in 1696. This fear was occasioned by the lack of coin in the High Peak after the reissue of currency due to the depredations of coiners. After witnessing crowd protest in Tideswell, the Earl of Devonshire's agent worried over the 'danger of insurrection amongst the miners in Derbyshire, upon their clipped money being reduced, when they had nothing else to supply it'. His letter to the Duke concluded with the advice that 'the best care' should be taken to 'suppress' any such rising, but subsequent exchange of letters recommended ameliorative action.[37] Again, the miners were unlikely to have been the only group affected by the debasement of their money. Like the London Apprentices of the 1640s, they were merely the most apparent and, to elite eyes, threatening body of men within the area.

Crowd protest in the eighteenth-century Peak Country betrays very similar forms of organization. Whether protesting over the price of food, the introduction of compulsory militia service or the debasement of currency, large crowds, growing in number as they moved, converged upon market towns either to redress grievances or to express their complaints to authority. The militia riots of 1796 and 1797 took exactly the same form as those which occurred in 1757 and 1760, in which crowds had burnt militia lists in marketplaces. Similarly, food riots in the 1790s and 1800 followed the same pattern as in 1757. Where complaint was voiced, it did not take the form of a deferential address. The 'great number of people' who gathered at Bakewell in 1757 to protest against the Militia Act 'raised a clamour against the Duke of Devonshire and threatened Chatsworth'. In an act of intimidated munificence, the Duke provided the crowd with 'great plenty of meat and drink'. Though 'their resentment dropt, . . . some of 'em said his Grace's liquor was not as good as they expected'. A few days later, Ashover miners followed Devonshire to Chesterfield to protest against the act. Perplexed by these developments, on his return to Chatsworth the Duke asked an overseer at Eyam Edge mine who happened to be at the House his opinion of the disturbances, adding miserably 'That he was sorry they had conceived so ill an opinion of him who strove to tread in the Steps of his Forfathers as much as he could.' The overseer refused to answer the Duke, saying that as an Eyam man his 'country was not Tenants to [the Duke]'.[38] Devonshire saw his forefathers' steps as following a paternalist path to social hierarchy, and was appalled that he might be

---

[37] BL, Add. MS 6668, fols. 210–14; PRO, SP32/274, fol. 131. For clippers in Ashbourne in 1698, see PRO, MINT15/17/27. I am grateful to Tim Wales for this reference.

[38] Thomas, 'Friends of democracy', 88, Hopkinson, 'Lead mining in eighteenth century Ashover', 5–6.

considered to have strayed from that route. But knowing the history of the Peak as we now do, we should not be so surprised that the men and women of the eighteenth-century Peak were so willing to reject the deference expected of them.

The pugnacity and independence of eighteenth-century Peak Country crowds bears comparison with the plebeian politics of the early seventeenth century. Eighteenth-century plebeians were unwilling to be pushed about by central authority, were unhappy about the high prices sometimes charged for food, were conscious of custom and sensitive to the infringement of their rights. But their struggles were defensive in a way that pre-civil war popular politics were not. The ambitions, methods and ideology of the plebeian politics of the early Stuart period had no equivalent in the eighteenth century. Individual conflicts in the eighteenth-century Peak add up to nothing larger: they do not speak to any political project or collective ambition. The politics of custom had become residual within local culture, as its larger meaning ossified into rigidity.

The contestation of authority remained a formative element of the confrontational system of social relations characteristic of pastoral-industrial eighteenth-century England. Ordered within social polarities which meant less in the more structurally differentiated environments of arable and urban communities, plebeian and elite were caught in a difficult balance.[39] The miner and cottager were sequestered from the gentleman and noble, their worlds unbridged by any substantial middle class or close concourse. Only the estate steward stood between the two, their sometimes worried letters to their sponsors providing us with a record of the polarized social relations of the period.[40] Yet as elite and plebeian interests and expectations collided, neither could win clear mastery over the other. Products of a defensive but rebellious culture, the Peak miners and cottagers were well capable of cocking a snoop at authority, but lacked the organizational resources to turn sullen hostility into the inspired politics of their predecessors. Similarly, noble and gentlemen could worry away at the fringes of the customs which protected plebeian community, but lacked the

---

[39] Thompson, *Customs in common*, chs. 1 and 2. For a reiteration of this view of eighteenth-century England, see most recently D. Hay and N. Rodgers, *Eighteenth-century English society* (Oxford, 1997). For a recent criticism of Thompson's interpretation, see P. King, 'Edward Thompson's contribution to eighteenth-century studies. The patrician-plebeian model re-examined', *Social History*, 21, 2 (1996), 215–28. Importantly, King suggests that Thompson's 'bipolar model' of social relations makes more sense in pastoral-industrial areas (such as the Peak) than in urban and agrarian England: *ibid.*, 221–5.

[40] For examples, see BL, Add. MS 6668, fols. 210–14; Hopkinson, 'Lead mining in the Eyam district', 96; Willies, 'The Barker family', 57. On the role of the estate steward, see D.R. Hainsworth, *Stewards, lords and people: the estate steward and his world in later Stuart England* (Cambridge, 1992), 48–75.

ability to sweep them away wholesale. Yet past habits still weighed upon local identities: eighteenth-century miners like William Hooson saw themselves as the inheritors of an independent tradition which imposed duties as well as rights. The importance of that perception must be given its due. Like other areas of eighteenth-century England where small-scale, semi-independent production remained important to household economies, a rebellious plebeian culture operated within the Peak. Such cultures of resistance were not produced mechanistically out of economics and social structure, but instead were actively maintained over generations. That Peak miners and cottagers possessed a habit of collective protest, like Cornish tinners, Kingswood colliers and Gloucestershire weavers, helped to reproduce a 'tradition of vigorous resistance' within local culture.[41] We might take the behaviour of the crowd at Grindlow in 1738 as representative of a larger social equation. The members of that crowd were conscious of the necessary bounds of their rebelliousness. Rhetorical statements of desperation and murderous intent were made, but violence was limited, even ritualistic. The object was to demonstrate a grievance and to effect immediate reformation, rather than to confront the armed force of the state.

Early seventeenth-century Peak plebeians had certainly not wanted to confront the authority of the state either. The awful, if distant, example of Robert Kett, and the closer case of the Midland rebels of 1607 helped to dissuade early seventeenth-century rioters from open rebellion. Across pre-civil war England, plebeians had found alternative ways of contesting elite authority than open rebellion or large-scale riot. The Peak miners provide one of the most inventive, original and stubborn examples of a wider phenomenon. In the course of building alliances, drawing out legal action, inventing and extending custom and engineering confrontations with their social superiors before higher authorities, they had often exhausted their opponents, and had sometimes won new rights into the bargain.

Crowd action had never been the only, or even the most important, form acquired by plebeian public politics in the early Stuart Peak. In contrast, in the eighteenth century crowd action became the central focus to the defence of the battered gains of earlier generations. A more sealed, defensive culture emerged out of the structural and cultural changes of the late seventeenth century. In part as a result of the compromise of the coping system, miners became more reconciled to the new distribution of power

[41] J.G. Rule, *The labouring classes in early industrial England, 1750–1850* (London, 1986), 348–51; A. Charlesworth and A. Randall, 'Comment: morals, markets and the crowd in 1766', *P&P*, 114 (1987), 200–13; Randall, *Before the Luddites*, 69–107; Rollison, *Local origins*, chs. 8–9; R.W. Malcolmson, 'A set of ungovernable people: the Kingswood colliers in the eighteenth century', in Styles and Brewer (eds.), *An ungovernable people*, 85–127.

within their industry, more prepared to accept and even to demand the opportunity of waged labour. Happy to probe the sore sensibilities of the Hanoverian state, some Peak villagers affected a Jacobitism under the very nose of the Whig stronghold at Chatsworth. Yet in a reversal of 1642, on the passage of the Jacobite army through the Peak in 1745 neither the Young Pretender nor the government was able to muster any visible support from amongst the mining villages.[42] Disengaged from the political world of their social betters, plebeians in the eighteenth-century Peak relegated themselves to an unambitious, fierce, dogged, defence of the residue of their rights.

[42] P. Kleber Monod, *Jacobitism and the English people, 1688–1788* (Cambridge, 1989), 105, 204, 319, 322, 143.

The making of the English working class in the Derbyshire Peak Country

To contemporaries and to modern social historians alike, the late eighteenth-century factory system seemed to spawn the class structure which subsequently dominated nineteenth- and twentieth-century Britain. There was something about the ordered, ugly, oppressive uniformity of the tall mills of northern England which seemed to call forth an ordered, ugly, oppressive, uniform class society. For both radical democrat and nostalgic Tory, the factory system marked the antithesis of the consensual, harmonious rural society which they imagined had existed before enclosure. William Cobbett and John Clare established the same connection between class, enclosure, immiseration and industry, as did, much later, Benjamin Disraeli and James Keir Hardie. The belief that late eighteenth-century Britain had experienced a moment of jolting transition in which it had moved from a harmonious rural society into an industrial class society was later given choate form in the terminology of industrial revolution.

As a region which experienced the early arrival of the factory system, in the shape of the establishment of Arkwright's mill at Cromford in 1771, perceptions of the Peak became central to changing views of industry and society in later eighteenth-century Britain. John Byng, who visited the Peak in 1790, recalled the tall cotton mills at Cromford: 'These cotton mills, seven stories high, and fill'd with inhabitants, remind me of a first rate man of war; and when they are lighted up, on a dark night, look most luminously beautiful.'[1]

In spite of their surreal, austere beauty, Byng found the cotton mills threatening. To him, they constituted an alien insertion into an ancient, natural, pre-industrial landscape:

these vales have lost all their beauties; the rural cot has given place to the lofty red mill, and the grand houses of overseers; the stream perverted from its course by sluices, and aqueducts, will no longer ripple and cascade. Every rural sound is sunk in the clamours of cotton works; and the simple peasant (for to be simple we must

[1] Andrews and Andrews (eds.), *Torrington diaries*, 252.

316

be sequestr'd) is changed into the impudent mechanic . . . I well know that a peasantry maintain'd by their own ground, or by the cultivation of others ground, must abide; but a fear strikes me that this . . . commerce may meet a shock; and then what becomes your rabble of artisans!!²

Just as nature had been corrupted by modernity and industry, so too had social relations. The 'simple peasant' of the pre-industrial Peak had been replaced by a threatening mass of industrial workers, whose birthplace 'in the cotton mills', had instilled in them 'blasphemy, and immorality'.³ Byng's view of industrialization helped to establish a dominant historical narrative which the British would subsequently recite in popular and academic forms over the succeeding two centuries, and which would suppress earlier histories of industrialization and social conflict.⁴

The story of the Industrial Revolution grew from the blur of observable contemporary reality, perception and assumption. It told of how a consensual, hierarchical, rural social world had been swept away by sudden, violent economic change. From that maelstrom had emerged for the first time a class society and (in some accounts) the class struggle. Byng's perception of the Peak reproduced that narrative. By the time that Arkwright had established his mill in 1771, educated opinion was already beginning to recast its view of mountainous regions. The Peak's landscapes came to be seen as romantic rather than as threatening.⁵ Thus Byng found Monsalldale a 'truly-romantic view'; around Youlgreave he observed 'a beautiful scenery of steep rocks'; the road to Hartingdon he thought was 'rocky, and romantic'.⁶ So, too, the native population of the Peak were no longer a frightening, barbarous collection of 'Peakrills', but became instead a quaint, pastoral people. Their cultural difference was assimilated as a romantic product of a peculiar landscape, and their long dependence upon the mining industry downplayed and even ignored. Thereby, the 'Peakrills' could be presented as a pre-industrial people whose social world had been rudely shattered by mass industrialization. Hence, although Byng could observe of the area around Youlgreave that 'All the country is scoop'd by lead mines', he could ignore the implications of this statement.⁷ For Byng, industry, and its concomitant social conflicts and discontents, had arrived in the region in 1771, at Cromford.

There was both truth and falsehood in this view of the late eighteenth-century Peak, and of the larger vision of social change which it sustained.

---

² *Ibid.*, 251.   ³ *Ibid.*, 433–4.
⁴ D. Cannadine, 'The past and the present in the Industrial Revolution, 1880–1980', *P&P*, 103 (1984), 131–49.
⁵ For this shift in perceptions of the Peak, see Bray, *Sketch*; BL, Add. MS 6670, fols. 319–323; Whetstone, *Truths*; Anon., *Account*.
⁶ Andrews and Andrews (eds.), *Torrington diaries*, 249, 250, 188.
⁷ *Ibid.*, 251.

We have seen in this book that the early modern Peak Country was not 'pre-industrial', and we have questioned the usefulness of such a term as a description of society and economics before the Industrial Revolution. We have also seen that social conflict had been a forceful, if intermittent, presence in social relations and popular culture before 1770, and that early modern plebeians had been quite capable of conceiving of society in terms of stark class polarities. Class was not made in the Industrial Revolution: but it was given a different expression. It is therefore possible to see the period between *c.* 1770 and 1800 as constituting an important breaking point in the history of the Peak Country.

After 1770, a variety of forces broke up the supports of the relatively closed world of plebeian politics in the Peak. As we have seen in Chapter 5, large-scale parliamentary enclosure set in after this date, in correspondence with the long decline of the lead industry. Methodism, hitherto an object of popular scorn, began to acquire a mass following. Similarly, new forms of labour organization developed amongst the miners. The first organized strike and lock-out in the history of the lead industry occurred in 1777. In that year, the owners of Hill Carr Sough, frustrated at the lack of progress in the works, ordered the miners to work on Sundays. In response, as the partners' minute book noted, 'the Club at Birchover have made an Order that no person who works at Hill Carr Sough (if he meets with a misfortune there) shall be relieved from their Box'. The 'Overseer' was therefore instructed to sack all those miners who refused Sunday work. The 'Box' to which the minute referred was an insurance fund, maintained by the miners around Birchover. Such Boxes often formed the source of early trade unionism, but references to them are unusual, typically surfacing only in records of disputes.[8] Evidence that the Birchover Box was not the sole focus for organized labour came in 1797 when High Peak miners met at Eyam to form a Miners' Friendly Society. Following the conventions of such rules, the published standing orders of the Society abjured discussion of politics. Yet contemporaries observed an intimate connection between the establishment of autonomous friendly societies and labour disputes in Derbyshire.[9]

There were good reasons for despondency amongst the Peak's inhabitants in the 1790s. The high price of food in those years, coupled with the sharpening of the enclosure movement and the collapse in lead prices, created a critical economic environment. Charles Whetstone remembered that at that time parliamentary enclosure had 'reduced, by their crafty and

---

[8] DRO, 200B/M1, fol. 27. On the role of box clubs, see C.R. Dobson, *Masters and journeymen: a prehistory of industrial relations, 1717–1800* (London, 1980), 38–46.
[9] *Rules for a friendly society of miners at Eyam*, 1797, DCL; Thomas, 'Friends of democracy', 32; Farey, *General view*, III, 572–3.

hard griping superiors, or their own honest simplicity' the miners and smallholders of the Peak to poverty. As an indication of the miners' desperation in these years, the free miners of Wensley lowered themselves to caving for scraps of ore. Initially opposed by the parish vestry of Wensley, as the practice spread across 'to alarming lengths throughout all the Wapentake', action at King's Bench was initiated by landowners in 1793. The court declared against the custom of caving in 1797.

Yet within the miners' desperation can also be detected continued strains of an independence of spirit and collective organization. The miners who were caving for ore in Wensley had formed themselves into a 'Partnership'. Upon being told to desist by the leading freeholders of the township, they 'treated him with much insolence & threatened to come & plunder his house'. Threatened by the price-setting of combinations of merchants, the free miners of Bradwell 'and its vicinity' organized a meeting to denounce 'the oreburners' who were 'at this juncture grinding the face of the Poor, and using the labouring miners very ill, by abating the prices of ore'.[10] Enclosure also engendered communal opposition. One frightened local gentleman wrote of how in July 1791 the enclosure commissioners met on Stanton moor to mark out that large common for division. They encountered 'a mob' who 'had assembled in their neighbourhood . . . the Comm[issione]rs had a narrow escape for their lives but that they were permitted to depart on a promise of not coming there again'. The author connected the Stanton 'mob' to the actions of the Sheffield crowd a few days later, who had broken into the gaol and burnt the house of a gentleman: 'They stuck up all over Sheffield printed Bills with the words *No King* in large characters; this I suppose is one mode of exerting the *Rights of Man*.'[11]

Suggestions that older forms of communal resistance could grow into the political radicalism of the early Industrial Revolution can be founded on more than the paranoid fears of the elite. Within the Peak as elsewhere, an enduring connection developed between organized labour, Methodism and political radicalism. In February 1792, a branch of the radical Sheffield Society for Constitutional Information was formed in Stoney Middleton, a mining village with a high proportion of Methodists. The intimate relationship between radicalism and print culture found its expression in the Peak Country in April 1793, when Thomas Bower, a bookseller of Winster, was arrested for selling editions of Tom Paine's *Rights of man*.

The organizational forms taken by semi-secret radicalism in the Peak at

---

[10] Whetstone, *Truths*, 16; BL, Add. MS 6676, fols. 130–60; SA, Bag C 587(71).
[11] MCL, Carill Worsley MS M35/2/44/41. Jeanette Neeson has recently suggested that enclosure encountered much more popular hostility in eighteenth-century England than has hitherto been supposed: see Neeson, *Commoners*, ch. 9.

the turn of the century suggest a spatial reordering of plebeian politics. Local radicals were drawn into a wider, inter-regional political organization. The growing town of Buxton, lying just outside the mining area, was listed as the centre of an organized network of some 330 radicals. In 1801, United Englishmen from Peak villages met with like-minded individuals from the towns around Manchester and Sheffield at Marple Bridge in north-east Cheshire. Their object was to establish a 'Society of Citizens' there and at Castleton, which would be maintained by force of arms. A government report later in that year claimed that 'emissaries of disaffection in Lancashire were attempting to convene a general meeting in Districts', which was to be centred upon the 'populous manufacturing districts in Derbyshire'. In the same year, the *Derby Mercury* warned of a plan to rally a force of radicals 'on the edge of Derbyshire to settle the affairs of the Nation'. We need not accept at face value exaggerated reports such as that which reached the Home Office in 1800 that the United Englishmen had levied some 50,000 people to their cause 'in Cheshire and Derbyshire' to see that insurrectionary plotters in the north-west assumed the existence of a pool of support within the Peak Country.[12]

The Luddite disturbances passed the heart of the Peak Country by, in 1812 touching only upon its southern fringes at Crich, and (in a recently discovered incident) its north-western bounds around New Mills.[13] None the less, the radicalism engendered by French Revolutionary ideas and rapid structural change had at least some roots in the deeper soil laid down by earlier habits of resistance. George Weightman, one of the leaders of the attempted rising at Pentrich in 1817, acquired his habit of insurrection from his participation in the militia riots around Bakewell in 1796. Like other radicals, and like many later socialists, Weightman was a Methodist.[14] In spite of the swift development of Methodism within the Peak in the 1780s and 1790s, the region did not possess its own Methodist circuit. Instead, like Peak Country radicalism, the organization and focus of its Methodism was centred upon Sheffield and Manchester. The torrent of class hatred charted in spies' reports to the Home Office, or in the threatening letters of the period, spoke of the immediate antagonism felt towards arbitrary government, exploitative employers, oppressive landlords and enclosing farmers. Many such words were tinged with the

---

12 Thomas, 'Friends of democracy', 42, 73, 78, 105–6; PRO, HO42/62, 28 July 1801, 31 August 1801; E. Fearn, 'The Derbyshire reform societies, 1791–1793', *DAJ*, 2nd ser., 88 (1968), 47–59. For the use of spies' reports in the investigation of underground radicalism, see especially R. Wells, *Insurrection: the British experience, 1795–1803* (London, 1983).

13 Thomas, 'Friends of democracy', 135–48; for Luddism in New Mills, see DRO, 1673Z/Z61; for gentry concerns in the Peak about Luddism, see DRO, D258M/41/18.

14 Thomas, 'Friends of democracy', 115; on the Pentrich rising, see J. Stevens, *England's last revolution: Pentrich, 1817* (Buxton, 1977).

rhetoric of a new political radicalism which communicated itself through print. The United Englishmen's card circulating in Castleton in 1801 required adherents to sign up to a political agenda which drew them beyond the smaller worlds of early modern social conflicts. Yet at the same time, the reported speech and actions of plebeians within the Peak at this time drew upon older standards and conventions. The enclosure commissioners on Stanton moor in 1791 were made to feel that they had made 'a narrow escape for their lives' from the 'mob'. The threat of armed force was there, like in the Grindlow riots of 1737; but the willingness to use it was not. We do not know how many Wensley miners had frequented Thomas Bower's Winster bookshop, where the *Rights of man* was on sale; but in its expropriatory impulse and threat, their reported speech of 1793 echoed rather more their ancestors' words in Grindlow in 1737, or Haddonfields in 1648, than Tom Paine's published rhetoric. Like the Luddites after them, and the Levellers before, the Bradwell miners spoke in a language of class drawn from a biblical idiom. Oppression and cruelty were seen as the source of class power, in which rich merchants were to be found 'grinding the face of the Poor'.

Like early modern enclosure rioters, this chapter has strayed beyond its bounds. We have roamed beyond the artificial border of early modernity, and ventured into the changed world of the early Industrial Revolution. This trespass finds its justification in two sources. First, a rough end-point in the plebeian politics of the Peak has been found. The historical characteristics of society, culture and popular politics in the Peak Country after 1770 have yet to be studied; what has been sketched here is only the crudest of caricatures. Yet it is suggestive. In the years which followed 1770, the economic and societal structures of the Peak began to twist into new forms. The appearance of a factory proletariat, combined with large-scale enclosure and the decline of the lead industry, shook loose some of the underpinnings of local plebeian politics. Methodism, political radicalism and organized labour developed within organizational structures which encompassed a wider area than the Peak Country, and which therefore created strong loyalties and new traditions which lay beyond the confines of the Peak's hills and valleys. The Ashover workers who signed up to the framework knitters' union founded their trade politics in the maintenance of regulations upheld within an industry which stretched through the South Midlands, rather than which sat within the Peak Country alone. Friendly societies within the Peak were organized on the same lines as those outside the region. Both underground and public radical organizations associated the Peak's radicals with those of Sheffield and Manchester.

In the 1790s, the plebeian culture *of* the Peak started to become a working-class culture *within* the Peak. The difference is important. One justification for the spatial and thematic demarcation of our study has been found in the intermingling of social conflict, custom, identities and cultures within a distinct and contemporaneously meaningful place in the early modern period: the Peak Country. In the latter third of the eighteenth century, that nexus in space began to break up. The effect was gradually to diminish the difference which had historically defined the plebeian politics of the Peak.

Our trespass lays claim to a second justification. Edward Thompson saw an autonomous, working-class political culture as born from the struggles of the period between 1780 and 1832. In his account, the making of the English working class was 'an active process', rather than a mechanistic product of structural change. Thus 'the working class did not rise like a sun at an appointed time. It was present at its own making'.[15] For Thompson, the period constituted a major breaking point in English social history. Yet within the violent fluctuations of discontinuity he traced connections to earlier struggles. Thompson's vision of class formation has been subject to increasing criticism. The long, painful birth of a working-class politics which Thompson charted, and its subsequent expression in Chartism, is now seen by many historians as rather the slow death of a sectionalist, artisanal politics. Exclusive of women and of the unskilled, crippled by the hangover of Whig ideas about natural rights, this politics is now considered to have had little to do with any unified, class-based political project. Instead, unable to face up to the realities of the permanence of industrial capitalism, artisanal radicalism and subsequently both Chartism and early socialism retreated into a nostalgic defence of fictional ancient rights and a yearning for a return to the land.[16]

This critique (much of it well founded in historical evidence, if sometimes driven by a misplaced iconoclasm) deprives Thompson's vision of class formation of its internal dynamic: its recognition of agency and movement within class politics. Unlike so many of his critics, Thompson recognized the diversity of earlier historical experiences on which the making of the English working class drew. In particular, his narrative remains founded upon an appreciation of the importance of earlier social, political and religious conflicts in the creation of working-class political ideology in the period of the Industrial Revolution.[17] We need not accept the entirety of

---

[15] Thompson, *Making*, 10.
[16] Stedman Jones, *Languages of class*, ch. 3, has had an enduring influence. For criticisms of this view of early working-class radicalism and Chartism, see N. Kirk, 'Class and the "linguistic turn" in Chartist and post-Chartist historiography', in Kirk (ed.), *Social class and Marxism*, 87–134; Wood, 'Place of custom', 59.
[17] Thompson, *Making*, 19–27; This appreciation is more apparent in his later work, especially *Customs in common*, chs. 1, 3, and *Witness against the beast: William Blake and the moral law* (Cambridge, 1993), chs. 1–7.

Thompson's account to see a distinct watershed in class politics and social relations as located in the 1780–1832 period. The importance of this disjuncture is best discerned from a long view of class formation. And here our trespass secures its second justification.

After 1832 a divided, uneven, but unmistakably working-class presence sits at the heart of politics, occupying a place which before 1770 was empty. A rather more standardized, rather less differentiated national working-class politics is apparent.[18] The qualifications are important; for regional difference continued, and continues, to play its part within working-class political culture.[19] Moreover, connections to earlier traditions remained. The exclusions of trade, honour, skill and gender by which groups like the Peak Country free miners had found their collective identity communicated themselves into the working-class culture of the nineteenth century. The identification with custom, the use of the law, the defence of quasi-legal institutions all formed important constituent elements of the political articulation of working-class interests in the early nineteenth century. Mystified by plebeian Jacobinism, a Peak free miner of the mid-seventeenth century might have found much in early nineteenth-century trade unionism quite comprehensible. Both traditions, after all, perceived of a binary opposition of class interest over the matter of custom, as 'Rich men' schemed to undo the legal and institutional fabric of rights and tradition within which the honour and independence of skilled working men were defined.

Like the radicals of the mid-seventeenth century, the ideologies of early nineteenth-century radicals and socialists were caught in a creative tension between a desire to return to lost liberties and a vision of a new society. Constructions of the historical past and images of possible futures blended within the radical and Chartist movements. In part, this ideological melange secured its blurred hegemony through its connection to surviving popular memories of lost rights. The radical and Chartist attachment to the land was not a product of a nostalgic conservatism. Instead, the fact of enclosure acted as a kind of metaphor out of which a radical historical narrative could be developed. As it weighed like a nightmare on the brains of the living, this sense of the past shaped and defined the broader culture of English radicalism, Chartism and early socialism.

Those local rights and customary laws which survived into the early nineteenth century – and they were rather more numerous and important than many social historians of that period, fixated upon the consequences of urbanization and industrialization, have imagined – continued to sustain the

---

[18] See G. Eley, 'Edward Thompson, social history and political culture: the making of a working-class public, 1780–1850', in Kaye and McClelland (eds.), *E.P. Thompson*, 12–49.
[19] Joyce, *Visions of the people*, chs. 11–12, conveys this regionalism with authority.

independence of poor plebeian and working-class households.[20] But their survival also suggested something of a world which the radicals imagined they had lost. Radicals constructed a vision of English history before the cataclysm of enclosure, in which an organic democracy of small producers, regulated by custom and good practice, was thought to have abided. Like all founder myths, this vision had at least some roots in historical reality. Moreover, survivals of earlier traditions and rights could operate upon local working-class cultures in ways which were unpredictable.

Working-class politics was not born fully formed out of the coal pit and the cotton mill. In the Forest of Dean and in Lanarkshire, traditions of free mining fed into later Chartism and organized trade unionism.[21] In Derbyshire, a hostile employing class and 'tyrannical landlords' still threatened mining custom in the nineteenth century. What remained of the free mining code was limited still further in these years; but never wholly obliterated. In a curious throwback to the seventeenth century, the free miners of Winster made complaint to the barmaster in the 1870s that they had been expelled from their works by the agents of a large mining concern.[22] Free mining continued within parts of the Peak, regarded by some landlords almost as a form of charitable poor relief, but yet by others as an infuriating infringement of private property.

With the decline of many English free mining communities after the late eighteenth century, some miners emigrated to North America. They took their laws and traditions with them. By the mid-nineteenth century, strangely similar versions of Derbyshire, Cornish and Forest of Dean customs were in operation beyond the frontier mining townships. While it lasted, the libertarian conditions of this 'poor man's paradise' led many miners back to a hostility to 'wage slavery'. Just as in the early modern Peak, these new mining customs were at first given the force of law before being undercut and eventually obliterated by large mining companies.[23]

---

[20] See for instance M. Reed, 'The peasantry of nineteenth-century rural England: a neglected class?', *History Workshop*, 18 (1984), 53–76.

[21] Campbell and Reid, 'The independent collier', 68–71; Fisher, *Custom, work and market capitalism, passim.*

[22] Bryan, *Matlock*, 300; Wright, *Longstone records*, 339; Farey, *General view*, I, 356, 364; Glover, *History of Derby*, I, 75; DRO, D161 Box 4/128; DRO, 1836M/L17.

[23] P.J. Naylor, 'John Burton of Bonsall, Derbyshire, and Iowa, USA 1795–1854', *BPDMHS*, 10, 1 (1987),4–12; M. Neuschatz, *The golden sword: the coming of capitalism to the Colorado mining frontier* (New York, 1986), 9–23; Raistrick and Jennings, *Lead mining, 325*; S. Dempsey, 'Mining district rules: popular law making on the American mining frontier', *BPDMHS*, 10, 4 (1988), 242–7; M. Lewis, *The mining frontier: contemporary accounts from the American West in the nineteenth century* (Oklahoma City, 1967), 7–19, 107; D.A. Smith, *Rocky Mountain mining camps: the urban frontier* (Indiana, 1967), 4, 47–8; R. Wilson Paul, *Mining frontiers of the far West, 1848–1880* (New York, 1963), 23–4, 169–75; J. Rowe, *The hard-rock men: Cornish immigrants to the North American mining frontier* (New York, 1974).

Genealogies of ideas and movements can reveal strange, repetitive cross-currents. In 1919, free mining was revived in the Winster area by a group of lead miners who had been blacklisted for their part in an earlier strike. Finance for their mining operations came from the Derbyshire Miners' Association. Finally limited and recodified in Acts of 1851 and 1852, the free mining laws which had first been specified in 1288 now fed into the syndicalism of early twentieth-century miners' unionism.[24]

That some Peak miners clung stubbornly to their rights to the bitter end amazed early twentieth-century observers and current labour historians alike. Comments of 1932 about the miners might as well have come from three hundred years earlier:

Deep down in every man born of this country there is an undefinable attitude that makes him part of the past. He looks into the future but little, but will fight with blind instinct and without reason for some immemorial nothing that brings him neither goods nor benefits except the simple satisfaction of having observed some nebulous right.[25]

Yet that 'nebulous right' continued to guarantee a measure of economic independence in the 1930s, and secured the remaining fragments of a collective identity. Again, the spirit connects to the past. William Hooson's eulogy of 1747 of his friend John Staley's defence of 'your Auncient Mineral Customs and Privilidges, acquired and settled many Ages ago, by the Care and Pains of your Worthy Ancestors', might easily be mistaken as evidence of the 'reactionary' and 'nostalgic' ideology of an anachronistic social group.[26] But Hooson's understanding of the past informed his vision of the future. His friend's defence of custom was motivated by the desire that 'Posterity might enjoy the benefit' of those rights.[27] In the late sixteenth and early seventeenth centuries, through their active political engagement, the miners of the Derbyshire Peak Country won a remarkable series of rights. After the Restoration, the generations which followed them settled down to a tenacious defence of their 'ancient' customs, such that even in the hard times of the 1930s it was still possible to avoid the humiliations of the Means Test by digging for ore in the King's Field.

---

[24] Willies, 'The working of the Derbyshire lead mining customs', 152; J.E. Williams, *The Derbyshire miners: a study in industrial and social history* (London, 1962), 538, 600–3.
[25] Williams, 'Derbyshire mining', 90.
[26] Quoting Campbell and Reid, 'Independent collier', 70.
[27] Hooson, *Miners' dictionary*, 198.

BIBLIOGRAPHY

MANUSCRIPT SOURCES

BRITISH LIBRARY, LONDON

Additional MS 24544 — Hunter's annotated copy of J. Brand, *Observations on popular antiquities* (London, 1813), I

Additional MS 32465 — Book of transcripts of mining customs, *c.* 1620

Additional MSS 64908–18 — Coke MSS

Additional MSS 6666–704 — Woolley MSS

Harleian MS 594 — 1563 ecclesiastical census

Harleian MS 6833 — Civil war papers

Lansdowne MS 231 — J. Aubrey, 'Remains of Gentilisme and Judaisme', 1687

Loan MS 16 — Court of mines royal minute book, 1662–70

CHATSWORTH HOUSE, BAKEWELL

BC: barmaster's collection

Deeds and charters

Unlisted seventeenth- and eighteenth-century mining documents

Unlisted 1634–8 book of rentals

William Senior's atlas

DERBY CENTRAL LIBRARY, DERBY

Pamphlet collection

Lead mining collection

DERBYSHIRE RECORD OFFICE, MATLOCK

D158M — Beresford MSS

D200B/M1 — Hill Carr sough minute book, 1777–90

D253 — Ashover parish records

D258M — Chandos-Pole-Gell MSS

D267Z/229c — Immanuel Bourne's letter, 1646

D504B — Brooke-Taylor MSS

D747 — Ashford chapelry and parish records

D776	Winster chapelry and parish records
D803M	Gresley MSS
D1038A	Hope parish records
D1232M	Sanders MSS
D1289B	Rieuwerts MSS
D1673Z/Z61	Letter concerning Luddites, 1812
D2270/1	Microfilm of Scottish Record Office GD345/824
D2057	Bakewell Parish records
D2143Z/Z1&2	Microfilm of PRO, RGO33
D3105	Bakewell parish records
D3644	Youlgreave parish records
QSB2, QSC	Quarter Sessions papers
QAB	Quarter Sessions petitions
Q/SO/1/1	Quarter Sessions order book, 1682–1703

HOUSE OF LORDS RECORD OFFICE, LONDON

Main papers 1624, 1642–8

JOHN RYLANDS LIBRARY, MANCHESTER

Bagshawe muniments
Nicholas MSS

LAMBETH PALACE LIBRARY, LONDON

Shrewsbury MSS
Talbot MSS

LICHFIELD JOINT RECORD OFFICE, LICHFIELD

B/C/5	Consistory Court cause papers
B/C/11	Wills and inventories
B/V/1	Visitation books

MANCHESTER CENTRAL LIBRARY, MANCHESTER

M35	Carill Worsley MSS

MIDDLE TEMPLE LIBRARY, LONDON

Treby's MSS law reports, 22–4 Chas II

NOTTINGHAMSHIRE ARCHIVES OFFICE, NOTTINGHAM

DD.FM 83/1	Book of profits and expenses, 1658, Haddon and Belvoir
DD.P	Portland MSS

NOTTINGHAM UNIVERSITY LIBRARY, NOTTINGHAM

Middleton MS, 4/126/11	1566 Wirksworth Great Barmote laws

PUBLIC RECORD OFFICE, LONDON

C 2, 3	Chancery, proceedings
C21	Chancery, country depositions, Elizabeth to Charles I
DL1	Duchy of Lancaster, bills and answers
DL3	Duchy of Lancaster, depositions, Henry VII to Mary
DL4	Duchy of Lancaster, depositions, Elizabeth to Victoria
DL5	Duchy of Lancaster, entry books of decrees and orders
DL6	Duchy of Lancaster, draft decrees
DL8	Duchy of Lancaster, draft injunctions
DL9	Duchy of Lancaster, affidavits
DL30	Duchy of Lancaster, manorial rolls
DL37	Duchy of Lancaster, chancery rolls
DL41	Duchy of Lancaster, miscellanea
DL42	Duchy of Lancaster, lease books
DL43	Duchy of Lancaster, rentals and surveys
DL44	Duchy of Lancaster, special commissions
E101	Exchequer, King's Remembrancer, various accounts
E112	Exchequer, King's Remembrancer, bills and answers
E126–8	Exchequer, King's Remembrancer, entry book, decrees and orders
E134	Exchequer, King's Remembrancer, depositions by commission
E178	Exchequer, King's Remembrancer, special commissions
E179	Exchequer, King's Remembrancer, Lay Subsidies
E317	Exchequer, King's Remembrancer, parliamentary surveys
HO42	Home Office, correspondence
IND1	Contemporary lists and alphabets
MINT15	Royal Mint, prosecutions for coinage offences
PC2	Privy Council registers
REQ2	Requests, proceedings
SP1	State Papers, Henry VIII
SP12	State Papers, Elizabeth I
SP14	State Papers, James I
SP16	State Papers, Charles I
SP18	State Papers, Interregnum
SP19	State Papers, Committee for the Advance of Money
SP23	State Papers, Committee for Compounding with Delinquents
SP25	State Papers, Council of State minute books
SP28	State Papers, Commonwealth Exchequer Papers
SP29	State Papers, Charles II
SP31	State Papers, James II
STAC2	Star Chamber, Henry VIII
STAC3	Star Chamber, Edward VI
STAC4	Star Chamber, Philip and Mary
STAC5	Star Chamber, Elizabeth I
STAC7	Star Chamber, Elizabeth I, addenda
STAC8	Star Chamber, James I
STAC9	Star Chamber, Charles I

SHEFFIELD ARCHIVES, SHEFFIELD

ACM   Arundel Castle muniments
BFM2   Bacon Frank MSS
Bag C   Bagshawe collection
Bar D   Barker deeds
BM   Beauchief muniments
CM   Crewe muniments
JC   Jackson collection
OD   Oakes deeds
PhC   Photocopy collection
SpSt   Spenser Stanhope collection
TC   Tibbetts collection
WWM   Wentworth Woodhouse muniments

CONTEMPORARY PRINTED BOOKS AND NEWSPAPERS

Aikin, J., *A description of the country from thirty to forty miles round Manchester* (London, 1795).
Anonymous, *Theeves, theeves, or a relation of John Gell's proceedings in Derbyshire* (London, 1642), BL, TT E. 100 (13).
The case of a publique business touching the mines in Darby-shire (*c.* 1649).
Two most strange wonders (London, 1661) BL, TT E. 1874 (4).
Account of the wonders of Derbyshire (London, 1779).
Bagshawe, W., *De spiritualibus pecci* (London, 1702).
Bourne, I., *A defence and justification of ministers maintenance by tythes* (1659).
Bray, W., *Sketch of a tour into Derbyshire and Yorkshire* (London, 1777).
Calthorpe, C., *A relation between the lord of a manor and the coppyholder his tenant* (London, 1635).
Camden, W., *Britannia* (1596; Eng. trans., London, 1610).
Cotton, C., *The wonders of the Peak* (London, 1681).
Gilpin, W., *Observations, relative chiefly to picturesque beauty made in the year 1772 on several parts of England*, 2 vols. (3rd edn, London, 1792).
Houghton, T., *Rara avis in terris, or the compleat miner* (London, 1681).
Leigh, C., *The natural history of Lancashire, Cheshire and the Peak in Derbyshire* (London, 1700).
Linden, D.W., *A letter to William Hooson* (London, 1747).
Pettus, J., *Fodinae regales, or the history, laws and places of the chief mines and mineral works in England, Wales and the English Pale in Ireland* (London, 1670).
Steer, G., *Compleat mineral laws of Derbyshire* (London, 1734).
Stringer, G., *English and Welsh mines and minerals discovered* (London, 1699).
Waller, W., *An essay on the value of mines* (London, 1698).
Whetstone, C., *Truths no. 1, or the memoirs of Charles Whetstone, or an exposition of the oppression and cruelty exercised in the trades and manufactures of Great Britain* (London, 1807).

NEWSBOOKS

Certain Informations
England's Memorable Accidents
The Kingdomes Faithfull Scout
Mercurius Elencticus
Mercurius Pragmaticus
The Moderate
The Moderate Messenger
The Modest Intelligencer
A Modest Narrative
A Perfect Diurnall
Perfect Occurrences

EDITIONS OF MANUSCRIPTS AND CONTEMPORARY PRINTED
WORKS, AND CALENDARS

Anonymous, 'The journal of Mr. John Hobson, late of Dodworth Green', in *Yorkshire diaries and autobiographies in the seventeenth and eighteenth centuries*, Surtees Soc., 65 (London, 1875), 245–300.
'Vills and freeholders of Derbyshire, 1633', *DAJ*, 1st ser., 6 (1884), 49–74.
'Letter from Derbyshire concerning lead-mining', *DAJ*, 2nd ser., 10 (1936), 130–2.
Andrews, C.B. and Andrews, F. (eds.), *The Torrington diaries: a selection from the tours of the Hon. John Byng (later Fifth Viscount Torrington) between the years 1781 and 1794* (London, 1954).
Bamford, S., *Early days* (London, 1849).
Bateson, E. (ed.), *Calendar of State Papers series, of the reign of William III*, 5 vols. (London, 1927–37).
Bickley, F. and Cantrell, J.D. (eds.), *Calendar of State Papers series, 1685–9*, (London 1960–72).
Bunyan, J., *The life and death of Mr. Badman* (1680; London, 1928 edn).
Clifford, J.G. and Clifford, F. (eds.), *Eyam parish register, 1630–1700*, DRS, 21 (Chesterfield, 1993).
Cox, J.C., 'A religious census of Derbyshire, 1676', *DAJ*, 1st ser., 7 (1885), 31–6.
Three centuries of Derbyshire annals, 2 vols. (London, 1890).
Cunningham, W., 'Common rights at Cottenham and Stretham in Cambridgeshire', *Camden Miscellany*, new ser., 12 (1910), 173–289.
Darnborough, G., 'A Wirksworth mine agent's letter', *BPDMHS*, 7, 6 (1980), 326.
Defoe, D., *A tour through the whole island of Great Britain* (1724–6; abridged edn, London, 1971).
Edwards, D.G., *Derbyshire Hearth Tax assessments, 1662–70*, DRS, 7 (Chesterfield, 1982).
Everett Green, M.A. (ed.), *Calendar of State Papers series, of the reign of James I*, 5 vols. (London, 1857–9).
Calendar of State Papers series, Commonwealth, 13 vols. (London, 1875–86).
Calendar of the Proceedings of the Committee for the Advance of Money, 1642–56, 3 vols. (London, 1888).
Calendar of the proceedings for the Committee for Compounding with Delinquents, 1643–60, 5 vols. (London, 1889–92).

Everett Green, M.A., Blakburne Daniell, F.H., and Bickley, F. (eds.), *Calendar of State Papers series, of the reign of Charles II*, 28 vols. (London, 1860–1938).

Farey, J., *A general view of the agriculture and minerals of Derbyshire*, 3 vols. (London, 1815).

Fletcher, W.G.D., 'Philip Kinder's MS "Historie of Darbyshire"', *Reliquary*, 23 (1882–3), 181–5.

Fowkes, D.V. and Potter, G.R. (eds.), *William Senior's survey of the estates of the first and second Earls of Devonshire, c. 1600–28*, DRS, 13 (Chesterfield, 1988).

Fuller, T., *The worthies of England* (1652; London, 1952 edn).

Gardiner, S.R. (ed.), *Reports of cases in the Star Chamber and High Commission*, Camden Society, new ser., 39 (1886).

Glover, S., *A history and gazetteer of the county of Derby*, 2 vols. (Derby, 1829).

Gratton, J., *Journal of the life of that ancient servant of Christ* (London, 1720).

Hamilton, W.D. (ed.), *Calendar of State Papers series, of the reign of Charles I*, 23 vols. (London, 1858–97).

Hardy, W.J., *Calendar of State Papers series, of the Reign of William and Mary*, 6 vols. (London, 1895–1906).

Historical Manuscripts Commission, *Report on the manuscripts of . . . the Duke of Portland*, 10 vols. (1886–1931).

Hooson, W., *The miner's dictionary* (1747; repr. Ilkley, 1979).

Hopkinson, G., *The laws and customs of the mines within the Wapentake of Wirksworth* (1644; repr. Nottingham, 1948).

Kiernan, D. (ed.), 'Lawrence Oxley's accounts', in D. Kiernan (ed.), *A seventeenth century Scarsdale miscellany*, DRS, 20 (Chesterfield, 1993), 121–44.

Lyon Turner, G., *Original records of early nonconformity under persecution and indulgence* (London, 1911).

Mander, J., *The Derbyshire miners' glossary* (Bakewell, 1824).

Manlove, E., 'The liberties and customs of the lead mines within the Wapentake of Wirksworth', repr. in W.W. Skeat (ed.), *Reprinted glossaries* (London, 1873), 9–20.

Morris, C. (ed.), *The journeys of Celia Fiennes* (London, 1947).

Roche Dascent, J., Penfold, P.A. *et al.* (eds.), *Acts of the Privy Council of England new series 1590–1631*, 28 vols. (London, 1899–1964).

Sharpe France, R. (ed.), *The Thieveley lead mines 1629–35*, Lancashire and Cheshire Record Society, 52 (Preston, 1947).

Toulmin Smith, L. (ed.), *The itinerary of John Leland in or about the years 1535–43*, 5 vols. (London, 1964).

Whiteman, A. and Clapinson, M. (eds.), *The Compton census of 1676: a critical edition*, British Academy Records of Social and Economic History, new ser., 10 (London, 1986).

BOOKS AND ARTICLES

Abrams, P., *Historical sociology* (Shepton Mallet, 1982).

Allan, D.G.C., 'The rising of the West Country, 1628–1631', *EcHR*, 2nd ser., 5, 1 (1952), 76–85.

Amussen, S.D., *An ordered society: gender and class in early modern England* (Oxford, 1988).

Appleby, J.O., *Economic thought and ideology in seventeenth century England* (Princeton, 1978).

Arriaza, A., 'Mounsier and Barber: the theoretical underpinning of the "society of orders" in early modern Europe', *P&P*, 89 (1980), 39–57.

Bagshawe, W.H.G., *A memoir of William Bagshawe . . . styled the apostle of the Peak* (London, 1887).

Barnatt, J. and Smith, K., *The Peak District: landscapes through time* (London, 1997).

Barry, J. and Brooks, C. (eds.), *The middling sort of people: culture, society and politics in England, 1550–1800* (Basingstoke, 1994).

Beer, B.L., *Rebellion and riot: popular disorder during the reign of Edward VI* (Kent, Ohio, 1982).

Bennett, M., ' "My plundered townes, my houses devastation": the civil war and North Midlands life', *Midland History*, 22 (1997), 35–50.

Berg, M., *The age of manufactures, 1700–1820* (London, 1985).

'Workers and machinery in eighteenth-century England', in J. Rule (ed.), *British trade unionism, 1750–1850: the formative years* (London, 1988), 52–73.

Berg, M. and Hudson, P., 'Rehabilitating the Industrial Revolution', *EcHR*, 2nd ser., 45, 2 (1992) 24–50.

Bettey, J.H., 'The revolts over the enclosure of the Royal Forest at Gillingham, 1626–1630', *Dorset Natural History and Archaeology Society*, 97 (1975), 21–4.

Blanchard, I.S.W., 'The miner and the agricultural community in late medieval England', *AgHR*, 20 (1970), 93–106.

Derbyshire lead production, 1195–1505', *DAJ*, 2nd ser., 91 (1971), 119–31.

The Duchy of Lancaster's estates in Derbyshire, 1485–1540, DRS, 3 (Chesterfield, 1971).

'Rejoinder: Stannator Fabulosus', *AgHR*, 22 (1974), 62–74.

'English lead and the international bullion crisis of the 1550s', in D.C. Coleman and A.H. John (eds.), *Trade, government and economy in pre-industrial England: essays presented to F.J. Fisher* (London, 1976), 21–44.

'Labour productivity and work psychology in the English mining industry, 1400–1600', *EcHR*, 2nd ser., 31 (1978), 1–21.

'Industrial employment and the rural land market 1380–1520', in R.M. Smith (ed.), *Land, kinship and life-cycle* (Cambridge, 1984), 227–75.

Russia's 'age of silver': precious-metal production and economic growth in the eighteenth century (London, 1989).

Bossy, J., *The English Catholic community 1570–1850* (London, 1975).

Bowles, C.E.B., 'Agreement of the freeholders of Eyam to the award for dividing Eyam pasture, 12th November 1702', *DAJ*, 1st ser., 20 (1898), 1–11.

Brailsford, H.N., *The Levellers and the English Revolution* (London, 1961).

Braylesford Bunting, W., *Chapel-en-le-Frith: its history and its people* (Manchester, 1940).

Brenner, R., 'Agrarian class structure and economic development in pre-industrial Europe', in T.H. Aston and C.H.E. Philpin (eds.), *The Brenner debate: agrarian class structure and economic development in pre-industrial Europe* (Cambridge, 1985), 10–63.

Brentnall, J.M., *William Bagshawe: the Apostle of the Peak* (London, 1970).

Brighton, J.T., *Royalists and Roundheads in Derbyshire* (Bakewell, no date).

Brushfield, T., 'Customs and notions at Ashford-in-the-water sixty years ago', *Reliquary*, 5 (1864–5), 11–14.

'A second notice of customs, notions and practices at Ashford-in-the-water sixty years ago', *Reliquary,* 5 (1864–5), 152–5.

Bryan, B., *Matlock: manor and parish, historical and descriptive* (London, 1903).

Bryson, W.H., *The equity side of the Exchequer: its jurisdiction, administration, procedures and records* (Cambridge, 1975).

Burt, R., 'Lead production in England and Wales, 1700–1770', *EcHR,* 2nd ser., 22, 2 (1969), 249–68.

'The international diffusion of technology in the early modern period: the case of the British non-ferrous mining industry', *EcHR,* 2nd ser., 45, 2 (1991), 249–71.

'The transformation of the non-ferrous metals industries in the seventeenth and eighteenth centuries', *EcHR,* 2nd ser., 48, 1 (1995), 23–45.

Bushaway, B., *By rite: custom, ceremony and community in England, 1700–1880* (London, 1982).

'"Tacit, unsuspected, but still implicit faith": alternative belief in nineteenth century rural England', in T. Harris (ed.), *Popular culture in England, 1500–1850* (Basingstoke, 1995), 189–215.

Campbell, A. and Reid, F., 'The independent collier in Scotland', in R. Harrison (ed.), *Independent collier: the coal miner as an archetypal proletarian reconsidered* (Sussex, 1978), 54–74.

Campbell, B.M.S., 'The population of early Tudor England: a re-evaluation of the 1522 muster returns and the 1524 and 1525 Lay Subsidies', *Journal of Historical Geography,* 7, 2 (1981), 145–54.

Cannadine, D., 'The past and the present in the Industrial Revolution, 1880–1980', *P&P,* 103 (1984), 131–49.

Capp, B., 'Separate domains? Women and authority in early modern England', in P. Griffiths, A. Fox and S. Hindle (eds.), *The experience of authority in early modern England* (Basingstoke, 1996), 117–45.

Carlin, N., 'Liberty and fraternities in the English Revolution: the politics of the London artisans' protests, 1635–1659', *International Review of Social History,* 39 (1994), 223–54.

Carr, J.P., 'Open field agriculture in mid-Derbyshire', *DAJ,* 2nd ser., 83 (1963), 66–81.

Carroll, W.C., '"The nursery of beggary": enclosure, vagrancy and sedition in the Tudor–Stuart period', in R. Burt and J.M. Archer (eds.), *Enclosure acts: sexuality, property and culture in early modern England* (Ithaca, 1994), 34–47.

C.E.L., *The 'saints and sinners' of Ashover* (Leicester, 1924).

Charles, L. and Duffin, L. (eds.), *Women and work in pre-industrial England* (London, 1985).

Charlesworth, A. and Randall, A., 'Comment: morals, markets and the crowd in 1766', *P&P,* 114 (1987), 200–13.

Clark, A., *Working life of women in the seventeenth century* (1919; 3rd edn, London, 1992).

Clark, A., *The struggle for the breeches: gender and the making of the British working class* (London, 1995).

Clark, J.C.D., *English society, 1688–1832* (Cambridge, 1985).

Clark, P., 'Popular protest and disturbance in Kent, 1558–1640', *EcHR,* 2nd ser., 29, 3 (1976), 365–82.

'Migration in England during the late seventeenth and early eighteenth centuries', in P. Clark and D. Souden (eds.), Migration and society in early modern England (London, 1987), 213–52.

Clark, P. and Slack, P. (eds.), Crisis and order in English towns, 1500–1700: essays in urban history (London, 1972).

Clay, C.G.A., Economic expansion and social change: England, 1500–1700, 2 vols. (Cambridge, 1984).

Collinson, P., De republica anglorum, or, history with the politics put back in (Cambridge, 1990).

Coveney, P.J. (ed.), France in crisis, 1620–1675 (Totawa, 1977).

Cressy, D., Literacy and the social order: reading and writing in Tudor and Stuart England (Cambridge, 1980).

Curry, P., 'Towards a post-Marxist social history: Thompson, Clark and beyond', in A. Wilson (ed.), Rethinking social history: English society, 1570–1920 and its interpretation (Manchester, 1993), 158–200.

Daniel, M., 'The early lead industry and the ancient demesne of the Peak', BPDMHS, 8, 3 (1982), 168–70.

'The origin of the barmote court system: a new theory', BPDMHS, 8, 3 (1982), 166–7.

Davidoff, L. and Hall, C., Family fortunes: men and women of the English middle class, 1780–1850 (London, 1987).

Davies, C.S.L., 'Peasant revolt in France and England: a comparison', AgHR, 21 (1973), 122–34.

Davis, J.C., 'Radicalism in a traditional society: the evaluation of radical thought in the English Commonwealth, 1649–60', History of Political Thought, 3, 2 (1982), 193–213.

Davis, N.Z., Society and culture in early modern France (Stanford, 1975).

Dempsey, S., 'Mining district rules: popular law making on the American mining frontier', BPDMHS, 10, 4 (1988), 242–7.

Dias, J.R., 'Lead, society and politics in Derbyshire before the civil war', Midland History, 6 (1981), 39–57.

Dobb, M., Studies in the development of capitalism (London, 1948).

Dobson, C.R., Masters and journeymen: a prehistory of industrial relations, 1717–1800 (London, 1980).

Doe, V.S., 'The common fields of Beeley in the seventeenth century', DAJ, 2nd ser., 93 (1973), 45–54.

Dow, F.D., Radicalism in the English Revolution (Oxford, 1985).

Eley, G., 'Edward Thompson, social history and political culture: the making of a working-class public, 1780–1850', in H.J. Kaye and K. McClelland (eds.), E.P. Thompson: critical perspectives (Oxford, 1990), 12–49.

Everitt, A., The community of Kent and the Great Rebellion, 1640–60 (Leicester, 1960).

The local community and the Great Rebellion (London, 1969).

Fearn, E., 'The Derbyshire reform societies, 1791–1793', DAJ, 2nd ser., 88 (1968), 47–59.

Fentress, J. and Whickham, C., Social memory (Oxford, 1992).

Fisher, C., Custom, work and market capitalism: the Forest of Dean colliers, 1788–1888 (London, 1981).

Fisher, F.N., 'Sir Cornelius Vermuyden and the Dovegang lead mine', DAJ, 2nd ser., 72 (1952), 74–118.

Fitton, R.S., The Arkwrights: spinners of fortune (Manchester, 1989).

Fletcher, A., 'Petitioning and the outbreak of civil war in Derbyshire', *DAJ*, 2nd ser., 93 (1973), 33–44.

The outbreak of the civil war (London, 1981).

Fletcher, A. and Stevenson, J., 'Introduction', in A. Fletcher and J. Stevenson (eds.), *Order and disorder in early modern England* (Cambridge, 1985).

Fletcher, J.M., 'Notes on the history of Tideswell and its manor', *DAJ*, 1st ser., 41, (1919), 1–37.

Ford, T.D. and Rieuwerts, J.H., *Lead mining in the Peak District* (1968; 3rd edn Matlock, 1983).

Foster, J., *Class struggle and the Industrial Revolution: early industrial capitalism in three industrial towns* (London, 1974).

Fox, A, 'Rumour, news and popular political opinion in Elizabethan and early Stuart England', *Historical Journal*, 40, 3 (1997), 597–620.

Frank, J., *The Levellers: a history of the writings of three seventeenth-century social democrats: John Lilburne, Richard Overton, William Walwyn* (Cambridge, Mass., 1955).

Gay, E.F., 'The Midland Revolt and the inquisitions of depopulation of 1607', *Transactions of the Royal Historical Society*, 2nd ser., 18 (1904), 195–244.

Gill, M.C., 'Mining and proto-industrialization', *British Mining*, 41 (1990), 99–110.

Gough, J.W., *The mines of Mendip* (Oxford, 1930).

Gowing, L., *Domestic dangers: women, words and sex in early modern London* (Oxford, 1996).

Gregg, P., *Free-born John: a biography of John Lilburne* (London, 1961).

Gurney, J., 'Gerrard Winstanley and the Digger movement in Walton and Cobham', *Historical Journal*, 37 (1994), 775–802.

Hainsworth, D.R., *Stewards, lords and people: the estate steward and his world in later Stuart England* (Cambridge, 1992).

Harris, L.E., *Vermuyden and the fens: a study of Sir Cornelius Vermuyden* (London, 1953).

Harris, T., *London crowds in the reign of Charles II: propaganda and politics from the Restoration until the Exclusion Crisis* (Cambridge, 1987).

'Problematising popular culture', in T. Harris (ed.), *Popular culture in England, 1500–1850* (Basingstoke, 1995), 1–27.

Hart, C.E., *The free miners of the Forest of Dean and the Hundred of St. Briavels* (Gloucester, 1953).

Hart, C.R., *The north Derbyshire archaeological survey to A.D. 1500* (Chesterfield, 1981).

Hatcher, J., 'Myths, miners and agricultural communities', *AgHR*, 22 (1974), 54–61.

Hay, D. and Rodgers, N., *Eighteenth-century English society* (Oxford, 1997).

Henstock, A., 'The Ashbourne inquiry of 1288: a reply', *BPDMHS*, 7, 2 (1978), 96–9.

Hey, D., *Packmen, carriers and packhorse roads: trade and communications in north Derbyshire and south Yorkshire* (Leicester, 1980).

The fiery blades of Hallamshire: Sheffield and its neighbourhood, 1660–1714 (Leicester, 1991).

'The Dragon of Wantley: rural popular culture and local legend', *Rural History*, 4, 1 (1993), 23–40.

Hill, C., 'The Norman yoke', in C. Hill, *Puritanism and Revolution: studies in interpretation of the English Revolution of the seventeenth century* (London, 1958), 58–125.

Reformation to Industrial Revolution (Harmondsworth, 1967).

The world turned upside down: radical ideas during the English Revolution (London, 1972).

Change and continuity in seventeenth century England (London, 1974).

Hilton, R. (ed.), *The transition from feudalism to capitalism* (London, 1976).

Hindle, S., 'Persuasion and protest in the Caddington common enclosure dispute, 1635–1639', *P&P*, 158 (1998), 37–78.

'The political culture of the middling sort in English rural communities, *c.* 1550–1700', in T. Harris (ed.), *The politics of the excluded in early modern England* (Basingstoke, forthcoming).

Hobsbawm, E., *Primitive rebels: studies in archaic forms of social movement in the 19th and 20th centuries* (New York, 1965).

Hodges, R., *Wall-to-wall history: the story of Roystone Grange* (London, 1991).

Holmes, C., 'The county community in Stuart historiography', *Journal of British Studies*, 19 (1980), 54–75.

'Drainers and fenmen: the problem of popular political consciousness in the seventeenth century', in A. Fletcher and J. Stevenson (eds.), *Order and disorder in early modern England* (Cambridge, 1985), 166–97.

Honeyman, K., *Origins of enterprise: business leadership in the Industrial Revolution* (Manchester, 1982).

Hopkinson, G.G., 'Lead mining in 18th century Ashover', *DAJ*, 2nd ser., 72 (1952), 1–21.

'Lead mining in the Eyam district in the eighteenth century', *DAJ*, 2nd ser., 80 (1960), 80–97.

Houlbrooks, R., *Church courts and the people during the English Reformation, 1520–1570* (Oxford, 1979).

'Women's social life and common action in England from the fifteenth century to the eve of the civil war', *Continuity and change*, 1 (1986), 171–90.

Houston, R.A., *Scottish literacy and Scottish identity: illiteracy and society in Scotland and northern England, 1600–1800* (Cambridge, 1985).

Howkins, A. and Merricks, L., '"Wee be black as hell": ritual, disguise and rebellion', *Rural History*, 4, 1 (1993), 41–53.

Hoyle, R.W., 'Lords, tenants and tenant right in the sixteenth century: four studies', *Northern History*, 20 (1984), 38–63.

'An ancient and laudable custom: the definition and development of tenant right in north-western England in the sixteenth century', *P&P*, 116 (1987), 24–55.

Hoyle, R.W. (ed.), *The estates of the English Crown, 1558–1640* (Cambridge, 1992).

Hudson, P., 'Proto-industrialisation: the case of the West Riding', *History Workshop*, 12 (1981), 34–61.

'The regional perspective', in P. Hudson (ed.), *Regions and industries: a perspective on the Industrial Revolution in Britain* (Cambridge, 1989), 5–40.

The Industrial Revolution (London, 1992).

Hughes, A., *Politics, society and civil war in Warwickshire, 1620–1660* (Cambridge, 1987).

'Local history and the origins of the civil war', in R. Cust and A. Hughes (eds.), *Conflict in early Stuart England: studies in religion and politics, 1603–42* (London, 1989), 224–53.

The causes of the English civil war (London, 1991).

Humphries, J., 'Enclosures, common rights and women: the proletarianization of families in the late eighteenth and early nineteenth centuries', *Journal of Economic History*, 50, 1 (1990), 17–42.

Hunt, C.J., *The lead miners of the northern Pennines in the eighteenth and nineteenth centuries* (Manchester, 1970).

Husbands, C., 'Regional change in a pre-industrial economy: wealth and population in the sixteenth and seventeenth centuries', *Journal of Historical Geography*, 13, 4 (1987), 345–59.

'Hearths, wealth and occupations: an exploration of the Hearth Tax in the later seventeenth century', in K. Schurer and T. Arkell (eds.), *Surveying the people: the interpretation and use of document sources for the study of population in the late seventeenth century* (Oxford, 1992), 65–77.

Ingram, M.J., *Church courts, sex and marriage in England, 1570–1640* (Oxford, 1987).

Johnson, K.H., 'Folklore and superstition in mines', *BPDMHS*, 5, 3 (1973), 156–9.

Johnson, M., *An archaeology of capitalism* (Oxford, 1996).

Joyce, P., *Work, society and politics: the culture of the factory in later Victorian England* (London, 1980).

Visions of the people: industrial England and the question of class, 1840–1914 (Cambridge, 1991).

Democratic subjects: the self and the social in nineteenth-century England (Cambridge, 1994).

'The end of social history?', *Social History*, 20, 1 (1995), 73–91.

Joyce, P. (ed.), *Class: a reader* (Oxford, 1995).

Kerridge, E., 'The revolts in Wiltshire against Charles I', *Wiltshire Archaeological and Natural History Magazine*, 57 (1958), 64–75.

Kershaw, S.E. 'Power and duty in the Elizabethan aristocracy: George, Earl of Shrewsbury, the Glossopdale dispute and the Council', in G.W. Bernard (ed.), *The Tudor nobility* (Manchester, 1992), 266–95.

Kiernan, D., *The Derbyshire lead industry in the sixteenth century*, DRS, 14 (Chesterfield, 1989).

'Twenty thousand miners can't be wrong!', *BPDMHS*, 11, 5 (1992), 249–53.

'Lawrence Oxley's accounts, 1672–81', in J.V. Beckett, J.P. Polack, D.M. Riden and D. Kiernan (eds.), *A seventeenth century Scarsdale miscellany*, DRS, 20 (Chesterfield, 1993), 121–44.

King, P., 'Gleaners, farmers and the failure of legal sanctions in England, 1750–1850', *P&P*, 125 (1989), 116–50.

'Customary rights and women's earnings: the importance of gleaning to the rural labouring poor, 1750–1850', *EcHR*, 2nd ser., 44, 3 (1991), 461–76.

'Edward Thompson's contribution to eighteenth-century studies. The patrician-plebeian model re-examined', *Social History*, 21, 2 (1996), 215–28.

Kiralfy, A., 'Custom in medieval English law', *Journal of Legal History*, 9, 1 (1988), 26–39.

Kirk, N., 'History, language, ideas and post-modernism: a materialist view', *Social History*, 19, 2 (1994), 221–40.

'Class and the "linguistic turn" in Chartist and post-Chartist historiography', in N. Kirk (ed.), *Social class and Marxism: defences and challenges* (Aldershot, 1996), 87–134.

Kirkham, N., 'The tumultuous course of the Dovegang', *DAJ*, 2nd ser., 73 (1953), 3–35.

'A royal mine in Netherhaddon?', *DAJ*, 2nd ser., 75 (1955) 20–35.

'Lead miners and royalists', *Derbyshire Miscellany*, 2, 5 (1961), 292–301.

Kishlansky, M.A., *The rise of the New Model Army* (Cambridge, 1979).

Parliamentary selection: social and political choice in early modern England (Cambridge, 1986).

Kleber Monod, P., *Jacobitism and the English people, 1688–1788* (Cambridge, 1989).

Kopperman, P.E., *Sir Robert Heath 1575–1649: window on an age* (London, 1989).

Kussmaul, A., *A general view of the rural economy of England, 1538–1840* (Cambridge, 1990).

Lachmann, R., *From manor to market: structural change in England, 1536–1640* (Madison, 1987).

Laslett, P., *The world we have lost: further explored* (London, 1965; 3rd edn, 1983).

Lawrance, H., 'The will of Lionel Tynley, lead-miner and merchant: died 19 November 1653', *DAJ*, 2nd ser., 5 (1931), 1–26.

Leftwich, A., *Redefining politics: people, resources and power* (London, 1983).

'Politics, people, resources and power', in A. Leftwich, (ed.), *What is politics? The activity and its study* (Oxford, 1984).

Levine, D., *Family formation in an age of nascent capitalism* (New York, 1977).

Levine, D. and Wrightson, K.E., *The making of an industrial society: Whickham, 1560–1765* (Oxford, 1991).

Lewis, M., *The mining frontier: contemporary accounts from the American West in the nineteenth century* (Oklahoma, 1967).

Lewis, W.J., 'Some aspects of lead mining in Cardiganshire in the sixteenth and seventeenth centuries', *Ceredigion*, 1 (1950–1), 177–92.

Lindley, K., *Fenland riots and the English Revolution* (London, 1982).

Maddox, R., *El Castillo: the politics of tradition in an Andalusian town* (Urbana, 1993).

Malcolm, J.L., *Caesar's due: loyalty and King Charles, 1642–6* (London, 1983).

Malcolmson, R.W., 'A set of ungovernable people: the Kingswood colliers in the eighteenth century', in J. Brewer and J. Styles (eds.), *An ungovernable people: the English and their law in the seventeenth and eighteenth centuries* (London, 1980), 85–127.

Manning, B., *The English people and the English Revolution* (1976; 2nd edn, London, 1991).

1649: the crisis of the English Revolution (London, 1991).

Manning, R.B., *Village revolts: social protest and popular disturbance in England, 1509–1640* (Oxford, 1988).

Martin, J.E., *Feudalism to capitalism: peasant and landlord in English agrarian capitalism* (Basingstoke, 1983).

Maclachlan, A., *The rise and fall of revolutionary England: an essay on the fabrication of seventeenth-century history* (Basingstoke, 1996).

McGlynn, F. and Tuden, A. (eds.), *Anthropological approaches to political behaviour* (Pittsburgh, 1991).

McMichael, J.R. and Taft, B. (eds.), *The writings of William Walwyn* (Athens, Ga., 1989).

Mendels, F.F., 'Proto-industrialization: the first phase of the industrialization process', *Journal of Economic History*, 32, 1 (1972), 241–61.

Meredith, R., 'The Eyres of Hassop, 1470–1640: I', *DAJ*, 2nd ser., 84 (1964), 1–51.

'A Derbyshire family in the seventeenth century: the Eyres of Hassop and their forfeited estates', *Recusant History*, 8, 1 (1965), 12–77.

'The Eyres of Hassop, 1470–1640: II', *DAJ*, 2nd ser., 85 (1965), 44–91.

Miller, E. and Hatcher, J., *Medieval England: rural society and economic change, 1086–1348* (London, 1978).

Millward, R, and Robinson, A., *The Peak District* (London, 1975).

Morrill, J.S., *The revolt of the provinces: conservatives and radicals in the English civil war, 1630–1650* (London, 1976).

Seventeenth century Britain, 1603–1714 (Folkestone, 1980).

The nature of the English Revolution (London, 1993).

Morrill, J.S. and Walter, J., 'Order and disorder in the English Revolution', in A. Fletcher, and J. Stevenson (eds.), *Order and disorder in early modern England* (Cambridge, 1985), 137–65.

Mousnier, R., *Peasant uprisings in seventeenth century France, Russia and China* (1967; Eng. trans., London, 1971).

Social hierarchies: 1450 to the present (1969; Eng. trans., London, 1973).

Naylor, P.J., 'John Burton of Bonsall, Derbyshire and Iowa, USA 1795–1854', *BPDMHS*, 10, 1 (1987), 4–12.

Neale, R.S., *Class in English history, 1680–1850* (Oxford, 1981).

Neeson, J., *Commoners: common right, enclosure and social change in England, 1700–1820* (Cambridge, 1993).

Neuchatz, M., *The golden sword: the coming of capitalism to the Colorado mining frontier* (New York, 1986).

Newby, H., *The deferential worker: a study of farm workers in East Anglia* (London, 1977).

Newton, S.C., 'The gentry of Derbyshire in the seventeenth century', *DAJ*, 2nd ser., 86 (1966), 1–30.

North, D.C., *Structure and change in economic history* (New York, 1981).

North, D.C. and Thomas, R.P., *The rise of the western world: a new economic history* (Cambridge, 1973).

O'Day, R., 'Immanuel Bourne: a defence of the ministerial order', *Journal of Ecclesiastical History*, 27, 2 (1976), 101–14.

Palliser, D.M., 'The trade gilds of Tudor York', in P. Clark and P. Slack (eds.), *Crisis and order in English towns, 1500–1700: essays in urban history* (London, 1972), 86–116.

Palmer, B.D., *Descent into discourse: the reification of language and the writing of social history* (Philadelphia, 1990).

Pendleton, J., *A history of Derbyshire* (London, 1886).

Pennington, R.R., *Stannary law: a history of the mining law of Devon and Cornwall* (Newton Abbot, 1973).

Perkin, H., *Origins of modern English society* (London, 1969).

Phythian-Adams, P., *Re-thinking English local history* (University of Leicester, Dept. of English Local History, Occasional Papers, 4th ser., No. 1, 1987).

Pocock, J.G.A., *The ancient constitution and the feudal law: a study in English historical thought in the seventeenth century. A reissue with retrospect* (Cambridge, 1987).

Prior, M., 'Women and the urban economy: Oxford, 1500–1800', in M. Prior (ed.), *Women in English society, 1500–1800* (London, 1985), 93–117.

Raistrick, A. and Jennings, B., *A history of lead mining in the Pennines* (London, 1969).

Randall, A., 'The industrial moral economy of the Gloucestershire weavers in the eighteenth century', in J. Rule (ed.), *British trade unionism, 1750–1850: the formative years* (London, 1988), 29–51.

Before the Luddites: custom, community and machinery in the English woollen industry, 1776–1809 (Cambridge, 1991).

Reddy, W.M., 'The concept of class' in M.L. Bush (ed.), *Social orders and social classes in Europe since 1500: studies in social stratification* (London, 1992), 13–25.

Reed, M., 'The peasantry of nineteenth-century rural England: a neglected class?', *History Workshop*, 18 (1984), 53–76.

Richardson, R.C., *The debate on the English Revolution revisited* (1977; 2nd edn, London, 1988).

Riden, P., 'The population of Derbyshire in 1563', *DAJ*, 2nd ser., 98 (1978), 61–71.

Rieuwerts, J.H., 'The inquisition or Quo Warranto of 1288', *BPDMHS*, 7, 1 (1978), 41–9.

'The earliest lead mine soughs in Derbyshire', *BPDMHS*, 7, 5 (1980), 241–315.

'Derbyshire lead mining and early geological concepts', *BPDMHS*, 9, 2 (1984), 51–100.

Rollison, D., *The local origins of modern society: Gloucestershire, 1500–1800* (London, 1992).

Rosser, G., 'Crafts, guilds and the negotiation of work in the medieval town', *P&P*, 154 (1997), 3–31.

Rowe, J., *The hard-rock men: Cornish immigrants to the north American mining frontier* (New York, 1974).

Rowlands, M.B., 'Continuity and change in an industrializing society: the case of the West Midlands industries', in P. Hudson (ed.), *Regions and industries: a perspective on the Industrial Revolution in Britain* (Cambridge, 1989), 103–31.

Rude, G., *Ideology and popular protest* (London, 1980).

Rule, J.G., *The experience of labour in eighteenth century industry* (London, 1981).

The labouring classes in early industrial England, 1750–1850 (London, 1986).

'The property of skill in the period of manufacture', in P. Joyce (ed.), *The historical meanings of work* (Cambridge, 1987), 99–118.

Russell, C., *Parliaments and English politics, 1621–1629* (Oxford, 1979).

The causes of the English civil war (Oxford, 1990).

Russell, C. (ed.), *Unrevolutionary England, 1603–1642* (London, 1990).

Samaha, J., 'Gleanings from local criminal-court records: sedition amongst the "inarticulate" in Elizabethan Essex', *Journal of Social History*, 8 (1975), 61–79.

Sassoon, D., *One hundred years of socialism: the West European Left in the twentieth century* (London, 1996).

Savage, M., 'Space, networks and class formation', in N. Kirk (ed.), *Social class and Marxism: defences and challenges* (Aldershot, 1996), 58–86.

Schochet, G.J., 'Patriarchalism, politics and mass attitudes in Stuart England', *Historical Journal*, 12, 3 (1969), 413–41.

Schofield, R.S., 'Dimensions of illiteracy in England, 1750–1850', in H. Graff (ed.), *Literacy and social development in the West* (Cambridge, 1981), 201–13.

Scott, J.C., *Domination and the arts of resistance: hidden transcripts* (Yale, 1990).

Scott, J.W., *Gender and the politics of history* (New York, 1988).

'The evidence of experience', *Critical Inquiry*, 17 (1991), 773–97.

Searle, C.E., 'Custom, class conflict and agrarian capitalism: the Cumbrian customary economy in the eighteenth century', *P&P*, 110 (1986), 106–33.

Sewell, W.H., 'How classes are made: critical reflections on E.P. Thompson's theory of working-class formation', in H.J. Kaye and K. McClelland (eds.), *E.P. Thompson: critical perspectives* (Cambridge, 1990), 50–77.

Sharp, B., *In contempt of all authority: artisans and riot in the west of England, 1586–1660* (Berkeley, 1980).

'Common rights, charities and the disorderly poor', in G. Eley and W. Hunt (eds.), *Reviving the English Revolution: reflections and elaborations on the work of Christopher Hill* (London, 1988), 107–38.

Sharpe, J.A., *Defamation and sexual slander in early modern England: the church courts at York*, Borthwick Papers, 58 (York, 1980).

Crime in seventeenth-century England: a county study (Cambridge, 1983).

'"Such disagreement betwyx neighbours": litigation and human relations in early modern England', in J. Bossy (ed.), *Disputes and settlements: law and human relations in the West* (Cambridge, 1983), 167–87.

Crime in early modern England, 1550–1750 (London, 1984).

'The people and the law', in B. Reay (ed.), *Popular culture in seventeenth century England* (London, 1985), 244–70.

Early modern England: a social history, 1550–1760 (London, 1987).

Sheail, J., 'The distribution of taxable population and wealth in England during the early sixteenth century', *Transactions of the Institute of British Geographers*, 55 (1972), 111–26.

Shimwell, D.W., 'Sheep grazing in Edale, Derbyshire, 1692–1747, and its effect on blanket peat erosion', *DAJ*, 2nd ser., 94 (1974), 35–40.

Sider, G.M., *Culture and class in anthropology and history: a Newfoundland illustration* (Cambridge, 1986).

Skipp, V.H.T., *Crisis and development: an ecological study of the Forest of Arden, 1570–1674* (Cambridge, 1978).

Slack, R., 'The economics of lead mining in sixteenth and seventeenth century Brassington', *BPDMHS*, 10, 5 (1989), 284–8.

Lands and lead-miners: a history of Brassington, in Derbyshire (Chesterfield, 1991).

'Free men or wage-slaves? The miners of the Wirksworth area in the 1650s', *BPDMHS*, 11, 6 (1992), 272–4.

Smith, D.A., *Rocky mountain mining camps: the urban frontier* (Indiana, 1967).

Smith Doxey, J., 'Notice of a clogg almanac, from Wirksworth, Derbyshire', *Reliquary*, 7 (1866–7), 173–4.

Snell, K.D.M., 'Deferential bitterness: the social outlook of the rural proletariat in the eighteenth and nineteenth centuries', in M.L. Bush (ed.), *Social orders and social classes in Europe since 1500: studies in social stratification* (London, 1992), 158–84.

Somerville, R., 'The Duchy of Lancaster Council and the Court of the Duchy Chamber', *Transactions of the Royal Historical Society*, 4th ser., 23 (1941), 159–77.

History of the Duchy of Lancaster, I: *1265–1603* (London, 1953).

Office-holders in the Duchy and County Palatine of Lancaster from 1603 (Chichester, 1972).

'Commons and wastes in north west Derbyshire: the High Peak "new lands"', *DAJ*, 2nd ser., 97 (1977), 16–22.

Spufford, M., *Contrasting communities: English villagers in the sixteenth and seventeenth centuries* (Cambridge, 1979).

Stafford, P., *The East Midlands in the early middle ages* (Leicester, 1985).

Stedman Jones, G., *Outcast London: a study in the relationship between classes in Victorian society* (Oxford, 1971).

Languages of class: studies in English working class history, 1832–1982 (Cambridge, 1983).

Steinberg, M.W., 'Culturally speaking: finding a commons between post- structuralism and the Thompsonian perspective', *Social History*, 21, 2 (1996), 193–214.

Stevens, J., *England's last revolution: Pentrich, 1817* (Buxton, 1977).

Stone, L., *The crisis of the aristocracy, 1558–1641* (Oxford, 1965).

The causes of the English Revolution, 1529–1642 (London, 1972).

Stoyle, M., *Loyalty and locality: popular allegiance in Devon during the English civil war* (Exeter, 1994).

Stretton, T., 'Women, custom and equity in the Court of Requests', in J. Kermode and G. Walker (eds.), *Women, crime and the courts in early modern England* (London, 1994), 170–89.

Tawney, R.H., *The agrarian problem of the sixteenth century* (London, 1912).

Taylor, B., *Eve and the new Jerusalem: socialism and feminism in the nineteenth century* (London, 1983).

Thirsk, J., *English peasant farming: the agrarian history of Lincolnshire from Tudor to recent times* (London, 1957).

'Seventeenth century agriculture and social change', *AgHR*, supplement 18 (1970).

The agrarian history of England and Wales. V.I: 1640–1750. Regional farming systems (Cambridge, 1984).

Thomas, K., *Religion and the decline of magic: studies in popular belief in sixteenth and seventeenth century England* (London, 1971).

'Age and authority in early modern England', *Proceedings of the British Academy*, 62 (1976), 205–48.

Man and the natural world: changing attitudes in England, 1500–1800 (Harmondsworth, 1983).

Thomas, M., 'The rioting crowd in eighteenth century Derbyshire', *DAJ*, 2nd ser., 95 (1975), 37–47.

Thompson, E.P., *The making of the English working class* (1963; 2nd edn, London, 1968).

'Patrician society, plebeian culture', *Journal of Social History*, 7, 4 (1974), 382–405.

Whigs and hunters: the origins of the Black Act (London, 1975).

'The grid of inheritance: a comment', in J. Goody, J. Thirsk and E.P. Thompson (eds.), *Family and inheritance: rural society in western Europe, 1200–1800* (Cambridge, 1976), 328–60.

'Eighteenth-century English society: class struggle without class?', *Social History*, 3, 2 (1978), 133–65.

Customs in common (London, 1991).

Witness against the beast: William Blake and the moral law (Cambridge, 1993).

Thwaites, W., 'Women in the market place: Oxfordshire, 1690–1800', *Midland History*, 9 (1984), 23–42.

Tolmie, M., *The triumph of the saints: the separate churches of London, 1616–1649* (Cambridge, 1977).

Underdown, D.E., 'Community and class: theories of local politics in the English

Revolution', in B.C. Malament (ed.), *After the Reformation: essays in honor of J.H. Hexter* (Manchester, 1980), 147–65.

Revel, riot and rebellion: popular politics and culture in England 1603–1660 (Oxford, 1987).

'Regional cultures? Local variations in popular culture during the early modern period', in T. Harris (ed.), *Popular culture in England, 1500–1850* (Basingstoke, 1995), 28–47.

Unwin, G., *Industrial organization in the sixteenth and seventeenth centuries* (Oxford, 1904).

Vernon, J., *Politics and the people: a study in English political culture, c. 1815–1867* (Cambridge, 1993).

'Who's afraid of the "linguistic turn"? The politics of social history and its discontents', *Social History*, 19, 1 (1994), 81–97.

Vincent, D., 'The decline of oral tradition in popular culture', in R. Storch (ed.), *Popular culture and custom in nineteenth century England* (London, 1982), 20–47.

Wallerstein, I., *The modern world-system, I: Capitalist agriculture and the origins of the European world-economy in the sixteenth century* (New York, 1974).

The modern world-system, II: Mercantilism and the consolidation of the European world-economy, 1600–1750 (New York, 1980).

Walter, J.D., 'Grain riots and popular attitudes to the law: Maldon and the crisis of 1629', in J. Brewer and J. Styles (eds.), *An ungovernable people: the English and their law in the seventeenth and eighteenth centuries* (London, 1980), 47–84.

'A "Rising of the people"? The Oxfordshire rising of 1596', *P&P*, 107 (1985), 90–143.

Walter, J.D. and Wrightson, K.E., 'Dearth and the social order in early modern England', *P&P*, 71 (1976), 22–42.

Wells, R., *Insurrection: the British experience, 1795–1803* (Gloucester, 1983).

Wiesner, M.E., 'Guilds, male bonding and women's work in early modern Germany', *Gender and History*, 1 (1989), 125–37.

Wightman, W.E., 'Open field agriculture in the Peak district', *DAJ*, 2nd ser., 81 (1961), 111–25.

Williams, C.J., 'The mining laws in Flintshire and Denbighshire', *BPDMHS*, 12, 3 (1994), 62–8.

Williams, D.E., *The Derbyshire miners: a study in industrial and social history* (London, 1962).

Williams, L.B., 'Derbyshire mining', *Mining Magazine*, 47, 2 (1932), 89–91.

Williamson, T., *Polite landscapes: gardens and society in eighteenth century England* (Stroud, 1995).

Willies, L., 'The Barker family and the eighteenth century lead business', *DAJ*, 2nd ser., 93 (1973), 55–74.

'The working of the Derbyshire lead mining customs in the eighteenth and nineteenth centuries', *BPDMHS*, 10, 3 (1988), 146–59.

'Management and workers at Miners Engine Mine, Eyam, in the mid-eighteenth century', *BPDMHS*, 11, 5 (1992), 146–60.

Wilson Paul, R., *Mining frontiers of the far west, 1848–1880* (New York, 1963).

Wood, A., 'Social conflict and change in the mining communities of north-west Derbyshire, c. 1600–1700', *International Review of Social History*, 38, 1 (1993), 31–58.

'Custom, identity and resistance: English free miners and their law, 1550–1800', in P. Griffiths, A. Fox and S. Hindle (eds.), *The experience of authority in early modern England* (Basingstoke, 1996), 249–85.

'Beyond post-revisionism? The civil war allegiances of the miners of the Derbyshire Peak Country', *Historical Journal*, 40, 1 (1997), 23–40.

'The place of custom in plebeian political culture: England, 1550–1800', *Social History*, 22, 1 (1997), 46–60.

'Migration and local identity in early modern England' (forthcoming).

'"Poore men woll speke one daye": plebeian languages of deference and defiance in England, c 1500–1640', in T. Harris (ed.), *The politics of the excluded in early modern England* (Basingstoke, forthcoming).

Woolrych, A., *Soldiers and statesmen: the General Council of the Army and its debates, 1647–1648* (Oxford, 1987).

Wright, G.T., *Longstone records* (Bakewell, 1906).

Wright, S.M., *The Derbyshire gentry in the fifteenth century*, DRS, 8 (Chesterfield, 1983).

Wrightson, K.E., *English society, 1580–1680* (London, 1982).

'The social order of early modern England: three approaches', in L. Bonfield, R.M. Smith and K.E. Wrightson (eds.), *The world we have gained: histories of population and social structure* (London, 1986), 177–202.

'Estates, degrees and sorts: changing perceptions of society in Tudor and Stuart England', in P. Corfield (ed.), *Language, history and class* (Oxford, 1991), 30–52.

'The enclosure of English social history', in A. Wilson (ed.), *Rethinking social history: English society, 1570–1920 and its interpretation* (Manchester, 1993), 59–77.

'Sorts of people in Tudor and Stuart England', in J. Barry (ed.), *The middling sort of people: culture, society and politics in England, 1550–1800* (Basingstoke, 1994), 28–51.

'The politics of the parish in early modern England', in P. Griffiths, A. Fox and S. Hindle (eds.), *The experience of authority in early modern England* (London, 1996), 10–46.

Wrightson, K.E. and Levine, D., *Poverty and piety in an English village: Terling, 1525–1700* (1979; 2nd edn, Oxford, 1995).

Wrigley, E.A., *Continuity, chance and change: the character of the Industrial Revolution in England* (Cambridge, 1988).

Wrigley, E.A. and Schofield, R.S., *The population history of England, 1541–1871: a reconstruction* (1981; 2nd edn, Cambridge, 1989).

Zagorin, P., *Rebels and rulers 1500–1660, I: Society, states and early modern revolution – agrarian and urban rebellions* (Cambridge, 1982).

Zell, M., 'Fixing the custom of the manor: Slindon, West Sussex, 1568', *Sussex Archaeological Collections*, 122 (1984), 101–6.

Industry in the countryside: Wealden society in the sixteenth century (Cambridge, 1994).

UNPUBLISHED DISSERTATIONS

Beats, L.N., 'Politics and government in Derbyshire 1640–60', PhD thesis, University of Sheffield, 1979.

Blanchard, I.S.W., 'Economic change in Derbyshire in the late middle ages, 1262–1540', PhD thesis, University of London, 1967.

Clark, R., 'Anglicanism, recusancy and dissent in Derbyshire 1603–1730', DPhil thesis, University of Oxford, 1979.

Davies, O.R.F., 'The Dukes of Devonshire, Newcastle and Rutland: 1688–1714. A study in wealth and political influence', DPhil thesis, University of Oxford, 1971.

Dias, J.R., 'Politics and administration in Nottinghamshire and Derbyshire, 1590–1640', DPhil thesis, University of Oxford, 1973.

Rieuwerts, J.H., 'A technological history of the drainage of the Derbyshire lead mines', PhD thesis, University of Leicester, 1981.

Robson, D., 'Some aspects of education in Derbyshire in the eighteenth century', PhD thesis, University of Sheffield, 1972.

Thomas, M., 'Friends of democracy: a study of working-class radicalism in Derbyshire, 1790–1850', MPhil thesis, University of Sheffield, 1984.

Willies, L., 'Technical and organisational development of the Derbyshire lead mining industries in the eighteenth and nineteenth centuries', PhD thesis, University of Leicester, 1980.

Wood, A., 'Industrial development, social change and popular politics in the mining area of north west Derbyshire, *c.* 1600–1700', PhD thesis, University of Cambridge, 1994.

INDEX

All local place-names are in Derbyshire, unless otherwise indicated.

Abney, 67
Africa, 72
agriculture, 93–5, 97
  communal systems of, 68–9, 177–8
  sheep farming, 53, 67–8, 108–9, 135, 245
Aldwark Grange, 207, 247
Alsop, 207
Amsterdam, 72
anthropology, 13, 15
Arkwright, Richard, 112, 114, 316–17
Armyn, Sir William, 20, 259–60
Ashbourne, 33, 68, 110, 302
Ashford, 30, 66, 68, 69–71, 81, 90, 120,
  136, 153, 177, 189, 190, 195, 204, 209,
  210–12, 214–15, 232–4, 236, 240,
  241, 242–5, 246, 258, 263, 275, 278,
  280, 291, 296, 297
Ashover, 114, 122, 185, 192, 195, 276, 304,
  306, 321
Assizes, 147, 280, 308
attorneys, 67–8, 161–2, 232, 233, 235, 242,
  244, 257–8
Aubrey, John, 7
Ayrshire, 124

Bagshawe, Thomas, 136, 235, 242
Bagshawe, William, 234, 272, 299
Bagshawe, William, Apostle of the Peak,
  191, 272, 299
Bakewell, 30, 55, 56, 63, 70, 81, 84, 90, 110,
  133, 147, 166, 224, 225, 231–7, 245–6,
  261, 262, 271, 274, 275, 297, 301,
  303–4, 305, 306, 320
Ball Eye mine, 76, 77, 199
Ballidon, 207
Bamford, William, 197
Baptists, 193
barmaster
  definition of, 44, 142–3
ideal role of, 167, 174, 206
jurisdiction, 139–43, 205–6, 245
leads miners' resistance, 219, 234, 242–3,
  262, 278–9
lease of office, 46, 58, 100, 186, 203, 206,
  207, 214–16, 219, 241
see also barmote courts; miners, claim right
  to elect barmaster
barmote courts
changing use of written evidence, 153,
  155
focus of miners' political organization,
  165, 169, 233, 241, 246, 263, 275, 278,
  287
growing complexity, 140, 142–3
juries, 51, 103, 122, 142–3, 160, 165,
  224, 229, 297
jurisdiction, 3, 103, 139–43, 164, 205–6
king's dish, 139–40, 170
origins, 137–8
similarities to Mendip and Forest of Dean
  miners' courts, 144
see also custom; free mining; miners;
  Wirksworth, Great Barmote of;
  Wirksworth, moothall of
Baslow, 236
Bawtry (Yorks.), 45, 72, 102
Beauchief, 57
Belvoir Castle (Leics.), 5
Berg, Maxine, 124
Bess of Hardwick, see Talbot, Elizabeth,
  dowager Countess of Shrewsbury
Birchover, 305, 318
boles, see lead industry, smelting
Bonsall, 46, 50, 66, 77, 183, 191, 207, 212,
  263, 304
Bourne, Immanuel, 192, 276
Bower, Thomas, 319, 321
Bowes, Lady Isabel, 24, 242

Bradborne, 207
Bradwell, 67, 81, 92, 108, 110, 321
Brailsford, H.N., 16
Brassington, 6–7, 33, 55, 77, 87–8, 135, 136, 212, 302
Braydon Forest (Wilts.), 262
Brenner, Robert, 118–19
Bristol, 72
Bunyan, John, 185
Burt, Roger, 117–18
Bushell, Thomas, 292
Buxton, 1, 55, 320
Byng, John, fifth Viscount Torrington, 316–17

California, 124
Calver, 177–8, 242, 306
Cambridgeshire, 136
Camden, William, 41
capitalism, 44, 103, 116–20
    organic development of, 123–4
    and social conflict, 120–3, 124
Carrier, Jennet, 24, 186–7, 219–20, 223–6, 253
Carrier, Richard, 166, 184, 186, 194, 219–26, 231, 241, 253, 274
Carsington, 55, 63, 77, 87–8, 223–4, 304
Castleton, 30, 55, 66, 81, 92, 108–9, 193–4, 195–6, 199, 237, 238–40, 320, 321
Catholicism, 192, 193, 272–3
Cavendish, Sir Charles, 244
Cavendish, Christiana, dowager Countess of Devonshire, 24, 236–7, 292
Cavendish, Sir William, Lord Cavendish, first Earl of Devonshire, 239, 243, 258
Cavendish, William, third Earl of Devonshire, 21, 99, 297
Cavendish, William, fourth Earl and first Duke of Devonshire, 312
Cavendish, William, third Duke of Devonshire, 149, 305, 310
Cavendish, William, fourth Duke of Devonshire, 312
Cavendish, William, fifth Duke of Devonshire, 310–11
Cavendish, William, first Earl and first Duke of Newcastle, 236, 274
Cavendishes, Earls and Dukes of Devonshire, 1, 5, 211, 239–40, 241, 247, 255
    estates, 69, 239, 242, 297
cavers
    attitude of law courts to, 149–50, 215, 310–11, 319
    definition, 24, 43, 76, 141, 176–8, 185
    nature of work, 58–9, 82
    number, 77, 79, 81
    poverty, 92

    production, 46, 52, 87–8
    see also custom, and male identities;
        custom, and women; miners, attitude to
        cavers; mining workforce,
        differentiation; women, work
census, of 1563, 53–6, 62–6
Chancery, Court of, 131, 148, 149, 160, 210, 211, 223, 224, 232, 242–4
Chartism, 249, 322–3
Charles I, King of England, 226, 230, 236–7, 257, 268, 270, 271, 288, 303
Charles II, King of England, 291, 303
Chatsworth House, 1, 5, 210, 239, 245, 274, 315
Chelmorton, 108, 134–5, 255
Cheshire, 36, 55, 114, 320
Chesterfield, 55, 236, 258, 271
Collinson, Patrick, 252
Consistory Court of Coventry and Lichfield, 131–2, 187, 223
Crich, 187
Clare, John, 316
Clark, J.C.D., 16
Clark, Peter, 111
class
    and economics, 17–19
    definitions of, 10–26, 316–18, 322–3
    and gender, 24–5
    languages of, 9, 15, 22–4, 206, 221–2, 277, 320–1
    and localism, 17, 28, 320–5
    and power, 19–21
    see also social conflict, as class conflict
coal mining, 93, 112, 116, 173, 181
Cobbett, William, 316
Coke, Sir John, 236–7
Cole Eaton, 247
Colorado, 124
common law, 136, 146, 164, 227, 229, 278
Common Pleas, Court of, 242, 285, 308
common rights, 20, 53, 67–9, 81, 107–9, 114, 134, 177–8, 251, 259–60
    inter-communal conflicts over, 66, 204, 212–13, 254
Commons, House of, 75–6, 147, 175, 235, 269, 275, 280, 284, 304
community
    attitudes to outsiders, 110–1, 169–70
    festivities, 27, 94, 189–90
    historiography, 188
    and magical beliefs, 195–200
    meanings of, 108, 172–3, 177–8, 188–91, 213
    and religion, 193–4
    social place, changing concepts of, 61–2, 177–8

community (*cont.*)
  see also agriculture, communal systems of;
    custom; miners; popular cultures;
    women, common interest; women, public
    roles
Cornwall, 268, 290, 291, 314, 324
Cotton, Charles, 2, 5, 7, 107
Council of State, 278, 284, 285–6
Cowley, 207
Crich, 110, 320
Cromford, 20, 46, 76, 77, 86–8, 98, 114,
    159, 203, 206, 225, 259–60, 262, 263,
    278, 316–17
cross-dressing, 193–4
Cullen, Lord, 308–10
custom
  ambiguities, 121
  and authority of age, 134–5
  and capitalism, 117–20, 306
  conflictual nature of, 127–8, 243–4,
    323–5
  defines compromise, 21, 243–5, 258, 279
  dynamism of, 128–9, 135, 138–9, 140–3,
    151, 243, 266, 306, 324
  legal meaning, 129, 135, 145, 147–9, 240
  and local culture, 128, 133–6, 160, 189,
    320–5
  local nature of, 128–9, 145–6
  and male identities, 24, 127, 132–5, 143,
    144, 169–74, 186, 249–50, 256, 261,
    323
  and memory, 127, 131–2, 140, 157,
    165–8, 170, 171–2, 214, 301, 307
  and office, 129, 177
  and oral culture, 130, 150–1, 157–60
  origins of, 127, 129, 137–8, 151, 205
  and political discourses, 136, 163, 252,
    289–91, 310–11
  and print, 159–60
  and property rights, 122, 124, 129,
    143–50, 163–4, 173
  and senses of the past, 128, 139, 161–2,
    163–9, 206, 325
  source of independence, 52, 71, 143,
    180–2, 254–5, 300–1, 314, 319, 323–5
  standardization of, 128, 159–60
  and women, 127, 132–3, 171–4, 185,
    186–7, 255
  and work, 128
  and writing, 128, 130, 135–6, 151–2,
    156–62, 288, 307
  see also agriculture, communal systems of;
    barmote courts; free mining; miners;
    popular politics; social conflict

Dale mine, 140

Darley, 63, 102, 237, 297, 304
Dean, Forest of (Glos.), 144, 169, 324
  Free Miners of, 169, 182, 227, 254, 260
Debankes, William, 159, 278–9, 288
Decazeville, 124
deference, 16, 20–2, 257, 258, 268, 272,
    297–8
  see also miners, deference.
Defoe, Daniel, 1–7, 105–7
depositions, 33, 58–9, 70, 102, 111, 130,
    161–2, 166, 171–4, 175, 183, 184,
    186–7, 209, 215, 221–2, 234, 240, 243,
    260
Derby, 33, 94, 102, 237, 271, 283
Derbyshire, ecological divisions of, 41
Derbyshire Miners' Association, 325
Derwent, 53, 55, 56, 62, 63, 66, 90
Devil, 196
Devil's Arse, 1, 195–6
Devonshire, Earls and Dukes of, *see*
    Cavendishes
Disraeli, Benjamin, 316
Dorset, 273
Dovegang mine, 76, 77, 86–8, 122, 147,
    219, 224, 225–31, 255, 261, 262, 263,
    272, 284, 293
Duchy of Lancaster,
  court of, 46, 70, 85, 111, 130–2, 140,
    141, 146, 147–8, 158, 183, 184, 185,
    203, 205–6, 207, 209, 210, 211,
    215–16, 220–3, 227–31, 238–48, 278,
    294, 295, 301–2, 303
  estates, 30, 43–4, 120, 131, 238–40
  leases, 109, 227–8, 239, 241, 297, 307,
    310
  policies, 66–7, 82–3, 102, 103, 108–9,
    120–3, 138–9, 147–8, 205, 214,
    227–31, 238, 272, 300
Duchy of Cornwall, 230
Duffield, 181, 262, 275, 284
Durham, Co., 72, 114

early modernity, 13–17, 321
East Anglia, 2, 218, 232
Edward VI, King of England, 166
Elizabeth I, Queen of England, 211
Elton, 59, 122, 135, 207, 212, 220, 222–3,
    301
economic history, 119
economics, 17, 18
enclosures, 33, 66–9, 102–3, 107–9,
    113–14, 133, 136, 204, 210–14, 234,
    242, 245, 247, 254–6, 299, 300, 306,
    318–19
English Revolution, 73, 147–8
  civil war in Peak Country, 274–8

historiography, 13, 267–9, 289
Leveller movement, 144, 252, 280–4,
   288–91, 321
popular allegiances, 241, 267–9, 271–4,
   281–4, 291–3
radicalism, 252, 275–7
social conflict during, 144–5, 248, 274–5,
   277–94, 297
Everitt, Alan, 252
Eyam, 59–62, 66, 81, 92, 94–7, 98–9, 101,
   107, 122, 156, 237, 304, 306, 307, 308,
   310, 312, 318
Eyre, Adam, 215–6
Eyre, Rowland (I), 136, 189, 214–16,
   241–2, 244
Eyre, Col. Rowland (II), 241–2, 271–2, 278,
   293
Eyre, Thomas, 215–16, 241–5
Eyres of Hassop, 192, 241, 274
Exchequer, Court of, 70, 82, 102, 130–2,
   146, 147, 148, 207, 209, 216, 223, 227,
   232, 234, 235–6, 259, 285, 303, 307

Fakenham (Norfolk), 250
fenlands, 70, 135–6, 218, 226–7, 232, 252,
   265, 289, 291
Ferne, John, 161–2, 173, 221, 225, 226,
   230, 259
Fiennes, Celia, 105–7
Fitzherbert, Sir John, 220, 276
Fletcher, Anthony, 16
Foljamb, Sir Francis, 122, 220, 222–3
Foljamb, Sir Godfrey, 46, 206
Foljamb, Henry, 203
Foljamb, Sir William, 242
Foljambs of Walton, 135, 239
Foolow, 114, 307
Fulwood, Christopher, 237, 258
free mining
   clarification of claim to, 142, 158, 161–2,
      180, 207, 216, 222–3, 238, 240, 244,
      262
   confusion concerning, 4
   conflict over, 5, 21, 117–18, 120–4,
      203–31, 238–48, 254–5, 259–66, 275,
      277–94, 300–3, 305–12, 318–19,
      324–5
   economic significance, 43, 46, 77–8, 81,
      102–3
   egalitarianism of, 143
   implications of enclosure for, 306–7
   nature of, 2, 4, 30–3, 118, 138
   origins, 2, 137–8
   persistence, 105, 112, 114, 123, 181–2,
      306, 324–5
   seasonality, 45

in United States, 124, 324
see also barmaster; barmote courts;
   custom; gentry and nobility, hostility to
   free mining; lead industry, manorial
   control of; miners; popular politics;
   social conflict

Gell, Col. Sir John (I), 23, 147, 232–7, 269,
   271–2, 275–6, 281, 293, 302
Gell, Sir John (II), 303
Gell, Sir Philip, 304, 305
Gells of Hopton, 58, 231
gender, *see* cavers, definition; class, and
   gender; community; custom, and male
   identities; custom, and women; miners,
   definitions of skill; miners, political
   project; women
Gentlewoman's Grove, 173, 183
gentry and nobility
   civil war divisions, 272
   class identity of, 26
   and county community, 263, 269–70
   as enclosers, 67
   hostility to free mining, 143–50, 203,
      206–12, 247, 278, 293–4, 301–3
   internal divisions, 241–2, 254
   and lead industry, 43, 58, 99–100, 120–3,
      174–5, 203–4
   popular perceptions concerning, 23
   perceptions of landscape and social order,
      144
   perceptions of miners, 1–8, 197, 232,
      259–60, 312
   post-Restoration unity, 296–7, 300
   small numbers in Peak Country, 3, 48, 62
   values of, 22
Gillingham Forest (Dorset), 262
Glossop, 210–12
Gloucestershire, 314
Godberhere, Thomas, 224–5, 260, 262
Great Hucklow, 81, 92, 234, 242, 299
Great Longstone, 68, 244, 306
Griffe Grange, 207, 302
Grindlow, 307, 308–10, 311, 314, 321

Hacker, Col. Thomas, 296
Haddon Hall, 239, 245, 277, 280
Haddon lordship, 30, 144, 239, 245–8, 251,
   263, 277–86
Haddonfields, 101, 279–81, 285–6, 293–4,
   295, 297, 300, 301, 310, 321
Hardie, James Keir, 316
Hardwick, Lord, 148
Harthill, 121, 122, 169, 275, 277–9, 284,
   286, 292, 306
Hartingdon, 30, 55, 66, 81, 102, 317

Hassop, 136, 242, 244, 306
Hassop Hall, 274
Hathersage, 192, 273
Hazelbadge, 121, 199, 247, 256, 261, 294
Heath, Sir Robert, 219, 225–31, 236, 255, 261, 263–4, 274, 275, 290, 293
Hearth Tax, 63–6, 89–93
Heaward, William, 280–2, 292
Henrietta Maria, queen consort to Charles I, 257
Hill, Christopher, 13, 252
Hillcar sough, 318
High Peak
  Hundred of, 24, 30, 58, 59, 63, 66, 77, 103, 110, 120, 131, 141, 144, 173–4, 207, 209–17, 231–48, 262, 272, 274, 318
  lordship of, 30, 102, 103, 108, 209, 238–9, 255
  manor of, 30, 66, 108, 138, 238, 275
High Stoole rake, 287
Highlow, 187
Hobbes, Thomas, 2, 7
Holmes, Clive, 252
Holmesfield, 76
Home Office, 320
Hooson, William, 8, 105–7, 137, 164, 167, 168–9, 176, 198, 305, 306, 314, 325
Hood, Robin, 144
Hope, 56, 59–62, 67, 70, 92, 94–7, 98–9, 110, 147, 156, 166, 224, 225, 231–7, 261, 262, 271, 274, 275, 297, 303–4, 305
Hopkinson, George, 137–8, 151, 167, 171, 276, 293, 302
Hopkinson, William, 293
Hopton, 303
households
  composition, 76, 179–80
  role in mining, 82, 105, 179–80
Hudson, Pat, 119
Hull (Yorks.), 45, 72, 99, 102, 271, 274
Humphrey, William, 57–60, 72, 74, 98, 113, 209–10

Ible, 302
Industrial Revolution, 9, 11, 98, 115–16, 124, 257, 316–17, 321–3
industrialization and early modern economy, 93–4, 97–8, 116
'Indies', 72

Jacobitism, 315

Kent, 291
Kenyon, Roger, 82–3, 104, 175, 182

Kett, Robert, 314
Kett's revolt of 1549, 250
King's Bench, Court of, 146, 147, 242, 280, 281, 284, 285, 294, 308, 319
King's (or Queen's) Field, *see* Duchy of Lancaster, estates
Kingswood (Glos.), 314

Lachmann, R., 118–19
Lanarkshire, 324
Lancashire, 36, 72, 114, 268
landholding, 50–1, 67–71, 92, 108
  see also miners, landholding
law
  contested nature of, 164
  and origins of capitalism, 118–9
  popular knowledge of, 135–6
  radical ideas concerning, 151, 289–90
  and state formation, 141, 150, 164
  see also custom; free mining; miners, legalism; popular politics, litigation
Lay Subsidies, 46–51
lead industry
  capital investment in, 49, 84–8, 99–102, 228
  capitalism, 89
  crown's duties upon, 75–6, 262, 270
  growth/decline, 42, 57–9, 114, 115
  historiography, 117–18
  manorial control of, 120–3, 166, 207, 209–10, 230, 240–1, 242–4, 245–7, 251, 290, 299, 301
  manorial duties upon, 44, 58, 100, 120–2, 138–43, 149, 166, 203–4, 206, 207, 214–16, 219–23, 242–4, 271
  mining technology, 74, 82–6, 99, 100–2, 104, 105–6, 114, 228
  production, 43, 44, 52, 56, 73, 85–8, 99–102, 114
  significance, 2, 72–3, 250–1
  smelting, 43, 45, 57–8, 101, 310
  wage labour in, 52, 76–7, 79, 81, 87–8, 117
lead markets, 45, 72–3, 102, 107
lead prices, 73–5, 81–2, 98, 102, 109, 241, 243–4, 270, 295, 298
  relation to population, 98
  relation to social conflict, 250–1
Leake, Sir Francis, first Baron Deincourt, 232–6
Leake, George, 203
Leakes of Sutton, 203, 232
Leftwich, Adrian, 253
Leicestershire, 246, 284
Leland, John, 41
Lenton, Priory of, 231

lesser gentry
  as enclosers, 68, 108
  involvement in lead industry, 68, 84–8,
    100–2, 108, 298–300
  wealth of, 48, 90
  see also miners, relations with lesser gentry
Lilburne, John, 289
Lindley, Keith, 252, 258
literacy, 152–62, 166–7
Little Hucklow, 67, 81, 92, 216, 234, 242
Little Longstone, 306
Litton, 22, 81, 136, 159, 168, 183, 234–5,
    242, 247, 260, 261, 262, 263, 299
Lords, House of, 149, 247, 279–80
London, 72, 146, 275, 288, 289, 312
lordship, definition of, 30
lot and cope, *see* lead industry, manorial
    duties upon
Luddism, 249, 320, 321

Manchester (Lancs.), 112, 320–1
Mandale rake, 84, 138
Manlove, Edward, 157, 176
Manners, Sir George, 247
Manners, Lady Grace, 24, 220, 247
Manners, Sir John, 166, 239, 245–7
Manners, John, eighth Earl of Rutland, 19,
    21, 22, 23, 77, 99, 121, 144, 147, 160,
    166, 237, 247–8, 256, 275, 277–86,
    296, 301
Manners, John, Lord Roos, ninth Earl and
    first Duke of Rutland, 101, 285, 297
Manners of Haddon, Earls and Dukes of
    Rutland, 5, 121, 222, 239, 241–2, 245
Manning, Roger, 251–2
manors, distribution, 30, 35, 218–19, 223,
    238–40
  see also lead industry, manorial control of;
    lead industry, manorial duties upon
Mansfield (Notts.), 94
Marple Bridge (Ches.), 320
marriage, seasonality of, 94–5
Martin, J.E., 118
Marxism, 10–15, 17, 118–9, 258
Mary I, Queen of England, 165
Mary, Queen of Scotland, 211
Matlock, 49, 50, 55, 62, 63, 66, 77, 90, 130,
    168, 182, 206, 263, 304
Medowplecke Grange, 21, 262
Mendips (Som.), 57, 59, 72, 144, 254, 262
mercantilism, 109–10
methodism, 191, 193, 318, 319–21
Middleton-by-Wirksworth, 46, 77, 87–8,
    207, 263
Middleton-by-Youlgreave, 237
middling sort, 19, 72, 107, 257–9, 298–9

Midland Rising of 1607, 232, 246, 265, 314
militia roll of 1638, 63–4, 71, 76, 78
Millclose mine, 114
miners
  acceptance into ranks of, 134, 169–70,
    171–2, 183
  alleged communism of, 144–5, 163, 277,
    280
  appearance, 7, 105, 106
  attitude to cavers, 43, 103, 174, 176–8
  attitude to poor, 110–11, 174, 176
  attitude to wage labour, 103–4, 121, 163,
    180–1, 182, 311
  by-employments, 183
  claim right to elect barmaster, 139–41,
    143, 166, 167, 206, 224, 278–9, 290–1,
    293
  collectors of documents, 161–2, 167, 259,
    301, 307
  coping system, 85–6, 104–5, 123, 180–1,
    308, 314–15
  defence of barmote jurisdiction, 137, 140,
    163–5, 290, 301, 305
  deference, 20–1, 203–4, 205–6, 243
  definitions of skill, 83, 105, 175–6, 180–1
  demand household franchise, 291
  diet, 95
  earnings, 19, 58–9
  economic position, 81–2, 84–8
  employment of wage labour, 84, 181, 182
  endogamy, 134
  geological ideas, 154, 197–8
  hostility to tithes, 84, 159–60, 167–8,
    223–6, 231–7, 271, 290, 303–5
  integration, 45, 47, 52, 70–1, 212, 254
  landholding, 50, 70–1, 74
  legalism, 23, 136, 146–7, 150–62,
    163–69, 256, 307
  and Leveller movement, 281–4, 288–91
  life-cycle, 182–3
  literacy, 153–6
  magical beliefs, 197–200
  nature of work, 44–5, 58–9, 82–5,
    105–7, 179–84
  networks, 159–60, 184, 219, 224–5,
    233–5, 259–61, 262–3, 287, 298
  office-holding, 50–1, 142–3, 225, 234,
    260, 262
  oral culture, 7, 153–5, 157–9, 160,
    166–9
  petitions, 75–81, 175, 178, 235, 236–7,
    262–4, 269–73, 280–2, 287, 290, 304,
    305
  political project, 204, 216, 219, 240, 246,
    262, 266, 288, 290–1
  poverty amongst, 92, 102–3, 107–8

miners (*cont.*)
  relations with lesser gentry, 85–6, 104,
    108, 158, 161–2, 205–6, 225, 228,
    257–9, 270, 278, 295, 298–300,
    304–5
  self-perception, 8, 24, 105, 158, 164,
    168–71, 173–4, 175–8, 249–50,
    260–2, 325
  sense of community, 33, 51, 143, 150,
    183–5, 190, 194, 270, 300–1
  strikes of, 181, 318, 325
  wealth, 47, 49
  see also, barmote courts; cavers; custom;
    free mining; gentry and nobility,
    perceptions of miners; lead industry;
    mining workforce; popular politics;
    social conflict
Miners' Friendly Society, 318
Mines Royal, 284–6
mining workforce
  differentiation, 43, 45, 74–6, 174–5, 229
  nature and organization of work, 44,
    82–4, 88, 99, 105–7, 179–87
  size and distribution of, 44, 59, 74–81, 97
  see also miners; cavers; households, role in
    mining; lead industry; women, work
Mitchell, John, 235, 236–7, 247, 259, 261,
    272
monastic granges, 53, 58, 67–8, 213, 220,
    239, 245
Monsalldale, 317
Monyash, 108, 258
Morrill, John, 16
Mousnier, Roland, 257–8
Muggletonians, 193

Nesthouse mine, 180
Netherhaddon, 56, 77, 99, 121, 122, 123,
    237, 245, 248, 275, 277–86, 300, 306
New Mills, 320
Newton Grange, 121, 219, 284, 293, 302
Nidderdale (Yorks.), 256, 265
Nigeria, 124
Norfolk, 268
North, D.C., 118–19
Northamptonshire, 246, 284
Nottingham (Notts.), 94, 237, 271
numeracy, 190

occupations, 61, 95–7, 175
Odin mine, 99, 108, 195
Oldfield, Raphe, 159, 234–7, 242, 259, 260,
    262, 299
orebuyers, 120–1, 235, 270, 301
Overhaddon, 81, 108, 263
Overton, Richard, 289

Oxford, 284

Paddock Torr mine, 85
Paine, Thomas, 319
parish registers, 59–62
Parker, Robert, 219–20
Parker, Thomas, 219–20
parliament, 263–4, 269, 278, 288
  see also Commons, House of; Lords,
    House of
past, popular senses of, 26, 198–200, 323–4
  see also custom
paternalism, 21, 244, 297
Peak Country
  administrative divisions within, 28–33
  climate, 36
  definitions of, 27, 33, 36, 55, 97–8, 253,
    263, 321–2
  elite perceptions of, 1–4, 7–8, 41, 316–17
  geography, 1, 28, 53, 55, 92–3
  as an industrial region, 74, 89–98, 100,
    115–16
  landscape, 5, 97, 108, 195
  material culture of, 36
  relations with agrarian regions, 93–4
  roads, 55
  see also lead industry
Peak Forest, 210–12, 238, 306
Peakrills, 1, 3, 5, 7, 36, 190, 317
Pentrich, 320
petitions, 22, 153–4
  see also miners, petitions
plebeian, meaning of, 11, 27, 313–14
poor relief, 102–3, 109–11, 114
popular cultures
  dynamic relationship with elite cultures,
    161–2, 259
  and local cultures, 26–37, 188, 323–5
  'reform' of, 196–7
  see also community; custom; miners;
    popular politics
popular politics
  and central state, 263–4, 269–71, 280–6,
    288, 290
  common purses, 209, 224, 232–6, 251–2,
    255
  definition, 4, 19, 252–4, 294
  depoliticization, 295, 300, 302, 313
  and early working-class radicalism,
    319–22, 323
  exploitation of gentry divisions, 207, 209,
    215–17, 220, 222, 226, 241–2, 243–5,
    254, 258, 274, 297
  historiography, 249–54, 264–5, 267–9
  leadership, 210–11, 232, 233–5, 257–61
  and literacy, 237, 289

litigation, 210–12, 215–16, 220–3, 231–7, 241–8, 251, 264–5, 278–9, 285, 307–8
localism, 159, 243, 249–50, 253–4, 262–3, 287, 318, 320–3
organization of, 23, 165, 221, 231, 238, 304, 310–11, 314–15
and print, 144–5, 271, 278–9, 280–4, 288–9, 310, 319
and riot, 133, 190, 204, 207, 209, 213–14, 219–20, 222, 229, 233–4, 236–7, 241– 4, 246–7, 255–9, 261, 262, 264–5, 274–5, 277–80, 285–7, 293–4, 295, 301–2, 307–15, 319–21
ritual, 265, 312
social basis of, 255, 257–61, 280–1, 286–7
tithe strikes, 231–7, 265
and violence, 264–5, 279–80, 285–6, 308–9, 319
see also custom; free mining; miners; social conflict; women, political roles
popular religion, 167–8, 184, 191–4, 272–3, 296, 318
population
distribution, 48, 53–66
increase/decrease, 57–66, 98–9, 109
migration, 33, 51–2, 110–11, 134, 188
Porschnev, Boris, 257–8
Postern, 94
postmodernism, 10–11, 17–18
poverty, 89
attitudes to, 109–10
distribution, 90–3
see also miners, poverty amongst
pre-emption of ore sales, *see* lead industry, manorial control of
Presbyterianism, 191, 193, 270, 272–3, 296, 299
Privy Council, 73, 211, 224, 227, 231, 235, 262, 269, 272, 288
protestation oath, 153, 269
proto-industrialization, 123
purcassers, *see* cavers
puritanism, 192, 268, 271, 273, 276
Putney debates, 144, 288

Quakerism, 192–3, 296
Quarter Sessions, 102, 111, 147, 175, 246, 280, 285, 287

Randall, Adrian, 124
Real del Monte, 124
rents, 109, 227–8, 245, 255
Ridge Hall, 136
riot, *see* popular politics, and riot

Robinson, Capt. Thomas, 280–2, 292–3
Roos, Lord, see Manners, John, Lord Roos, ninth Earl of Rutland
Rowland, 242, 306
Rowsley, 247

Sanders, Col. Thomas, 271, 275–6, 283–4
Savile, Sir George, first Marquis of Halifax, 307
Scarsdale, Hundred of, 36, 304
Schofield, R.S., 94
schools, 155, 157
Settlement Act, 111
Sharp, Buchanan, 258
Sheffield (Yorks.), 55, 319, 320–1
Sheldon, 66, 68, 70, 81, 92, 172–3, 244, 278
Shottle, 94
Shrewsbury, Earls of, *see* Talbots
Smerrill Grange, 220, 222
Snitterton, 46, 63, 207
social conflict
absence, 53, 204–5
as class conflict, 277–8, 287–8, 292–4
and custom, 119–24, 127–8, 159, 161–2, 204, 210, 221, 246, 313–14
defines local identities, 134, 249–50, 260–1, 313–14
growth, 214
historiography, 216–17, 225, 258, 260, 313–14
intensity in Peak Country, 218, 221, 252, 277
localism, 15, 118, 123–4
in pastoral-industrial areas, 218, 251–2, 268, 314
and social history, 14–15, 17
see also class; custom; enclosures; free mining; gentry and nobility; miners; popular politics
social history, 10–18, 119
socialism, 10, 25, 249, 323
sociology, 15
Somerset, 264
space, senses of, 33, 66, 134–6, 172, 177, 212–13, 240–1, 253
Staffordshire, 36, 55, 72, 114, 190, 284, 286, 292
Stanton, 68, 219, 246, 247, 306, 319
Star Chamber, Court of, 46, 131, 146, 186, 190, 222, 226, 227, 234, 235, 242, 243–4, 246, 251, 260
Stathom, Sir John, 150–1, 152
Steeple Grange, 121, 207, 219, 221
Stevenson, John, 16
Stoney Middleton, 66, 69, 92, 237, 255, 304–5, 306, 307, 319

Stoyle, Mark, 273
Stuarts, Restoration of, 37, 72, 89, 98, 99, 102, 108, 110, 111, 155, 182, 223, 237, 296, 301
Suffolk, 268

Taddington, 108, 172–3, 234, 255
Talbot, Elizabeth, dowager Countess of Shrewsbury, 24, 210, 214, 239
Talbot, George, sixth Earl of Shrewsbury, 3, 58, 67, 120, 207, 209–12, 214, 216–17, 219, 231, 239, 240, 243, 274
Talbot, Gilbert, seventh Earl of Shrewsbury, 207, 209, 214, 239
Talbots, Earls of Shrewsbury, 231, 297
Tawney, R.H., 119
Tearsall rake, 85, 104
Terling (Essex), 299
textile industries, 56, 112, 114, 116, 132
Thieveley (Lancs.), 82–3
Thirsk, Joan, 70
Thompson, E. P., 11–12, 16, 17, 107, 127, 264, 300–1, 322–3
Tideswell, 59, 67, 70, 81, 110, 113, 147, 166, 216, 224, 225, 231–7, 238, 242, 256, 261, 262, 263, 271, 274, 275, 294, 297, 299, 302, 303–4, 305, 312
Tissington, 110, 219, 220, 222–3
tithe disputes, 84, 131, 168–9, 186, 219–20, 223–6, 231–7, 257–9, 260–1, 262, 271–2, 274, 284, 303–5
Tynley, Lionel, 76, 270

Underdown, David, 16, 267–9, 273

Vermuyden, Sir Cornelius, 86, 101, 227–31, 264, 275
Vernon, Sir George, 239, 245
Vernon, Richard, 245
Vernon, Roger, 203
Vernons of Haddon, 56, 245

Wales, 72, 102, 268
Walton, 122
Walwyn, William, 289
Wardlow, 67, 70, 81, 92, 232
Warwickshire, 246
Weber, Max, 13, 17
Wensley, 46, 63, 77, 85, 104, 183, 207, 302, 319, 321
West Country, 2, 226–7, 258, 260, 265, 267–8
Western Rising of 1628–31, 250, 258
Westminster, central courts, 128, 130–3, 135, 136, 152, 162, 164, 172, 225, 256, 278, 288, 305

and writing, 67–8, 152, 222
Whetstone, Charles, 188–9, 191, 193, 318–19
Whissonsett (Norfolk), 250
Wigwell Grange, 134, 150, 219
Willersley Grange, 207
Wingfield Hall, 276
Winster, 68, 101, 104, 110, 149, 212, 242, 263, 319, 321, 324, 325
Wirksworth
  Great Barmote, 103, 140–3, 159, 170–1, 207, 222, 238, 263
  manor, 4, 21, 30, 50, 132, 134, 139–43, 148, 166, 226–31, 255
  moothall, 4, 49, 170–1
  parish, 30, 56, 59–62, 63, 66, 98–9, 156, 160, 166, 184, 186, 194, 223–6
  township, 33, 43, 46, 49, 53, 77, 87–8, 89–90, 92–8, 102, 170–1, 173, 181, 186– 7, 191, 192, 207, 225, 263, 271, 274
  Wapentake, 30, 33, 43, 46, 47, 56, 71, 110, 114, 120, 122, 131, 142, 148, 166, 170–1, 180, 203–4, 205–9, 219–23, 225, 226, 233, 238, 247, 262, 263, 271, 272, 275, 291, 293, 301, 319
work, *see* cavers, nature of work; custom, and work; free mining; lead industry; miners; mining workforce; women, work
working class, and gender, 25
women
  common interest, 187, 256
  literacy, 152, 154, 156
  political roles, 6, 19, 25, 255–7, 309, 311
  property rights, 173, 186, 270
  public roles, 171–3, 185–7, 256–7
  work, 6–7, 46, 83, 105, 133, 172, 174, 179–80, 184–6, 255
  see also custom, and women
Wright, William, 237, 292
Wrightson, Keith, 16–17, 253–4
Wrigley, E.A., 94
Wye, 81

Yatestoop mine, 101, 105, 110, 149
yeomanry, 48, 90
  and lead industry, 43, 76
  as enclosers, 68
Yorkshire, 72, 93, 112, 116, 268
Youlgreave, 21, 36, 59–62, 66, 81, 90, 94–5, 98–9, 110, 138, 169, 183, 237, 238, 242, 246, 263, 271, 275, 284, 286, 287, 292, 293, 294, 297, 305, 317

Zagorin, Perez, 16

Cambridge Studies in Early Modern British History

Titles in the series

The Common Peace: Participation and the Criminal Law in Seventeenth-Century England*
CYNTHIA B. HERRUP

Politics, Society and Civil War in Warwickshire, 1620–1660
ANN HUGHES

London Crowds in the Reign of Charles II: Propaganda and Politics from the Restoration to the Exclusion Crisis*
TIM HARRIS

Criticism and Compliment: The Politics of Literature in the England of Charles I*
KEVIN SHARPE

Central Government and the Localities: Hampshire, 1649–1689
ANDREW COLEBY

John Skelton and the Politics of the 1520s
GREG WALKER

Algernon Sidney and the English Republic, 1623–1677
JONATHAN SCOTT

Thomas Starkey and the Commonwealth: Humanist Politics and Religion in the Reign of Henry VIII
THOMAS F. MAYER

The Blind Devotion of the People: Popular Religion and the English Reformation*
ROBERT WHITING

The Cavalier Parliament and the Reconstruction of the Old Regime, 1661–1667
PAUL SEAWARD

The Blessed Revolution: English Politics and the Coming of War, 1621–1624
THOMAS COGSWELL

Charles I and the Road to Personal Rule
L. J. REEVE

George Lawson's 'Politica' and the English Revolution
CONAL CONDREN

Puritans and Roundheads: The Harleys of Brampton Bryan and the Outbreak of the Civil War
JACQUELINE EALES

An Uncounselled King: Charles I and the Scottish Troubles, 1637–1641
PETER DONALD

Cheap Print and Popular Piety, 1550–1640*
TESSA WATT

The Pursuit of Stability: Social Relations in Elizabethan London
IAN W. ARCHER

Prosecution and Punishment: Petty Crime and the Law in London and Rural Middlesex, c. 1660–1725
ROBERT B. SHOEMAKER

Algernon Sidney and the Restoration Crisis, 1677–1683
JONATHAN SCOTT

Exile and Kingdom: History and Apocalypse in the Puritan Migration to America
AVIHU ZAKAI

The Pillars of Priestcraft Shaken: The Church of England and its Enemies, 1660–1730
J. A. I. CHAMPION

Steward, Lords and People: The Estate Steward and his World in Later Stuart England
D. R. HAINSWORTH

Civil War and Restoration in the Three Stuart Kingdoms: The Career of Randal MacDonnell, Marquis of Antrim, 1609–1683
JANE H. OHLMEYER

The Family of Love in English Society, 1550–1630
CHRISTOPHER W. MARSH

The Bishops' Wars: Charles I's Campaign against Scotland, 1638–1640*
MARK FISSEL

John Locke: Resistance, Religion and Responsibility*
JOHN MARSHALL

Constitutional Royalism and the Search for Settlement c. 1640–1649
DAVID L. SMITH

Intelligence and Espionage in the Reign of Charles II, 1660–1685
ALAN MARSHALL

The Chief Governors: The Rise and Fall of Reform Government in Tudor Ireland, 1536–1588
CIARAN BRADY

Politics and Opinion in Crisis, 1678–1681
MARK KNIGHTS

Catholic and Reformed: The Roman and Protestant Churches in English Protestant Thought, 1604–1640
ANTHONY MILTON

Sir Matthew Hale, 1609–1676: Law, Religion and Natural Philosophy
ALAN CROMARTIE

Henry Parker and the English Civil War: The Political Thought of the Public's 'Privado'
MICHAEL MENDLE

Protestantism and Patriotism: Ideologies and the Making of English Foreign Policy, 1650–1668
STEVEN C. A. PINCUS

Gender in Mystical and Occult Thought: Behmenism and its Development in England
B. J. GIBBONS

William III and the Godly Revolution
TONY CLAYDON

Law-Making and Society in Late Elizabethan England: The Parliament of England, 1584–1601
DAVID DEAN

Conversion, Politics and Religion in England, 1580–1625
MICHAEL C. QUESTIER

Politics, Religion, and the British Revolutions: The Mind of Samuel Rutherford
JOHN COFFEY

King James VI and I and the Reunion of Christendom
W. B. PATTERSON

The English Reformation and the Laity: Gloucestershire, 1540–1580
CAROLINE LITZENBERGER

Godly Clergy in Early Stuart England: The Caroline Puritan Movement c. 1620–1643
TOM WEBSTER

Prayer Book and People in Elizabethan and Early Stuart England
JUDITH MALTBY

Sermons at Court, 1559–1629: Religion and Politics in Elizabethan and Jacobean Preaching
PETER E. MCCULLOUGH

Dismembering the Body Politic: Partisan Politics in England's Towns, 1650–1730
PAUL D. HALLIDAY

Women Waging Law in Elizabethan England
TIMOTHY STRETTON

The Early Elizabethan Polity: William Cecil and the British Succession Crisis, 1558–1569
STEPHEN ALFORD

The Polarisation of Elizabethan Politics: The Political Career of Robert Devereux, 2nd Earl of Essex
PAUL E.J. HAMMER

The Politics of Social Conflict: The Peak Country, 1520–1770
ANDY WOOD

*Also published as a paperback